ENGLISH LITERATURE
AND
BRITISH PHILOSOPHY

PATTERNS OF LITERARY CRITICISM

General Editors

MARSHALL McLUHAN

R. J. SCHOECK

ERNEST SIRLUCK

ENGLISH LITERATURE
AND
BRITISH PHILOSOPHY

A Collection of Essays
Edited with an Introduction by
S. P. ROSENBAUM

The University of Chicago Press
Chicago & London

154792

THE UNIVERSITY OF CHICAGO PRESS, CHICAGO 60637
THE UNIVERSITY OF CHICAGO PRESS, LTD., LONDON

© 1971 by The University of Chicago. All rights reserved
Published 1971. Printed in the United States of America

International Standard Book Number: 0–226–72656–8 (clothbound)
0–226–72657–6 (paperbound)
Library of Congress Catalog Card Number: 71–157147

Only connect . . .
       E. M. Forster

Everything is what it is, and not another thing.
       Bishop Butler

CONTENTS

vii

INTRODUCTION

In identifying the literature as English and the philosophy as British, the title of this collection of critical essays may seem to suggest a distinction without a difference. Most of the philosophers discussed here were Englishmen; several of the writers were not. Yet *English* and *British* do not always work the same way with the word *literature* as they do with the word *philosophy*. English literature very often refers to the language of the literature rather than the nationality of its practitioners. Thus one can without paradox describe W. B. Yeats or T. S. Eliot as writers of English literature. British philosophy, however, usually refers to philosophy done in Britain or by Britons. Thus, again, it is not paradoxical that the great British philosophers Bacon and Wittgenstein wrote philosophical masterpieces in Latin and German.

This difference in meaning between the way we frequently describe English literature and British philosophy is worth emphasizing in a volume of essays that seek to relate literature and philosophy. The usefulness of seeing connections between literature and philosophy can be lost if their fundamental differences are forgotten. Only some relations are equations. That is why this anthology has two mottos. Against the novelist E. M. Forster's famous epigraph "Only connect . . ." we need to balance the philosopher Bishop Butler's celebrated tautology, "Everything is what it is, and not another thing."

I

The range of connections that the essays in this anthology display has been given definite limitations so that the anthology will have a certain emphasis. The boundaries of English literature and British philosophy were chosen, to begin with, because Britain has a long and very rich literary as well as philosophical history, and it is not unnatural to expect its literary and philosophical achievements to interact. Before searching abroad for philosophical influences on authors of English literature we might first look to see how they responded to the philosophy that was most immediately available to them. This kind of inquiry assumes, of course, that literature does make use of philosophy, though it is an assumption that some modern critics have questioned along with the whole activity of examining ideas in literature. It has been maintained, for instance, that poetry is written with images or words rather than ideas—as if ideas existed somehow apart from their symbolization. The aridity that results when ideas are theoretically exiled from literary criticism is often alleviated in practice by their return under such aliases as "image," "symbol," or "myth." Given the general meanings of the word *idea*, the interesting question is not whether there are ideas in literature but *how* they exist there. The explicit philosophical statement is but one way and not always the most interesting. "Heard philosophies are sweet," observed George Santayana, "but those unheard may be sweeter." How ideas are used in literature also bears on the problem of whether or not literature conveys knowledge. The truth or falsity of ideas in literature is a function of the ways in which they are used in specific types and works of literature. Few would deny that such literature as *The Republic, De rerum natura*, or *The Decline and Fall of the Roman Empire* expresses propositions. Whether, and in what ways, lyrics, tragedies, and novels also embody statements that are true or false is not something to dogmatize about.

The very richness of English literature and British philosophy presents anthological problems, and in order to keep this collection of essays coherent, additional limitations have had to be imposed on its scope. For those writers who received a classical education the philosophy most available to them was most likely ancient philosophy. A useful anthology could be made of essays on the significance of Greek, Hellenistic, and Roman thought for English writing. Another anthology could demonstrate the long influence of the great "British" medieval philosophers, an excellent example of which would be the way Gerard Manley Hopkins was stimulated by the ideas of Duns Scotus. But neither collection would show the particular kinds of relations that exist between native philosophical traditions and vernacular literatures. To display these relations in English literature and British philosophy is the aim of this anthology, and therefore connections between classical, medieval, and to some extent renaissance philosophy and English literature have been omitted.

With one exception, the essays chosen here have also been

limited to a single type of connection between English literáture and British philosophy, namely the impact of philosophy on literature. This restriction is not as severe for British philosophy as it might be for French or German because on the whole English literature has not influenced British philosophy in noteworthy ways. There are exceptions, and George Pitcher's essay on Lewis Carroll and Wittgenstein documents one of them in this anthology. (There have also been British philosophers who have written valuably on English literature; John Laird, Samuel Alexander, and Stuart Hampshire are examples in this century; another is Gilbert Ryle, whose essay on Jane Austen and Shaftesbury comes within the scope of the anthology and is included here.) By restricting the essays to those in which philosophy affects literature, it has been possible to include the major British philosophers, though obviously many major authors have had to be omitted; Augustan and Victorian poets are those most conspicuously absent.

The general imperviousness of British philosophy to the influence of English literature suggests that this philosophy amounts to something more than just a collection of philosophers associated with Britain. In a concise history of British philosophy written for *The Encyclopedia of Philosophy*, Anthony Quinton quotes the great American philosopher Charles Sanders Peirce's account of tendencies that unite British philosophers:

> From very early times, it has been the chief intellectual characteristic of the English to wish to effect everything by the plainest and directest means, without unnecessary contrivance. . . . In philosophy, this national tendency appears as a strong preference for the simplest theories, and a resistance to any complication of the theory as long as there is the least possibility that the facts can be explained in the simpler way. And, accordingly, British philosophers have always desired to weed out of philosophy all conceptions which could not be made perfectly definite and easily intelligible, and have shown strong nominalistic tendencies since the time of Edward I, or even earlier.

"The chief intellectual characteristic of the English" has not produced comparable unifying tendencies in English literature, though the inclinations Peirce identifies are not unrecognizeably alien to the literature either. And some of the philosophers most influential for English literature have been largely apart from the central tradition in British philosophy. The Cambridge Platonists are one example, Alfred North Whitehead is another. Because their influence is widely known, essays on them have not been included here. For the same reason Herbert Spencer is missing too, although with Spencer it is also questionable how important his ideas were for any really enduring works of English literature. The more unfamiliar connections existing between English literature and the main British philosophical tradition are what most of the essays in this anthology explore.

One final restriction on the kinds of connections represented in this anthology needs to be mentioned before considering some of the reasons why the most characteristic British philosophy has seemed largely irrelevant to many modern critics and scholars of English literature. The field of philosophy has been interpreted fairly strictly. There are no discussions here of the impact of deism or Darwinism on English literature; science and theology, the neighbors of philosophy, have been ignored in selecting essays so that the anthology could concentrate on ideas that were unambiguously philosophical. For the same reason the work of the quasi-philosophical figure of the sage, which John Holloway has identified and studied in Victorian literature, has also been excluded. The distinctions here between the philosopher, the scientist, the theologian, and the sage are not invidious. They simply distinguish areas that, if included in the scope of this anthology, would blur its focus on philosophy and literature. Philosophy, after all, has its own disinctive value for the study of literature. If philosophy is the study of ideas as such, the best place to begin examining ideas expressed, embodied, and assumed in literary works would appear to be there. Conceptual analysis can, both directly and by analogy, further critical analysis. The study of ideas that are characteristically philosophical in content and origin can also avoid to a large degree a serious inadequacy in the history of ideas. In his essay "Philosophy, Literature, and the History of Ideas," R. S. Crane has argued that the "unit-ideas" Arthur O. Lovejoy so influentially studied represent "not so much what the writers in whose treatises, essays, poems, or novels we find them are thinking *about* as what they are thinking with," and to talk about them in separation from the particular activity of reasoning by which they are ordered and defined in philosophic discourse is to talk about them merely as floating commonplaces or themes. . . .

The discursive context of a philosophical idea may also illuminate its imaginative transmutation into something rich and strange in literature and even suggest related ideas that have less recognizably accompanied the change.

II

"Descartes, Locke, and Newton took away the world and gave us its excrement instead." Yeats's observation in *Pages from a Diary* is the succinct expression of a belief that many students of English literature are in sympathy with, and that Frank Kermode has shown is part of the Symbolist inheritance of modern English literary history. It was Whitehead, however, who gave the theory behind this feeling its most elegant and influential philosophical formulation. In the lectures he published in 1920 under the title *The Concept of Nature*, Whitehead protested against "the bifurcation of nature into two systems of reality," one of which was "the nature apprehended in awareness" and the other,

the nature which is the cause of awareness. The nature which is the fact apprehended in awareness holds within it the greenness of the trees, the song of the birds, the warmth of the sun, the hardness of the chairs, and the feel of the velvet. The nature which is the cause of awareness is the conjectured system of molecules and electrons which so affects the mind as to produce the awareness of apparent nature.

In the early chapters of his widely read *Science and the Modern World*, which appeared five years later, Whitehead traced the historical development of this bifurcation to its culmination at the end of the seventeenth century in a mechanistic scientific philosophy. The aesthetic consequences of this philosophy were illustrated by Whitehead in a famous passage on the implications of Locke's distinction of primary and secondary qualities:

The primary qualities are the essential qualities of substances whose spatio-temporal relationships constitute nature. The orderliness of these relationships constitutes the order of nature.

The occurrences of nature are in some way apprehended by minds, which are associated with living bodies. . . . But the mind in apprehending also experiences sensations which, properly speaking, are qualities of the mind alone. These sensations are projected by the mind so as to clothe appropriate bodies in external nature. Thus the bodies are perceived as with qualities which in reality do not belong to them, qualities which in fact are purely the offspring of the mind. Thus nature gets credit which should in truth be reserved for ourselves; the rose for its scent: the nightingale for his song: and the sun for his radiance. The poets are entirely mistaken. They should address their lyrics to themselves, and should turn them into odes of self-congratulation on the excellency of the human mind. Nature is a dull affair, soundless, scentless, colourless; merely the hurrying of material, endlessly, meaninglessly.

For Whitehead the bifurcation of nature amounted to the ruin of modern philosophy—a ruin that could be undone, however, by a philosophy of organism such as Whitehead propounded. The reaction of romantics like Wordsworth (and Yeats) to the disjunction of the aesthetic and the scientific helped point the way, according to Whitehead, toward an organic concept of nature that would recombine fact and value.

It is difficult to overestimate the influence of Whitehead's theory on English literary studies. Men as diverse as Basil Willey, Edmund Wilson, and F. R. Leavis have acknowledged its importance. In a recent distinguished anthology devoted to the intellectual backgrounds of modern literature and ranging in its one thousand pages from Kant to Sartre, Whitehead is the only British philosopher included. Part of Whitehead's influence comes from the way his theory appears to reinforce an even more celebrated hypothesis about English literary history, which Whitehead's theory may actually have helped to formulate. The year after Whitehead's bifurcation theory was set forth in *The Concept of Nature*, T. S. Eliot wrote a review of the metaphysical poets for the *Times Literary Supplement* in which, borrowing from the vocabulary of Remy de Gourmont, he stated his famous thesis of the dissociation of sensibility. Seventeenth-century poets, Eliot wrote, "possessed a mechanism of sensibility which could devour any kind of experience," but after them "a dissociation of sensibility set in, from which we have never recovered. . . ." Thought and feeling were separated and poetry became by fits sentimental or reflective, but it was rarely able to embody a unified sensibility in which thought was felt "as immediately as the odour of a rose." As a serious student of philosophy, Eliot knew who Whitehead was; Eliot was familiar with *Principia Mathematica* and it is not at all unlikely that he would have been very interested in a new work by Whitehead on a subject much closer to his own philosophical interests than symbolic logic had been. In Whitehead's view of the bifurcation of nature Eliot may have found another clue to the explanation of the bifurcation of poetic sensibility that he had felt in English poetry since the later seventeenth century, and that French criticism in the nineteenth and twentieth centuries had helped him describe. Whitehead's and Eliot's theories are, of course, very different. One is essentially about the history of ideas, the other about the history of poetry. Nature and sensibility are quite different things. Whitehead and Eliot were in complete disagreement about the significance of English romantic poetry for their hypotheses, one seeing it as a protest against the split and the other finding a confirmation of the split in the poetry. (Whitehead's discussion of the romantic reaction to empirical philosophy did not accompany his original formulation of the bifurcation theory, however.) Yet each theory postulates a profound division in man's experience, and each locates that division historically toward the end of the seventeenth century. The difference between "causal" and "apparent" nature in Whitehead's theory cannot be equated with the imbalance of thought and feeling in Eliot's, but the two can be correlated—and in fact they have been repeatedly by historians and critics of English literature.

Whatever the merits of Whitehead's interpretation of the results of the new philosophy, it has led to a remarkable oversimplification of the importance of British philosophy for English literature. The conclusion that Locke and the scientists who influenced him have ruined modern philosophy has been applied to literature, and Locke emerged as an important cause of the dissociation of sensibility. The consequences for literature of the British tradition in philosophy, as summarized, for example, by Peirce, have gone unconsidered, and philosophy since Locke has been seen as sustaining the split, though Berkeley, Mill, and Bradley have sometimes been recognized as exceptions. The development of British thought has been dichotomized into a Bentham versus Coleridge melodrama.

With Whitehead's assistance what was originally a theory of poetry has often been converted into a theory of literature that takes no account of the relations between British philosophy and English fictional and nonfictional prose.

The moral of this anthology is not that British philosophy is good for English literature, but that those who want to understand the literature of England ought not to dismiss the philosophy that usually was closest to it with allusions to the bifurcation of nature or the dissociation of sensibility. Excremental exclamations will not help much either. We need instead to become aware of the varieties of relevance that British philosophy has for English literature, and the essays of this anthology have been brought together for this end. British philosophy's relevance to English literature is by no means always flattering to the philosophy. Whitehead's theory, incomplete and partial as it is, has identified some prominent features of British philosophy that English authors have reacted to strongly. But these and other responses can best be seen by considering together the subjects, methods, and conclusions of the essays that follow. The essays are arranged in approximate chronological order by writer or period, but they can be better compared according to whether they relate poetry (or poetics), fiction, or nonfiction to philosophy.

III

Though Whitehead does not mention him in *Science and the Modern World*, William Blake is perhaps the best illustration of Locke's negative influence. Northrop Frye's essay on the case that Blake developed against Locke reveals how the poet reacted to such features of the philosopher's thought as the division between sensation and reflection (which could be interpreted as a variant of the bifurcation of nature), the apparent passivity of the mind required by empiricism, and the reliance on ordinary sense experience as a criterion of reality. Blake's hostility to empiricism, unlike Coleridge's, extended back to Bacon; Coleridge called Bacon the British Plato, and Blake did not think very much of Plato either. R. S. Crane has pointed out, in an analysis of Locke's *An Essay concerning Human Understanding* (reprinted in *The Idea of the Humanities*) that both Blake and Coleridge as well as other Romantic propagandists conceived of Locke as "a philosopher for whom the sources of human knowledge are all external to the mind in sense-experience and the mind itself is a passive recipient of impressions from without or at most a mechanical manipulator of the simple ideas it has derived from these." Crane goes on to demonstrate that this is only a part of the truth about Locke's *Essay*; in Locke's account of the passive and limited ways of our knowing there is also to be found a complementary emphasis on the activity of the mind and on the possibilities of knowledge. The interesting point for Blake's poetry, however, is the use he made of his own idea of Locke. Locke's empiricism provided Blake with a needed opposition, an epistemological model that Blake could take as the threat of enslavement necessary for him to create his own system. The result can illuminate both Blake and Locke.

But the visionary's antipathy for the empiricist is not extendable without important qualification to romantic theory in general. M. H. Abrams's discussion of the romantics' use of organic and mechanical metaphors of perception is a useful piece to read alongside Frye's particular examination of one romantic's revulsion against the new philosophy. Abrams expounds the empiricist assumptions of eighteenth-century theories of artistic creation, showing both their difficulties and the problems that alternative organic theories encounter. In assessing the relevance of British philosophy for English literature —especially in the work of a figure like Coleridge—it is important to realize how syncretic Coleridge's critical theory was; in Abrams's words, it utilized "not one, but two controlling analogues, one of a machine, the other of a plant. . . ." Abrams also indicates how, contrary to Whitehead's belief, Wordsworth was still more indebted than Coleridge to eighteenth-century British philosophy, for he refused to make a complete separation of the organic from the mechanical.

The influence of British philosophy on English poetry and poetics is visible long before the romantics, of course. R. L. Brett's essay on Thomas Hobbes indicates how, through his influence on Dryden and others, Hobbes became a founding father of the eighteenth century. Unlike Dryden, Milton was not an admirer, however. Marjorie Hope Nicolson argued in 1926 that Hobbes provided Milton with a useful antagonist in theology as well as in moral and political philosophy. Nicolson concluded that although the whirligig of time may bring

S. P. ROSENBAUM

Hobbes's reputation to nought, he would still be known for the opposition he provoked. Ironically the whirligig of time has reduced Milton's reputation instead, and Hobbes's fame as a moral and political philosopher may be greater today than it has ever been. In the eighteenth century Hobbes's linguistic theories affected Augustan literary style, and his interest in the psychology of literature has made Hobbes one of the ancestors of nineteenth- and twentieth-century critical theory. Hobbes's importance for literature is not incompatible with the sharp separation of reason and imagination that Brett describes as characteristic of "the positivist temper" of Hobbes's thought. But before we diagnose Hobbes as an early manifestation of the dissociation of sensibility, it is worth noting that T. S. Eliot, for one, preferred him as a writer to Sir Thomas Browne.

Eliot himself was deeply influenced by philosophy. In fact both the leading modern English poets seriously studied British as well as ancient and continental philosophers, Eliot at the beginning of his career, and Yeats toward the end of his. The importance of Eliot's doctoral dissertation on the philosophy of F. H. Bradley has become clear since Anne C. Bolgan edited it for publication in 1964. In an essay taken from the book that she is completing on Eliot and Bradley, Bolgan outlines the philosophical background of Eliot's work and shows how particular ideas of post-Kantian idealism are part of "the Brad-leyan filament" that she finds running throughout Eliot's most important poems. Yeats's study of philosophy, which he under-took seriously after finishing the first version of *A Vision*, shared with Eliot's a dominant interest in British idealism. Yeats preferred Berkeley's brand of idealism. (Berkeley was the one empiricist Blake could tolerate as well.) Donald Davie argues in his essay that Yeats was interested in Berkeley not just because the bishop was an eighteenth-century Irishman. Berkeley's recently reinterpreted Augustan idealism fitted in with the growing anti-romanticism that Davie sees in Yeats's later career. Berkeley's critique of Locke also helped to make the world a little less excremental for Yeats. Yet the common-sensical and even skeptical elements of British idealism as found in both Berkeley and Bradley ought not to be overlooked, for they were also congenial to the poetry of Eliot and Yeats.

The attention that has been paid to the philosophical back-grounds of English poetry in general and romanticism in particular has tended to obscure the quite different philosophical origins of the novel. In drawing an analogy between philosophical and novelistic realism, Ian Watt implicitly reveals that the bifurcation of nature was not a serious matter for the eighteenth-century novelist. Locke's epistemology and Thomas Reid's Scottish commonsense philosophy postulated a dualistic correspondence between the individual's senses and external reality that parallels the novel's basic concern with the relation of man to his environment. Watt's discussion of the significance of time to the fundamental preoccupations of the novel illustrates how crucial epistemological realism was for the rise of the novel.

A paradigm case of the importance of epistemological realism for the novel and of British philosophy for English literature is found in the influence of John Locke on Laurence Sterne. Locke's doctrine of the association of ideas which developed out of his empiricism has been seminal for psychology and for fiction. Ernest Tuveson explores the well-known connections between Locke and Sterne and finds new ones. The suggestion that the reformer in Locke influenced the satirist in Sterne adds a moral dimension to the influence that the new empirical philosophy had on the rise of the novel. The last essay in this anthology shows how the realism of this new philosophy, as reformulated by G. E. Moore, underlay the fiction of a twentieth-century novelist. The editor discusses there how Virginia Woolf came to know and read Moore, and how his epistemological realism is assumed in her fiction. The influence of Moore's thought and personality was mediated to Virginia Woolf through the relatives and friends who are grouped together as the members of Bloomsbury. Their profound debt to Moore's ethics is not news, though the way Moore's epistemology provided the basic assumptions for Virginia Woolf's major novels has never been analyzed. In a reasonably strict philosophical sense of the word, her art is about perception.

Perhaps the most celebrated encounter of English literature and British philosophy, at least in modern times, also took place between a novelist and a philosopher. The brief, intense, and revealing relationship of D. H. Lawrence and Bertrand Russell illustrates, together with Virginia Woolf's experience, the potential significance of personal relationships as one form in which philosophy and literature can interact. Some details of

Lawrence's and Russell's extraordinary friendship are known through Lawrence's letters and Russell's portrait of Lawrence. The partisans of each have had their say and drawn their conclusions about the sterility of philosophy or the madness of art. Michael L. Ross has gone beyond these to demonstrate how the relationship informs Lawrence's fine story, "The Blind Man," and how the story makes a complex comment on the relationship. If Lawrence's and Russell's encounter was indeed symbolic, as many have said, Ross shows that something more interesting than the black and white of two cultures is being symbolized.

The debt of nineteenth-century English fiction to British moral philosophy is reflected in two essays written by philosophers in this anthology. Gilbert Ryle's discussion of Jane Austen's novels begins by pointing out the concern with theoretical questions of human nature and conduct that they share with moral philosophy. Ryle then suggests that, directly or otherwise, Shaftesbury provided Jane Austen with the general moral position and vocabulary that she used in her fiction. Jerome B. Schneewind argues that the neglect of intuitionism by historians of literature and philosophy has led to a misvaluing of the utilitarianism that conflicted with it throughout Victorian ethics and fiction. Schneewind urges that not only the novelist but the philosopher "presents the world as justifying a certain attitude or outlook," and he demonstrates how an outline of the central convictions of the utilitarian and intuitionist can be used to clarify the moral outlook of different philosophical novels.

The art of prose that we lamely describe as nonfiction bears witness as much as poetry or fiction to the varieties of relevance that British philosophy has for English literature. What David Hume's empiricism did for Edward Gibbon's history is a particularly good example. Louis Kampf's essay briefly discusses the connection between Hume's skepticism and Gibbon's irony, and the context of Kampf's discussion in a book on modernism suggests the contemporaneity of the philosopher and the historian. Two great British philosophers, Francis Bacon and John Stuart Mill, are also of major significance in English literature through their achievements as writers of nonfiction. Mill's work has been considered as a whole by critics and philosophers while Bacon's essays and longer philosophical works have tended rather to be studied separately from each other. Stanley Fish indicates, however, that Bacon's essays are based on a conception of the mind set forth in his *Novum Organum* and *The Advancement of Learning*. By analyzing the organization and style of the essays, Fish shows how Bacon used them as a kind of rudimentary conceptual analysis that relieves the reader of possible misjudgments. The essays are not merely philosophical expositions because it is in the experience as much as in the conclusions of the essays that the philosophy works. The literary experience embodies the philosophical point. The relationship between philosophic method and the rhetorical strategies of prose style is also examined by Alan Donagan in the work of Mill and F. H. Bradley. A commonplace of modern literary study is that the style of a good piece of literature is an integral part of the work. Yet according to Donagan little attention has been given to the significance of the prose styles of Victorian philosophers. Donagan's examination of the styles of Mill and Bradley reveals how their distinctive philosophies appear to require distinctive styles, and how their stylistic flaws are indicative of ethical limitations. There is an implicit moral here for the study of other literary forms: a writer's style may embody basic philosophical assumptions that are unstated, as it were, except through his style.

Finally, there is Lewis Carroll. As a mathematical logician his philosophical stature is short—yet he influenced modern British philosophy more than any other English writer. Because British philosophy has not been especially literary in its concerns, the competition here may not have been very stiff. Nevertheless George Pitcher's essay shows that the parallels between Lewis Carroll and Ludwig Wittgenstein are not trivial. Through the influence on Wittgenstein—one could add Russell and not just because he looked somewhat like the Mad Hatter—the significance of Lewis Carroll has increased. The present has modified the tradition of the past, as Eliot said it could, and we are beginning to see the author of the Alice books as something more than a comic Victorian children's writer. He may yet come to be included among the very greatest Victorian authors. Pitcher's study details how Lewis Carroll's vision of nonsense resembles the very meaningful sense of Wittgenstein. For an introduction to twentieth-century linguistic analysis one

S. P. ROSENBAUM

could do worse than read the extraordinary language philosopher who wrote *Alice in Wonderland* and *Through the Looking-Glass*.

With Lewis Carroll and Wittgenstein we are on the edge of a different type of inquiry. Everything being what it is and not another thing, the connecting of philosophy to literature is not the same as the connecting of literature to philosophy. The ways that literature can be seen to inform philosophy is material for another anthology than one whose essays examine the kinds of significance that British philosophy has had for various forms, periods, and authors of English literature.

IV

Even within the confines of this anthology's limited intentions it has not been possible to include all the pieces that I would have liked to. For reasons of emphasis, range, balance, and space it was not possible to include, for example, J. M. Cameron's study of how Hume's empiricism shaped Cardinal Newman's thought, or the examination by Sharon Kaehele and Howard German of Iris Murdoch's *The Bell* in terms of her own philosophical ideas. I would also have liked to include studies that do not appear to be written yet. A promising subject, to take a final example, is that formidable Cambridge idealist John McTaggart Ellis McTaggart. He turns up in his own person in no less formidable a work than Dorothy Richardson's *Pilgrimage;* he also received fan letters from Thomas Hardy, who wrote that in *The Dynasts* he was trying to do something of the same thing that McTaggart was doing in *Some Dogmas of Religion.*

But I am more than grateful for the studies that are available, and I wish to thank the authors and publishers for permission to use them. I am also grateful to the general editors of the Patterns of Literary Criticism series for inviting me to contribute this anthology. I am particularly indebted to R. J. Schoeck for his patience and counsel, and to Stanley Fish, Anne C. Bolgan, and Michael L. Ross for allowing their unpublished work to appear for the first time in *English Literature and British Philosophy*.

University College, Toronto   S. P. R.

I

STANLEY FISH

Georgics of the Mind: Bacon's Philosophy and the Experience of His Essays

And surely if the purpose be in good earnest not to write at leisure that which men may read at leisure, but really to instruct and suborn action and active life, these Georgics of the mind, concerning the husbandry and tillage thereof, are no less worthy than the heroical descriptions of Virtue, Duty, and Felicity.

The Advancement of Learning

I

There has been a general recognition in the twentieth century of the close relationship between Bacon's *Essays* and his critique of philosophic method. In 1871 Edward Arber could still write that the essays are "no essential part" of Bacon's real work, "the proficiency and advancement of knowledge,"[1] but in 1923 R. S. Crane pointed out that these "Counsels Civill and Morall" speak directly to a need first articulated in *The Advancement of Learning;*[2] and five years later Jacob Zeitlin was referring to this same body of materials as "a science of pure selfishness."[3] This view of the *Essays* opened the way for a consideration of their successive revisions, which were seen to correspond to the successive stages of philosophic inquiry. Thus, in the 1597 version, Bacon is "content to offer us the *disjecta membra*" without the ordering superstructure of a "methodical scheme,"[4] while

This essay is a version of a chapter from the author's forthcoming book, *Self-Consuming Artifacts: Studies in Seventeenth Century Prose and Poetry*.

[1] *A Harmony of Bacon's Essays* (London, 1871), p. xxvii.

[2] R. S. Crane, "The Relation of Bacon's *Essays* to his Programme for the Advancement of Learning," in *Schelling Anniversary Papers* (New York, 1923), pp. 87–105.

[3] Jacob Zeitlin, "The Development of Bacon's *Essays* and Montaigne," *JEGP* 27 (1928): 503.

[4] Zeitlin, p. 507.

in the 1625 *Essays* these discrete observations are related to one another and to the abstraction they collectively illuminate by "a clear and explicit organization."[5] This description of the essays and of their progress is now standard: Bacon, Douglas Bush tells us in his volume of the *Oxford History of English Literature*, "wished to fill a gap in practical psychology and ethics, to contribute to . . . knowledge of the genus *homo*" (196). Paoli Rossi takes his text from Bush and treats the essays as "another contribution to that science of man to which Bacon dedicated for many years the best part of his inexhaustible energies."[6] And for Brian Vickers, the most recent of the commentators, the connection between these "literary productions" and the scientific labors of Bacon's philosophic program is not a point of issue; he assumes it, and goes on to draw illuminating parallels between the style of the *Essays* and the methodology of the *Novum Organum* and other works.[7]

Yet, for all this unanimity, the casual judgments these critics make on the *Essays* suggest that they do not really understand what is "scientific" about them. For the most part they take their cue from Bacon's praise of Machiavelli:

. . . we are much beholden to Machiavel and others, that write what men do and not what they ought to do. For it is not possible to join serpentine wisdom with the columbine innocency, except men know exactly all the conditions of the serpent.

(3: 430–31)[8]

To know exactly what men do. This seems to be a call for "objectivity," for accurate and disinterested observation of particulars; and objectivity is the quality most commonly attributed to the *Essays*.

. . . his method was that of the detached, impersonal observer, his presentation was concise, dogmatic, formal.

(Zeitlin, 518–19)

[5] Crane, p. 97.

[6] Paoli Rossi, *Francis Bacon: From Magic to Science* (London, 1968), p. 187.

[7] Brian Vickers, *Francis Bacon and Renaissance Prose* (Cambridge, 1968), p. 53.

[8] References are to the *Works* edited by James Spedding, R. L. Ellis, and D. D. Heath (London, 14 volumes, 1857–74), hereafter referred to as *Sp.*, followed by the appropriate volume number.

In the *Essays* his attitude is conditioned by the whole rationale of the work towards dispassionate objective observation and analysis.

(Vickers, 133)

. . . Bacon's cool objectivity . . . represents also the attitude of the scientific analyst who does not gossip and ramble, whose mind is a dry light.

(Douglas Bush)[9]

It [the style of the *Essays*] thus represents a clear parallel to the scientific style of report.[10]

But if the *Essays* are objective in fact, analytic in method, impersonal in tone, and practically instructive in purpose, they are not, according to these same critics, without their problems. Zeitlin is uncomfortable with the "baldly analytic or coldly intellectual consideration" of the topics Bacon treats and he sees the essays as a battle between the "two spirits" that fight for the author's soul, the spirit of the scientist and the spirit of the moralist (512, 510). Bush speaks of the "utilitarian motives" that "keep Bacon's *Essays* in the category of admired books rather than among the well-thumbed and beloved" (197); and he notes the simultaneous presence of "some wholly admirable counsels of moral wisdom and public and private virtue" and "an atmosphere of 'business', of cold-blooded expediency, and sometimes of unscrupulous self-interest" (196).

In short, the characterization of the *Essays* as objective, dispassionate, and concisely analytic is hardly borne out by the collective response of those who so characterize them. An impersonal report does not leave its readers wondering about the inner life of the author; nor does it encourage speculation as to whether its own focus is "traditional," "utilitarian," "moral," or blurred. A student of Bacon criticism may be excused if he asks, only half in jest, will the real Bacon's *Essays* please stand up?

The difficulty, I think, lies in the assumed equation of "scientific" and "objective"; for this involves the further assumption that Bacon's concern as a scientist is wholly with the form of his presentation. I would suggest, however, that his primary

[9] Douglas Bush, *English Literature in The Earlier Seventeenth Century* (Oxford, 1962), p. 195.

[10] H. Fisch, *Jerusalem and Albion* (London, 1964), p. 29.

concern is with the *experience* that form provides, and further, that this experience, rather than the materials of which it is composed, is what is scientific about the *Essays*. I believe such a hypothesis to be consistent with the psychological emphasis of Bacon's theoretical writings and with his repeated classification of styles according to their effect on readers and hearers; but for now I prefer to rest my case on the primary evidence and proceed inductively, in good Baconian fashion, to the discovery of general principles.

Let us begin by examining a section of the 1625 essay, "Of Love":

> You may observe, that amongst all the great and worthy persons (whereof the memory remaineth, either ancient or recent) there is not one that hath been transported to the mad degree of love: which shews that great spirits and great business do keep out this weak passion. You must except nevertheless Marcus Antonius, the half partner of the empire of Rome, and Appius Claudius, the decemvir and lawgiver; whereof the former was indeed a voluptuous man, and inordinate; but the latter was an austere and wise man: therefore it seems (though rarely) that love can find entrance not only into an open heart, but also into a heart well fortified, if watch be not well kept.
>
> (6: 397)

Everything about the first sentence serves to inspire confidence in its contents. Before a reader reaches the main statement, he has been assured (by the parenthesis) that it is based on exhaustive research. Both the rhythmic and argumentative stresses fall on the phrase "there is not one," and nothing that follows qualifies this absoluteness. The formal conclusion of the "which" clause is hardly necessary—it is clearly implied—but it does add to the impression of completeness and finality, especially since the opposition of "great" and "weak," "business" and "passion," is so strongly pointed. The form of the whole is almost syllogistic, moving from the primary proposition—"there are great and worthy persons"—to the secondary proposition—"not one of them hath"—to the inevitable therefore—"which shows that." In short, the reader is encouraged in every way possible to confer the status of "truism" or "axiom" on the assertion this sentence makes. Of course, there are potential ambiguities. As we read it for the first time, "You may observe" is simply a rhetorical formula which allows us to anticipate something unexceptionable; but, strictly speaking, that formula includes the possibility of *not* taking the action referred to: You may observe, or, on the other hand, you may not observe. The material in the parenthesis contains a similar "logical out," since it acknowledges indirectly the possibility of there being a whole body of great and worthy persons whereof *no* memory remains, persons whose existence would call into question the validity of the generalization that follows. Still, there is no reason for a reader to indulge in such quibbles and every likelihood, if my description of the sentence's effect is accurate, that he will not.

But no sooner has Bacon's axiom been established, then he begins to qualify it, and insofar as he has accepted it, the reader participates in the act of qualification. Indeed he has no choice, for in contrast to the permissive "may," Bacon begins the next sentence with a commanding "You *must* except"; and as the exceptions are enumerated, the force of the original statement is less and less felt, in part because the prose is making so many new demands on the reader. The sentence proceeds in fits, and each stage of it seems momentarily to be the final one. First Marcus Antonius and Appius are set apart from other "great men," and this is a simple enough (mental) action; but then these two are distinguished from one another and the reader is obliged to construct categories for them: both are "great" and subject to the passion of love; but while the weakness (voluptuous and inordinate) of one suggests an explanation for his subjugation—i.e., Marcus Antonius can be "handled" without disturbing the validity of the axiom—the qualities of the other (wise and austere) prevent us from raising this explanation to the level of a general truth. And meanwhile, the emphasis of the entire experience has shifted from the original assertion to the classification of its exceptions, so that it now seems that *no* great man is immune from the infection of love.

At this point, the words "and therefore" promise relief from this rather strenuous mental activity. Presumably a new and more inclusive axiom will be forthcoming, one that takes into account the fact of Marcus Antonius and Appius Claudius. But unlike the first (and now discredited) axiom, this one is qualified even before it is offered. The firm conclusiveness of "therefore" gives way to the equivocation of "seems" and then to the near negativity of "though rarely." By the time the reader reaches the actual statement, its status is so unclear that the question of record—whether or not great men and mad lovers constitute mutually exclusive classes—is only further muddled. The last tail-like phrase, "if watch be not well kept," introduces a new variable—the "vigilance factor"—which would seem to make it even more difficult to formulate a generally applicable rule.

What are we to make of this confusion? Is this the Francis Bacon whose revisions, Vickers tells us, are always in the direction of "extending, clarifying and focusing"? (231) One can answer in the affirmative, I think, if the focus of inquiry is shifted from the essay's nominal subject, love, to what I believe to be its real subject, the inadequacy of the commonly received notions about love. That is, if anything is being "clarified" here, it is the extent to which the confidently proffered pronouncement of the first sentence does not hold up under close scrutiny; and, moreover, the reader's experience of that clarification is somewhat chastening, since it involves the debunking of something he had accepted without question. Of course Bacon has assured this acceptance by surrounding his generalization with the paraphernalia of logical discourse and enclosing it in a rhythmically satisfying syntactical structure; but this deception (if deception is the proper word) is essential to his strategy, and that strategy is adumbrated in the Preface to *The Great Instauration* and in the first book of the *Novum Organum*.

II

Although the goal of Bacon's work is the orderly disposition of an objective reality, his primary concern in the early stages of that undertaking is with his tools, and chief among these is the human mind itself. In the plot of *The Great Instauration* and especially in the first book of the *Novum Organum*, the mind has the role of villain. Its principal crimes are

1. *A tendency to fly up too quickly to generalizations:*

> The mind longs to spring up to positions of higher generality, that it may find rest there; and so after a little while wearies of

experiment . . . this evil is increased by logic, because of the order and solemnity of its disputations.

(xx)[11]

2. *A tendency, not unrelated to (1), to identify its own sense of order with the cosmic order:*

It is a false assertion that the sense of man is the measure of things. On the contrary, all perceptions, as well of the sense as of the mind, are according to the measure of the individual and not according to the measure of the universe.

(xli)

The human understanding is of its own nature prone to suppose the existence of more order and regularity in the world than it finds.

(xlv)

3. *A tendency to ignore or suppress whatever does not accord with its own notions:*

The human understanding when it has once adopted an opinion (either as being the received opinion or as being agreeable to itself) draws all things else to support and agree with it. And though there be a greater number and weight of instances to be found on the other side, yet these it either neglects and despises; or else by some distinction sets aside and rejects; in order that by this great and pernicious predetermination the authority of its former conclusions may remain inviolate.

(xlvi)

4. *A tendency to assent to forms—logical, rhythmical, syntactical—rather than to empirical evidence:*

If you look at the method of them [presently received systems] and the divisions, they seem to embrace and comprise everything which can belong to the subject. And although these divisions are ill filled out and are, but as empty cases, still to the common mind they present the form and plan of a perfect science.

(lxxxvi)

It [the syllogism] is a thing most agreeable to the mind of man. For the mind of man is strangely eager to have something fixed and immovable, upon which in its wanderings and disquisitions it may securely rest.

(*De Aug., Sp.* 4: 428)

[11] References to the *Novum Organum* and the Preface to *The Great Instauration* are to *The English Philosophers From Bacon to Mill,* ed. E. A. Burtt (New York, 1939).

According to Bacon, these defects of the understanding are responsible for the confused state of knowledge at the present time, and unless they are remedied, no progress is possible. Of course in one sense the problem is insoluble, since these are "errors common to human nature" (xlii); but the least (and the most) we can do is provide "true helps of the understanding" so that "as far as the condition of mortality and humanity allows, the intellect may be . . . made capable of overcoming the difficulties and obscurities of nature" (p. 15). By "helps" Bacon means the method of induction, a manner of "collecting and concluding" whose principal force is to protect the mind against itself. The general rule is given in aphorism lviii—"let every student of nature take this as a rule, that whatever his mind seizes and dwells upon with particular satisfaction is to be held in suspicion"—and in practice this is translated into a determined delaying action:

> The understanding must not . . . be allowed to jump and fly from particulars to remote axioms and of almost the highest generality.
>
> (civ)

> The induction which is to be available for the discovery and demonstration of sciences and arts, must analyze nature by proper rejections and exclusions: and then after a sufficient number of negatives, come to a conclusion on the affirmative instances.
>
> (cv)

One must take care not to accept an axiom until it has been tried in the fire of "rejection and exclusion," and even then the acceptance should be provisional, leaving open the possibility that the discovery of new particulars will challenge its adequacy. This is a question not only of method but of communication. That is, the "cautions" Bacon would institute look in two directions, to the compilers of systems and to those who will come after them. If the mind of man is wont to assume completeness in a science merely because the form of its presentation has the *appearance* of completeness, that form must be altered accordingly. In place of an "artificial method" with full and articulated divisions, Bacon recommends "short and scattered sentences not linked together," aphorisms that will not give the impression that "they pretend or profess to embrace the entire art" (lxxxvi). For his part, he promises to "so present . . . things naked and open, that my errors can be marked and set aside before the mass of knowledge be further infected by them" (12). To each experiment, he will "subjoin a clear account of the manner in which I made it; that men knowing exactly how each point was made out, may see whether there be any error connected with it and may arouse themselves to devise proofs more trustworthy" (21). It will be the business of his presentation to "arouse" men rather than to "force or ensnare" their judgments(12).

This concern with a method of communication that neutralizes the errors the understanding is prone to is on display everywhere in Bacon's writings. There is now, he complains in *The Advancement of Learning*, "a kind of contract of error between the deliverer and the receiver: he that delivereth knowledge desireth to deliver it in such form as may be best believed; and he that receiveth knowledge desireth rather present satisfaction than expectant inquiry." Such a form of delivery—Bacon terms it "Magistral"—is proper for the transmission of settled truths, but tends to discourage futher inquiry. Far more fruitful is the way of "Probation" whereby knowledge is "delivered and intimated . . . in the same method wherein it was invented" (404).[12] The opposition of "Magistral" and "Probative" is transferred in the same work to another pair of terms, "Methods" and "Aphorisms," and the advantages claimed for Aphorisms are exactly those claimed for the new induction:

> . . . the writing in Aphorisms hath many excellent virtues, whereto the writing in Method doth not approach.
>
> For first, it trieth the writer, whether he be superficial or solid: for Aphorisms, except that they should be ridiculous, cannot be made but of the pith and heart of sciences; for discourse of illustration is cut off; recitals of examples are cut off; discourse of connexion and order is cut off; descriptions of practice are cut off; so there remaineth nothing to fill the Aphorisms but some good quantity of observation: and therefore no man can suffice, nor in reason will attempt, to write Aphorisms, but he that is sound and grounded. But in Methods . . . a man shall make a great shew of art, which if it were disjointed would come to little. Secondly, Methods are more fit to win consent or belief, but less fit to point to action; for they

---

[12] *Sp.*, vol. 3.

carry a kind of demonstration in orb or circle, one part illuminating another, and therefore satisfy; but particulars, being
dispersed, do not agree with dispersed directions. And lastly,
Aphorisms, representing a knowledge broken, do invite men to
enquire farther; whereas Methods, carrying the shew of a total,
do secure men, as if they were at furthest

(405).

Again, the distinction and the evaluation are made on the basis
of psychological effect rather than literal accuracy. The content of aphorisms is not necessarily more true than the content
of methodical writing; but one form has a more salutary effect
than the other because it minimizes the possibility that the
mind, in its susceptibility, will take the internal coherence of
an artful discourse for the larger coherence of objective truth.
Like induction and the way of Probation, writing in aphorisms
sacrifices present satisfaction to the hope of a fuller knowledge
in the future.

Later in *The Advancement of Learning,* Bacon turns to
a consideration of the "wisdom touching Negotiation or
Business," and here too the emphasis is on the dangers of a
procedure which facilitates the mind's tendency to rest in the
notions it already possesses:

The form of writing which of all others is fittest for this variable
argument of negotiation and occasion is that which Machiavel
chose wisely and aptly for government; *discourse upon histories
or examples.* For knowledge drawn freshly and in our view out
of particulars, knoweth the way best to particulars again. And it
hath much greater life for practice when the discourse attendeth
upon the example than when the example attendeth upon the
discourse. For this is no point of order, as it seemeth at first,
but of substance. For when the example is the ground . . . it is
set down with all circumstances, which may sometimes control
the discourse thereupon made and sometimes supply it, as a
very pattern for action; whereas the examples alleged for the
discourse sake are cited succinctly and without particularity,
and carry a servile aspect toward the discourse which they are
brought in to make good.

(453)

When a discourse is controlled by examples, its form is discovered rather than imposed and its general conclusions are
independent of the author's preconceptions which, indeed,

may be altered in the process of discovery; but when the examples carry a "servile" aspect to the discourse—that is, when they are brought in to make it good or left out because they do not make it good or are distorted so that the "axiom now in use" can be "rescued and preserved"—those preconceptions are allowed to limit what can be discovered. As A. N. Whitehead has put it, in an aphorism Bacon would have admired, "Our problem is . . . to fit the world to our perceptions, and not our perceptions to the world."[13]

III

We are now in a position to define more precisely the relationship between Bacon's *Essays* and his method of scientific inquiry. The point of contact, of course, is the *experience* the *Essays* give. If we return to the passage from "Of Love," and recast my analysis in the vocabulary of the *Novum Organum* and *The Advancement of Learning*, it becomes obvious that Bacon's strategy in that essay is dictated by his conception of the human understanding and its needs. First the reader is presented with an axiom-like statement enclosed in "such form as may be best believed, and not as may be best examined." The sentence is "rounded"; the progression of its thought is apparently logical; its parts "carry a kind of demonstration in orb or circle, one . . . illuminating another, and therefore satisfy." In short, the mind's desire "to have something fixed and immovable, upon which in its wanderings and disquisitions it may securely rest" has been gratified. (One should note in this connection that the sentence flatters the reader, since it allows him to include himself among "all the great and worthy persons.")

But, unexpectedly, the examples that follow do not "attend upon the discourse" but begin instead to "control and supply" it. The reader is "aroused" from his complacency and becomes involved in a refining operation in which the commonly received notion is subjected to the test of "proper rejections and exclusions." Qualification follows upon qualification with the double result that the original axiom is discredited—it is not sufficiently "wide" (*N.O.*, 1: cvi) to include "new particulars"—and the possibility of formulating another is called into question.

---

[13] *The Limits of Language*, ed. Walker Gibson, p. 14.

What then is the value of this experience? Obviously, it has not yielded the promised clarification of the nature of love, but in Bacon's scale of values it has yielded much more:

1. a felt knowledge of the attraction generalities have for the mind and therefore a "caution" against a too easy acceptance of them in the future;

2. an awareness of the *unresolved* complexity of the matter under discussion;

3. an open and inquiring mind, one that is dissatisfied with the state of knowledge at the present time.

In short, the demands of the prose have left the reader in a state of "healthy perplexity," neither content with the notion he had been inclined to accept at the beginning of the experience, nor quite ready to put forward a more accurate notion of his own.

My description of the essay, or, more precisely, of its effects, is noteworthy for an omission; it says nothing at all about the nominal subject, love; but as I have suggested earlier, the real subject of the essay is what men think about love, or, perhaps, *how* men think about love; and I would suggest further that the same formula should be applied to the other essays which are about how men think about friendship and fortune and dissimulation and studies and so on. This of course would tend to make all of the essays one large essay in the root sense of the word—one continuing *attempt* to make sense of things, with the emphasis on the "making sense of" rather than on the "things." The alternative (and more usual) view is well represented by Anne Righter:

> . . . the 1625 edition is not a tidy knitting together of various ideas which interested Bacon; it is an accumulation of disparate pieces as difficult to generalize about, or to connect internally, as Donne's *Songs and Sonets*, and it is to be read in a not dissimilar fashion.[14]

This statement has been endorsed recently by Vickers who adds that the *Essays* were "not . . . composed from a consistent impelling attitude or plan" (132). Mrs. Righter and Vickers are no doubt correct if one looks for a consistency of content or attitude (remember the "two" Bacons who trouble Zeitlin

[14] "Francis Bacon," in *The English Mind*, ed. H. S. Davies and G. Watson (Cambridge, 1964), p. 26.

and Bush); but there is, I think, another kind of consistency to the essays, a consistency of experience, which in turn is a reflection of what might be called an "impelling plan." The *Essays* are to be read not as a series of encapsulations or expressions, but as a process, a refining process that is itself being enacted by the reader; and to some extent, the question, in any one essay, of exactly what abstraction is being refined, is secondary.

Thus, in the 1625 essay "Of Love," for example, the title merely specifies the particular area of inquiry within which and in terms of which the reader becomes involved in a characteristic kind of activity, the questioning and testing of a commonly received notion. The excerpt analyzed above is followed in the 1625 text by a sentence that begins: "It is a poor saying . . ." The "poor saying" in question turns out to be one of Epicurus', but the phrase might well apply (as it seems to for a moment) to the generalization that has dominated the essay to this point, "amongst all the great and worthy persons . . . there is not one . . ." Indeed the true focus of the essay is the many "poor sayings" that have accumulated about this one abstraction; and the purpose of the essay is to initiate a search for "better sayings," sayings more in accordance with the observable facts.

This same pattern—the casual proffering of one or more familiar and "reverenced" witticisms followed by the introduction of data that calls their validity into question—is found everywhere in Bacon's *Essays*. A particularly good example is the late essay "Of Usury" which moves immediately to the point other essays make only indirectly:

> Many have made witty invectives against Usury. They say that it is a pity the devil should have God's part, which is the tithe. That the usurer is the greatest sabbath-breaker, because his plough goeth every Sunday. That the usurer is the drone that Virgil speaketh of;
> *Ignavum fucos pecus a praesepibus arcent.* That the usurer breaketh the first law that was made for mankind after the fall, which was, *in sudore vultus tui comedes panem tuum;* not, *in sudore vultus alieni* [in the sweat of thy face shalt thou eat bread —not in the sweat of another's face]. That usurers should have orange-tawny bonnets, because they do judaize. That it is against nature for money to beget money; and the like.

No practiced reader of Bacon's *Essays* will be likely to miss the sneer in "and the like"; and its effect is retroactive, extending back to the governing verb phrase, "They say . . ." In other essays, "They say . . ." will appear in slightly changed form as "men say" or "as has been thought," while "and the like" will be shortened to "and such"; but the implication is always the same: what men say and think about things may be far from the truth about them. In this case, the current sayings are "poor" because they have not been formulated with a view to the facts of the human condition:

> I say this only, that usury is a *concessum propter duritiem cordis;* [a thing allowed by reason of the hardness of men's hearts:] for since there must be borrowing and lending, and men are so hard of heart as they will not lend freely, usury must be permitted. Some others have made suspicions and cunning propositions of banks, discovery of men's estates, and other inventions. But few have spoken of usury usefully. It is good to set before us the incommodities and commodities of usury, that the good may be either weighed out or culled out; and warily to provide, that while we make forth to that which is better, we meet not with that which is worse.
>
> (*Sp.*, 6: 473–74)

In the *Novum Organum*, Bacon uses the phrase "sciences as one would" to refer to internally coherent, but objectively inaccurate, systematizations of knowledge: "For what a man had rather were true he more readily believes" (xlix). Here, in "Of Usury," the object of the philosopher's contempt is "morality as one would," a morality of wishful thinking based on "what men ought to do" rather than on "what men do." Such a morality, he implies, may well be immoral (useless), for it leaves a man ignorant of and defenseless against the real complexity of the situations that will confront him. It is a mistake to term the essays a "science of pure selfishness," if by that one means that they advocate selfishness: the essays advocate nothing (except perhaps a certain openness and alertness of mind), they are descriptive, and a description is ethically neutral, although if it is accurate, it may contribute to the development of a true, that is, responsible, ethics.

The making of "witty invectives" or of unrealistic rules is, as Bacon says in the second paragraph, "idle." Talk of the "abolishing of usury," for instance, "must be sent to Utopia"

(475). Bacon is even more vehement in "Of Suspicion," another late essay: "What would men have? Do they think those they employ and deal with are saints?" (454). In "Of Riches," the reader is warned, "have no abstract nor friarly contempt of them" (460). And the tone of the essays in this connection is established at the very beginning, in "Of Truth":

> Doth any man doubt, that if there were taken out of men's minds vain opinions, flattering hopes, false valuations, *imaginations as one would, and the like,* but it would leave the minds of a number of men poor shrunken things, full of melancholy and indisposition, and unpleasing to themselves?
>
> (377-78)

Taking out of the reader's mind all vain opinions, flattering hopes, false valuations, imaginations as one would, and the like, is the business of these essays. There is no room in Bacon's program for illusions, and especially not for the illusions projected naturally by the order-loving, simplicity-imposing, human understanding.

"Of Usury," however, is not typical of the essays because so much of the work is done *for* the reader. In the more characteristic essay, the "vain opinions" and "false valuations" are exposed gradually, and then only after the reader has been given an opportunity to accept them or to let them go by unchallenged. "Of Adversity" is such an essay, and for our purposes it has the advantage of being brief enough to be quoted in full:

> It was a high speech of Seneca (after the manner of the Stoics), *that the good things which belong to prosperity are to be wished; but the good things that belong to adversity are to be admired.* Bona rerum secundarum optabilia; adversarum mirabilia. Certainly if miracles be the command over nature, they appear most in adversity. It is yet a higher speech of his than the other (much too high for a heathen), *It is true greatness to have in one the frailty of a man, and the security of a God. Vere magnum habere fragilitatem hominis, securitatem Dei.* This would have done better in poesy, where transcendences are more allowed. And the poets indeed have been busy with it; for it is in effect the thing which is figured in that strange fiction of the ancient poets, which seemeth not to be without mystery; nay, and to have some approach to the state of a Christian; that *Hercules, when he went to unbind Prometheus*

(by whom human nature is represented), *sailed the length of the great ocean in an earthen pot or pitcher*; lively describing Christian resolution, that saileth in the frail bark of the flesh through the waves of the world. But to speak in a mean. The virtue of Prosperity is temperance, the virtue of Adversity is fortitude; which in morals is the more heroical virtue. Prosperity is the blessing of the Old Testament; Adversity is the blessing of the New; which carrieth the greater benediction, and the clearer revelation of God's favour. Yet even in the Old Testament, if you listen to David's harp, you shall hear as many hearse-like airs as carols; and the pencil of the Holy Ghost hath laboured more in describing the afflictions of Job than the felicities of Salomon. Prosperity is not without many fears and distastes; and Adversity is not without comforts and hopes. We see in needle-works and embroideries, it is more pleasing to have a lively work upon a sad and solemn ground, than to have a dark and melancholy work upon a lightsome ground: judge therefore of the pleasure of the heart by the pleasure of the eye. Certainly virtue is like precious odours, most fragrant when they are incensed or crushed: for Prosperity doth best discover vice, but Adversity doth best discover virtue.

(Sp., 6: 386)

In one of the more recent editions of the essays, "high" is glossed as "presumptuous," but this is hardly the meaning that will occur to the casual reader as he first moves into the essay. More likely he will assume, too easily, perhaps, but naturally, that by "high" Bacon intends "elevated" or "exalted" or "lofty," even "noble"; and in the same way, the parenthetical "after the manner of the Stoics" will seem at first to be a point of identification rather than a criticism. Only after the last word is read is the meaning of "high" clarified, and even then "presumptuous," while it is more accurate than "noble," does less than justice to the felt experience of the word's complexity. An understanding of that complexity is the chief product of the essay, which is finally more about "high speeches" (for which read "poor sayings" or "abstract" or "friarly") and their relationship to what is than it is about "adversity."

This first "high speech" exhibits many of the characteristics Bacon associates with the delivery of knowledge "in such form as may be best believed and not as may be best examined." This is the form Bacon condemns in the *De Augmentis* because it "seemes more witty and waighty than indeed it is":

> The labour here is altogether, *That words may be aculeate, sentences concise, and the whole contexture of the speech and discourse, rather rounding into it selfe, than spread and dilated* . . . Such a stile as this we finde more excessively in *Seneca* . . . it is nothing else but a hunting after words, and fine placing of them.[15]

The "fine placing" of the words results in a pointed and schematic prose in which the argument is carried more by the clinking harmony of like endings than by the "matter." In short, one assents to the form, which is designed to satisfy the physiological needs of the receiving consciousness, rather than to the content; and this makes the Senecan style, at its most mannered, as debilitating as the "sweet falling . . . clauses" of an extreme Ciceronianism; for both persuade by alluring and short-circuit the rational processes.

Williamson has noted how carefully Bacon's translation preserves the Senecan mannerisms, and even perfects them: "Bacon duplicates Seneca's balance, suggests his transverse like-endings, but adds alliteration to the parallelism of the second member." And he adds, "If this form be considered accidental, it may be argued that the similarities could have been, but are not, avoided."[16] The similarities are not avoided because Bacon wishes to secure, at least momentarily, the extreme Senecan effect, the unthinking acceptance of this "high speech." The reader is allowed to anticipate a comfortable and untaxing journey through the essay, and this expectation is strengthened by the first word of the next sentence, "Certainly." But the second word of the sentence is "if," and suddenly the hitherto sharp outlines of the discussion are blurred. "Certainly, if" is a particularly concise instance of a pattern that appears everywhere in the essays: words like "surely," "doubtless," "truly," and phrases like "in truth," "it is doubtless true," "certainly it is true," suggest strongly that what follows is to be accepted without qualification; but within a word or a phrase or, at most, a sentence, Bacon drops in one of another group of words and phrases—"but," "except," "although," "nevertheless," "and yet," and the most devastating of all, "it is *also* true." The result is a change in the quality of the reader's attention, from

[15] *De Aug.*, trans. Gilbert Wats (Oxford, 1640), p. 29.
[16] *The Senecan Amble* (London, 1951), p. 117.

complacency to a kind of uneasiness, an uneasiness that takes the (perhaps subconscious) form of a silently asked question: "What, exactly, is the truth about———?" At that moment the reader is transformed from a passive recipient of popular truth into a searcher after objective truth, and this transformation follows upon the transformation of the essay from a vehicle whose form is designed to secure belief into an instrument of inquiry and examination.

This is, perhaps, too great a burden to place on the phrase "Certainly, if" in "Of Adversity." Its effect is less dramatic; it simply introduces doubt where there had been none before, and that doubt, while it is unfocused, nevertheless extends to the word "adversity," which does appear in a prominent position. (Incidentally, this is the only function of the sentence, to foster doubt and uncertainty; that is, its purpose is not communicative or expressive, but rhetorical; Bacon is not really interested in whether or not miracles can be defined as "the command over nature.") The reader's active involvement in the essay begins with the next sentence, which returns to the concept of "highness." However straightforwardly the first "high" had been accepted, there is something uncomfortable and awkward about the comparative "higher," and of course with the parenthesis ("much too high for a heathen") the word can no longer be taken as honorific. It is here that the meaning "presumptuous" comes into play and with it an implied hierarchy of authorities—heathen vs. Christian. This second "high speech," then, will be viewed with more suspicion than the first, and that suspicion will be confirmed and given body by its association in the following sentence with "poesy" and "transcendences." A third meaning of "high" now emerges—"unreal" or "remote from the world of facts"—a meaning reinforced by the phrase "strange fiction." Together with "heathen," "poesy," and "transcendences," "strange fiction" forms a system of related terms that begin to displace "adversity" as the subject of the essay. In this system, "mystery" occupies an ambiguous position: on one hand it shares with poetry "and the like" the taint of "fantasy"; and on the other it looks ahead to the more respectable category of "Christian." But that word too, coming as it does at the end of the series, cannot escape the pejorative associations that have been clustering around "high" and its equivalences. The opposition of "heathen" to "Christian" now seems less firm and controlling than it did a few moments ago, and the reader is further away than ever from knowing the "truth" about adversity, largely because the authorities contending for his attention have been overtly or implicitly discredited.

In short, the effect of the first half of the essay is to disabuse the reader of whatever confidence he may have had in the sayings of heathen philosophers, poets, traffickers in mysteries, or even Christians. At this point Bacon introduces another of his "code phrases"—"But to speak in a mean"—which will be read by the initiated as, "Now that we've taken note of the opinions men commonly hold on the subject, let us look to the truth of the matter." In "Of Usury" the phrase is "to speak usefully" and in "Of Cunning," "To say truth," while in "Of Truth" the distinction implied by all these is made more fully: "To pass from theological and philosophical truth, to the truth of civil business" (*Sp.*, 3: 378). In terms of the methodology of philosophic inquiry, "theological truth" is no more to be honored than any other body of commonly received notions. One of the most remarkable statements in the *Novum Organum* is this variation on the biblical commonplace, "Render therefore unto Caesar the things which be Caesar's" (*Luke*, 20:25):

> . . . some of the moderns have with extreme levity indulged so far as to attempt to found a system of natural philosophy on the first chapter of Genesis . . . from this unwholesome mixture of things human and divine there arises not only a fantastic philosophy but also an heretical religion. Very meet it is therefore that we be sober-minded, and give to faith that only which is faith's.
>
> (lxv)

Being "sober-minded" means speaking "usefully" or "in a mean," descending from the aery heights where adversity is characterized by the image of the frail bark of flesh sailing through the waves of the world (this is almost comical) to the level plain of empirical observation and a plainer style: "The virtue of Prosperity is temperance, the virtue of Adversity is fortitude. . . . Prosperity is the blessing of the Old Testament; Adversity is the blessing of the New." But these speeches, while they are less "lively" and metaphorical than the others, are still "high" in the all-important sense of being above the facts; and moreover the parallel members and the pointed schemes operate to secure the kind of facile assent Bacon is always warning against. Once again knowledge is being delivered "In such form as may best be believed" and once again Bacon breaks the spell of his cadenced rhythms with a characteristic qualification: "Yet, even ..." But the qualifying statement has a rhythm of its own in addition to a network of patterned oppositions—"David's harp"—"pencil of the Holy Ghost," "hearse-like airs" —"afflictions of Job," "carols"—"felicities of Salomon"—and for the third time the reader is encouraged to relax while his powers of judgment are taken over by the movement of the prose. The transverse patterning continues—"Prosperity"—"fears and distastes," "Adversity"—"comforts and hopes"—as the distinction between the two abstractions becomes increasingly blurred. The argument, which is, of course, rhetorical rather than logical, is helped along by the unheralded reintroduction of "lively" language. Amidst talk of "embroideries" and "lightsome grounds," the emotional and physical realities of adversity fade, and when Bacon concludes "Judge therefore of the pleasure of the heart by the pleasure of the eye" he is in fact urging something his style has already effected. As the final sentence unfolds, the reader is once more in the position he occupied at the beginning of the essay, the passive receiver of "high speeches," assured by an introductory "Certainly" that nothing will be required of him but a nod of the head. The sentence itself is the "highest" speech imaginable, complete with an elaborate and fanciful simile and ending with a perfect and pointed *isocolon*. But the effect is spoiled, intentionally of course, by a single superfluous phrase—"or crushed"—which not only upsets the symmetry of the parallel members, but serves, for the last time, to arouse the reader from the intellectual lethargy he has fallen into. Supposedly offered as a synonym for "incensed," "crushed" is instead a comment on it and on "precious odours" and "fragrant" too, revealing what "incensed" and all incense-like "high speech" is designed to hide, the hard, and ultimately saving, truth. Without it the last pair of neat antitheses—"Prosperity doth best discover vice, but Adversity doth best discover virtue"—would have been received with the reverence we usually accord comforting *sententiae*, but with its near-onomatopoetic sound ringing in our ears, the response is more likely to be, "that's all very nice, but...." The essay ends, then, as it began, with a "high speech," but in between the two the deficiencies of any speech that flies above the facts have again and again been exposed along with the attraction such speeches hold for the mind of the reader. The question of the nature of "adversity" is no more settled here than the question of the nature of "love" is settled in that essay. In fact, the experience of the essay is *un*settling, and therefore it meets Bacon's criteria for "useful" and "fruitful" discourse, discourse, which, because it does not pretend to completeness, invites men "to enquire farther."

IV

The movement characteristic of this essay, the uneasy and unsettling juxtaposition of *sententiae* and observations from the "real world," has not gone unnoticed by the critics who for the most part regard it as an accidental by-product of Bacon's revisions:

. . . compositions which were originally pervaded by an atmosphere of clear moral stimulation were overlaid with considerations of immediate practical utility, till their primary inspiration became altogether obscured.

(Zeitlin, 514)

In the later editions . . . although the ligatures are good, unlike elements are joined and chronology is ignored.

(A. W. Green)[17]

The assumption is that the presence in a single work of "unlike elements" is regrettable, and in some sense, unintentional— Bacon either lost control of his form in the successive editions or unwittingly allowed the essays to become a battleground for the warring elements of his personality. But "Of Adversity" is a late essay, as are others in which the same pattern can be seen. The "accidents-of-revision" theory will not hold water, no more than will Vickers' assertion that Bacon is without a plan: "Bacon . . . added new material at any moderately suitable point, without much thought to the overall development" (132). These statements are further evidence of a general failure to see that the coherence of the *Essays*—singly and as a whole— inheres in the experience they provide. A study of the revisions, with a view to the changes effected in the reader's response, will, I think, reveal a determined effort to make the *Essays* the kind of experience I have been describing.

17 A. W. Green, *Sir Francis Bacon* (Twayne, 1966), p. 84.

Let us turn once again to the essay "Of Love," but this time in its 1612 guise, a perfectly straightforward piece of conventional moralism:

> LOVE is the argument alwaies of *Comedies*, and many times of *Tragedies*. Which sheweth well, that it is a passion generally light, and sometimes extreme. Extreame it may well bee, since the speaking in a perpetuall *Hyperbole*, is comely in nothing, but *Loue*. Neither is it meerely in the phrase. For whereas it hath beene well said, that the *Archflatterer* with whom al the petty-flatters haue intelligence, is a Mans selfe, certainely the louer is more. For there was neuer proud Man thought so absurdly well of himselfe, as the louer doth of the person loued: and therefore it was well said, that it is impossible to loue, and to bee wise. Neither doth this weakenes appeare to others only, and not to the party loued, but to the loued most of all, except the loue bee reciproque. For it is a true rule, that loue is euer rewarded either with the reciproque, or with an inward and secret contempt. But how much the more, men ought to beware of this passion, which loseth not onely other things, but it selfe. As for the other losses, the Poets relation doth wel figure them: That hee that preferred *Helena*, quitted the gifts of *Iuno* and *Pallas*. For whosoeuer esteemeth too much of amorous affection, quitteth both riches and wisdome. This passion hath his flouds in the verie times of weakenesse; which are great prosperity, and great aduersitie. (though this latter hath beene lesse obserued) Both which times kindle loue and make it more feruent, and therefore shew it to be the childe of folly. They doe best that make this affection keepe quarter, and seuer it wholly from their serious affaires and actions of their life. For if it checke once with businesse, it troubleth Mens fortunes, and maketh Men, that they can no waies be true to their own endes.

> (*Sp.*, 6: 557–58)

This admirably structured paragraph answers to the idea most people (who have not read them) have of Bacon's *Essays*. The argument moves smoothly from one point to the next; the prose is "pithy" and aphoristic; the moral vision clear and unambiguous. The first two sentences seem almost to generate what follows: Comedy and Tragedy are used to specify the two chief characteristics of love, its excessiveness and its triviality ("lightness"). This "division" is then expanded into an indictment of love as an unworthy passion that interferes with the "serious affaires and actions of . . . life." The example of

Paris is brought in to "prove" Bacon's thesis, and the essay ends with a predictable and unexceptionable exhortation: avoid love, especially when it threatens to make you forsake your "own endes."

Much of this is retained in 1625, but the additional materials work a profound change in the tone of the essay and completely transform the phrases and sentences that have been carried over from the earlier version. The nature of this change can be seen by a comparison of the two openings:

> Love is the argument alwaies of *Comedies*, and many times of *Tragedies*. Which sheweth well, that it is a passion generally light, and sometimes extreme.
>
> (*Sp.*, 6: 557)

> The stage is more beholding to Love, than the life of man. For as to the stage, love is ever matter of comedies, and now and then of tragedies; but in life it doth much mischief; sometimes like a syren, sometimes like a fury.
>
> (*Sp.*, 6: 397)

In place of the easy correspondence between life and the stage, we now have a clear separation of the two, and a suggestion that the view of love projected on the stage is an oversimplification. This implied criticism extends to the whole of the earlier essay, which, like other presentations whose coherence is merely formal, excludes more of the truth than it contains. Bacon's additions operate to break that coherence, and to substitute for the almost physical satisfaction of a "closed" experience the greater satisfaction of a fuller understanding. Specifically, the emphasis is shifted from the prescriptive moral—avoid love—to the difficulty, if not impossibility, of doing so. This is clearly the effect of the passage analyzed at the beginning of this paper. The first sentence holds out the promise of an easy and formulaic distinction between wise men and mad lovers; but as exceptions to it are admitted, that formula becomes less and less reliable, until the phrase "if watch be not well kept" discards it altogether by transferring the responsibility from the labels to the individual. Wise man or fool, austere man or voluptuary; it doesn't seem to matter; love can always find entrance into a heart that is not constantly on guard against it. Later, when the two versions of the essay coalesce, sentiments that had seemed unexceptionable in the tightly controlled framework of 1612 now ring somewhat hollowly in the looser, but more inclusive, framework of 1625. This is particularly true of that most familiar of proverbs, "it is impossible to love and be wise." In the earlier essay that old saw is accepted without qualification or reservation as the inevitable conclusion to the arguments preceding it; but in 1625, with the examples of Marcus Antonius and Appius Claudius fresh in our memories, the response to that same sententia is made up of equal parts of skepticism and wonder. It may indeed be "well said" that "it is impossible to love and be wise," but is it *true?* After all, Bacon's original assertion, that "amongst all the great and worthy persons . . . there is not one that hath been transported to the mad degree of love" was also "well said," as was, presumably, the "poor saying" of Epicurus. Not that the reader will flatly reject this "saying"; the conflicting evidence is itself too inconclusive for anything so drastic. The effect of Bacon's revisions is never to cancel out what had been asserted previously, but to qualify it: something assumed to be true on the basis of what now appears to be inadequate evidence is not declared false (necessarily); rather, something else is declared to be true *also*. And if the fact of the two "true things" poses difficulties for the logically oriented consciousness, well, that's life. And that is also the experience of a Bacon essay.

In addition to inserting new material and (as a consequence) repositioning the old, Bacon achieves his complicating effects by slightly altering the phrasing of individual sentences. In 1612, the reader is advised that "they doe best that make this affection keep quarter, and sever it wholly from their serious affaires." In 1625 a single clause is added, but it makes all the difference in the world: "They do best who, *if they cannot but admit love,* yet make it keep quarter and sever it wholly from their serious affairs." In the light of the revised essay's emphasis on the difficulty of keeping love out, the parenthetical qualification is more than a gesture. The sentence, in its expanded form, reflects the delicate and shifting relationship between the absoluteness of a moral imperative ("morality as one would") and the realities of a difficult world, and serves as a further reminder to the reader that there are no easy answers.

As is often the case, the later essay is given a new conclusion, one that reveals more baldly than anything else the transformation that has been wrought in the vehicle:

I know not how, but martial men are given to love: I think it is but as they are given to wine; for perils commonly asked to be paid in pleasures. There is in man's nature a secret inclination and motion towards love of others, which if it be not spent upon some one or a few, doth naturally spread itself toward many, and maketh men become humane and charitable as it is seen sometimes in friars. Nuptial love maketh mankind; friendly love perfecteth it; but wanton love corrupteth and embaseth it.

(398)

A statement like "I know not how" would have been unthinkable at the beginning of the essay. The posture usually assumed by the moral essayist does not allow for an admission of ignorance. But by this time, a more assertive stance would be out of place. Both the speaker and the reader have long since given up the illusion that love could be easily defined or contained; all we can do for the present is note the operation of this strange passion. It is a fact that martial men are given to love, but aside from a hardly serious reference to an old wives' tale, there is no explanation for the fact. Bacon must resort to the evasion of positing a "secret inclination" whose visible effects are the actions we group under the rubric "love." In this penultimate sentence love becomes a kind of disease spreading of its own volition into every corner of our varied lives. So powerful is this force that it literally overwhelms the qualitative distinctions we usually make between its manifestations. "Humane" and "charitable" love lose their positive associations and become just two more instances of this "spreading"; the religious life is less a noble and chosen calling than it is an involuntary response to an irresistible urge. An essay that began by identifying a "mad degree" of love and implying the existence of other, more manageable degrees, concludes by suggesting that all love is uncontrollable and, perhaps, mad. In the end, Bacon does return to the pointed prose and neat schematizations of the opening paragraph, but the familiar and comforting labels—"nuptial," "friendly," "wanton"—are here nothing but the skeletal remains of a simpler vision that is no longer ours.

And this is of course, exactly as Bacon would have it; for it is his intention, to borrow the words of an Englishman nearly contemporary, to purge our intellectual ray so that it is once more fit and proportionable to Truth, the object and end of it.

II

R. L. BRETT

Thomas Hobbes

At the heart of the philosophy of Thomas Hobbes (1588–1679) lies this combination of strict empiricism with a rationalist and deductive method. His epistemology and psychology rest upon the conviction that all our knowledge ultimately derives from sense experience, for as he writes in the opening chapter of *Leviathan* (1651), ". . . there is no conception in a man's mind, which hath not at first, totally, or by parts, been begotten upon the organs of sense. The rest are derived from that original" (1: i).[1] Hobbes also argues that we can only obtain knowledge which is universally true by proceeding deductively from exact definitions, and by a process of reasoning, to link these in a logically necessary chain of argument. Philosophy, for Hobbes, is no other than reasoning.

This kind of logical empiricism leads in Hobbes to a dualism in knowledge itself.

> There are of KNOWLEDGE two kinds; whereof one is *knowledge of fact:* the other *knowledge of the consequence of one affirmation to another.* The former is nothing else, but sense and memory, and is *absolute knowledge;* as when we see a fact doing, or remember it done: and this is the knowledge required in a witness. The latter is called *science* [i.e. exact and universally valid knowledge]; and is *conditional;* as when we know, that *if the figure shown be a circle, then any straight line through the centre shall divide it into two equal parts.* And this is the knowledge required in a philosopher; that is to say, of him that pretends to reasoning.
>
> (1: ix)

Reprinted from *The English Mind: Studies in the English Moralists Presented to Basil Willey,* edited by Hugh Sykes Davies and George Watson, pp. 30–54. Copyright 1964 by Cambridge University Press. Reprinted by permission of the author and publisher.

[1] *Leviathan*, ed. Michael Oakeshott (Oxford, 1946), p. 7. All quotations from *Leviathan* are from this edition.

The first kind of knowledge is entirely of particulars; it is an absolute knowledge, for facts are neither true nor false but simply facts. Even history is only a record of particular facts, and according to Hobbes a study of it cannot lead to generalizations which are necessarily true. No doubt a study of history will give a man wisdom, and past experience will enable him to look to the future with some "foresight"; it will give him what Hobbes calls "prudence." But "experience concludeth nothing universally,"[2] and history and prudence are not knowledge as understood by the philosopher.

Nor does science (in the modern sense that is, and not as used by Hobbes, who equates it with philosophy) provide us with certain and universal truth. For mathematics he had a great admiration, and it was on first looking at the works of Euclid, at the age of forty, he tells us, that he "fell in love with geometry," delighted "not so much by the theorems as by its way of reasoning." But for the experimental method he had no sympathy. In spite of his early and close association with Bacon, he scarcely mentions him in his writings, and his attitude to the Royal Society and all it stood for was almost contemptuous. Science when based on observation and induction cannot give us real knowledge.

But though Hobbes distinguishes between philosophical and empirical knowledge, he believes that it is the former and not the latter which is concerned with cause and effect. Experience cannot discern any causal relation between particulars; this is the result of reasoning. He defines philosophy at the beginning of *De corpore* as ". . . such knowledge of effects or appearances, as we acquire by true ratiocination from the knowledge we have first of their causes or generation: And again, of such causes or generations as may be from knowing first their effects"[3] God is ruled out as a subject for philosophical speculation, for God, as a matter of definition, is uncaused. He does not deny the existence of God, but considers it a matter of faith and not knowledge. Knowledge then, in its philosophical sense, and as described by Hobbes, is distinct from experience, from history, from science, and from theology. Its limits are very sharply drawn; its concern is with cause and effect, and as we

[2] *Discourse on Human Nature*, in *English Works of Thomas Hobbes*, ed. William Molesworth (London, 1840), 4: 18.

[3] *English Works*, ed. Molesworth (London, 1840), 1: 3.

shall see in a moment, only with these in a very special and restricted sense.

According to Hobbes a relationship between the two kinds of knowledge he has defined is effected by the use of language. Man, along with all the animal world, is endowed with perception, but alone among the animals he has the power of reflection and is self-conscious. The instrument of this power is his ability to use language. Hobbes refers to language in many places in his writings and devotes an entire chapter of *Leviathan* to it. Briefly, his account of language is that it enables man to pass from a knowledge of particulars to general notions. We attach names to the images of sense-perception as an aid to memory, and then we relate these names by putting them in propositions. But language is not only a medium of thought, it is a means of communication. Hobbes distinguishes four uses of language. The first of these connects it with reason; ". . . to register what by cogitation we find to be the cause of any thing, present or past; and what we find things present or past may produce, or effect"; the second sees it as communication, "to show to others that knowledge which we have attained"; the third considers it as persuasion, "to make known to others our wills and purposes, that we may have the mutual help of one another"; and the fourth views it simply as a source of aesthetic pleasure; "to please and delight ourselves and others, by playing with our words, for pleasure or ornament, innocently" (1: iv).

The power language has as a medium of thought is drastically restricted by Hobbes's nominalism. Though language enables us to pass from particulars to general notions, Hobbes does not believe that universals have any existential validity. They are simply names given to a class of individual beings as a kind of shorthand reference.

> Of names, some are *proper,* and singular to one only thing, as *Peter, John, this man, this tree*; and some are *common* to many things, *man, horse, tree*; every of which, though but one name, is nevertheless the name of divers particular things; in respect of all which together, it is called an *universal*; there being nothing in the world universal but names; for the things named are every one of them individual and singular.
>
> (1: iv)

Reason, which is nothing more in Hobbes than reasoning, is the power of joining names together in propositions which are seen to be self-evident. But though we can transcend the particularity of brute fact and make generalizations, these are true only in a very limited sense. For generalizations are only about names and not about the real world. It was this profound skepticism that caused J. S. Mill, who admired Hobbes as "one of the clearest and most consecutive thinkers whom this country or the world has produced," to criticize Hobbes's theory of logic.

> The only propositions of which Hobbes' principle is a sufficient account are that limited and unimportant class in which both the predicate and the subject are proper names. . . . But it is a sadly inadequate theory of any others. That it should ever have been thought of as such, can be accounted for only by the fact that Hobbes, in common with the other Nominalists, bestowed little or no attention upon the *connotation* of words and sought for their meaning exclusively in what they *denote;* as if all names had been (what none but proper names really are) marks put upon individuals; and as if there were no difference between a proper and a general name, except that the first denotes only one individual and the last a greater number.[4]

It follows from Hobbes's nominalism that when he says philosophy is concerned with cause and effect, he does not mean cause and effect as they are empirically verified by physical science. Causation for him is a concept of logic, it is what is logically demonstrable and not what is empirically verifiable. Hobbes believes that he proceeds deductively from purely empirical axioms which introspection declares to be self-evident, but the identification of causality with logical entailment is a rationalist assumption which is really incompatible with his empiricism. Even body and motion, which for Hobbes are the two great principles from which he deduces his philosophical system, are not proved by observation. Sensation, which is the source of all our knowledge, demands a belief in both body and motion. Without body there could be no motion and without bodies being moved so as to act upon our sense organs there could be no sensory experience. Body and motion are prerequisites for our having any knowledge at all.

Hobbes is equally forthright in his declaration that the knowledge gained by reasoning is only conditional and not absolute.

---

[4] *A System of Logic* (London, 1843), 1: 5: 2.

And therefore, when the discourse is put into speech, and begins with the definitions of words, and proceeds by connexion of the same into general affirmations, and of these again into syllogisms; the end or last sum is called the conclusion; and the thought of the mind by it signified, is that conditional knowledge, or knowledge of the consequence of words, which is commonly called SCIENCE.

(1: vii)

The function of reason is to frame propositions which are analytical. Hobbes sees the work of reason as best exemplified in mathematical calculation, which starts from certain agreed premises and arrives at its conclusions by logical necessity.

This implies that reason is concerned not with ends but means. If, for instance, men desire peace (and Hobbes thinks that everyone would be ready to accept this hypothesis), reason will indicate the means by which we can ensure it, and his *Leviathan* contains a long succession of arguments which he thinks are demonstrably true to show how this can best be done. The end itself is not dictated by reason, for value is not a matter of reasoning, it is simply the object of men's desire.

But whatsoever is the object of any man's appetite or desire, that is it which he for his part calleth *good*: and the object of his hate and aversion, *evil*; and of his contempt, *vile* and *inconsiderable*. For these words of good, evil and contemptible, are ever used with relation to the person that useth them: there being nothing simply and absolutely so; nor any common rule of good and evil, to be taken from the nature of the objects themselves.

(1: vi)

If reason is to perform its task efficiently, it must employ language which is as concise, clear, and unambiguous as possible. The first stage in the process of reasoning is accurate definition, for "in the right definition of names lies the first use of speech; which is the acquisition of science" (1: iv). But even this preliminary is difficult, for our use of words is biased by self-interest and emotion.

. . . in reasoning a man must take heed of words; which besides the signification of what we imagine of their nature, have a signification also of the nature, disposition, and interest of the speaker. . . . And therefore such names can never be true grounds of any ratiocination. Nor more can metaphors and

tropes of speech: but these are less dangerous, because they profess their inconstancy; which the other do not.

(1: iv)

Given exact definitions, we can proceed "to assertions made by
connexion of one of them to another," and then to "the con-
nexions of one assertion to another, till we come to a knowledge
of all the consequences of names appertaining to the subject in
hand" (1: v). The opposite of this is to employ "metaphors, and
senseless and ambiguous words, [which] are like *ignes fatui*; and
reasoning upon them is wandering amongst innumerable
absurdities" (1: v).

But Hobbes believes that language is more than simply an
instrument of reason. We have seen that he distinguishes logical
discourse from persuasion and teaching, and from language as
a means of aesthetic pleasure. Logic is one thing, rhetoric and
poetry are quite different.

Hobbes's interest in literature lasted all his life. His earliest
published work was a translation of *The Peloponnesian War* of
Thucydides (1629) and amongst his last publications were his
verse-translations of Homer's *Iliad* and *Odyssey* (1673–76).
Writing of the latter in his preface to the *Fables*, Dryden said
that Hobbes had turned to poetry "as he did mathematics, when
it was too late," but nevertheless Hobbes's work was remarkable
for some one approaching ninety. As a young man he had
counted among his friends Ben Jonson, Lord Herbert of Cher-
bury, and the Scottish poet, Robert Aytoun. Of this period
John Aubrey tells us that "Before Thucydides, he spent two
yeares in reading romances and playes, which he haz often
repented and sayd that these two yeares were lost of him."[5]
But Hobbes's love of literature never left him. His friends in
later life included Waller, Cowley, and Davenant, and his writings show not only a speculative interest in literary questions,
but a mastery of style, a brilliant concision, and a deft use of the
telling phrase.

While he was tutor to William Cavendish, son of the Duke of
Devonshire, Hobbes dictated to his young pupil an abstract of
Aristotle's *Rhetoric*. It was published as *A Briefe of the Art of
Rhetorique* and was entered in the Stationers' Register in 1636.

[5] Aubrey, *Brief Lives*, ed. Andrew Clark (Oxford, 1898), 1: 361.

This rather free and condensed version of Aristotle's treatise is an early work and partly a translation, and it does not necessarily represent Hobbes's mature views, but it still has a certain interest. In the second chapter of the *Briefe*, where he defines rhetoric, he writes: "Proofs are, in *Rhetorick*, either *Examples*, or *Enthymemes*, as in *Logick, Inductions*, or *Syllogismes*. For an *Example* is a short *Induction*, and an *Enthymeme* a short *Syllogisme;* out of which are left as superfluous, that which is supposed to be necessarily understood by the hearer; to avoid prolixity."[6] When he came to elaborate his own system of logic he left no place for induction, and "Examples," being all particular, were held to prove nothing. But "Examples" could still provide practical wisdom and graphic illustrations of truths which had been arrived at by other means, and this is one of the functions Hobbes assigns to literature. So also it is possible for literary discourse to condense long chains of logical argument and to relieve the monotony of syllogistic reasoning by rhetorical devices. His own prose gives a vivid demonstration of how to write philosophy with style, of how to achieve persuasiveness without sacrificing logical consistency.

There is nothing in this contrary to the traditional theory of the period. On the first of these points Hobbes is echoing Sidney, who wrote of the poet in his *Apologie for Poetrie*: "whatsoever the Philosopher sayth shoulde be doone, hee [i.e., the poet] giveth a perfect picture of it in some one, by whom hee presupposeth it was doone. So as hee coupleth the generall notion with the particular example."[7] The second point reaffirms Bacon's definition of "the office of Rhetoric" in the *Advancement of Learning*, which is ". . . to apply and recommend the dictates of reason to imagination in order to excite the appetite and will."[8] The development of Hobbes's philosophy, however, brought some changes in his literary theory. These

[6] *A Briefe of the Art of Rhetorique* (1681 edition), ch. 2. Father W. J. Ong, S.J., in his "Hobbes and Talon's Ramist Rhetoric in English," *Trans. Cambridge Bibliographical Society*, 1 (1951), argues that Hobbes's definition of an enthymeme derives not from Aristotle but Ramus. There may be some truth in this, but his contention that Hobbes was a Ramist in logic is unlikely. On a point of central importance they are divided; Hobbes was a nominalist whereas Ramus was a realist.

[7] *Apologie*, ed. J. Churton Collins (Oxford, 1907), p. 17.

[8] *The Philosophical Works of Bacon*, ed. J. M. Robertson (London, 1905), p. 535.

occur in his later writings, and it is in the *Answer to D'Avenant* that their nature and extent are most evident. In this he leans heavily on Aristotle's *Poetics*. For instance, ". . . the subject of a Poem," he writes, "is the manners of men, not natural causes; manners presented, not dictated; and manners feigned, as the name of Poesy imports, not found."[9] But when he relates poetry to his own theory of knowledge he is more original and controversial. In a famous passage in which he presents his theory of the poetic imagination he writes:

> Time and Education begets experience; Experience begets memory; Memory begets Judgement and Fancy; Judgement begets the strength and structure, and Fancy begets the Ornaments of a Poem. The Ancients therefore fabled not absurdly in making memory the Mother of the Muses. For memory is the World (though not really, yet so as in a looking glass) in which the Judgement, the severer Sister, busieth her self in a grave and rigid examination of all the parts of Nature, and in registering by Letters their order, causes, uses, differences, and resemblances; Whereby the Fancy, when any work of Art is to be performed findes her materials at hand and prepared for use.[10]

Here Hobbes's empiricist psychology is brought into use to explain the literary imagination. The outside world, by impinging on our sense-organs, produces images in our minds; when the objects themselves are no longer present these images are stored in memory, which Hobbes describes as no other than "decaying sense."[11] This store of sensory images gives rise to judgment and fancy (or imagination). Fancy is the ability to discern likenesses between things, whereas judgment is the power of distinguishing differences; together they make up wit, which is the facility for linking one idea to another. "The former, that is, fancy, without the help of judgment, is not commended as a virtue: but the latter which is judgment, and discretion, is commended for itself, without the help of fancy" (1: viii). We can understand why Hobbes makes judgment responsible for "the strength and structure" of a poem, for he continues,

[9] *The Answer to D'Avenant*, in *Critical Essays of the Seventeenth Century*, ed. J. E. Spingarn (Oxford, 1908), 2: 56.

[10] *Op. cit.*, 2: 59.

[11] *Leviathan*, 1: ii.

... without steadiness, and direction to some end, a great fancy
is one kind of madness; such as they have, that entering into any
discourse, are snatched from their purpose, by every thing that
comes in their thought, into so many, and so long digressions,
and parentheses, that they utterly lose themselves.

(1: viii)

Nor does he contradict what he says in his *Answer to D'Avenant*, when he maintains in *Leviathan* that "In a good poem,
whether it be *epic*, or *dramatic*; as also in *sonnets, epigrams*, and
other pieces, both judgment and fancy are required: but the
fancy must be more eminent; because they please for the ex-
travagancy; but ought not to displease by indiscretion" (1: viii).
But poetry is one thing, logical discourse another. When truth
is our concern there is scarcely a place for fancy.

In demonstration, in counsel, and all rigorous search of truth,
judgment does all, except sometimes the understanding have
need to be opened by some apt similitude; and then there is so
much use of fancy. But for metaphors, they are in this case
utterly excluded. For seeing they openly profess deceit; to
admit them into counsel, or reasoning, were manifest folly.

(1: viii)

Fancy, then, according to Hobbes, is not only the younger
sister: she must put herself in tutelage to the elder if she is to
be useful as well as beautiful. When indeed she becomes the
handmaid of philosophy, her accomplishments are almost as
great as civilization itself.

But so far forth as the Fancy of man has traced the ways of true
Philosophy, so far it hath produced very marvellous effects to
the benefit of mankinde. All that is beautiful or defensible in
building, or marvellous in Engines and Instruments of motion,
whatsoever commodity men receive from the observations of
the Heavens, from the description of the Earth, from the account of Time, from walking on the Seas, and whatsoever
distinguisheth the civility of Europe from the Barbarity of the
American savages, is the workmanship of Fancy but guided
by the Precepts of true Philosophy. But where these precepts
fail, as they have hitherto failed in the doctrine of Moral vertue,
there the Architect, Fancy, must take the Philosophers part
upon her self.[12]

[12] *The Answer to D'Avenant*, ed. cit., 2: 59–60.

The word "doctrine" in the last sentence of this passage has led some commentators[13] to suggest that Hobbes considers moral philosophy bankrupt and thinks poetry can take its place. But the word is used here in its older sense of "teaching," and he is making the traditional point that poetry can be a better moral teacher than philosophy because it provides example as well as precept. Great and genuine as his admiration for the power of the imagination undoubtedly is, it never leads him to the belief that poetry allows us to dispense with philosophy.

There is a good deal in Hobbes's account that is unoriginal. The conception of poetry as a more persuasive way of teaching morality than philosophy can achieve is almost a commonplace in Renaissance rhetoric and poetic. What gives his account novelty is his empiricist psychology and theory of knowledge. No one before Hobbes has paid much attention to the mental processes involved in writing literature, and his description of the writer's mind at work proved so convincing that it became generally accepted by his contemporaries. There were strong objections to his philosophy, especially from the Cambridge Platonists, but it was left to a later generation to realize that if the philosophy were at fault, it was likely that the theory of literature derived from it would also be unsatisfactory.

The central weaknesses of Hobbes's philosophy when looked at from the standpoint of literature—and indeed from any standpoint—are his restriction of reason to the process of reasoning and his belief that the mind can arrive at truth only by logical demonstration. This leaves literature with only two roles; it can propagate truths arrived at by reasoning, and it can entertain. Truth for Hobbes was a property of propositions; the notion that truth can be adumbrated in myth, symbol, and image was simply the chimera of a distempered mind. A theory of imagination of the kind advanced by Coleridge, which sees the imagination as an "agent" of the reason, or, as Wordsworth put it in *The Prelude*, "reason in her most exalted mood," would have been quite alien to the positivist temper of his thought. For him there is no interplay of reason and imagination by which the mind is given greater insight, no reciprocity between symbol and concept which will extend the boundaries

[13] Cf. D. G. James, *The Life of Reason* (London, 1949).

of man's knowledge.[14] The relation between reason and imagination is that of master and servant; judgment controls the excesses of fancy, which must always have a subordinate position.

The difference between these two conceptions of the imagination is shown by the analogies Hobbes and Coleridge use to describe the imagination. With Hobbes the process of imagination is little more than a review of the images stored in the memory. For him imagination and memory are almost identical.

> This *decaying sense*, when we would express the thing itself, I mean *fancy* itself, we call *imagination*, as I said before: but when we would express the decay, and signify that the sense is fading, old, and past, it is called *memory*. So that imagination and memory are but one thing, which for divers considerations hath divers names.[15]

The images he uses to describe the imaginative process are humble and even pedestrian; it operates ". . . as one would sweep a room, to find a jewel; or as a spaniel ranges the field, till he find a scent; or as a man should run over the alphabet, to start a rhyme" (1: iii).[16] How different from Coleridge's "divine analogy,"[17] which sees the imagination ". . . as a repetition in the finite mind of the eternal act of creation in the infinite I AM."[18] In some respects, then, Hobbes is a tradition-

[14] The failure to realize this detracts from the value of C. D. Thorpe's account of Hobbes's theory of imagination in *The Aesthetic Theory of Thomas Hobbes* (Ann Arbor, 1940).

[15] *Leviathan*, 1: ii.

[16] That this account influenced literary critics is seen in both Dryden and Dennis. In the preface to *Annus Mirabilis* (London, 1667), Dryden writes: "The faculty of imagination in the writer . . . like a nimble spaniel, beats over and ranges through the field of memory, till it springs the quarry it hunted after"; *Essays*, ed. W. P. Ker (Oxford, 1900), 1: 14. And the dog turns up again with canine fidelity in Dennis's *Remarks on the Dunciad*: "For Memory may be justly campar'd to the Dog that beats the Field, or the Wood, and that starts the Game; Imagination to the Falcon that clips it upon its Pinions after it; and Judgment to the Falconer who directs the Flight and who governs the whole"; *Critical Works of Dennis*, ed. E. N. Hooker (Baltimore, 1939–43), 2: 363.

[17] Cf. letter to Richard Sharp (15 January 1804), in which Coleridge calls the imagination "a dim Analogue of Creation"; *Collected Letters of Coleridge*, ed. E. L. Griggs (Oxford, 1956), 2: 1034.

[18] *Biographia Literaria*, ch. 13.

alist who repeats the Renaissance orthodoxy that poetry combines pleasure and instruction. In other and important respects he is an innovator, bringing to criticism a new and more sophisticated awareness of the mental processes involved in literary composition. His empiricist psychology and his skeptical philosophy were to have a decisive influence upon critical theory and literary discourse in the period that followed.

One of the chief effects of Hobbes's philosophy on contemporary poetry lay in its "demythologizing" tendency. Professor Willey, in his *Seventeenth Century Background,* was one of the first to draw attention to the fate of the heroic poem in an age of science, and to show how the status of the epic declined in the rarified atmosphere of the Royal Society. But it was not only science that put the future of the epic in jeopardy. Hobbes, for all his interest in epic, was equally influential in bringing about a change of attitude toward it. Indeed, his interest was partly responsible, for it led him to express his views with a cogency that his contemporaries found difficult to rebut.

A turning point in the fortunes of epic poetry was the appearance in 1651 of Davenant's unfinished epic *Gondibert,* which, as well as the author's own preface, was preceded by Hobbes's *Answer to D'Avenant* and prefatory poems by Waller and Cowley. These men had given much thought to the role of the epic in the new climate of intellectual opinion created in the mid-seventeenth century. Davenant's preface and Hobbes's *Answer* were both written in Paris, where all these writers were in exile, and their authors no doubt took part in the discussions which were starting there on this subject. Davenant begins his preface by calling in question the authority of Homer and Virgil. He censures both for what he considers an unwarrantable intrusion of the supernatural in their poems. Homer

. . . doth too frequently intermixe such Fables as are objects lifted above the Eyes of Nature; and as he often interrogates his Muse, not as his rational Spirit, but as a *Familiar,* separated from his body, so her replys bring him where he spends time in immortal conversation, whilest supernaturally he doth often advance his men to the quality of Gods, and depose his Gods to the condition of men.

Virgil, too, is equally to blame; since ". . . He hath so often led

him [the reader] into Heaven and Hell, till by conversation
with Gods and Ghosts he sometimes deprives us of those natural
probabilities in Story which are instructive to humane life."[19]
It is not that Davenant wishes to remove religion from the
epic; he chooses a Christian subject for his poem and believes
that poetry can be the handmaid of religion. But his theme
is Christian virtue rather than dogma, and he dispenses with
any mythological framework, even of the kind which received
Scriptural sanction. Similarly, when Cowley's *Davideis* appeared in 1656, it emphasized the historicity of the biblical
narrative and tried to accommodate the traditional Christian
cosmology to contemporary scientific discovery. Religious
imagery there certainly is in *Davideis*, but as Thomas Sprat
observed in his *Life and Writings of Cowley* (1668)—and it is
significant that he uses Hobbes's terminology to make his point
—"His Fancy flow'd with great speed, and therefore it was very
fortunate to him that his Judgment was equal to manage it.
He never runs his Reader nor his Argument out of Breath."[20]

Hobbes himself, in his *Answer to D'Avenant*, quite explicitly
repudiates the supernatural in epic poetry. He approves
Davenant's departure from the customary invocation to God
and the poet's claim to heavenly inspiration.

> In that you make so small account of the example of almost all
> the approved Poets, ancient and modern, who thought fit in the
> beginning, and sometimes also in the progress of their Poems,
> to invoke a Muse or some other Deity that should dictate to
> them or assist them in their writings, they that take not the laws
> of Art from any reason of their own but from the fashion of
> precedent times will perhaps accuse your singularity. . . . But
> why a Christian should think it an ornament to his Poem, either
> to profane the true God or invoke a false one, I can imagin no
> cause but a reasonless imitation of Custom, of a foolish custome,
> by which a man, enabled to speak wisely from the principles of
> nature and his own meditation, loves rather to be thought to
> speak by inspiration, like a Bagpipe.[21]

Nature, he maintains, is the final criterion, and we are left in
little doubt that the concept is to be interpreted in terms of
matter and motion in accordance with his own philosophy.

[19] *Critical Essays of the Seventeenth Century*, ed. Spingarn, 2: 2.
[20] *Critical Essays of the Seventeenth Century*, 2: 130.
[21] *Ibid.*, 2: 58–59.

Thomas Hobbes

For as truth is the bound of Historical, so the Resemblance of truth is the utmost limit of Poeticall Liberty. In old time amongst the Heathen such strange fictions and Metamorphoses were not so remote from the Articles of their Faith as they are now from ours, and therefore were not so unpleasant. Beyond the actual works of nature a Poet may now go; but beyond the conceived possibility of nature, never.[22]

The test of probability derives of course from Aristotle, but with him it had meant internal consistency rather than correspondence to the natural order, and embraced even a "probable impossibility." With Hobbes, probability means simply what is likely to be verified by experience, and for him the empirically verifiable has nothing to do with knowledge in the philosophical sense. All that the epic poet can do is to present characters and events, whether true or false, which by example might point the way to virtue. This is made manifest in his much later "Preface concerning the Vertues of an Heroique Poem" (1675), prefixed to his translation of Homer's *Odyssey*, where he tells us that ". . . the Designe [of an epic poem] is not only to profit, but also to delight the Reader. By Profit, I intend not here any accession of Wealth, either to the Poet, or to the Reader; but accession of Prudence, Justice, Fortitude, by the example of such Great and Noble Persons as he introduceth speaking, or describeth acting."[23]

The epic will present the reader with feigned experience and like experience itself this will provide no more than a knowledge of particulars. Poetry is *poiema*, that is, a making or fiction; it is not *logos*, or rational knowledge. We may agree with Hobbes that poetry is *poiema* and not *logos*, but the trouble is that his philosophy leaves no possibility of any living relation between the two. Poetic images are merely the reflection of sensory objects in the mirror of our minds and can never become symbols which stimulate the reason to frame new concepts. Even the power of poetry to foster virtue may be ineffective, "For," as he admits, "all men love to behold, though not to practice, Vertue." But with this gone all that epic can do is to entertain; its high religious purpose and supernatural reference have vanished. Hobbes is not afraid to admit this consequence. "So that at last the work of an Heroique Poet is no more but to

22 *Ibid.*, 2: 62.
23 *Ibid.*, 2: 68.

furnish an ingenuous Reader (when his leisure abounds) with the diversion of an honest and delightful Story, whether true or feigned."[24]

Not only is knowledge divorced from experience in Hobbes's system, but it is separated from faith. This separation of faith and knowledge was not peculiar to Hobbes, of course, for many of his contemporaries, especially those who looked to the Royal Society for guidance, were inclined to agree that knowledge is a matter of secondary causes. So impressive were the achievements of scientific method that it was easy to assume that what was real was a world of atoms in motion, explicable in mathematical terms, whose only relation to God was that of a machine that has been set going by a divine clockmaker. As Cudworth, the Cambridge Platonist, pointed out, such a view made ". . . God to be nothing else in the world, but an idle spectator of the various results of the fortuitous and necessary motions of bodies . . . and made a kind of dead and wooden world, as it were a carved statue, that hath nothing neither vital nor magical at all in it."[25]

It was a view difficult to reconcile with traditional Christian belief, and one that changed the character of poetry. For the writer of epic, who had traditionally been regarded as someone between a priest and prophet, it could only provide a diminished status. It is true that the Royal Society included in its ranks poets as well as scientists, and that Cowley, one of its earliest and most enthusiastic members, was himself an epic poet. But it is significant that the *Davideis* was never finished, and few have thought it a successful poem. Johnson in his *Life of Cowley* put his finger on its chief defect when he wrote, "Cowley gives inferences instead of images," for it rarely rises above literal discourse to the level of symbol and myth. Yet in spite of all this, we have to remember that this was the age which achieved the greatest epic in English literature, *Paradise Lost,* and the question arises of how Milton succeeded in such an accomplishment. Professor Willey and others have given convincing answers, and all that is required here is to bring out a few salient points which relate the discussion to Hobbes.

[24] *Ibid.*
[25] *The True Intellectual System of the Universe* (London, 1678), ed. J. Harrison (London, 1845), 1: 220–21.

On nearly every important issue of religion, philosophy, and poetry, Hobbes and Milton are absolutely divided. In writing of Milton, John Aubrey tells us that "His widowe assures me that Mr. T. Hobbs was not one of his acquaintance, that her husband did not like him at all, but would acknowledge him to be a man of great parts, and a learned man. Their interests and tenets did run counter to each other."[26] Hobbes believed that we can know nothing of God, that all the qualities we attribute to him have no significance in reality; for, he writes: ". . . in the attributes which we give to God, we are not to consider the signification of philosophical truth; but the signification of pious intention, to do him the greatest honour we are able."[27] But for the Christian, who believes that God was revealed in Christ, there is real meaning in attributing goodness and mercy and other qualities to the godhead. God, the Christian believes, was revealed in history; the Incarnation, indeed, is the central point which gives the historical process pattern and meaning. Hobbes on the other hand, saw history as a series of meaningless particulars from which, at best, we can derive only the virtue of prudence. It is this conviction of history, and especially biblical history, as having meaning, which is the mainspring of Milton's poem.

The main theme of *Paradise Lost* is not, as is so often supposed, Man's Fall but his Redemption. Milton's poem is concerned not only with original sin but with the intervention in history of the second Adam and with the reconciliation he brings. Nevertheless, a good deal of the action lies outside history and beyond the bounds of human experience, and he sees the historical events themselves as a divine drama. The biblical story is both history and myth. Milton is even prepared to accept pagan myth as a prefiguration of the truth revealed in Scripture, and as a Christian poet is ready to believe that fiction can embody truth. In Raphael's speech to Adam, which describes Satan's rebellion, he is also perhaps indicating the difficulties of his own task:

[26] Aubrey, *Brief Lives*, ed. A. Clark, 2: 72. For an excellent discussion of the philosophical and religious differences between the two men, cf. M. H. Nicolson, "Milton and Hobbes," *Studies in Philology* (1926), 23: 405–33.

[27] *Leviathan*, 2, xxxi.

> High matter thou enjoin'st me, O prime of Men,
> Sad task and hard; for how shall I relate
> To human sense th'invisible exploits
> Of warring Spirits? . . .
> . . . how, last, unfold
> The secrets of another world, perhaps
> Not lawful to reveal? Yet for thy good
> This is dispensed; and what surmounts the reach
> Of human sense I shall delineate so,
> By likening spiritual to corporal forms,
> As may express them best.[28]

Milton was sustained in his writing, he believed, by the heavenly Muse who visited him in sleep and inspired his imagination; unlike Hobbes he did not consider that his divine assistance turned him into a "bagpipe," but rather that it made his poetry an instrument of the truth.[29] Hobbes was contemptuous of such a suggestion.

> For if a man pretend to me, that God hath spoken to him supernaturally and immediately, and I make doubt of it, I cannot easily perceive what argument he can produce, to oblige me to believe it. . . . To say he hath spoken to him in a dream, is no more than to say he dreamed that God spake him.[30]

For Milton, not only the Bible, but the whole of experience is a means of knowing God; the world of nature is not simply particular concrete objects which by pressure on our senses bring about images in the mind. It is rather a secondary revelation of its Creator. Raphael, in addressing Adam, does not commit himself to any precise description, but suggests something of the relation between the natural and the supernatural, when he says,

> . . . what if Earth
> Be but the shadow of Heaven, and things therein
> Each to other like, more than on Earth is thought?
> (5: 574–76)

[28] *Paradise Lost*, 5: 563–74.

[29] In his *Reason of Church Government* (1642) Milton had written that the great epic on which he was embarking would be guided by help not "to be obtained by the invocation of Dame Memory and her Siren daughters, but by devout prayer to that eternal Spirit who can enrich with all utterance and knowledge." This is in direct contradiction to Hobbes's theory of the imagination.

[30] *Leviathan*, 3: xxxii.

This was a difficult doctrine for Milton to hold, for it was a matter of Puritan conviction that the world of Grace and the world of Nature had been rent asunder by the Fall, and in some respects the new scientific rationalism was easier to combine with Puritanism than was Renaissance humanism. Milton's achievement in *Paradise Lost* was, then, a precarious one,[31] and in *Paradise Regained* and *Samson Agonistes* he turned to a literal presentation of the historical and biblical narrative and a style largely devoid of rhetorical figures. But if his Puritanism left him disposed to accept a dualism between the natural and supernatural, it did not lead him to accept Hobbes's division of reason and faith.

Reason and faith in Hobbes are not merely separate but almost antithetical, and we should not think there is any conscious irony when he tells us that ". . . it is with the mysteries of our religion as with wholesome pills for the sick; which swallowed whole, have the virtue to cure; but chewed, are for the most part cast up again without effect."[32] In Milton reason and faith are almost synonymous. Reason is that part of man which approximates to the divine nature, and his treatment of the Fall suggests that he regarded it as the overthrow of reason by the passions. Hobbes, on the other hand, affirmed that reason is the servant of the passions. "For the thoughts are to the desires, as scouts, and spies, to range abroad, and find the way to the things desired" (1: viii). With Milton reason is divine illumination, an active principle in man which is more than the faculty of intellection; it makes judgments of value and conduces to virtue. The best known passage in which Milton advances this Platonic conception is in Book 5 of *Paradise Lost*, where Raphael describes for Adam's benefit the great chain of being which reaches from grossest matter to the life of the spirit. Coleridge chose this passage as a heading for the famous chapter

[31] Marvell realized something of this when he wrote in "On Mr. Milton's Paradise Lost,"

> . . . the Argument
> Held me a while misdoubting his Intent,
> That he would ruine (for I saw him strong)
> The sacred Truths to Fable and Old Song.

That Milton recognized this difficulty I have tried to show in my *Reason and Imagination* (Oxford, 1960), chap. 2.

[32] *Leviathan*, 3: xxxii.

in *Biographia Literaria* in which he defines the poetic imagination. For Milton, as for Coleridge (at any rate if we interpret the passage as Coleridge does), the reason is a product of both the imagination and the understanding. It works both discursively and intuitively; with man the truth will most often be reached through logical discourse, but at times he will reach the angelic heights of direct apprehension. Matter, Raphael tells Adam, will

> . . . by gradual scale sublim'd
> To vital spirits aspire, to animal,
> To intellectual, give both life and sense,
> Fansie and understanding, whence the Soule
> Reason receives, and reason is her being,
> Discursive, or intuitive; discourse
> Is oftest yours, the latter most is ours,
> Differing but in degree, of kind the same.
> (5: 483–90)

Reason and freedom are identical for Milton; man is perfectly free when he obeys reason and is enslaved only when governed by his passions. Unlike Hobbes, who argued that the will is simply the last link in a chain of determined mental processes, he believed man to be free to choose between his reason and his passions. God made man a rational being and man is free when he acts in accordance with his own nature.

> But God left free the Will; for what obeys
> Reason is free; and Reason he made right.
> (9: 351–52)

This difference between their conceptions of the reason lies at the basis of their different political philosophies. Hobbes's system of thought envisaged a time when men lived in a state of nature, before society had become organized. The life of natural man, in his most famous phrase, was "solitary, poor, nasty, brutish, and short," for every man lived in a chaos of competition with his fellows. It was to deliver themselves out of this miserable condition that men contracted to vest supreme authority in a sovereign who should exercise power over them. Their motives in doing this were fear of each other and the desire for peace. This account, which is as mythological as anything in the book of Genesis, is very different from Milton's view of how society came into being. For Milton, unfallen man was in no need of government; Adam and Eve before the Fall lived in a state of concord which was founded upon the rule of reason. Obedience to reason meant individual freedom and an identity of interest between them. Except for the Fall their progeny could have continued living in a community of free wills all recognizing the sway of reason, which is no other than the law of God. If men were rational they would realize that their interests are all identical, and there would be hardly any need for government in the authoritarian sense. But because men are fallen and have allowed their passions to usurp the place of reason, government becomes necessary, and men's sinfulness will lead, on occasion, to the emergence of tyranny. Milton puts this theory into the mouth of the archangel Michael, who tells Adam,

> . . . yet know withall,
> Since thy original lapse, true Libertie
> Is lost, which alwayes with right Reason dwells
> Twinnd, and from her hath no dividual being:
> Reason in man obscur'd, or not obeyed,
> Immediately inordinate desires
> And upstart Passions catch the Government
> From Reason, and to servitude reduce
> Man till then free . . .
>   . . . Tyrannie must be,
> Though to the Tyrant thereby no excuse.
> Yet sometimes Nations will decline so low
> From Vertue, which is Reason, that no wrong,
> But Justice, and some fatal curse annext
> Deprives them of their outward Libertie,
> Their inward lost.
>   (12: 82–101)

Both men regard authoritarian government as a result of man's sinful nature, but Hobbes believes it to be the best that can be achieved, whereas Milton thinks that if man would obey the dictates of reason he could establish democratic rule. Good government, according to Milton, depends upon self-government; for Hobbes it must always be imposed from outside.

If Milton wrote in conscious opposition to Hobbes, in Dryden we meet someone who was in many respects his professed disciple. Aubrey describes Dryden as Hobbes's "great admirer" and says that he "oftentimes makes use of his doctrine in his plays—from Mr Dryden himself."[33] A good deal has been written already of Hobbes's influence on Dryden. Professor Bredvold[34] has indicated the extent of Dryden's debt to Hobbes in the plays, and it has long been recognized that the various accounts of poetic composition in Dryden's work, especially that in the preface to *Annus Mirabilis*, owe a great deal to Davenant and Hobbes. But we can also perceive the effect of Hobbes on Dryden's own poetry.

Dryden, although first an Anglican and then a Roman Catholic, was, as he himself tells us, skeptical by temperament, and this natural disposition was strengthened by the intellectual pressures of his times. It is perfectly possible to combine philosophical skepticism with religious faith, as we see in the anti-metaphysical character of so much theology today. But such a combination was more difficult for an Anglican in the second half of the seventeenth century, since Anglican theology from the time of Hooker had insisted on the reasonableness of the Christian religion. It was because he felt the Latitudinarian tendency of the Church of England to be the beginning of a slippery slope that Dryden retreated to the safer position of rendering unto faith the things that are faith's and to reason the things that are reason's. Such a circumscription of reason does not necessarily derive from one source, of course, but the kind of separation of reason and faith to be found in Hobbes's writings was undoubtedly congenial to Dryden's mind. The fear that rational theology was likely to end in deism led Dryden to embrace the Roman Catholic faith, but its presence is already manifest in *Religio Laici* (1682), written to defend the Anglican position. The magnificent opening lines of this poem express the Hobbesian view that reason is not a speculative but a practical faculty; reason does not show us the ultimate truth but enables us to live ordered and decent lives.

> Dim as the borrow'd beams of Moon and Stars
> To lonely, weary, wandring Travellers
> Is Reason to the Soul: And as on high
> Those rowling Fires discover but the Sky
> Not light us here; So Reason's glimmering Ray

[33] Aubrey, *Brief Lives*, ed. A. Clark, 1: 372.
[34] *The Intellectual Milieu of John Dryden* (Ann Arbor, 1934).

> Was lent, not to assure our doubtful way,
> But guide us upward to a better Day.

The ending of *Religio Laici* is even more in the manner of Hobbes, for here reason is frankly subordinated to a political end; public order is the great good and if reason runs counter to this, it is better to disregard it.

> 'Tis some Relief, that points not clearly known,
> Without much hazard may be let alone:
> And after hearing what our Church can say,
> If still our Reason runs another way,
> That private Reason 'tis more Just to curb,
> Than by Disputes the publick Peace disturb.
> For points obscure are of small use to learn.

The acceptance of this dualism between reason and faith, together with an admiration for the poetry of Davenant and Cowley, might well have led to a coolness toward Milton on Dryden's part. But Dryden was too good a critic not to recognize the greatness of *Paradise Lost*. His writings in many places express his admiration for the epic and his own unfulfilled aspiration to write in this form. "Heroic Poetry . . . has ever been esteemed, and ever will be, the greatest work of human nature."[35] Nor is he ready to join those who wish to "demythologize" the epic. Horace, he writes, ". . . taxed not Homer, nor the divine Virgil, for interesting their gods in the wars of Troy and Italy; neither, had he now lived, would he have taxed Milton, as our false critics have presumed to do, for his choice of a supernatural argument."[36] And yet we cannot be unaware of the great gulf between Milton and Dryden. The above quotations come from "The Author's Apology for Heroic Poetry," which Dryden prefixed to *The State of Innocence and Fall of Man* (1677), an opera based upon *Paradise Lost*. To move from Milton's epic to Dryden's opera is more than to exchange the splendor of Milton's blank verse for the rather trite quality of Dryden's rhymed couplets. We have changed our entire world. Such is Milton's genius that we feel in reading *Paradise Lost* that we are being presented with eternal truths of a cosmic significance; in Dryden the same "great argument" has been trimmed to meet the needs of a stage entertainment.

[35] *Essays of Dryden*, ed. W. P. Ker, 1: 181.
[36] *Ibid.*, pp. 189–90.

Such a comparison is unfair, of course, for Milton's poem was the fruit of years of preparation and composition, while Dryden's opera, according to Johnson, was written in a month. But this fact in itself establishes the point we are making. For all Dryden's admiration for the epic, his genius flowered in other forms; forms which he often had to devise or adapt to suit his own talents and the material available. The work which best illustrates how he matched his individual genius to the situation in which he found himself is *Absalom and Achitophel* (1681-82). This poem is written in the heroic manner, and like *Paradise Lost* its central scene is the temptation and fall of the hero. Although it is in the strict sense an occasional poem, Dryden raises the theme of rebellion to a universal significance, on a political if not a cosmic level. It is not difficult, indeed, to catch echoes of Milton, but its total effect owes more to Hobbes. If Absalom's fall is the overthrow of reason by the passions, we are left in little doubt that reason's chief end should be to secure settled government and that Dryden considers this best achieved by the absolute sovereignty of the monarch.

> Yet, if the Crowd be Judge of fit and Just,
> And Kings are onely Officers in trust,
> Then this resuming Cov'nant was declar'd
> When Kings were made, or is for ever bar'd . . .
>
> For who can be secure of private Right,
> If Sovereign sway may be dissolv'd by might?
> Nor is the Peoples Judgment always true:
> The most may err as grossly as the few.
>   (ll. 765–82)

If the style is heroic, so is much of the characterization. And yet the poem lacks not only epic dimensions but a purely epic purpose. In chapter 9 of the *Leviathan*, Hobbes had categorized the objects of poetry as "magnifying" and "vilifying," and that of rhetoric as "persuading." Dryden's poem combines all three. Dryden was not the first, of course, to bring poetry and rhetoric together, but he does so in a very individual manner, one which probably owes something to Hobbes. Hobbes, it will be remembered, had followed Aristotle in suggesting that rhetorical discourse depends upon example and enthymeme. Earlier poets had employed both of these, but never to such an extent as Dryden. In *Religio Laici, The Hind and the Panther*,

Thomas Hobbes

and *Absalom and Achitophel* they became the chief features of his style. No one before him had brought poetry so close to logical discourse; he was, as Johnson observed, "the first who joined argument with poetry," and "sentences were readier at his call than images." There were other forces, such as the work of the Royal Society, which helped to bring about the *rapprochement* between poetry and prose at this time, but one can hardly doubt, considering Dryden's debt to Hobbes in so many other ways, that here too Hobbes was a decisive influence. His insistence on clear and distinct ideas and his distrust of metaphor are reflected in the simplicity and concision of Dryden's style. But more than this, his belief that truth is reached by propositions linked together in consecutive argument finds its most appropriate poetic form in the rhymed couplet.

Hobbes's philosophy was one of the most powerful influences that brought about the approximation of poetry to rhetoric in the Augustan period. But there were other forces counterbalancing this which were to draw poetry and poetics away from rhetoric toward aesthetics. In many ways the history of eighteenth-century poetic theory can be recounted in terms of the gradual ascendancy of aesthetic concepts over rhetorical ones. Hobbes himself in the *Answer to D'Avenant* had echoed the Horatian maxim *ut pictura poesis* when he wrote, "Poets are Painters,"[37] and Dryden developed this theme in an essay on "The Parallel betwixt Painting and Poetry," which he prefixed to a translation of Du Fresnoy's *De arte graphica* (1695). With the turn of the century poetry was seen once more not only as verbal discourse but as analogous to the plastic arts. The growing regard for landscape which derived from painting, and the new interest in the nature of aesthetic experience which revealed itself in discussions of the beautiful and the sublime, were accompanied by a rebirth of imagery. But imagery now had a somewhat different function; it came increasingly to be used for description and the symbolization of feeling, and less as a vehicle for meaning. The eighteenth century started as an age of sense but it ended as one of sensibility.

It might be thought that Hobbes's philosophy would have been inimical to this development, but this is not wholly true.

[37] *Critical Essays of the Seventeenth Century*, ed. Spingarn, 2: 61.

63

The influence of a great thinker is often self-contradictory, and must be seen in the opposition he provokes as much as in the assent he commands. If the immediate effect of Hobbes's thought was to bring poetry closer to rhetoric, we must remember that he stands at the beginning of English aesthetics. In particular, his discussion of literature in psychological terms was an innovation, and had repercussions which have lasted to the present day. Psychological criticism turned attention from the work of art itself to its effectiveness and, for good or ill, hastened the dissolution of fixed literary "kinds." It gave a new importance to questions both of artistic creation and aesthetic experience; concepts such as genius and the sublime may have been difficult to account for in terms of his psychology, but it is doubtful if eighteenth-century critics would have formulated them but for Hobbes.

We often forget that Hobbes believed man to be a creature of the passions. Good, according to him, lies in the satisfaction of the appetites: a doctrine which manifested itself, in critical theory, in the concept of taste and the decline of rational standards, and which led in literature to a more plangent expression of the feelings. Such a doctrine could accord with a liberal and optimistic notion of human nature, but in Hobbes it is accompanied by a fundamental pessimism. This is reflected in his view of society as something achieved almost in opposition to human nature and without any foundation in natural law, and in a deep skepticism concerning man's knowledge. Both the optimism and the pessimism are present in Augustan literature and are brought together in Pope's famous paradox about man as "the glory, jest, and riddle of the world!"

Hobbes, though he was disliked and feared by more people than admired him, was one of those thinkers whose influence is too great and pervasive to trace in detail. Whether in opposition or allegiance, those who followed him were obliged in no small measure to think in the categories which he had framed and to write in a language he had helped to form. His contemporary, Leibniz, could rightly say that Hobbes was "among the deepest minds of the century." Leibniz could not foresee the future but, if he had been able to do so, he might have added that Hobbes was also one of the founding fathers of the century to come.

III

IAN WATT

Realism and the Novel

Mr. Douglas Grant has lately expressed in these pages his dissatisfaction with the present state of novel criticism. Most recent
attacks on the problem have been carrying out the program
put forward by R. P. Blackmur: "the novel needs precisely the
same kind of attention, . . . from the same untenable position,
that in the last twenty years or so, we have been giving
poetry."[1] I share Mr. Grant's feeling that this approach may be
rejecting too much that is true in previous views on the nature
of the novel genre, and that these traditional views need to be
re-interpreted, not rejected. The view that I am trying to re-
interpret here is an elementary one: that the novel is essentially
different from poetry, because it is a new literary form which
characteristically uses language in a primarily respresentational,
referential, or realistic way. It would follow that analyses of the
symbolic complexity of a novel must take account of its primarily realistic nature.

It will at once be objected that the term realism is so vague
and banal as to be unhelpful, and that it cannot in any case be
used as though it were self-explanatory. Further, that its use
tends to be polemic—to suggest that all writers before Flaubert
were unresisting victims of a penchant for the unreal. These
objections seem obviously true and what follows here is an
attempt to explain and re-interpret one meaning of "realism"
which will make clearer the historical development and the
formal methods of the novel genre as a whole.

Descriptively, "realism" means primarily "minute fidelity of
representation." It was first used in something like this sense in
France, in 1835, to describe the "vérité humaine" of Rembrandt,

From *Essays in Criticism* (October 1952), 2: 376–96, reprinted by permission of the author and F. W. Bateson.

[1] "For a Second Look," *Kenyon Review* (1949) 11: 7–10.

as opposed to the "idéalité poétique" of neoclassical painting.[2] Later its use was extended to literature and finally consecrated by a particular literary school, with the appearance in 1856 of *Réalisme*, a literary journal edited by Duranty. The term in England recapitulates its history in France, being applied first to art by Ruskin, in *Modern Painters*, in 1856, and later to literature, by Swinburne in 1880.[3] This historical connection of the term "realism" with the French school which adopted it has continued to influence its English usage; for it often carries with it the odium aroused by the low subjects and allegedly immoral tendency of the French Realists, and especially of their successors, the Naturalists. The term has another and more definitely pejorative sense, arising from the association of realism with minute detail: realism as photographic, as a copy of the appearance, not the reality of things. In our time, realism has acquired another kind of odium, connected with the previous two: it evokes "Ibsen and Zola dealing with the reality of life in joyless and pallid words,"[4] contrasted with the richer and more complex conceptions of symbolism and post-symbolism; and suggests a realistic literature that is *a priori* formless and boring, and which certainly offers small opportunity for feats of interpretative criticism.

It is not surprising, therefore, that the term "realism" has on the whole been avoided by modern critics of the novel, except to be peremptorily dismissed. True there are some qualified uses of the term which are not pejorative. "Social realism," as used by the Marxist school of critics, extends approbation to those novels whose representation of social reality accords with the views held by the user of the term.[5] "Moral realism" has a general use to indicate unwilling assent to the truth of the picture of life given by such writers as Swift— unwilling because the truths are not pleasant or flattering. And lastly, the use of the terms "realized" and "realization" to express commendation for imagery, and, more broadly, the conviction that a writer's words in some way genuinely correspond to his

---

[2] Bernard Weinberg, *French Realism: the Critical Reaction* (London, 1937), p. 114.

[3] O.E.D. But Swinburne wrote of the "modern realist" in 1870.

[4] J. M. Synge, Preface, *The Playboy of the Western World*.

[5] E.g. George Lukacs, *Studies in European Realism* (London, 1950), pp. 5–14.

experience, is similarly subjective. These three uses have one element in common: they applaud some correspondence between a literary work and the view of reality held by the user; and they therefore have the disadvantage that they ultimately involve us in a metaphysical rather than a literary problem—the nature of reality.

This issue cannot be wholly avoided. Broadly speaking, all uses of the term "realism" which are not purely historical eventually involve an imputation of correspondence between the work of art under discussion and "reality." This being so, it seems logical to turn to those professionally concerned with the analysis of concepts—the philosophers—to see what light they can shed upon the nature of modern literary realism.

I

By a paradox that will surprise only the neophyte, the term realism in philosophy is most strictly applied to a view of reality diametrically opposed to that of common usage. Scholastic philosophy is realist because it holds that it is universals, classes, or abstractions, and not the direct and concrete objects of sense-perception, which are the true "realities." This, at first sight, appears unhelpful. For in the novel, more than in any other genre, general truths only exist *post res*; they can only be elicited from the concrete cases of individual characters in particular situations. Nevertheless, a consideration of scholastic realism helps us to focus one of the characteristics of the novel which is representative of a major trend in modern thought. For, from Descartes on, the general philosophical outlook, however various and contradictory in many other respects, has not been colored by a belief in universals. The characteristic literary form of the modern period, and the only one which is substantially new, the novel, came into being in a period whose intellectual orientation was most decisively separated from its classical and medieval heritage by its rejection of universals.

This basic change of intellectual climate allotted a new meaning to the word realism, which was more optimistic about the objective truth of particular observations by individuals. Modern epistemological realism, which begins with Descartes and Locke, and receives its first full formulation by Reid in the middle of the eighteenth century, holds the view that the external world is real, and that our senses give us a true report of it.[6] This tenet does not in itself throw much light on literary realism, nor on the uniqueness of the novel's method of describing reality. For one thing, almost everyone, in all ages, has in one way or another been forced to some such conclusion about the external world by his own experience; and consequently all literature has to some extent been exposed to the same epistemological naïveté. What is important to the novel in modern philosophical realism is less specific: it is the kind of problem which it has raised, and the way of thought which it has introduced.

For instance, the central problem which realism has had to face has been that of dualism, to which Descartes gave a historically unprecedented importance: How can the individual mind know anything that is external to it? If we put this problem in terms of literature, it becomes the familiar one of the relation of the individual to his environment, a problem which, though not, of course, exclusive to any form of literature, is nevertheless more directly and exhaustively the subject of the novel than of other forms. The way of thought which realism has made necessary bears an equally close relation to the novel: both have been individualist, critical, introspective, antitraditional, and mainly concerned with eliciting truth from the evidence of particulars. We can at least try to find what closer correspondences exist between this general philosophical orientation, and realism in the novel.

That the founder of modern realism was a dualist suggests a solution to two apparent contradictions to the view that the novel is basically a realistic genre: that which interprets "realism" in the novel as closely equivalent to materialism; and that which sees such modern figures as Henry James, Virginia Woolf, or James Joyce as nonrealist.

The French realists, and even more the Naturalists, were often accused of making the environment the dominating factor in their works, and especially its economic aspect. The accusation was assisted, no doubt, by the fact that the word realism, among its other ambiguities, has a similarly materialist, and economic sense. "Res," as a material object, has given rise to the opposition of "real" as opposed to "personal" estate; the first

[6] I base my generalizations about philosophical realism on S. Z. Hasan's *Realism* . . . (Cambridge, 1928), chaps. 1–2.

meaning of "real" given in Johnson's *Dictionary* is "relating to things not persons." Many novelists have followed Balzac in being hypnotized by the spectacle of the fluctuations of man's real estate. Yet it is obvious that in any ordinary sense of the word, no novelist has limited himself to material things; all have dealt with persons, and their interest in the material has been a new emphasis not a total change in the novel's subject-matter. This sense of realism is surely an extreme literary pole which parallels a philosophical extreme: that which has suggested that *only* the external world is real.

At the other extreme, the exponents of the subjective novel— James, Proust, Virginia Woolf, and Joyce—undoubtedly reacted from the French realist school, but they are still realists. They may surely best be seen as an opposite swing in the larger development of literary realism: and an exact parallel to the other extreme of epistemological realism, the internal, subjective, introspective, and solipsist direction to which Descartes tended, and which led to the idealism of Berkeley and the skepticism of Hume. However, although Descartes gives priority to the internal objects of consciousness—the ego's awareness of doubt or thought—external objects are also eventually found to be real. So in the novel, the most extreme subjectivists eventually place the individual in relation to the external world. It has been a classic theme. All the great novelists, from Richardson on, have portrayed the interplay of the subjective experience of the individual with the external realities of the environment. Proust gives us—among other things—a document of Cartesian introspection: but it is an introspection which reveals the external as well as the internal world. Henry James's technical triumphs can be seen as a new solution of the old dualist problem: the reader is absorbed into the subjective consciousness of the characters, and from that point of disadvantage he sees obliquely and ironically revealed the vision of the external social facts, the furies of money, class, and culture, which are the real determinants of subjective experience, although hardly glimpsed by their human agents, and only recognized by the reader when the story is done: all this in service of the novel's aim—"a direct impression of life"[7]—Lockean phrase. Virginia Woolf's method is based

[7] The exact relation of Henry James to philosophical realism can be gauged from A. E. Lovejoy's essay on the affinities of Pragmatism with

upon a conviction that what she shows us is more real, more existent, than the external facts presented by Mr. Bennett; her claim is surely to be more of a realist than he is. Joyce is the climax of the novel's epistemological realism. Molly Bloom's daydream and the objects in her husband's drawer[8] are defiantly unadulterated samples of the adjustment of literary manner to the opposite poles of realism, subjective and objective: they are the *reductio ad absurdum* of dualism.

II

The analogy of philosophical dualism, then, helps us to see the homogeneity of the novel's development: and both may be subsumed under the term "realism," because both are results of a similar epistemological bent. This epistemological bent suggests that the "realism" of the novel is a matter of its approach to "reality": its representational technique. The elements of this technique will now be shown to be related to the individualist, antitraditional, and particularizing tendencies which epistemological realism has inherited from Descartes and Locke.

By the individualist tendency I mean only the fact that since the *Meditations* of Descartes the pursuit of truth has been conceived as something wholly in the power of the unaided individual to achieve, and wholly independent of the body of past thought. The ego has only to turn the mind to the immediately apprehended data of consciousness to achieve truth. The analogy of this procedure with the novel is twofold: it applies to the relation of the novelist to his work, and to the relation of the novel to the reader. Each relation is private; that is, the novelist writes alone, and the novel's reader is also alone. There is no relationship, no acknowledged contact, except through the novel, which is, as it were, the printed equivalent of the data of consciousness which one individual has recorded, and another can overlook: the novel gives a private view of those individual experiences which are the source of reality and truth, and its value is judged, not by reference to other literature, or to accepted dogma, but by the authenticity of its report, the extent

---

Natural Realism, in *Essays in Critical Realism* (London, 1920), especially p. 76.

[8] *Ulysses* (London, 1922), pp. 673–75, 690ff. I have received very valuable criticism on this and other points from Mr. J. C. Hodgart.

to which the novelist convinces the reader that a real epistemological observation is being conducted. If the reader is convinced that the novel's picture of its subject is accurate, the
novelist has done the main part of his job.

The individualist tendency of philosophical realism is closely
related to its critical, antitraditional, and innovating bent:
departure from established norms of thought and action is
likely to lead to discoveries of truth. The novel embodies
similar features in its form and content. It is in itself formless,
compared with other literary forms; since the recording of
individual experience is its primary aim, no formal conventions
about the way it is done are necessary, or even possible. Just as
Descartes' greatness resides in the thoroughness of his doubts
about past views of truth, so the novel has tended to set aside
traditional wisdom in favor of the truth that each individual
must continually experience anew. The novel is therefore well-
named. It rejects innate ideas. It is the vehicle of a culture which
since the sixteenth century has set a new value on originality.[9]
Whereas older cultures have tended to make conformity to tradition the main test of truth, modern culture has continuously
held as its aim the discovery of new truths, the reshaping of
reality, an aim which would previously have seemed both impossible and undesirable. And it is in this intellectual climate that
the older forms of literature, whose plot and essential theme
have been a matter of recapitulation rather than discovery, have
been challanged by the novel whose criterion is truth to individual experience, which is always unique, and therefore always
new. It will surely be agreed that it is more damaging for a novel
to be an imitation in form or matter than is the case in any other
kind of literature.

The innovating, antitraditional tendency of realist thought is
reflected in the novel's plot. Of the classical genres only comedy
was supposed to have an invented plot; but, since the Renaissance at least, it had tended to prefer old ones. Only with the
novel did an invented plot become the rule. The action or plot
was thereby enabled to express exactly the experience of life

[9] See Max Scheler, *Versuche zu einer Soziologie des Wissens* (Munich
and Leipzig, 1924), p. 104ff; "Four Romantic Words" in Logan Pearsall
Smith, *Words and Idioms* (London, 1947), pp. 87–91; Elizabeth L. Mann,
"The Problem of Originality in English Literary Criticism, 1750–1800,"
P.Q. (1939), 18: 106–18.

which the novelist wished. This has a further advantage: the fact that the plot is not already known gives the reader a sense of the discovery of a human experience which is real although as yet unknown to him, whereas that of classical tragedy or epic gives the reader a sense of a reminder, rather than a sense of a new revelation.

The invention of the plot and its characters by the novelist has an importance which it is difficult to exaggerate. It means that the novel is new in the sense of contemporary, and thus tends to find a more immediate resonance in the experience of the reader. It is also new in the sense that its story is unknown to the reader. And finally, it is new in the sense that it permits a new individual discovery of reality to be embodied in plot as freely as the method of Descartes and Locke allowed their thought to spring from the immediate facts of consciousness.

III

The third way in which the methods of realist thought are paralleled by the novel's technique is the rejection of universals, and the pursuit of truth through the particulars of individual experience. This is a significant alteration of the way in which reality is conceived. It is a matter, not of universals, but of particulars. Truth, for Locke, has as its basis the senses which "at first let in particular ideas and furnish the yet empty cabinet" of the mind.[10] The new philosophical attitude had its echoes among the critics of the eighteenth century, whose classical values defended the "general" against the growing forces of those who preferred the particular in art and literature.[11] Much has been written on this theme recently, and it has even come to be seen as the most universal feature of romantic and post-romantic literatures that, in various ways, the particular, not the general, the "object as it is," became the main focus of

[10] *Essay Concerning Human Understanding,* Bk. I, ch. I, sect. 15.

[11] On general aspects of this controversy, David Lovett, "Shakespeare as a Poet of Realism in the eighteenth century," *E.L.H.*, (1935), 2: 267–89, Scott Elledge, "The Background and Development in English Criticism of the Theories of Generality and Particularity," *P.M.L.A.* (1947), 62: 147–82, and W. K. Wimsatt, "The Structure of the 'Concrete Universal' in Literature," *P.M.L.A.* (1940), 19: 225–36; and as it affects the novel, Houghton W. Taylor, "Modern Fiction and the Doctrine of Uniformity," *P.Q.* (1940), 19: 225–36, and "Particular Character": an Early Phase of a Literary Evolution," *P.M.L.A.* (1945), 60: 161–74.

literary attention. The ways of thought encouraged by philosophical realism could only emerge in literature after the established traditions had been broken down, and it took nearly two centuries. Then "individualism," "the eye on the object," "the primary affections and duties," and "the real language of men" found their full literary expression.[12]

In this context, the position of Stendhal and Balzac, and of their successors the Realist school, and the Naturalists, has always been clear; they have always been seen as parts of the French romantic movement. But what of the English realist novelists of the eighteenth century? One strand of their romantic filiation has long been seen: "sentimentalism" as a precursor of romanticism. But this has in the past tended to set Richardson, and Sterne, "sentimentalists," in opposition to Defoe, Fielding, and Smollett as "realists." In the analysis which follows, another line of filiation will be followed, based, not on any emotional tendency, but on literary method: a method alike in one thing at least—its concern for the more accurate representation of human life by paying attention to the objective dimensions of human existence, and the way in which the truth of any report of an action is ordinarily verified.

All literature, of course, is in some sense an imitation of life, and since Aristotle at least the question of verisimilitude[13] had occupied an important, though not, until the nineteenth century, a dominating position in the critical arena. For both classical and neoclassical literature and criticism were dominated by literary forms such as epic and tragedy which are not primarily concerned with realism. So it was very difficult for the spirit of realist inquiry to lodge itself in the accepted literary forms of the past, even though their critical theory made a good deal of the need for verisimilitude. It was much easier in the novel, a form which was at first denied the status of literature, and attempted only to be mistaken for real life. It had to face

[12] See, for instance, Geoffrey Tillotson, "Arnold and Pater: Critics Historical, Aesthetic and Otherwise," *Essays and Studies by Members of the English Association,* ed. G. Rostrevor Hamilton (1950), pp. 47–57; Bertrand H. Bronson, "The Double Tradition of Dr. Johnson," *E.L.H.* (1951), 18: 102–3.

[13] See Richard McKeon, "Literary Criticism and the Concept of Imitation in Antiquity," *M.P.* (1936), 34: 1–35; Ralph C. Williams, "Two Studies in Epic Theory," *M.P.* (1924), 22: 133–58. (The first study deals with verisimilitude in Italian and French romance.)

the technical problems raised by the attempt to create "a direct impression of life," and it had to face it without a preconceived idea of literary verisimilitude. There are, of course, many technical problems in the representation of individual experience, and it cannot be claimed that the eighteenth-century novelists solved all of them; but some of the essential ones seem to have been raised by them for the first time. The elementary needs for the description of the particulars of human experience, it will be agreed, are those of time and place, and of the identity of the individuals concerned. We can at least begin to define the methodological realism of the novel and the place of the eighteenth-century English novelists in its development by considering its innovations in the treatment of these factors.

The treatment of the time and space dimensions is one of the most striking differences between the novel and romance. Coleridge noted the "marvellous independence and true imaginative absence of all particular time and space in the *Faerie Queen*.[14] But the novel and ordinary life have at least this in common: our impressions of them in the mind are indissolubly linked with a particular temporal and spatial context. The first way in which a speaker or writer can persuade us in ordinary life that anything actually happened is to tell us where and when. This difference of the role of time in novel and romance is representative of the difference between modern and ancient thought on the matter.

Time was not an essential dimension of reality as Plato conceived it; and in general, the thought of Greece and Rome was colored by a belief in the supreme reality of ideas, "universals . . . that . . . were changeless and immovable and eternal."[15] Nothing happened on earth, or could happen, which was in essence new. Consequently, classical literature portrayed, not what passes in the mind, but what is and always has been in it; it attempted to reflect the immanent realities of the world order, not the continuously new collocations of sensations as they occur in each individual mind. Criticism reflected this denial of the importance of time; for the "Unity of Time" is surely a

---

[14] Nonesuch edition, p. 333.

[15] Samuel Alexander, *Time, Space and Deity* (1920), *cit.*, Wyndham-Lewis, *Time and Western Man* (London, 1927), p. 155.

denial of the importance of time as a dimension of human life; immanent patterns of life can be as well unfolded in the space of a day as in the space of a lifetime.

In a different way, the classical literary roles of time equally denied the force of time as we experience it, as duration and succession. The winged chariot and the grim reaper, whose occasional and dramatic interventions in human affairs make us forget the reality of those human affairs which exist in the ordinary time dimension, remind us instead of the superior status in reality of the life which is conceived *sub specie aeternitatis.*

Such a view of time is still present in Elizabethan literature. Troy and medieval England are only two different, and not very different, backgrounds against which the wheel of time churns out the same eternally applicable *exempla.* Later, in *Pilgrim's Progress*, we have the same abstract and unparticularized sense of the passage of time as in the romances and Shakespeare's history plays.[16] But, if the modern sense of time was as yet unrepresented in literature, it was already active in philosophy. Time was an essential dimension of reality to the new exponents of individualist and introspective thought, from Montaigne and Descartes onward.[17] Our apprehension of time was an essential psychological problem in Locke;[18] and in the seventeenth century, both in history and in science, the time dimension was given a new importance as both fields of study became more scientific in their aims and methods.

Here again we can find a general correlation between the modern realistic movement—specifically here in its psychology and its world-view—and the realism of the novel. For the novel also gives time a new and important place both in its method of narration, and in its general view of life. E. M. Forster sees as one of the two roles of the novel, the portrayal of "life by time,"[19] which has been added to literature's more ancient role, the portrayal of "life by values." The portrayal of

[16] Some of the evidence is presented in Mable Bulland, *The Presentation of Time in the Elizabethan Drama* (New Haven, 1912).

[17] Georges Poulet, *Études sur le Temps Humain* (Edinburgh, 1949), deals with the change from medieval to modern ideas of time in chapters one to three.

[18] *Essay Concerning Human Understanding*, Bk. 2, chs. xiv, xv.

[19] *Aspects of the Novel* (London, 1927), pp. 28–31.

"life by time" is a necessary part of the novel's wider and more general concern with particularity and minuteness of description. As T. H. Green wrote in his *Estimate of the Value and Influence of Works of Fiction in Modern Times* (1862), the greater part of life cannot be represented in literature "simply from its slowness";[20] but the beginnings of such a representation can be found in Defoe and the slowed down tempo of his narration.

The time element has a further importance in the novel. That an event happened at a particular time is a piece of information that is important for the authenticity it bestows. And when we have the impression that all the actions narrated are part of the same time continuum, they take on a different status: a story becomes a novel. The novel, Forster has said, is a narrative where one thing happens and therefore another thing happens.[21] The time dimension must be made real before we can feel that a character is the product of his past actions, and that the pattern of all the characters and actions is one of cause and effect.

It is evident that plot and character do not have this kind of authenticity in romance: but that they do in Defoe, and in later novels. In a sense, Defoe's time-schemes are careless and ill contrived: the time scales of the novels are often both contradictory in themselves, and inconsistent with their historical setting.[22] Still, the main effects of a particularized presentation of time are there. Although the events described are actually recounted decades after they actually happened to Crusoe, Moll Flanders, and Roxana, they are set upon a general autobiographical time scale which is presented in some detail. The main events are so narrated as to give the impression of their occurring in the historic present, and the details of these events are depicted through a closer or more discriminated time-dimension than had been previously embodied in narrative.

Richardson took the process a stage further. The letter form gives us a sense that all is happening at the present time. And the device—clumsy though it is in many respects—also slowed

[20] *Works,* ed. Nettleship (London, 1888), 3: 36.

[21] *Aspects of the Novel,* pp. 82–83.

[22] The most complete account of these errors is to be found in Paul Dottin, *Daniel De Foe et ses Romans* (Paris, 1924), vols. 2 and 3.

down the time-scale of events to one very near that of actual experience. Characters and events, for the first time, are set upon a time scale not of years, but of hours and minutes. It is probably true to say that the decisive technical factor which has caused so general an assent to the view that Richardson is the first novelist, is his development of a form of narrative which is composed entirely of what he called "critical situations . . . with what may be called instantaneous descriptions and reflections."[23] It was this unprecedentedly thorough kind of particularity as regards the time scale, this close attention to the details of the succession of actions, which was the basis of his achievement and influence; it did for the novel what Griffith's technique of the "close-up" did for the film: took the audience closer to the object than had ever been done before. Later novelists could absorb his closeness to the realized scene without necessarily adopting his epistolary technique.

It is interesting to note that the importance of the time dimension to the novel's methodological realism is supported by the innovations of the two other most original novelists of the century.

Fielding ridiculed the Richardsonian use of the present tense in *Shamela*,[24] and the day by day method of narration in *Tom Jones*.[25] But he, too, felt the need to give an authentic time scale to *Tom Jones*: it was probably the first work to be composed with the aid of an almanac, so that the phases of the moon for instance, in the novel, are correctly located for the year 1745.[26]

Sterne's treatment of time is the *reductio ad absurdum* of the philosophical-realist view of time. The story of the Shandy family has an external temporal realism, in that enough is said to make it possible to date all the events on the historical time scale:[27] it has an internal temporal realism in that the actual sequence of narration follows the subjective succession of ideas

[23] Preface, *Clarissa*.

[24] Letter 6.

[25] Book 2, ch. 1.

[26] This was shown by F. S. Dickson (Wilbur L. Cross, *Henry Fielding* [New Haven, 1918], 2: 189–93).

[27] Theodore Baird, "The Time Scheme of *Tristram Shandy* and a Source," *PMLA* 51 (1936): 803–20: *Tristram Shandy*, Bk. 2, ch. vi, Bk. 3, chs. xviii, xix, Bk. 4, ch. xxxii.

in the author's mind: and finally, Sterne proposes a total correspondence between the duration of his fictional events and the reader's experience of them—one hour's reading to every hour in the hero's waking life. If the novelist, then, takes temporal verisimilitude to its logical conclusion, his novel can never be completed. In seeing this Sterne is foreseeing later contradictions in the realist novel's technique, which also have their parallel in later realist philosophy. One of the greatest of the contemporary exponents of realism, Bertrand Russell, has named his paradox of time, the "Tristram Shandy."[28]

In this, as in many other respects, space is the necessary correlative of time:

> What is actual is actual only for one time
> And only for one place.

The individual, particular case is defined by its position in space and time.[29] The methodological realism of the novel pays a closer attention to both these aspects of reality than other forms. It is not easy to differentiate the two: the terms "minute" and "present," applying to both time and place description, show this, and Proust's novel is the *locus classicus* of their indivisibility. Still, it is necessary to indicate briefly how the eighteenth-century novelists made a break from the unparticularized locations of other literary forms, and began to give the novel its spatial particularity.

Place is unparticularized and general in romance, tragedy, and, to a large extent, in comedy. Shakespeare, Johnson tells us, "had no regard to distinction of time or place,"[30] and in this respect *Pilgrim's Progress* and *Candide* are as unlike the novel as Sidney's *Arcadia*. But Defoe, though lacking the careful precision that has become customary in the novel, sets his novels in particular places, and by occasional details or, more rarely, by set passages of description such as are found in *Robinson Crusoe*, gives us enough of the spatial setting of his novels to convince us of their authenticity. Then Richardson—here again

---

[28] *Principles of Mathematics* (London, 1937), pp. 358–60.

[29] Coleridge points out that our idea of time is 'always blended with the idea of space' in *Biographia Literaria*, ed. Shawcross (London, 1907), 1. p. 187.

[30] Preface to Shakespeare, in *Johnson on Shakespeare*, ed. Raleigh (London, 1908), pp. 21–22.

occupying the central place in the development of the methodological realism of the novel—gives such detailed descriptions of the surroundings of Clarissa that there is an anticipation of Balzac in the way the Harlowe mansion becomes a pervasive operating force, a physical and moral environment which is a part of the total effect. Fielding, once again, must be placed between Richardson's particularity and the more generalized spatial setting of romance. But he, Smollett, and Sterne all give us a definite, tangible, physical environment.

IV

Particular time and place combine in Locke to give the principle of individuation; a specific *locus* in both dimensions is what distinguishes an individual object from the others belonging to the same class.[31] The same principle operates in the novel. The individualization of character is clearly related to the development of means for the rendering of the objective conditions of its existence. Of these, a specific time and place are primary conditions for the differentiation of the individual from the type. This differentiation is an important part of the contrast between the characters of the romance and the novel. A convenient way of showing the contrast is to consider the way their characters are named. Proper names in philosophy raise the problem of the relation of the individual and the class; so in the novel the realistic technique required a break with the traditional practice of giving characters class-names.[32] John Dennis reflected the current view when he wrote that since "poetical persons are general," they need only be "barely named."[33] But if the persons of the novel are to have the same status as those of life, their names must imitate those of real persons. Sir Toby Belch, or Mr. Badman will not do, and nor will Chloe who has no surname and is "common as the Air." So the novel established the practice of using real names, a practice which the novelists disregard at the peril of sacrificing the kind of reality which we ordinarily accord the characters in novels. As Henry James said of Trollope's "ambiguity of mind

[31] *Essay*, Bk. 2, ch. xxvii.

[32] There is a résumé of English practice in Charlotte Sennenwald's "Die Namengebung bei Dickens; eine Studie über Lautsymbolik," *Palaestra*, 203 (1936): 15–38.

[33] *Works*, ed. E. N. Hooker (Baltimore, 1939–43), 1: 45.

as to what constitutes evidence"—"A Mr. Quiverful with four-
teen children is too difficult to believe in. We can believe in the
name and we can believe in the children; but we cannot manage
the combination."[34]

At all events, it will be agreed that the novel has, by the use
of real names, symbolized its intention of dealing with the same
social world, in the same descriptive way, as we practice in
ordinary life. And, once again, we find that the development
of the novel's realistic methodology in this respect too is initiated
by the eighteenth-century English novelists. Defoe, casually and
sometimes contradictorily it is true, gives his main characters
ordinary names.[35] Richardson does so in a more thoroughgoing
manner, and at the same time introduces considerations of
symbolic appropriateness without detracting from realism, in
such names as Clarissa Harlowe and Robert Lovelace. Fielding
combines the old and the new literary tradition by compromis-
ing—creating a world where some characters have general
names—Allworthy and Western—whereas others have particular and realistic ones—Tom Jones and Mrs. Fitzpatrick. And
Sterne takes the naming conventions of realism to their *reductio
ad absurdum* by making the name Tristram Shandy the unique
symbol of the bearer's destinies.

V

There are many other matters in which the novel's essential
particularity of method could be demonstrated. Perhaps the
most important of them is language. One of the earliest causes
of trouble which philosophical realism hit on was the fact that
words did not all, or equally, stand for real objects: and Defoe's
language is surely in closer agreement than any previous work
of fiction had been with Locke's definition of the function of
words in the *Essay concerning Human Understanding*: "to
convey the knowledge of things."[36] For until Defoe narrative
was dominated by the traditional view of the literary function
of language: which was, briefly, to transform "things" into the
appropriate linguistic status of the literary genre which was

[34] *Partial Portraits* (London, 1888), p. 118.
[35] I have dealt with this theme in some detail in "The Naming of Characters in Defoe, Richardson, and Fielding," *R.E.S.* 25 (1949): 322–38.
[36] Bk. 3, ch. x, sect. 25.

being practiced. To each genre there was a special linguistic decorum; and to each character or incident, a suitable rhetoric. This use of language necessarily subordinated, if it considered at all, the referential suitability of words to considerations based, not on life, but on literature, on a traditional interpretation of nature or reality. But, by the eighteenth century, some of the unreality involved in this use of language was being seen. Dennis, for example, echoed Locke's view that figurative speech was an abuse of language: "No sort of imagery can ever be the language of grief. If a man complains in simile, I either laugh or sleep."[37] He had in mind, as Johnson later, the actual behavior of an individual suffering grief, as the true standard; and such a standard of verisimilitude could be fully incorporated only in the novel which was new and therefore had no linguistic decorums except those of ordinary speech, the newspaper, and the private letter. Since then the novel has usually used language in a way that was mainly referential, that took for its main criterion the correspondence of the word with the object or action denoted.

The point hardly needs exemplifying in Defoe, Richardson, or Sterne. All three, in their own way, achieve a new closeness of correspondence between the words and the imagined reality they are dealing with. Fielding is to some extent an exception—his prose is intermediate between the purely referential and the literary and generalizing. Indeed, his language, and his formal structure in general, are outside the main tradition of realism in the novel. For Fielding summarizes, rather than reports, experience: and all particular events and characters are expressed with some degree of generality. The reader cannot imagine himself to be in the role of the scientist eavesdropping on a new exploration of reality: the prose immediately informs him that exploratory operations have long since been accomplished, and that he is privileged to have been spared the labor, and to be presented instead with a summary of findings. We are reminded that a patent selectiveness of vision is something which, for the most part, tends to destroy our credence in the report. When this selectiveness, operating in the language and the structure of a novel, becomes noticeable, it impairs the realistic method's pretense of merely putting us in possession of

[37] Preface, "Passion of Byblis," 1692, *Works,* 1: 2.

all the relevant data. In extreme cases—say, in *La Princesse de Clèves* and *Les Liaisons Dangereuses*—an extreme selectiveness on the part of the reporter forces us to doubt the reality of the report while admiring the skill of the reporter; whereas at the opposite extreme, the diffuseness of Defoe and Richardson tends to act as a guarantee of the authenticity of their report.

This is not, of course, to deny the appropriateness of ordinary stylistic and structural criteria to the novel; but only to suggest that they have not there the same primacy as in poetry; and that they must be imposed unobtrusively upon a text which is first and foremost the verbal equivalent of real referents in human life, Flaubert's "le réel écrit." This primarily referential technique of the novel helps to explain why defects of style have less weight in the critical evaluation of a novelist—Richardson, Dickens, Hardy, Balzac, Dostoevsky, for instance—than of a poet; also, why the novel is the most translatable of the genres. And—taking the primarily referential function of language in the novel a step further—the same contrast explains why historical and literary commentary are so much less necessary for its appreciation: the novel must supply its own footnotes.

VI

So much for our analogy. It is not intended as exact. Philosophy is one thing and literature is another. Nor is the question of the influence of philosophy on the novel being raised. The analogy does not really depend on the appropriateness of the word "realism" in its philosophical or its literary sense: but only on the supposition that some general features of modern thought may help to explain various formal and historical aspects of the novel for which "realism" seems a moderately convenient term.

One or two objections perhaps require brief attention. First of all, it may be said that the decisive implication of realism derives from its use as an antonym of "idealism." This opposition obtains in two spheres, epistemological and psychological. The realist-idealist controversy in philosophy seems to support rather than undermine the historical parallel of realism proposed above: since neoclassicism which opposed the particularity of the novel genre had a distinctly idealist or Platonizing tendency;[38] and modern idealism is a tendency which has clearly not been embodied in the novel.

But the usual sense of the antonym, of course, is ethical, or psychological. It makes "realism" stand for something more accurately to be found in the controversies aroused by naturalism: briefly, a low view of the human scene. George Boas expresses the view thus: "realism became the explaining of all acts as the effects of discreditable causes."[39] This use of "realism" has certainly been active in the literary history of the novel. The Ephesian matron's story was "realistic" because it shows that sexual appetite is stronger than wifely sorrow; fabliaux, farces, and picaresque tales are "realistic" because economic or carnal motives have priority of place in the description and explanation of behavior. And on these grounds, the eighteenth-century novelists are found to be "realistic" because Moll Flanders is a thief and Pamela a hypocrite[40] and Tom Jones a fornicator.

This view of realism seems to me to fit our proposed analogy. The tendency of the novel's realism, like that of philosophical realism, is critical. The search for real explanations of human behavior, leads to the rejection of the more flattering pictures of man supported by many established ethical, social, and literary codes: and it may well come to put "low views" in their place. But this view of "realism" is incomplete, and tends to obscure the real development of the novel. Since "higher motives" are the preserve of tragedy, the novel, as has often been said, appears to have got closer historical affinities with comedy, which has always been allowed to deal with the baser realities and particularities. This view, implicitly, is taking "a low view" of the novel. For this reason. The time-hallowed Aristotelian dichotomy of the separate tragic and comic realms, which is in accord with most classical literary practice, excludes wholeness of representation. It imposes an *a priori* suitability of literary and linguistic treatment upon social types and classes. This

---

[38] See Louis I. Bredvold, "The Tendency towards Platonism in Neo-Classical Aesthetics," *E.L.H.* 1 (1934): 91–119.

[39] *A Primer for Critics* (Baltimore, 1937), p. 131.

[40] As, for instance, is argued in William White, "Richardson: Idealist or Realist?" *M.L.R.* 34 (1939): 240–41.

dichotomy is not practiced in early Christian literature. As Auerbach has brilliantly demonstrated, humble people, and *sermo humilis*, are found in its most serious literature; in the Gospels, in medieval religious drama, in the lives of the saints, and in Dante.[41] But the *stil-trennung*, the segregation of matter and manner, was re-imposed in neoclassical literature, and it remained for the novel to make a complete break with any overtly prejudged attitudes and decorums to its subject matter. It is—at least in contrast with previous genres—omnivorous, and independent in its treatment of any kind of reality. This brings us back to the epistemology of the novel: its basic technique is a pretense that reality, the facts of experience, are being allowed to speak for themselves; that it is merely a mirror of the internal and external world, and so any overtly comic, tragic, pastoral, or romance bias conflicts with the pretended objectivity of the reflecting medium. This methodological, quasiscientific attitude inherent in the novel was first formulated by the French realists: but they drew attention to what seems to be a more universal fact about the novel's method. If an ethical bias to "the low" is apparent in their work they have failed in the larger sense of realism. Certainly their filiation from romanticism, with its attack on the segregation of the genres, is clearer if we take a wider view of realism than that which equates it with taking the low moral view of man: their originality was to take "low" subjects as seriously as "high" ones.

To have pretended to describe reality as it is apprehended by individual experience has certainly been characteristic of the novel form. And it would be difficult to deny, and superfluous to demonstrate, that in the last two hundred years the majority of readers have found in the novel the literary form which most closely satisfies the requirements of the correspondence of art to life. This is not to deny the view that complete realism in any art is ultimately impossible and in any case undesirable.[42] Nor even that, to a large extent, the methodological realism we have

[41] *Mimesis: dargestellte Wirklichkeit in der Abendländischen Kultur* (Berne, 1945).

[42] As is argued in Martin Lebowitz, "Concerning Realism in Literature," *Journal of Philosophy* 39 (1924): 358.

been concerned with is not itself a convention.[43] Still, the present disrepute of "realism" should not be allowed to blind us to the fact that there are important differences in the degree to which various literary forms imitate reality; that the novel's technique allows for a more direct expression of many of the dimensions in which individual, particular experience is set; and that this represents a genuine literary discovery which is an essential part of the achievement of the great novelists.

So much for the main argument. One further implication of realism is worth suggesting. The novel, from Richardson onward, has seemed to many people to be qualitatively different from other literary forms in the closeness of the reader's identification with the characters. The first example I have found of the term "identification" used in this sense is significant: "Prêtez-moi la magie de m'identifier avec eux" De Sade begs of Richardson's *Clarissa*.[44] This fullness of identification renders the novel peculiarly liable to the charge of providing "substitute living" or "vicarious experience." And it is surely a result, no doubt regrettable, of the novel's methodological realism. For the technique of the cinema, which makes even stronger use and abuse of identification, is after all an extreme development of the literary technique we have been discussing: photographic realism.

[43] See, Kenneth Burke, *Counterstatement* (New York, 1931), pp. 182, 218, 238.

[44] *Idées sur les Romans,* ed. Uzanne (Paris, 1872), p. 13.

IV

ERNEST TUVESON

Locke and Sterne

That Laurence Sterne should have admired John Locke's *Essay concerning the Human Understanding* seems at first as odd as anything in *Tristram Shandy*. Yet Sterne himself gave unmistakable testimony that Locke's great treatise had a most important influence on his own life and work. He ranked the *Essay* with the Bible as the books that had affected him most. Allusions to Locke, Lockian terminology, even exhortations to read—really read—the master, abound in *Tristram Shandy*. "It was his glory," Tristram exclaims, "to free the world from the lumber of a thousand vulgar errors." Wilbur Cross remarked that "the famous Essay became Sterne's companion to the end of life and coloured much of his own thinking."[1] But this statement leaves the most interesting questions to be answered. What does the apparently, dry, proper, commonsense mind of Locke have in common with that of the mercurial Yorick? First, of course, the literary artist, whose subject is the human personality, was impressed by the fact that it was Locke who had finally written "a history-book . . . of what passes in a man's own mind." But what really was Sterne's attitude towards the history-book of the understanding? Did Locke merely give Sterne the idea for a superb joke, the ludicrous possibilities of association of ideas, around which the vast learning and rich comedy of *Tristram* are put together, rather as the Pavilion at Brighton was built around the Oriental room the Prince Regent happened to acquire? It has been said that Sterne makes out of Locke something that is not Locke. Is Sterne, perhaps, satirizing the new way of ideas? Even though accepting the Lockian

From *Reason and the Imagination: Studies in the History of Ideas, 1600–1800*, edited by J. A. Mazzeo (New York and London, 1962), pp. 255–77. Copyright 1962 by Columbia University Press and Routledge & Kegan Paul, Ltd. Reprinted by permission of the author and publishers.

[1] *The Life and Times of Laurence Sterne* (New Haven, 1909), p. 33.

account as inescapably true in general, is he entering a humanistic protest against what new psychology made of human dignity? And what about many fundamental attitudes of Sterne—his faith in sentiment, for example—for which there seems to be no parallel in Locke?[2] Without attempting to treat exhaustively this problem, which indeed reaches to the very heart of Sterne's significance, and without presuming in an essay of this length to document every point fully, I shall attempt to indicate a new line of enquiry. I suggest, to put it briefly, that, in order to understand what Locke meant for Sterne, we should stand off at a greater distance. Instead of being preoccupied with the many detailed "sources," we should try to see what was Locke's ultimate purpose in studying the human mind. Then, perhaps, we can perceive a similarity between that purpose and Sterne's.

To begin with, it is essential to recognize *why* Locke became interested in re-examining the ways of the mind and what he proposed in the *Essay* to accomplish. He was not a "researcher," in a modern sense of the word, investigating for the sake of truth pure. Nor was he a true systematic philosopher, concerned to bring all aspects of thought under the heads of a consistent structure; after all, he called his book by the modest name of "essay," rather than "treatise" or "theory." Hence, perhaps, some of the loose ends and ambiguities of his work, which, indeed, may have increased its appeal to the great imaginative writer who was so keenly aware of the loose ends and ambiguities in human nature. I shall not repeat here what I said before about the general significance of Locke's study for the literary artist.[3] The essential thing, it seems to me, is that he was not primarily either scientist or philosopher, but reformer. In *The Conduct of the Understanding*, a kind of manifesto he wrote at the end of his life, he sets forth what had motivated him far more fully than he could in the more formal writings.

[2] Among studies dealing in whole or in part with this subject, I may list the following: Kenneth MacLean, *John Locke and English Literature of the Eighteenth Century* (New Haven, 1936); Theodore Baird, "The Time-Scheme of *Tristram Shandy* and a Source," *PMLA* 51 (1936): 803 ff.; John Traugott, *Tristram Shandy's World* (Berkeley and Los Angeles, 1954); and Ian Watt, *The Rise of the Novel* (Berkeley and Los Angeles, 1957).

[3] *The Imagination as a Means of Grace: Locke and the Aesthetics of Romanticism* (Berkeley and Los Angeles, 1960).

It becomes clear that his essays on the social contract, on civil right, on education, and on the mind all are branches of one tree. They grow out of a desire to further a radical reform, so sweeping that it would reach into every aspect of culture. I say "further," since, to appreciate Locke and what he represents, we must look beyond him, and realize that he is only one figure, although a central one, in a great movement of Western thought. It was with that movement, not merely with one writer, that Sterne was connected; it was not merely Locke the original observer of the mind, but Locke the center of a liberating force that appealed so strongly to Sterne.

The source of the movement (at least according to most of its participants in the earlier stages) was Bacon; and Locke justifies his study of the mind by the "great lord Verulam's authority" (*The Conduct*, sec. 1). There was a growing conviction that Western Europe was being smothered by an intellectual heritage which, like a heavy layer of smog, prevented men from seeing nature as it really is. Sterne's images present with great exactitude the intellectual world of his time. He asks the question that incited this revolution:

> Tell me, ye learned, shall we for ever be adding so much to the *bulk*—so little to the *stock*— . . . Are we for ever to be twisting, and untwisting the same rope? for ever in the same track—for ever at the same pace?
>
> *(Tristram Shandy*, 5, chap. 1)

Is Man, he asks, the image of God, the ray of divinity, etc., "to go sneaking on at this pitiful—pimping—pettifogging rate?" A whole new departure was necessary, Bacon had proclaimed, if man was not to suffer for ever, a pitiable creature: pitiable not because of necessity but because of his own folly and ignorance in binding himself in chains of his own forging. An essential part of the reform would be the examination of our own minds, to learn why we had got so far off the course God had intended for us; hence the "idols" of the tribe and of the cave. Locke's investigation is an extended and detailed carrying out of such hints, rather inspirations, as these following; and, as we shall see, Sterne's work is an extended imaginative embodiment of these germinal ideas:

> For it is a false assertion that the sense of man is the measure of things. On the contrary, all perceptions as well of the sense as

of the mind are according to the measure of the individual and not according to the measure of the universe. And the human understanding is like a false mirror, which, receiving rays irregularly, distorts and discolours the nature of things by mingling its own nature with it.

(*Novum Organum*, Book 1, Aphorism xli)

For every one (besides the errors common to human nature in general) has a cave or den of his own, which refracts and discolours the light of nature; owing either to his own proper and peculiar nature; or to his education and conversation with others; or to the reading of books, and the authority of those whom he esteems and admires; or to the differences of impressions, accordingly as they take place in a mind preoccupied and predisposed or in a mind indifferent and settled; . . .

(Aphorism xlii)

Locke cites in the *Novum Organum* as the authority of his work: "That it is absolutely necessary, that a better and perfecter use and employment of the mind and understanding should be introduced." The Royal Society, dedicated to carrying on the Baconian mission, condemned the "old talkative arts" as Sprat, in the *History* of the Society, called them. He associated the Restoration with the new enterprise, and his words could be the motto of the Enlightenment that was beginning: ". . . as it began in that time, when our Country was freed from confusion, and slavery; So it may, in its progress, redeem the minds of Men, from obscurity, uncertainty, and bondage."[4] Part of the essence of Locke's *Essay* is in Sprat, including the proposal for a reform of language and the call for a straight, honest look at the two natures: the nature without; and the human nature within, to be observed by honest, unbiased introspection.

Europe possessed what Sterne called the "lumber-rooms of learning," of elaborate and "fantastical" ideas, for which "metaphysical" became the contemptuous term. To get rid of them was necessary if nature was to be reconquered; but to attack them one by one was to cut off the Hydra's heads. We must find their source, in the mind itself. Knowing what it is, we can be on the alert—against ourselves; and we can judge ourselves and our lives as they really are.

[4] Thomas Sprat, *History of the Royal Society* (London, 1667), p. 58.

Locke carried this most basic investigation into details as Bacon had not done, and did so in a different spirit from that of Hobbes. It is unnecessary to give anything like a full account of Locke's famous theory. We need only recall here that knowledge is in no way innate; thus no philosophy could clothe itself in an imprescriptible authority, for nothing is above the test of experience. The test, moreover, of common experience, and of the common, but alert mind. But most people's minds are like Uncle Toby's picture of the "smoak-jack;—the funnel unswept, and the ideas whirling round and round about in it, all obfuscated and darkened over with fuliginous matter!" To clear the understanding, to let light into it—for Locke imaged activity as "seeing"—is the desideratum. We must realize, moreover, that when we perceive, and even when we think most profoundly, we do not participate in ultimate reality. We perceive not reality but the sense impressions that something—we can never know just what—causes. Locke's constant effort to reduce the intellectual pride in which dogmatism grows emphasizes Bacon's point that perceptions are "according to the measure of the individual and not according to the measure of the universe." But, one may ask, is not all this the ultimate in pessimism? Why did Bacon, and Locke, with their hopes for the future of the race, seem to beat us out of all certainty about our knowledge? The answer is their confidence that we *can* know our inner selves; and by knowing what we are, we can find our true relation to reality. Locke, the good pedagogue, had no desire to abase the mind; he hastens to assure us that we are able to deal quite adequately, in a utilitarian way, with the real world. What we must not do is to exaggerate what we can comprehend: we must not proudly assume that our minds can soar to grasp the final causes, or penetrate into the heart of the universe. But we can be certain that the mind, as part of what we should now call its biological endowment, has the power to arrange the simple ideas, the impressions, in patterns that enable the animal man to cope with the environment. So much God has granted us, and no more.

Locke attacks the traditional view that the mind is an independent, incorporeal, self-contained being, inhabiting its tenement of clay for a term, engaged in a constant struggle to maintain its dominance over a partner to which it is intrinsically and infinitely superior. Maybe a certain quantity of matter is endowed with the powers of receiving impressions and of "reflecting" on its own operations. In any case, the mind is in, not outside and above nature. In a suggestive section of *The Conduct of the Understanding,* he compares that power itself to a physical organ; thus the mind is like a "sinew," which must be gradually strengthened (sec. 28). "Knowing is seeing," he says elsewhere. Knowledge is perceiving, by an "internal sense," the agreement or disagreement of the simple ideas. (See the *Essay,* 2: i, 4; 4: i.) The fact of intellection is physical; and a corollary is that sense impressions, emotional drives, and reflection are all not separate operations of a soul and a body, but ultimately components of an organic process. All this, of course, is quite alien to the traditional complete separation of body and mind. The problem is not to attempt to find, as Cartesians had attempted to do, some point of contact between alien entities, but to realize that the *body thinks.*

The issue, I believe, was of the greatest importance for Sterne. Mr. Shandy's ludicrous speculations about "so noble, so refined, so immaterial, and so exalted a being as the *Anima,* or even the *Animus,* taking up her residence, and sitting dabbling, like a tadpole, all day long, both summer and winter, in a puddle, —" present the issue, the burlesque language exactly hitting the center of the problem. Body and mind, Tristram speculates, are "exactly like a jerkin, and a jerkin's lining;—rumple the one —you rumple the other" (3, chap. 4). Body and mind appear as integral parts of one garment. A reason for Sterne's "indecencies" may be here. Swift and Pope and many others had satirized the "stoic pride" of those who imagine they can transcend the physical impulses. Man loves to talk about himself as if he were a celestial being, but, since he is not, he constantly falls into prudishness and hypocrisy. The debate between the Shandys and Slop exposes asceticism in religion. In *A Sentimental Journey,* Yorick asks, "What trespass is it that man should have [passions]? or how his spirit stands answerable to the Father of spirits but for his conduct under them. If Nature has so wove her web of kindness that some threads of love and desire are entangled with the piece—must the whole web be rent in drawing them out?" By showing us how mind and body are one nature, how words and gestures, for example, bring to all minds associations supposed to be lower than the spirit, he uses an old satirical method to make his point. Bodily impulses help the spirit realize man's natural, therefore divinely purposed end, for those impulses are themselves part of the spiritual being. Swift's scatology seems intended to warn us to be on our guard constantly against the physical side, and not to preen ourselves with a false confidence that we have ever conquered it. Sterne, however, calls for a co-operation of the two; let us, he urges, be "natural." But opinion has given us a fictitious impression that the two are enemies, and thus the "natural" man has been divided against himself. "REASON is, half of it, SENSE; and the measure of heaven itself is but the measure of our present appetites and concoctions—" (7, chap. 13). "Soul and body are joint-sharers in every thing they get . . ." (9, chap. 13).

Sterne remained with Locke, and, despite his keen interest in psychology, showed no sign of going along with the more "up-to-date" post-Lockians of the Hartley school. Certainly Locke's own attitude towards the mind was more acceptable to Sterne than the mechanical system envisaged by the pure associationists. Sterne could never think of mental activity as the mere setting up of connections in a neural machine. Locke thought that, even if the mind be matter, still at the center was a living, sensitive something, capable of self-awareness. He solved the vexed problem of personal identity (to his own satisfaction, if not to that of others) with the statement that "*Self* is that conscious thinking thing,—whatever substance made up of (whether spiritual or material, simple or compounded, it matters not)—which is sensible or conscious of pleasure and pain, capable of happiness or misery, and so is concerned for itself, as far as that consciousness extends" (*Essay*, 2: xxvii. 17).

The "self" of Locke is transformed into the "sensibility" of Sterne, which Yorick apostrophizes in *A Sentimental Journey* as "source inexhausted of all that's precious in our joys, or costly in our sorrows! thou chainest thy martyr down upon his bed of straw—and 'tis thou who lift'st him up to HEAVEN— Eternal fountain of our feelings!—'tis here I trace thee—and this is thy 'divinity which stirs within me.' " New values have been added to the "self": it is now also the agency of aesthetic and ethical experience. We exist to feel. The more the chords of our senses, external and internal, are touched, the more we

become spiritual beings in the true sense of the word. The idea
that the mind is a physical organ finally could lead to opposite
kinds of response. One would make everything mechanical; the
spiritual is eliminated, as in the young Godwin. On the other
hand, the physical could be absorbed into the spiritual, as in
Romanticism generally. Emotion, impulse, raw sensation, could
take on values previously reserved exclusively to the soul.
Purely physical experience takes on spiritual excellence, and, in
Carlyle's phrase, nature is "supernaturalised." The sensibility,
the divinity within us, must be exercised, as the mind must be
strengthened. When we feel compassion for another, as often
as we are in love, even when we suffer, we resemble the "great
SENSORIUM of the world! which vibrates, if a hair of our heads
but falls upon the ground, in the remotest desert of thy
creation—." The capacity for intense feeling for others as well
as self is the prerogative that man and God share. Illusory
opinion, however, by cutting off as unworthy many sources of
stimulus for the sensibility, has withered many souls. The end
of life is not the contemplation of the Aristotelian tradition, but
an exquisite awareness.

Locke, as I have indicated, assumed that there is a direct,
unmediated intuitus of truth when the understanding sees the
ideas arranged in proper order. Thus he condemned the operations of formal logic as usually unnecessary and ofter misleading. The inference is that the more elaborately reasoned a
theory is, the more we should suspect it. Sterne illustrates the
point in common and simplified imagery, in Volume 3, chapter
40 of *Tristram Shandy*. Locke believed that the common man
can see the truth at least as clearly as the specialist. The idea, of
course, is essential to the whole Enlightenment; the Royal
Society, as Sprat reported, preferred the language of artisans
to the terms of art. Uncle Toby, the least philosophical and most
uncomplicated person in *Tristram Shandy*, at once accounts for
the sense of duration in the same manner as Locke—" 'Tis owing,
entirely, . . ." to the "succession of our ideas"—although, he
says, he understands the "theory of that affair" no more than
his horse. By simply observing his own mind without preconceptions as to what he would discover, he solved the puzzle
that had baffled the philosophers.

In the eighteenth century there was growing a reliance on the
immediate response to experience—a reliance that to be sure

went beyond what Locke himself would have approved.[5] If the understanding has operated so inefficiently, if the faults of thinking are so deeply imbedded in the mind, may not the intuitive, even instinctive response to a situation—before ratiocination—be the most trustworthy? Shaftesbury and Thomas Burnet suggested and Hutcheson developed the theory of an "inner sense," corresponding to the outer ones, that reacts with pleasure or displeasure to situations as reflected in the mind's eye; it perceives good and bad as the outer sense perceives, or seems to perceive color. There is a movement in Sterne from the sermon in Volume 2 of *Tristram Shandy*, with its definition of "conscience" as a sort of monitor or judge in the mind, recalling Adam Smith's "third person" who views our conduct from without, to the unqualified emphasis on immediate sensibility in *A Sentimental Journey*. The development is typical of the times.

The opinions of the understanding, unfortunately, can break the circuits nature has set up, which should operate as naturally and instantly as the reflexes. Theological dogmas are among the worst offenders. In *A Sentimental Journey*, Yorick, influenced by his acquired prejudices, rejects the poor monk, whom he sees as an abstraction created by generations of preaching and propaganda. The reality, the pitiable human being, has been replaced by an artificial entity. But, a moment later, as the figure crowds back into his imagination, his natural reactions reassert themselves, and he responds in the right, the natural manner, with sympathy. This is an example of the sentimental education we all need, and it demonstrates the part the imagination can play in restoring us to ourselves. Yorick's sermon on "Vindication of Human Nature" gives another instance of opinion destroying the harmonious operation of natural benevolence. There are selfish and unscrupulous persons in the world, to be sure; and logic, universalizing instead of looking into the heart, has produced the doctrine that human nature is innately evil. What is the consequence?

> . . . to involve the whole race without mercy under such detested characters, is a conclusion as false, as it is pernicious; and

[5] The "moral sense" theory owed much, as it seems to me, to Lockian psychology, even though Locke himself was dubious about the idea. See my article "The Origins of the 'Moral Sense,'" *HLQ* 11 (1948): 241.

was it in general to gain credit, could serve no end, but the rooting out of our nature all that is generous, and planting in the stead of it such an aversion to each other, as must untie the bands of society, and rob us of one of the greatest pleasures of it, the mutual communications of kind offices; and by poisoning the fountain, rendering everything suspected that flows through it.[6]

The title *The Life and Opinions of Tristram Shandy, Gentle-man* hints strongly at the relation of this book to Locke's reform. The epigraph of Volumes 1 and 2, from Epictetus, is translated: "It is not actions but opinions concerning actions, which disturb men."[7] For, as Locke says in the following eloquent passage, opinions are the most dynamic things in our lives.

Temples have their sacred images, and we see what influence they have always had over a great part of mankind. But, in truth, the ideas and images in men's minds are the invisible powers, that constantly govern them; and to these they all universally pay a ready submission. It is, therefore, of the highest concernment, that great care should be taken of the understanding, to conduct it right, in the search of knowledge, and in the judgments it makes.

(The Conduct of Understanding, sec. 1)

Sterne, employing the comic and satirical imagination, shows us how opinions rise; by taking us into other minds, and primarily into his own, for that is what he can know best, he gives concrete reality to what Locke had discussed. Sterne, like most satirists, aims at pride. In the sermon "Job's Account of Life," he asks:

Does not an impartial survey of man—the holding up this glass to shew him his defects and natural infirmities, naturally tend to cure his pride and cloath him with humility, which is a dress that best becomes a short-lived, wretched creature?

But the pride satirized is not that which Swift or Pope had attacked. The glass most satirists hold up reflects the deviations from a "norm" and contrasts its objects with the ideal of the reasonable man. Sterne's mirror reflects the mind in its hidden

[6] *The Sermons of Mr. Yoricke* (Oxford and Boston, 1927), 1: 83.

[7] I have used, for *Tristram Shandy*, the indispensable edition of James A. Work (Odyssey Press), whose translation this is.

operations, underneath the appearance of reason on which we all pride ourselves. He seeks to correct our smug assumption that all within our heads is neat and orderly, and that the mad and even the eccentric are different in *kind* from ourselves.

Tristram Shandy frequently is classified as a novel and fitted, although not without awkwardness, into the history of that form. To be sure, Sterne's influence on the techniques of such modern novelists as Virginia Woolf is not to be denied; but, I should suggest, neither the evocation of the atmosphere of the mind nor the presentation of character in the round is a primary intention for him. Sterne connected his work with those of Rabelais, Cervantes, and Swift. The first named, as Erich Auerbach has pointed out, had a serious purpose underneath the jest: "a fruitful irony which confuses the customary aspects and proportions of things, which makes the real appear in the super-real, wisdom in folly, rebellion in a cheerful and flavorful acceptance of life."[8] Rabelais and Swift and Sterne, for all their differences, had in common the fact that they lived in times of great change and they were aware of the need for shaking up sacrosanct and ossified opinions; they used satirical comedy, in their respective ways, as a kind of solvent to break up the crystallizations of thought. To change the figure, Sterne, with Locke, saw the need for letting air and light into the stuffy world of Europe, represented by the little world of the Shandys. Rabelais tells us that the drug within the box is more valuable than the outside promises and that the subjects treated are not so foolish as the title suggests. The wise reader will search for the deeper meaning as a dog breaks open a bone to get at the marrow. Perhaps with the precedent in mind, Sterne said that he wrote a "careless kind of civil, nonsensical, good-humored *Shandean* book, which will do all your hearts good—. And all your heads, too,—provided you understand it." He assumed the role of the jester, whose cap and bells license him to tell home truths to his exalted audience. For the epigraph to Volumes 3 and 4, he expanded the *Policraticus* of John of Salisbury: "in quibus fuit propositi semper, a jocis ad seria, a seriis vicissum ad jocos transire." What wisdom do we learn? It is that we are beholding the human family; we look into the glass the author holds up and we behold—our own minds. So

8 "The World in Pantagruel's Mouth," in *Mimesis: The Representation of Reality in Western Literature*, transl. Willard Trask.

comprehensive a scope called for a different, a more "civil" satire. Sterne could write the more biting kind, also; but his purpose, it may be, called for the persona of Yorick, the most attractive of Shakespeare's jesters, or for that of the ill-fated but romantic Tristram. In disagreeing with Locke's condemnation of wit, however, Sterne associated himself with the tradition of Rabelais and Swift rather than with the new, more and more biteless, "good-humored" comedy with which he was to be identified in the years after his death.

Finding the reasons for the prevalent "obscurity and confusion" of thought was, as I have remarked, the first cause of Locke's investigation. Mr. Shandy, that universal philosopher, identified some obvious ones—"dull organs," "slight and transient impressions made by objects," "a memory like unto a sieve" (2, chap. 2). We may add to these the dominance of passion over reason. That is to say, the usual explanation for human error and folly was in terms of physical defects or ethical fault. Locke's contribution was to identify other sources of error, which are indigenous to the mind. One is the tendency, without any reason of self-interest or passion, to construct towering, well organized theories giving every appearance of being true:—but, unfortunately, false, because, like the webs constructed by the Spider in Swift's *Battle of the Books,* they are spun from the mind and not based on the facts of nature. Man loves to spin these gossamers: a harmless enough amusement, if only they were not often accepted as true. "Who knows not what odd notions many men's heads are filled with, and what strange ideas all men's brains are capable of?" (*Essay,* 4: v. 7). It could well be the epigraph of *Tristram Shandy.* The vast extent of human thought, philosophy, religion, science, literature, medicine, is seen as a hothouse of grotesque and fantastic growths. Sterne's purpose is to make us see these growths as they are, exposing them to raillery by setting forth parodies of them. The prodigious Slawkenbergius is akin to the heroic Scriblerus. But Slawkenbergius is much closer to ourselves. Hence, perhaps, we feel an affection for the German Gothic marvel greater than we feel for the pedants of earlier satirists.

Mr. Shandy is the ordinary man touched by this kind of folly. He emulates, at a humbler distance, the eminent philosophers who have imposed their fancies on the world. Swift regarded system-makers and conquerors as the great scourges of the human race. Sterne in fact took a dark view of them also, but he shows us humor under what seems to be a different and kindlier light. Mr. Shandy constructs his wondrous hypotheses for the sheer joy of hypothesizing. He is constantly trapped in odd dilemmas that exist only within his own brain, and he recalls Locke's warning that "The eagerness and strong bent of the mind after knowledge, if not warily regulated, is often an hindrance to it." (*The Conduct*, sec. 25.) He is one of those who, as Locke again says, "stick at every useless nicety, and expect mysteries of science in every trivial question or scruple." Amusing as he is, he still represents a class that Sterne's age especially feared. He "was systematical, and like all systematick reasoners, he would move both heaven and earth, and twist and torture every thing in nature to support his hypothesis" (1, chap. 19). The difficulty is that we are all system-makers, at least in potentia, and so we are easily dazzled and misled by theories which attract us more than does the plain face of truth. Madame du Chatelet expressed the attitude of her time when she wrote: "Les hipothèses deviennent le poison de la philosophie quand on les veut passer pour la vérité."[9]

Mr. Shandy takes on a further meaning, however, when we remember that the age was in its way as paradoxical as a Shandean hypothesis. On one side was the bugaboo of the system, and everyone was glad that the world was progressing beyond the darkness of scholasticism. Yet no century, not even the thirteenth, was fonder of constructing systems; only this period could have produced the tribe of Whiston and his many successors, who explained the whole geological history of the earth from Creation to Judgment on the basis of one idea. Titles of systems published in this age, of both moral and natural philosophy, would fill a volume. What, then, impels people, against their own principles, into this extravagance? Most of Mr. Shandy's theories, Tristram says, "I verily believe, at first enter'd upon the footing of mere whims, and of a vive la Bagatelle"; and he warns the reader, as Locke had done, "against the indiscreet reception of such guests, who, after a free and undisturbed entrance, for some years, into our brains,—at length claim a kind of settlement there." (1, chap. 19).

[9] Quoted by Ira O. Wade, in *Voltaire and Candide* (Princeton, 1959). See his clear summary of the problem of hypotheses in this time.

Locke and Sterne

Tristram Shandy rides along on what Locke has identified as the "association of ideas," and it has the distinction of being the first literary work to exploit thoroughly this discovery. Sterne continued to use the phrase in Locke's meaning, disregarding later psychological theorists who described all mental activity as fortuitous combinings of impressions; therefore, the term means for Sterne the combinations which by chance form outside the reflective activity of the understanding. Simple ideas enter into associations (and there is the feeling that they do indeed act independently, motivated by forces beyond and sometimes unknown to the understanding) which do not correspond to anything in nature. These combinations, once formed, "always keep in company, and the one no sooner at any time comes into the understanding, but its associate appears with it; and if they are more than two which are thus united, the whole gang, always inseparable, show themselves together" (Essay, 2: xxxiii.5). Today we are so constantly bombarded by these gangs that it is hard for us to realize the shocking effect of Locke's chapter. It inaugurated a Copernican revolution in psychology, even though its full implications for advertising and propaganda did not begin to be realized until the nineteenth century. To Sterne it was not merely a novelty, the source of another and promising kind of humor. He was, for example, one of the first to realize what manipulated associations—consciously created by new magicians of the mind—could achieve. The contrast between Mr. Shandy's and Trim's respective orations on death leads to an important although seemingly off-hand observation. Mr. Shandy is a natural rhetorician, of the old school, "proceeding from period to period, by metaphor and allusion, and striking the fancy as he went along" (phrases, by the way, adapted from Locke's severe criticism of rhetorical arts); but Trim, by a simple, perfectly managed gesture, dropping his hat, created an immediate, unreasoned association of impressions, producing a much greater effect on the heart than did Mr. Shandy's rhetorical philosophizing (5, chap. 7). Then Sterne is moved to recommend Trim's hat to "Ye who govern this mighty world and its mighty concerns with the engines of eloquence." They were slow to wake up to the possibilities of this wonderful device, but of what they have done with it since, we are only too sadly aware. Locke did distrust appeals to fancy in metaphors and analogies, but how would he have regarded this new and more powerful method of enchaining the mind?

Locke, then, described in detail the idols of the tribe and of the cave. Some are intrinsic to the psyche itself; and we are at the mercy of forces within our own minds which seem to carry on their own life and which, Locke went so far as to say, may be irresistible. We can only understand them and try to avoid the situations, especially in childhood, that liberate them. He first identified what we should call obsession, and showed how ubiquitous it is. We recall Mr. Shandy when we read this passage:

> we may find that the understanding, when it has a while employed itself upon a subject which either chance, or some slight accident, offered to it, without the interest or recommendation of any passion; works itself into a warmth, and by degrees gets into a career wherein, like a bowl down a hill, it increases its motion by going, and will not be stopped or diverted. . . .
>
> (*The Conduct*, sec. 45)

Behind this interesting phenomenon is a "troublesome intrusion of some frisking ideas which thus importune the understanding, and hinder it from being better employed." What a suggestion the antics of the "frisking ideas" might have provided for Sterne! "Strange combination of ideas," he explains, "the sagacious *Locke*, who certainly understood the nature of these things better than most men, affirms to have produced more wry actions than all other sources of prejudice whatsoever" (1, chap. 5). Having emphasized the point so strongly, Locke, we might expect, would proceed to show how great superstitions, wars, and persecutions have come out of the waywardness of the mind. But there is none of the portentousness we expect from Freudian studies of abnormality. Sterne, with his genius for language, uses Locke's own word to describe the illustrations Locke gives—"wry." They are congenial to the spirit of Sterne, sometimes even in language as well as in substance. Comic-grotesque, most of them are taken from commonplace episodes of life. Sterne, of course, recalls the statement of the general principle of association, but Locke's concrete suggestions may well have had their influence also. Some people, Locke recounts, see in the dark "a great variety of faces, most commonly very odd ones, that appear to them in a train one after another." There was a lady "of excellent parts," who had got to be past thirty without having had such an experience, and doubted its possibility; but, sure enough, "some time after drinking a large dose of dilute tea," she did see exactly such a variety of faces (*The Conduct*, sec. 45). There is the strange case of the young gentleman

> who having learnt to dance, and that to great perfection, there happened to stand an old trunk in the room where he learnt. The idea of this remarkable piece of household stuff had so mixed itself with the turns and steps of all his dances, that though in that chamber he could dance excellently well, yet it was only whilst that trunk was there; nor could he perform well in any other place, unless that or some other trunk had its due position in the room.
>
> (*Essay*, 2: xxxiii. 16)

People may be oblivious to the company, so that "when by any strong application to them they are roused a little, they are like men brought to themselves from some remote region; whereas in truth they come no farther than their secret cabinet within, where they have been wholly taken up with the puppet, which is for that time appointed for their entertainment." Here are sketches for Shandean portraits.

How Sterne probed dogmas may be shown by the Shandys' discussion of duration and time, in volumes 2 and 3. Time, we hardly need to be reminded, has always been a puzzle, but the eighteenth century found itself in one of its oddest dilemmas with regard to the problem. It found itself confronted by two quite contradictory but seemingly irrefutable conclusions. The pillars of the Newtonian universe were the conceptions of absolute space and absolute time. As Miss Nicolson has shown in *Mountain Gloom and Mountain Glory*, the space in which the planets move came to be identified with infinity and to be considered a divine attribute. Absolute time in like manner came to be identified with eternity and also to form an attribute of deity. Must not our experience, logically, share in this majestic and invariable march which carries everything in the universe? How, if nature forms a great and harmonious system, could any part go its own eccentric way, or exist in its own private time?

But, Locke had demonstrated from introspection, our sense of "duration," which gives rise to the complex idea of time, is purely subjective—owing, as Uncle Toby notes, "entirely to the succession of our ideas." As we observe the ideas pass before our inner eye, reflected as it were on the screen of consciousness, we form the idea of duration, from the intervals between the impressions. But how uncertain, how completely subjective this is! Time may be "long" or it may be "short"; we lose time entirely, Locke tells us, when we are asleep, for without consciousness it does not exist for us. If Adam and Eve, when they were alone in the world, "instead of their ordinary sleep, had passed the whole twenty-four hours in one continued sleep, the duration of that twenty-four hours had been irrecoverably lost to them, and been for ever left out of their account of time" (*Essay*, 2: xiv. 5). If this wholly subjective sense of duration is, as Locke believed, the foundation for the idea of time, on what a shaky foundation must be based our apprehension of the cosmos! The confidence of the whole Enlightenment that the two histories—of the inner life, and of nature—must harmoniously fit within one ordered universe could be challenged at this point. Sterne saw the dilemma more clearly than did the philosophers, for even Hume felt that the question of time, although not answered satisfactorily by Locke, could be quite nicely solved.

Sterne used the old debate about the interpretation of Aristotle's observations on "unity of time" in the drama as the vehicle for his presentation of the paradox. Our inner experience, as we observe the succession of ideas—itself subject to moods and passions—is what we really know. The critics who demanded that the chronological time of the action of a play must correspond exactly with the measured time elapsed in presenting it had got this inner experience hopelessly confused with the march of the universe. But it is with the inner life that the literary artist, whether dramatist or narrator, is concerned. If he is successful, he governs the consciousness of the spectator, causing the ideas to pass before it, slowly or rapidly as the mood he creates may dictate. "The train and succession of our ideas," Sterne assures his readers, "is the true scholastic pendulum,—and by which, as a scholar, I will be tried in this matter,—abjuring and detesting the jurisdiction of all other pendulums whatever" (2, chap. 8).

Yet, as Theodore Baird has shown in a perceptive article cited above, Sterne does not abandon "all other pendulums whatever." Behind the apparent ramblings and inconsequences of the book is a carefully worked out plot which has a consistent time sequence, fixed not only by Shandy family history but also by references to important events of Europe in the reigns of William and Mary and of Anne. That is, the characters do have both external and internal histories. Sterne avoids the dangers lurking in the "stream of consciousness" technique, which may give the reader a feeling of remaining stationary as impressions float aimlessly by. Enclosed and self-contained as the Shandean world is, we are reminded of its existence in the greater one, as Uncle Toby's fortifications reflect the great campaigns of Louis XIV and the allies. So we never lose the feeling that the significance of the whole work transcends the story of one small group of humor figures.

Obviously, the book does not exist for the sake of the plot. As in many learned satires, the story serves partly as convenience, a scaffolding that supports the material in which the author is primarily interested. It wins and delights the reader, so that he will follow the author's "digressions" into the various realms of the mind. Here I can try to point out only one of the manifold functions of the plot of *Tristram Shandy*. The plot gives the author the opportunity to do something no one had ever deliberately done in this way before, because the key had not been available before the new psychology: to show how the mind works in reconstructing a story out of memory. He anticipates, he recalls associations, a simple event calls forth reflections and associated stories; his whole personality, with its interests and special character, becomes involved and gradually emerges. A formally organized, logical plot delights the understanding, and Tristram keeps lamenting that he cannot tell his story in that way. At the end of Volume 6, he draws a series of kinky lines illustrating the advance of the action, which he contrasts with an absolutely straight line drawn, in significant symbolism, with the aid of a "writing-master's ruler (borrowed for that purpose)." Artificiality, in the emblem of the writing-master and his ruler, contrasts with the natural movement of the mind. But Sterne warns us, as he does elsewhere, that this is not to be taken too literally: "In a word, my work is digressive, and it is progressive, too,—and at the same time" (1, chap. 22). Neither is the work, like a "stream of consciousness" novel, a look into the mind in undress. It is, indeed, a "conversation." The affectation of whimsy covers a development of effects. We come to know the Shandy family, as we come to know most families, not in a systematic way, but bit by bit, puzzling pieces of information gradually coming to fit into a pattern, and a unique atmosphere coming to be sensed. To understand people, with all their oddities and eccentricities which really constitute personality, we should discover them naturally, as we do in the disorganized but revealing course of ordinary experience. Again, however, although we observe people and events from within Tristram's consciousness, we are not imprisoned in that subjective world. As we have the history of Europe establishing points of reference for the divagations of the Shandy family, so we observe Tristram himself from the outside—in the person of his alter ego, Yorick. We have an objective description and estimate of his appearance and his character as they are after he had become a man, and we return to Tristram with a new insight.

Those two curious but very important phenomena of the mind, fantastical opinionizing and association of ideas, are for Sterne as for Locke central problems of life. But Sterne's evaluation of them differs from that of Locke himself. The moral of *Tristram Shandy*, if so formal a word can be applied to such a creation, is the danger of Opinion itself. The impulse to erect theories on every subject, to elaborate, distinguish, force everything into an artificial order, constantly threatens to narrow and distort the psyche. The over-busy intellect intrudes upon and threatens to dominate the direct reactions to impression. Many instances are scattered throughout *Tristram Shandy*. Ernulphus' anathema is representative. The hatred engendered by squabbling over logical but essentially unreal theological opinions leads to this glorious but terrible exercise of the imagination. The wonderfully elaborate condemnation of fellow human beings to all kinds of frightful punishments, for nothing but a disagreement in logic, shows how the chords of sympathy can be severed.

A supreme irony in this book is the demonstration of how

Locke's own attack on false and obscure reasoning can be perverted to produce exactly what he tried to eliminate. Mr. Shandy prides himself on his deep reading of the *Essay*, but his educational program is one ideally designed to produce in the child exactly what Locke most deplored. One of Locke's most cherished points was that words must have precise and concrete meanings. A word corresponds to a simple idea. Even an abstract word may designate one simple quality—e.g., whiteness—isolated from many different groups of simple ideas. The substitution of words for things had been one of the most fruitful sources of error. However, the gradual but accurate process of stocking the mind with ideas derived only from experience is too slow for Mr. Shandy. Ordinarily, he explains, a single word represents an idea, and, "when the mind has done that with it—there is an end,—the mind and the idea are at rest,—until a second idea enters;—and so on" (5, chap. 42). How much better to multiply ideas without waiting for the experience! Hence his astounding scheme for using the "auxiliaries"—to set the soul a going by herself upon the materials as they are brought her; and by the versatility of this great engine, round which they are twisted, to open new tracks of enquiry, and make every idea engender millions." And so back to opinion-spinning.

In contrast, there are Uncle Toby's inveterate association of every idea with his military game, and his inability to follow learned discourse. Instinctively kind and benevolent, he is a secular saint, but he seems to be hopelessly impractical in this world. Thus we tend to see him, with Mr. Shandy's eyes, as both lovable and irritating. Again, however, the deeper meaning is not what appears on the surface. One of Yorick's functions is to expose these prejudiced judgments. Thus when Trim, who shares much of Toby's character, repeats the ten commandments (having to begin with the first, since they form a train of ideas and go together), he inspires one of Mr. Shandy's typical orations. It is all rote learning, he says, believing he is applying Locke's principle that words are substituted for things, and that we must know truth by experience. He will lay out Aunt Dinah's legacy in "charitable uses (of which, by the bye, my father had no high opinion) if the corporal has any one determinate idea annexed to any one word he has repeated." Whereupon the corporal replies that the words mean he allowed his

parents, when old, "three halfpence a day out of my pay";
and Yorick exclaims "thou art the best commentator upon that
part of the Decalogue; and I honour thee more for it, corporal
Trim, than if thou hadst had a hand in the *Talmud* itself" (5,
chap. 32). A chapter could be written on the many signifi-
cances of this episode. It can only be noted here that the story
points up the meaning of Locke in a way that, we may be sure,
would have delighted him. The comparison of Trim's answer
and the Talmud suggests that concrete meaning, represented by
action, is vastly superior to the multiplication of elaborate but
abstract interpretations and allegories. The story has implications also for benevolism, an emotion which, as was to become
clear, could easily be merely a self-indulging luxury.

The truth about Uncle Toby is rather different from what
we at first expect. He epitomizes the immediate, forthright,
response to experience, and can hardly be the absurd but
saintly fool we at first take him for. He it is who discovers,
without reading, the explanation of duration. He defends his
taking up the profession of arms with a real eloquence that
contrasts with the pompous rhetoric of Mr. Shandy. He teaches
Tristram the lesson about compassion, in the episode of the fly,
with an instinct for truly effective pedagogy. His compassion
for Le Fever—based, by the way, on old military comradeship
as well as on the general sense of sympathy—produces the
great act of *practical* benevolence in the book. An important
sign post to his real nature is the contrast between his and Mr.
Shandy's respective humors. Tristram informs us that Mr.
Shandy gave himself up to his great "TRISTRA-*poedia*," or institute for the boy's education, "with as much devotion as ever
my uncle *Toby* had done to his doctrine of projectils.—the
difference between them was, that my uncle *Toby* drew his
whole knowledge of projectils from *Nicholas Tartaglia*—My
father spun his, every thread of it, out of his own brain,—or
reeled and cross-twisted what all other spinners and spinsters had
spun before him, that 'twas pretty near the same torture to him"
(5, chap. 16). Thus the one derives his information from a
factual authority, even if an old one, while the other is a web-
spinner of theories.

But what are we to say of his comic obsession with curtins
and horn works? Here Sterne, I should suggest, makes a
departure from Locke. As we read the latter's examples of the

involuntary association of ideas, we may wonder, a little, whether they are so unfortunate after all. They provide spectators with innocent amusement, and most of them are quite harmless; they may even provide the victim himself with a kind of pleasing and consoling illusion. Sterne shared the common faith of his generation that the system of the universe reflects the benevolence of its Creator. Are the strange obsessions and curious quirks of the mind nothing but pointless oddities or nuisances? May they not ease our way through this life, which Sterne, beneath his gaiety, felt so deeply to be troubled and sad? May they not compensate for sorrows and disappointments, enabling us to "Shandy it" through this mortal life with a fair share of the joy we should all have? The erratic fortune of the Shandys has robbed Uncle Toby of his profession and his ideal. He is not really a perennial ineffectual, for he has mastered a difficult and hard profession and has served bravely in war. Is not his hobby-horse a kindly provision in the scheme of things, filling up the void in his life? And, indeed, as Sterne asks, why should we begrudge each other our hobby-horses if we ride peaceably down the King's highway, and if we do not attempt to force our humors on others?

Alas, however, we do not tolerate one another. Our opinions become sacred truths, above the test of experience. Mr. Shandy's hypotheses are backed only by his impetuous and domineering personality, but those of others, just as odd and illusory in their ways, have acquired the support of powerful institutions and turned into instruments of repression. We try to understand what we cannot understand, and, trying to peer into the empyrean, we lose our way in this world.

I might summarize all this by comparing, once again, Rabelais and Sterne. To the former the new learning of the Renaissance provided a lever by which he could move the mass of dead ideas and institutions that lay like a heavy weight on the human spirit in his time. For Sterne, it seems to me, Locke's *Essay concerning the Human Understanding* performed a somewhat comparable function. It was not that Locke and Sterne agreed in everything, but that Locke had, so to speak, wiped clean the window of the soul of the false ideas that had hitherto obscured it. Now we are in a position to look into ourselves, and, armed with that knowledge, begin to regain our place in the great system. Sterne, in a passage of *Tristram Shandy* about

"Nature," that true deity of the age, expressed the meaning of his own work and much of the significance of Locke's as well:

> She, dear Goddess, by an instantaneous impulse, in all *provoking cases*, determines us into a sally of this or that member—or else she thrusts us into this or that place, or posture of body, we know not why—But mark, madam, we live amongst riddles and mysteries—the most obvious things, which come in our way, have dark sides, which the quickest sight cannot penetrate into; . . . so that this, like a thousand other things, falls out for us in a way, which tho' we cannot reason upon it,—yet we find the good of it, may it please your reverences and your worships —and that's enough for us.
>
> (4, chap. 17)

V

LOUIS KAMPF

Gibbon and Hume

The consciousness of liberty, that open consideration of our moral, artistic, and political maxims, is partially based on our awareness of history: To look at the past with some sense of its own nature, its own character, is to become aware of its many possibilities, of the directions history might have taken. It is a commonplace that our feelings about the past tell us something about the present. Now our sense of there being a history—that is, a past which we have to reconstruct, rather than a clear and simple sequence of separate events which leads up to the present and to the future—is one particular aspect of modernism's necessity for criticism; or perhaps, one of its causes. Since we do not feel ourselves developing logically from the sequence of events immediately prior to us, a chronicle of those separate events cannot reasonably give us a convincing account of the past. It has too often been said that the distinguishing mark of modern historical writing is its emphasis on fact. The reverse is closer to the truth: Only as the exclusive emphasis on fact begins to lose its importance will real historical concerns be ready to appear. For only then do we become capable of dealing with the nature of development itself, rather than casually assuming that the listing of a succession of events implies a developmental sequence. Once history stops being a simple recital of political facts, its most urgent concern is likely to be with causality. For history will have to *construct* a narrative, and thereby connect events which had once stood alone, which had provided their own connection. Hume, while discussing the association of ideas

From Chapter Two, "Skeptical Doubts," in *On Modernism: The Prospects for Literature and Freedom* by Louis Kampf (Cambridge, Massachusetts), pp. 80–90. Copyright 1967 by The M. I. T. Press. Reprinted by permission of author and publisher. The title "Gibbon and Hume" has been supplied by the editor.

(in *An Inquiry Concerning Human Understanding*), suggests how these connections are to be made:

> To return to the comparison of history and epic poetry, we may conclude from the foregoing reasonings that as a certain unity is requisite in all productions, it cannot be wanting to history more than to any other; that in history the connection among the several events which unites them into one body is the relation of cause and effect, the same which takes place in epic poetry.

Hume, it is clear, sees historical writing not as a recital of events but as an intellectual and imaginative effort on the part of the historian dealing with those events. The connections he needs to make might force him, as they did Montesquieu and Voltaire, to consider aspects of man's life in society other than the political. After all these years, does not the question of just what knowledge is relevant to historical narrative still form a lively bone of contention? Does not today's historian need to make the critical decision whether such semirespectable fields as social anthropology and psychoanalysis will really provide him with historical knowledge; whether they will connect the events of the past; whether they are events in themselves? In any case, the historian (and his reader) now bears the burden of making the proper connections. And we shall need to do more than connect those events among themselves. Since *we* are making the connections, we shall have to consider the relation of the present to the past: How else are we to get a proper perspective on our causal associations? Futhermore, the reader, since he is relying on the historian's connections, will have to question that historian's relation to the events described—indeed, the historian should do so himself. There is no way out of it, we shall have to write and rewrite our histories.

For Edward Gibbon, the connective link between events in *The History of the Decline and Fall of the Roman Empire* is provided, naturally enough, by the search for the causes of that decline and fall. Gibbon's motive for this search—what connects him to his material and lends it shape—lies in his intellectual attitudes, in his Humean skepticism. He sees his work as the epic (and recall Hume's association of the epic and history) of the decline and fall of humane rationality, of that civilized urbanity which had reached its summit during the age of the Antonines. This attitude, in turn, connects Gibbon's work to his own times, for he is writing the epic of the Enlightenment, the age in which rational intellect had to combat the dark cloud of ignorance, much as it did during the decline of the Roman empire.[1] Being the epic of the Enlightenment, the work must, of course, be an ironic mock-epic. For the skeptic, the necessary critical function reveals only the decline and fall; the reconstruction which will emerge after the destruction of the present is the work of the future, and of this no epics can be written, only utopias. *The Dunciad*, with its mocking vision of doom, rather than Voltaire's *La Henriade*, is the epic of the eighteenth century. For the latter is a conscious lie; it is not about the heroism of the past or present; it is, indeed, a utopia, a plan for an enlightened future.

An intellectual of the Enlightenment cannot look at the history of Christianity, even if he is a believer, as an early chronicler might have done. For one thing, someone like Hume will be constantly aware that what we see and hear may be a function of our historical moment, that the conditions of the moment may allow us to see some events but not others. Thus we—the historian, the present age, the reader—by our awareness of these subtle determinants, become as much a part of any modern account of the past, as that past itself. Gibbon points this out when he discusses the chronicles written by many of the Gnostic sects:

> Each of these sects could boast of its bishops and congregations, of its doctors and martyrs, and, instead of the four gospels adopted by the church, the heretics produced a multitude of histories, in which the actions and discourses of Christ and of his apostles were adapted to their respective tenets.

That each sect apparently composed its sacred accounts in order to justify itself teaches Gibbon, first of all, that religion has a history. If the Church had to choose four official gospels, then that choice itself might have a history—it might, in fact, be connected to other events. Worst of all, the Church, like the sects, might have made its choice for the purpose of self-justification. The assumption that the four gospels were adopted simply because god willed it becomes highly suspect or, at least, problematic. Indeed, the gospels have entered the realm of history.

[1] The notion of *The Decline and Fall* as an epic was suggested to me by Harold L. Bond's *The Literary Art of Edward Gibbon* (Oxford, 1960).

Second of all, and of greater importance to us, the historical practice of the sects teaches Gibbon that religious history ought to have the same standards as any other history; more strongly, it shows him that we should bring to religious history the same canons for belief which we use in dealing with our own personal pasts. But this last notion, which would seem to be trivial and somewhat obvious, does present us with difficulties—not only for religious history, but for history in general.

I shall look at some of these difficulties as they concern Gibbon, our first modern historian. It strikes me that Gibbon, rather than Voltaire, is the first major historian who gives us some sense of being our contemporary. The reason for this is of the greatest importance: Gibbon's modernity stems from the feeling he creates that history, rather than being a straightforward narrative of events, is composed of a series of problems each of which must be looked at with a good deal of philosophical subtlety. But let us examine Gibbon's procedure in the following passage; it is almost at the very end of his famous Chapter 15, the chapter which deals with the causes of mass conversion during the early years of the Christian faith:

> But how shall we excuse the supine inattention of the Pagan and philosophic world to those evidences which were presented by the hand of Omnipotence, not to their reason, but to their senses? During the age of Christ, of his apostles, and of their first disciples, the doctrine which they preached was confirmed by innumerable prodigies. The lame walked, the blind saw, the sick were healed, the dead were raised, daemons were expelled, and the laws of Nature were frequently suspended for the benefit of the church. But the sages of Greece and Rome turned aside from the awful spectacle, and pursuing the ordinary occupations of life and study, appeared unconscious of any alterations in the moral or physical government of the world. Under the reign of Tiberius, the whole earth, or at least a celebrated province of the Roman empire, was involved in a praeternatural darkness of three hours. Even this miraculous event, which ought to have excited the wonder, the curiosity, and the devotion of mankind, passed without notice in an age of science and history.

Gibbon's real subject, it should be clear, is the nature of historical evidence: His epistemological concerns have become, necessarily, part of the fabric of his narrative. The cutting irony of his remarks should be readily apparent to any of us modern unbelievers—or even to believers of a skeptical frame of mind. Now Gibbon's irony is not simply a means of beating the censor; it is an almost unavoidable consequence of his difficulties with the theory of knowledge. Gibbon draws the reader into his description: We have to interpret the meanings of the events along with him; we must decide which way the irony cuts. This collaboration is not based on any system of mutually shared beliefs; it depends, rather, on our mutual doubts, our doubts about the judgments we make of others' experience.

Hume, in trying to resolve his Cartesian doubts concerning the possibility of knowledge, has told us that historical knowledge must at some point be based on experience:

> We learn the events of former ages from history, but then we must peruse the volume in which this instruction is contained, and thence carry up our inferences from one testimony to another, till we arrive at the eyewitnesses and spectators of these distant events.

Only the testimony of someone who has experienced an event can make that event believable. But a Christian's experience may include the witnessing of miracles. The problem lies in just what and whose statements we believe to be connected to *actual events;* not whether those statements are based on someone's experience. We must ultimately make a judgment of the validity of the eyewitness's experience. Hume, unfortunately, tells us at one point in his argument that the chief principle by which we connect statements with events, causality, being a mental operation based on a species of instinct, is as incomprehensible in relation to ordinary events as it is to prodigies of nature. Hume's (extremely convincing) argument, by internalizing the problem of knowledge, has deprived us of any legitimate argument for challenging the connection between the believer's experience (his impression) and the actual event. As a result, we are left to deal with the miraculous—to the unbeliever, the incredible—only in terms of irony. The believer may take the report of a miracle at face value; the skeptic is likely to know better.

Gibbon's treatment of the evidence for miracles, indeed his general approach to historical sources, rests on Hume's speculations and conclusions about these subjects in his philosophical writings. The insistence on the naturalistic approach to all problems, on bringing the laws of secular history to bear on religious history, and the search for natural causes to explain the general acceptance of miracles—all these are equally the concern of the philosopher and the historian. The motives Hume posits for the acceptance of miracles, in Section X of *An Inquiry Concerning Human Understanding,* are almost identical to those Gibbon attributes to the early Christians in his Chapter XV. Finally, there is Hume's own irony in dealing with the miraculous:

> There is another book in three volumes (called *Recueil des Miracles de l'Abbé Paris*) giving an account of many of these miracles, and accompanied with prefatory discourses, which are very well written. There runs, however, through the whole of these a ridiculous comparison between the miracles of our Saviour and those of the Abbé, wherein it is asserted that the evidence for the latter is equal to that of the former, as if the testimony of men could ever be put in the balance with that of God himself, who conducted the pen of the inspired writers. If these writers indeed were to be considered merely as human testimony, the French author is very moderate in his comparison, since he might, with some appearance of reason, pretend that the Jansenist miracles much surpass the other in evidence and authority.

We ought to look at this footnote of Hume's in the context of his argument; for Hume's irony depends on his having clearly demonstrated that the evidence for Christ's miracles is as unacceptable as those for the Abbé's, that if we accept the evidence for the earlier prodigies we should, a fortiori, accept that for the more recent ones. Hume's basic argument is easily summarized: It is that an observer's report, if it is to be acceptable and believed, must correspond to the general course of our experience. What then are we, people living now, to make of miracles if we have never experienced any? Here are Hume's thoughts:

> A miracle is a violation of the laws of nature; and as a firm and unalterable experience has established these laws, the proof against a miracle, from the very nature of the fact, is as entire as any argument from experience can possibly be imagined. . . . The plain consequence is (and it is a general maxim worthy of our attention) that no testimony is sufficient to establish a mira-

cle unless the testimony be of such a kind that its falsehood would be more miraculous than the fact which it endeavors to establish.

Hume's point is, in short, that if we believe nature to be lawful, there is no logical basis for accepting any evidence for miracles; we would not believe one if we saw it with our own eyes. For Hume's contemporaries, and for us, there is no reasonable way of avoiding these conclusions: We are, in our empirical sense of evidence, products of the Enlightenment and therefore weigh the evidence of the past, including earlier historical accounts, in accordance with the laws of nature. Along with Hume, we are likely to make comments of the following sort:

> It forms a strong presumption against all supernatural and miraculous relations that they are observed chiefly to abound among ignorant and barbarous nations. . . . When we peruse the first histories of all nations, we are apt to imagine ourselves transported into some new world where the whole frame of nature is disjointed, and every element performs its operations in a different manner from what it does at present.

Here is a wholly modern attitude toward the writing of history, an attitude which is constantly aware that historical knowledge is dependent on the epistemology of the knower and that epistemologies change with the passage of time. Hume asks the most basic, and therefore most difficult, questions about the *foundations* of historical knowledge. These questions are posed simply on the basis of his researches in "mental geography"; and if we are familiar with these, we know that Hume will inevitably reach the conclusion that our perception of history—the connections we make, the causes we impute—may often depend on our personal feelings, on the psychological states which our time has made possible for us.

This modern attitude toward the philosophy of history is the dominant theme of Gibbon's practice as an historian. Here is Gibbon wondering about belief in the resurrection:

> At such a period, when faith could boast of so many wonderful victories over death, it seems difficult to account for the scepticism of those philosophers who still rejected and derided the doctrine of the resurrection.

Gibbon leaves us—indeed, makes us deal with—the problem of

whom one believes, the Christian doctors or the pagan philosophers. To do this we must decide what our standards for evidence are; how else are we to come to terms with Gibbon's
meaning? It is obvious that some people at some time believed
in miracles. If the Christian believer accepts the early miracles,
why should he not accept recent ones? One way of dealing with
the problem, Gibbon points out, is to assume that god withdrew his special dispensation from a sinful world, and, as a
result, the occurrence of miracles came to an end. But this
assumption, Gibbon illustrates, leads to some serious difficulties:

> And yet, since every friend to revelation is persuaded of the
> reality, and every reasonable man is convinced of the cessation,
> of miraculous powers, it is evident that there must have been
> *some period* in which they were either suddenly or gradually
> withdrawn from the Christian church. Whatever area is chosen
> for that purpose, the death of the apostles, the conversion of the
> Roman empire, or the extinction of the Arian heresy, the insen-
> sibility of the Christians who lived at that time will equally
> afford a just matter of surprise. They still supported their pre-
> tensions after they had lost their power.

At whatever time we place the disappearance of the miraculous, there will still be a number of superstitious souls who
experience miracles. Why should we reject the evidence of
their senses? Gibbon, after posing the question and embarrassing
us with the impossibility of an answer, decides to drop it altogether. He changes his approach to the problem, and bypasses
it in Humean fashion. He will not question the evidence for
miraculous events, since, as Hume has taught us, there is no
sure way of connecting evidence to event—miraculous or
ordinary—in any case; instead, he will change the ground of the
question to the psychology of belief, and ask why people
accepted the reality of Christian miracles. Just a few of his
devastating imputations follow:

> Whatever opinion may be entertained of the miracles of the
> primitive church since the time of the apostles, this unresisting
> softness of temper, so conspicuous among the believers of the
> second and third centuries, proved of some accidental benefit
> to the cause of truth and religion. . . . The primitive Christians
> perpetually trod on mystic ground, and their minds were exer-
> cised by the habits of believing the most extraordinary events.
> They felt, or they fancied, that on every side they were in-

cessantly assaulted by daemons, comforted by visions, instructed by prophecy, and surprisingly delivered from danger, sickness, and from death itself, by the supplications of the church. The real or imaginary prodigies of which they so frequently conceived themselves to be the objects, the instruments, or the spectators, very happily disposed them to adopt, with the same ease, but with far greater justice, the authentic wonders of evangelic history.

Gibbon has tried to illustrate, with deadly success, that the belief in miracles is based entirely on one's psychological predisposition to believe. Chapter 15 of Gibbon's work is, almost in its entirety, an illustration of this proposition earlier formulated by Hume. We learn that the success of Christianity —that is, the acceptance of its miracles—depended wholly on a combination of accidental circumstances properly exploited by the Church. The truth or falsity, the rationality or absurdity of Christianity's doctrines had little, if anything, to do with it.

The psychological predispositions for belief were readily available to the early Church. For us, matters are likely to be different. We are bound to exploit our knowledge that belief is grounded in the psychology of individual human beings; we might be tempted to induce those predispositions necessary for the desired belief by the clever use of propaganda —as, indeed, the Jesuits and a number of evangelical sects often did. For a man of the Enlightenment, this psychological predisposition might be shaped by the history he knows, in the view he takes of the past, and by the manner in which he consciously appropriates historical epochs. The writing of secular history becomes a substitute for hagiography. Its purpose is ideological and propagandistic; its real concern, the present and the future. Think of the underlying reasons for Voltaire's portrayal of the age of Louis XIV; and think of Gibbon's purpose in stressing the rationality and politeness of the age of Augustus. One of the possibilities of Gibbon's work is that it will succeed, by drawing the reader into its mode of apprehension, in creating a psychological predisposition which will eventually produce an enlightened attitude toward men and society which will reject the gathering forces of darkness, the irrationality, and "the cloud of critics." This attitude demands Gibbon's irony: To absorb it in reading *The Decline and Fall* is to affirm one's capacity for doubt, one's capacity to remain sane. For our perception of Gibbon's irony not only connects us with his work and with the past; much more importantly, it makes it possible for us to deal with the oppositions created by our own, and Gibbon's theory of knowledge.

VI

NORTHROP FRYE

Blake's Case Against Locke[1]

That an eighteenth-century English poet should be interested in contemporary theories of knowledge is hardly surprising. Blake had carefully read and annotated Locke's *Essay Concerning Human Understanding* in his youth, though his copy has not turned up. But as Locke, along with Bacon and Newton, is constantly in Blake's poetry a symbol of every kind of evil, superstition, and tyranny, whatever influence he had on Blake was clearly a negative one. The chief attack on Locke in the eighteenth century came from the idealist Berkeley, and as idealism is a doctrine congenial to poets, we should expect Blake's attitude to have some points in common with Berkeley's, particularly on the subject of the mental nature of reality,

From Chapter One, "The Case Against Locke," in *Fearful Symmetry* by Northrop Frye (Princeton, New Jersey), pp. 14–29, 435–37. Copyright 1947 by Princeton University Press. Reprinted by permission of the author and the publisher. The title "Blake's Case Against Locke" has been adapted by the editor.

[1] All references to Blake's own works are accompanied by the page reference to *The Writings of William Blake*, ed. Geoffrey Keynes, 3 vols., London, 1925. These page references are preceded by the letter "K" and the number of the volume. The Arabic numeral following a reference to an engraved poem is the number of the plate; following a reference to *A Descriptive Catalogue*, it is the number of the page in the original edition; following a reference to *A Vision of the Last Judgment*, it is the number of the page of the Rossetti MS; following a reference to marginalia it is the number of the page in the copy annotated by Blake. This variety of reference is confusing, but not easily avoidable. The following abbreviations for Blake's works have been employed:

A.R.O.	*All Religions Are One*
D.C.	*A Descriptive Catalogue*
G.P.	*The Gates of Paradise*
M.	*Milton*
M.H.H.	*The Marriage of Heaven and Hell*
N.N.R.	*There Is No Natural Religion*
V.L.J.	*A Vision of the Last Judgment* (Rossetti MS)

expressed by Berkeley in the phrase *esse est percipi*: "to be is to be perceived":

> Mental Things are alone Real; what is call'd Corporeal, No-body Knows of its Dwelling Place: it is in Fallacy, & its Existence an Imposture. Where is the Existence Out of Mind or Thought? Where is it but in the Mind of a Fool?[2]

The unit of this mental existence Blake calls indifferently a "form" or an "image." If there is such a thing as a key to Blake's thought, it is the fact that these two words mean the same thing to him. He makes no consistent use of the term "idea." Forms or images, then, exist only in perception. Locke's philosophy distinguishes sensation from reflection: the former is concerned with perception, the latter with the classification of sensations and the development of them into abstract ideas. These latter afford inclusive principles or generalizations by which we may build up the vast unselected mass of sense data into some kind of comprehensible pattern. The eighteenth century's respect for generalization comes out in Samuel Johnson, who dwells frequently on the "grandeur of generality," saying that "great thoughts are always general," and that "nothing can please many, and please long, but just representations of general nature."[3] Blake, evidently, thinks differently:

> What is General Nature? is there Such a Thing? what is General Knowledge? is there such a thing? Strictly Speaking All Knowledge is Particular.

> To Generalize is to be an Idiot. To Particularize is the Alone Distinction of Merit. General Knowledges are those Knowledges that Idiots possess.[4]

Blake is discussing Reynolds' theories of painting, but as one of his main points against Reynolds is the Lockian basis of his aesthetics, it is quite safe to use these quotations here. The second remark, though of course itself a generalization, means that the image or form of perception is the content of knowledge. Reflection on sensation is concerned only with the mere memory of the sensation, and Blake always refers to Locke's reflection as "memory." Memory of an image must always be

---

[2] V.L.J. 95: K3, 162.
[3] *Lives of the Poets*: "Cowley" and "Pope."
[4] Marg. to Reynolds, 61: K 3, 25; and xcviii: K3, 13.

less than the perception of the image. Just as it is impossible to do a portrait from memory as well as from life, so it is impossible for an abstract idea to be anything more than a subtracted idea, a vague and hazy afterimage. In fact, it is far less real than an afterimage. Sensation is always in the plural: when we see a tree we see a multitude of particular facts about the tree, and the more intently we look the more there are to see. If we look at it very long and hard, and possess a phenomenal visual memory, we may, having gone away from the tree, remember nearly everything about it. That is far less satisfying to the mind than to keep on seeing the tree, but, though we no longer have a real tree, we have at least a memory of its reality. But the abstract idea of "tree" ranks far below this. We have now sunk to the mental level of the dull-witted Philistine who in the first place saw "just a tree," without noticing whether it was an oak or a poplar.

But even the idea "tree" retains some connection, however remote, with real trees. It is when we start inferring qualities from things and trying to give them an independent existence that the absurdities of abstract reasoning really become obvious. We do this as a kind of mental shorthand to cover up the deficiencies of our memories. Blake says, in a note on Berkeley's *Siris*:

> Harmony and Proportion are Qualities & not Things. The Harmony and Proportion of a Horse are not the same with those of a Bull. Every Thing has its own Harmony & Proportion, Two Inferior Qualities in it. For its Reality is its Imaginative Form.[5]

This implies, for one thing, that "proportion" means nothing except in direct relation to real things which possess it; and for another, that the differences between the proportions of a bull and a horse are infinitely more significant than the mere fact that both of them have proportion. In short, things are real to the extent that they are sharply, clearly, particularly perceived by themselves and discriminated from one another. We have said that the idea "tree" represents a dull and vague perception of the forms of trees; but such a word as "proportion," taken by itself, represents a flight from reality that even a dense fog

[5] Marg. to Berkeley's *Siris*, 213: K3, 355.

or a pitch-black night could be no more than a mere suggestion of. The first point in Blake to get clear, then, is the infinite superiority of the distinct perception of things to the attempt of the memory to classify them into general principles:

> Deduct from a rose its redness, from a lilly its whiteness, from a diamond its hardness, from a spunge its softness, from an oak its heighth, from a daisy its lowness, & rectify everything in Nature as the Philosophers do, & then we shall return to Chaos, & God will be compell'd to be Eccentric if he Creates, O happy Philosopher.[6]

The acceptance of the *esse-est-percipi* principle unites the subject and the object. By introducing the idea of "reflection" we separate them again. The abstract philosophers say that things do not cease to exist when we stop looking at them, and therefore there must be some kind of nonmental reality behind our perception of them. Thus Locke attempts to distinguish the "secondary qualities" of perception from "primary qualities" which he assigns to a "substratum" of substance. A still cruder form of the same theory is atomism, the belief in a nonmental and unperceived unit of the object-world. "An atom," Blake said, is "a thing which does not exist"[7]—as of course it does not, in the sense in which he meant the word. Democritus had ex-pounded this theory in classical times: it had been developed by Epicurean philosophers, and Bacon, who "is only Epicurus over again," and whose "philosophy has ruined England," had been enthusiastic about Democritus.[8] Newton's corpuscular theory of light belongs to the same method of thought.[9] Atom-ism is another attempt to annihilate the perceived differences in forms by the assertion that they have all been constructed out of units of "matter." If we try to visualize a world of tiny particles all alike, we again summon up the image of a dense fog or a sandstorm which is the inevitable symbol of general-ization. How could forms have been developed out of such a chaos? There is no "matter": there is a material world, but that is literally the "material" of experience, and has no reality apart

[6] Marg. to Lavater's *Aphorisms on Man*, 532: K1, 107.

[7] Letter to Cumberland, Apr. 12, 1827: K3, 392.

[8] Marg. to Reynolds, 35: K3, 20.

[9] See the poem beginning "Mock on, Mock on, Voltaire, Rousseau": K2, 214.

from the forms in which it subsists, except as an abstract idea on the same plane as that of "proportion."

If to be is something else than to be perceived, our perceptions do not acquaint us with reality and we consequently cannot trust them. We are then forced back on altering the method of perception in the hope that something more real will turn up. Bacon, whose "first principle is Unbelief,"[10] started a program of conducting experiments for this purpose. Blake is quite ready to admit that "the true method of knowledge is experiment"[11]; but he insists that everything depends on the mental attitude of the experimenter. If you cannot accept what you see as real, the fact that you see it in a microscope or a test tube makes no difference. Anyone who, like Descartes, begins by doubting everything except his own doubts, will never end in certainties, as Bacon promises. Where is the certainty to come from? Blake is never tired of ridiculing Locke's

> Two Horn'd Reasoning, Cloven Fiction,
> In Doubt, which is Self contradiction.[12]

and he asks ironically what would happen if the object took the point of view of the subject:

> He who Doubts from what he sees
> Will ne'er Believe, do what you Please.
> If the Sun & Moon should doubt,
> They'd immediately Go out.[13]

This last remark has a double edge. The attempt to separate the object from the subject gets us no further than a mere hypothesis of the "substratum" or "atom" type. But, if the mountain will not go away from Mohammed, Mohammed can always go away from the mountain. Locke's "reflection" is designed to withdraw the subject from the object, to replace real things with the shadowy memories of them which are called "spectres" in Blake's symbolism. But all that can be produced from this must be spun out of the philosopher's own bowels like a spider's web, a fantastic and egocentric daydream. Hence, while the Epicurean atomist and the solipsist or navel-gazer are

[10] Marg. to Reynolds, 61: K3, 25.
[11] A.R.O., Argument: K1, 131.
[12] G.P. 5: K3, 348.
[13] "Auguries of Innocence": K2, 235.

superficially opposed to one another, the attempt to separate the subject and the object is common to them both, and consequently they differ only in emphasis. We shall meet with extensions of this principle later on.

Berkeley draws a distinction, though his treatment of it is not as thorough as it might be, between the ideas we have of the existence of other things and the "notion" we have of our own existence. We know that we are a reality beyond others' perceptions of us, and that if *esse est percipi*, then *esse est percipere* as well.

Now insofar as a man is perceived by others (or, in fact, by himself), he is a form or image, and his reality consists in the perceived thing which we call a "body." "Body" in Blake means the whole man as an object of perception. We need another word to describe the man as a perceiver, and that word must also describe the whole man. "Soul" is possible, though it has theological overtones suggesting an invisible vapor locked up in the body and released at death. Blake will use this word only with a caution:

> Man has no Body distinct from his Soul; for that call'd Body is a portion of Soul discern'd by the five Senses.[14]

At the time that he wrote the aphorisms referred to above he used the rather cumbersome term "Poetic Genius" for reasons that will presently appear: "the Poetic Genius is the true Man," he says, and "the body or outward form of Man is derived from the Poetic Genius."[15] The commonest word, however, is "mind," and Blake frequently employs it. We use five senses in perception, but if we used fifteen we should still have only a single mind. The eye does not see: the eye is a lens for the mind to look through. Perception, then, is not something we do with our senses; it is a mental act. Yet it is equally true that the legs do not walk, but that the mind walks the legs. There can be therefore no distinction between mental and bodily acts: in fact it is confusing to speak of bodily acts at all if by "body" we mean man as a perceived form. The only objection to calling digestion or sexual intercourse mental activities is a hazy associ-

[14] M.H.H. 4: K1, 182.
[15] A.R.O. 1: K1, 131.

ation between the mind and the brain, which latter is only one organ of the mind, if mind means the acting man. It is perhaps better to use some other word. If man perceived is a form or image, man perceiving is a former or imaginer, so that "imagination" is the regular term used by Blake to denote man as an acting and perceiving being. That is, a man's imagination is his life. "Mental" and "intellectual," however, are exact synonyms of "imaginative" everywhere in Blake's work. "Fancy" also means the imagination: "fantasy," on the other hand, relates to the memory and its "spectres."

To be perceived, therefore, means to be imagined, to be related to an individual's pattern of experience, to become a part of his character. There is no "general nature," therefore nothing is real beyond the imaginative patterns men make of reality, and hence there are exactly as many kinds of reality, as there are men. "Every man's wisdom is peculiar to his own individuality,"[16] and there is no other kind of wisdom: reality is as much in the eye of the beholder as beauty is said to be. Scattered all through Blake's work are epigrams indicating this relativity of existence to perception:

> Every Eye sees differently. As the Eye, Such the Object.
>
> Every thing possible to be believed is an image of truth.
>
> The Sun's Light when he unfolds it
> Depends on the Organ that beholds it.[17]

Blake does not deny the unity of the material world: a farmer and a painter, looking at the same landscape, will undoubtedly see the same landscape:

> . . . All of us on earth are united in thought, for it is impossible to think without images of somewhat on earth.[18]

This fact has its importance in Blake's thought; but the reality of the landscape even so consists in its relation to the imaginative pattern of the farmer's mind, or of the painter's mind. To get at an "inherent" reality in the landscape by isolating the common factors, that is, by eliminating the agricultural qualities from the farmer's perception and the artistic ones from the painter's, is

---

[16] M. 4: K2, 309.
[17] Marg. to Reynolds, 34: K3, 20; M.H.H. 8: K1, 185; G.P.: K3, 338.
[18] Marg. to Lavater (conclusion): K1, 116-17.

not possible, and would not be worth doing if it were. Add more people, and this least common denominator of perception steadily decreases. Add an idiot, and it vanishes.

The abstract reasoner attempts to give independent reality to the qualities of the things he sees, and in the same way he tries to abstract the quality of his perception. It is to him that we owe the association of mind and brain. The intellect to him is a special department concerned with reasoning, and other departments should not meddle with it. Emotion is another department, formerly ascribed to the heart, and still retaining a fossilized association with it. As for the sexual impulse, that is "bodily"; that is, it belongs to a third department called "body" by a euphemism. Thought being largely reflection, it is an "inward" activity: those who specialize in "outward" activity are not thinkers, but the practical people who do things. Scientists should be trained to see the sun as a fact; artists to see it emotionally as beautiful. That is, the artist's imagination is not concerned with seeing things, but with seeing an abstraction called the "beauty" in things; the scientist does not see anything either, but merely the "truth" in it. Thus we get Philistines saying that if we add any enthusiasm about beauty to our perception of things it will blur the clarity with which we see them; while the sentimental assert that the warm-blooded mammalian emotional perception which tenderly suckles its images is superior to the reptilian intellectual who lays cold abstract eggs. This last is a point of view with which Blake's is often confused.

All this pigeonholing of activity is nonsense to Blake. Thought *is* act, he says.[19] An inactive thinker is a dreamer; an unthinking doer is an animal. No one can begin to think straight unless he has a passionate desire to think and an intense joy in thinking. The sex act without the play of intellect and emotion is mere rutting; and virility is as important to the artist as it is to the father. The more a man puts all he has into everything he does the more alive he is. Consequently there is not only infinite variety of imaginations, but differences of degree as well. It is not only true that "every eye sees differently," but that "a fool sees not the same tree that a wise man sees," and that "the clearer the organ the more distinct the object."[20] Hence if existence is

[19] Marg. to Bacon's *Essays*: K2, 172.
[20] M.H.H. 7: K1, 184; D.C. 37: K3, 108.

in perception the tree is *more* real to the wise man than it is to
the fool. Similarly it is more real to the man who throws his
entire imagination behind his perception than to the man who
cautiously tries to prune away different characteristics from
that imagination and isolate one. The more unified the perception, the more real the existence. Blake says:

> "What," it will be Question'd, "When the Sun rises, do you not
> see a round disk of fire somewhat like a Guinea?" O no, no, I
> see an Innumerable company of the Heavenly host crying,
> "Holy, Holy, Holy is the Lord God Almighty."[21]

The Hallelujah-Chorus perception of the sun makes it a far
more real sun than the guinea-sun, because more imagination has
gone into perceiving it. Why, then, should intelligent men
reject its reality? Because they hope that in the guinea-sun they
will find their least common denominator and arrive at a common agreement which will point the way to a reality about the
sun independent of their perception of it. The guinea-sun is a
sensation assimilated to a general, impersonal, abstract idea.
Blake can see it if he wants to, but when he sees the angels, he
is not seeing more "in" the sun but more of it. He does not see
it "emotionally": there is a greater emotional intensity in his
perception, but it is not an emotional perception: such a thing
is impossible, and to the extent that it is possible it would produce only a confused and maudlin blur—which is exactly what
the guinea-sun of "common sense" is. He sees all that he can see
of all that he wants to see; the perceivers of the guinea-sun see
all that they want to see of all that they can see.

In Blake the criterion or standard of reality is the genius; in
Locke it is the mediocrity. If Locke can get a majority vote
on the sun, a consensus of normal minds based on the lower
limit of normality, he can eliminate the idiot who goes below
this and the visionary who rises above it as equally irrelevant.
This leaves him with a communal perception of the sun in which
the individual units are identical, all reassuring one another that
they see the same thing; that their minds are uniform and their
eyes interchangeable. The individual mind thus becomes an
indivisible but invariable unit: that is, it is the subjective equivalent of the "atom." Blake calls the sum of experiences common
to normal minds the "ratio," and whenever the word "reason"

[21] V.L.J. 91-95: K3, 162.

appears in an unfavorable context in Blake, it always means "ratiocination," or reflection on the ratio.

There are two forms of such ratiocination. There is deductive reasoning, or drawing conclusions from a certain number of facts which we already possess, a process in which every new fact upsets the pattern of what has already been established: "Reason, or the ratio of all we have already known, is not the same that it shall be when we know more."[22] Then there is inductive reasoning, which is equally circular because it traces the circumference of the universe as it appears to a mediocre and lazy mind:

> The bounded is loathed by its possessor. The same dull round, even of a universe, would soon become a mill with complicated wheels.[23]

We distinguish between voluntary and involuntary activities, between conscious and unconscious planes of the mind, and it is from this that Blake's idea of degrees of imagination is derived. "My legs feel like a walk" is recognized to be a half-humorous figure of speech; but "my heart beats" is accepted as literal. It is not altogether so: the imagination beats the heart; but still the automatic nature of the heartbeat is not in question. Blake's objection to Locke is that he extends the involuntary action into the higher regions of the imagination and tries to make perceptive activity subconscious. Locke does not think of sight as the mind directing itself through the eye to the object. He thinks of it as an involuntary and haphazard image imprinted on the mind through the eye to the object. In this process the mind remains passive and receives impressions automatically. We see the guinea-sun automatically: seeing the Hallelujah-Chorus sun demands a voluntary and conscious imaginative effort; or rather, it demands an exuberantly active mind which will not be a quiescent blank slate. The imaginative mind, therefore, is the one which has realized its own freedom and understood that perception is self-development. The unimaginative is paralyzed by its own doubt, its desire to cut parts of the mind off from perception and parts of perception out of the mind, and by the dread of going beyond the least common denominator of the "normal." This opposition of the freedom of the acting

[22] N.N.R. II, ii: K1, 130.
[23] N.N.R. II, iv: K1, 131.

mind and the inertia of the response to an external impression will also meet us again.

Such freedom is extravagant only if there is no inner unity to the character of the perceiver. Perceptions form part of a logically unfolding organic unit, and just as an acorn will develop only into an oak, and not just any oak but the particular oak implicit in it, so the human being starts at birth to perceive in a characteristic and consistent way, relating his perception to his unique imaginative pattern. This is what Blake means when he explodes against the denial of innate ideas with which Locke's book opens:

> Reynolds Thinks that Man Learns all that he knows. I say on the Contrary that Man Brings All that he has or can have Into the World with him. Man is Born Like a Garden ready Planted & Sown. This World is too poor to produce one Seed.

> Innate Ideas are in Every Man, Born with him; they are truly Himself. The Man who says that we have No Innate Ideas must be a Fool & Knave, Having No Con-Science or Innate Science.[24]

It perhaps should be pointed out that Locke is denying what from Blake's point of view would be innate generalizations, and Blake does not believe in them any more than Locke does. Blake is protesting against the implication that man is material to be formed by an external world and not the former or imaginer of the material world. We are not passively stimulated into maturity: we grow into it, and our environment does not alter our nature, though it may condition it. Blake is thus insisting on the importance of the distinction between wisdom and knowledge. Wisdom is the central form which gives meaning and position to all the facts which are acquired by knowledge, the digestion and assimilation of whatever in the material world the man comes in contact with.

Sense experience in itself is a chaos, and must be employed either actively by the imagination or passively by the memory. The former is a deliberate and the latter a haphazard method of creating a mental form out of sense experience. The wise man will choose what he wants to do with his perceptions just as he will choose the books he wants to read, and his perceptions will

[24] Marg. to Reynolds, 157: K3, 41; and 58: K3, 24-25.

thus be charged with an intelligible and coherent meaning. Meaning for him, that is, pointing to his own mind and not to, for instance, nature. It thus becomes obvious that the product of the imaginative life is most clearly seen in the work of art, which is a unified mental vision of experience.

For the work of art is produced by the entire imagination. The dull mind is always thinking in terms of general antitheses, and it is instructive to see how foolish these antitheses look when they are applied to art. We cannot say that painting a picture is either an intellectual or an emotional act: it is obviously both at once. We cannot say that it is either a reflective or an active process: it is obviously both at once. We cannot say that it is "mental" or "bodily"; no distinction between brain-work and handwork is relevant to it. We cannot say that the picture is a product of internal choice or external compulsion, for what the painter wants to do is what he has to do. Art is based on sense experience, yet it is an imaginative ordering of sense experience: it therefore belongs neither to the "inside" nor the "outside" of the Lockian universe, but to both at once.

The artist is bound to find the formless and unselected linear series of sense data very different from what he wishes to form, and the difficulties inherent in this never disappear for him. The composition of music is an imaginative ordering of the sense experience of sound, yet so different from random sense experience of sounds that the latter for most composers is a nuisance to their composing and must be shut out of their ears. The painter is even worse off, for though Beethoven's deafness did not destroy the hearing of his imagination, the painter cannot shut his eyes. For Blake the acquiring of the power to visualize independently of sense experience was a painful and laborious effort, to be achieved only by relentless discipline. But at the same time the senses are the basis of all art. No painter ever painted an abstract idea; he paints only what he can visualize, and art owes its vividness and directness of impact, as compared with reasoning, to the fact that the concrete is more real than the general.

It is, then, through art that we understand why perception is superior to abstraction, why perception is meaningless without an imaginative ordering of it, why the validity of such ordering depends on the normality of the perceiving mind, why that normality must be associated with genius rather than mediocrity, and why genius must be associated with the creative power of the artist. This last, which is what Blake means by "vision," is the goal of all freedom, energy, and wisdom.

But surely it is absurd to connect this with the *esse-est-percipi* doctrine. To be is to be perceived; therefore the object is real in proportion as the perceiver is a genius; therefore a tree is more real to a painter than to anyone else. This sounds dubious enough, and more so when we raise the question: what is the reality of a painted tree? If it is painted from life, it is an imitation of life, and must therefore be less real; if it is visualized independently of sense experience, does it not come out of the memory just as abstract ideas do? And if the whole work of art in which it occurs is an imaginative ordering of experience, then similarly the work of art is an imitation or a memory of experience. According to Plato the bed of sense experience, itself an imitation of the form or idea of the bed, is imitated by the painter. And while it is not surprising that Blake should be fond of pointing out that the Muses Plato worshiped were daughters of memory rather than imagination, there is still Plato's argument to meet.

Now it is true that we derive from sense experience the power to visualize, just as Beethoven derived from his hearing the power to "visualize" sounds after he had lost it. It may even be true that we do not visualize independently of sense without the help of memory. But what we see appearing before us on canvas is not a reproduction of memory or sense experience but a new and independent creation. The "visionary" is the man who has passed through sight into vision, never the man who has avoided seeing, who has not trained himself to see clearly, or who generalizes among his stock of visual memories. If there is a reality beyond our perception we must increase the power and coherence of our perception, for we shall never reach reality in any other way. If the reality turns out to be infinite, perception must be infinite too. To visualize, therefore, is to realize. The artist is *par excellence* the man who struggles to develop his perception into creation, his sight into vision; and art is a technique of realizing, through an ordering of sense experience by the mind, a higher reality than linear unselected experience or a second-hand evocation of it can give.

It is no use saying to Blake that the company of angels he sees surrounding the sun are not "there." Not where? Not in a gaseous blast furnace across ninety million miles of nothing, perhaps; but the guinea-sun is not "there" either. To prove that he sees them Blake will not point to the sky but to, say, the fourteenth plate of the Job series illustrating the text: "When the morning stars sang together, and all the sons of God shouted for joy." *That* is where the angels appear, in a world formed and created by Blake's imagination and entered into by everyone who looks at the picture. It appears, then, that there are not only two worlds, but three: the world of vision, the world of sight and the world of memory: the world we create, the world we live in and the world we run away to. The world of memory is an unreal world of reflection and abstract ideas; the world of sight is a potentially real world of subjects and objects; the world of vision is a world of creators and creatures. In the world of memory we see nothing; in the world of sight we see what we have to see; in the world of vision we see what we want to see. These are not three different worlds, as in the religions which speak of a heaven and hell in addition to ordinary life; they are the egocentric, the ordinary and the visionary ways of looking at the same world.

The fact that in the world of vision or art we see what we want to see implies that it is a world of fulfilled desire and unbounded freedom. The rejection of art from Plato's *Republic* is an essential part of a vision of the human soul which puts desire in bondage to reason, a vision of a universe turning on a spindle of necessity, and an assumption that a form is an idea rather than an image. Works of art are more concentrated and unified than sense experience, and that proves that there is nothing chaotic about the unlimited use of the imagination. Hence an antithesis of energy and order, desire and reason, is as fallacious as all the other antitheses with which timid mediocrity attempts to split the world. Imagination is energy incorporated in form:

> Energy is the only life, and is from the Body; and Reason is the bound or outward circumference of Energy.[25]

Blake's poem *Visions of the Daughters of Albion* ends in an apotheosis of desire; *Jerusalem* in one of intellect. Those who have succeeded in mentally separating the inside from the out-

[25] M.H.H. 4: K1, 182.

side, the top from the bottom, the convex from the concave, will call these poems hopelessly inconsistent with each other. But a thinker who has no desire to think cannot think, and thus all thought, like all sexual intercourse, is a fulfillment of desire. And one who desires but cannot imagine what it is he wants is not getting very far with his desire, which, if it were real, would attempt to achieve an intelligible form.

Nearly all of us have felt, at least in childhood, that if we imagine that a thing is so, it therefore either is so or can be made to become so. All of us have to learn that this almost never happens, or happens only in very limited ways; but the visionary, like the child, continues to believe that it always ought to happen. We are so possessed with the idea of the duty of acceptance that we are inclined to forget our mental birthright, and prudent and sensible people encourage us in this. That is why Blake is so full of aphorisms like "If the fool would persist in his folly he would become wise."[26] Such wisdom is based on the fact that imagination creates reality, and as desire is a part of imagination, the world we desire is more real than the world we passively accept.

Now of course the arts are only a few of many social phenomena which are summed up in such words as "culture" or "civilization." These words in fact give a much clearer idea of what Blake means by "art." The religious, philosophical, and scientific presentations of reality are branches of art, and should be judged by their relationship to the principles and methods of the creative imagination of the artist. If they are consistent with the latter, they fulfill a necessary function in culture: if they are not, they are pernicious mental diseases.

We have said that the artist uses ideas, but *qua* artist is not otherwise concerned with their truth. This exactly corresponds to the doctrine that reality is in the individual mental pattern. As compared with religion, for instance, art keeps the pragmatic individual synthesis, whereas religion as generally understood is both dogmatic and communal. The religious synthesis, therefore, in trying to fulfill the needs of a group, freezes the symbols both of its theology and ritual into invariable generalities. Religion is thus a social form of art, and as such both its origin in

[26] M.H.H. 7: K1, 184.

art and the fact that its principles of interpretation are those of art should be kept in mind:

> The Religions of all Nations are derived from each Nation's different reception of the Poetic Genius, which is every where call'd the Spirit of Prophecy.[27]

"All Religions are One" means that the material world provides a universal language of images and that each man's imagination speaks that language with his own accent. Religions are grammars of this language. Seeing is believing, and belief is vision: the *substance* of things hoped for, the *evidence* of things not seen.

A metaphysical system, again, is a system; that is, an art-form, to be judged in terms of its inner coherence. "Every thing possible to be believ'd is an image of truth," which means a form of truth, and if Plato's or Locke's philosophy makes sense in itself, it is as truly a form or image of reality as a picture, and an image of the same kind. To try to verify a philosophical or religious system in relation to an objective nonmental "truth" is to dissolve an imaginative form back into the chaos of the material world, and this kind of verification will destroy whatever truth it has. Even in science there is no use looking beyond the human mind for reassurance. As a matter of fact in stressing the concrete and the primacy of sense experience Blake is much closer to the inductive scientist than to the "reasoner," and his unfavorable comments on science always relate to certain metaphysical assumptions underlying the science of his day laid down by Bacon and Locke. As long as science means knowledge organized by a commonplace mind it will be part of the penalty man pays for being stupid; the value of science depends on the mental attitude toward it, and the mental attitude of Bacon and Locke is wrong. As for history, that, even when it has overcome the difficulty of having to deal with documents which are invariably a pack of lies, is a linear record of facts like our daily sense experience, and has like it to be ordered by the imagination. "Reasons and opinions concerning acts are not history," says Blake: "Acts themselves alone are history"[28]—history is

---

[27] A.R.O. 5: K1, 132.

[28] D.C. 44: K3, 111. For his view of the trustworthiness of records in history cf. Marg. to Watson, 15-16: K2, 165.

imaginative material to be synthesized into form, not memory to be reflected upon.

Blake is not simply rationalizing his own job to the limit: his defense of the supremacy of art is a well-established one in literary criticism, and he has no wish to curtail the variety of culture. He does not say that science is wrong; he says that a commonplace mind can make a wrong use of it. He does not say that philosophy is quibbling; he says it would be if philosophers had no imagination. And still less has his teaching to do with that of most of those who tell us that we should make our lives a work of art and live beautifully. The cultivators of "stained-glass attitudes" do not usually mean by beauty the explosion of energy that produces the visions of the dung-eating madman Ezekiel.

Whatever may be thought of Blake's doctrine of the imagination, one thing should be at least abundantly clear by now. Any portrayal of Blake as a mystical snail who retreated from the hard world of reality into the refuge of his own mind, and evolved his obscurely beautiful visions there in contemplative loneliness, can hardly be very close to Blake. That identifies his "imagination" with his interpretation of Locke's "reflection," which is unnecessarily ironic. It is true that we often confuse the imaginary with the imaginative in ordinary speech, and often mean, when we say that something is "all imagination," that it does not exist; but such modes of speech and thought, however intelligible in themselves, cannot be used in interpreting Blake.

Though Blake is an interesting eighteenth-century phenomenon even in philosophy, Locke's reputation can perhaps be left to take care of itself. To meet the difficulties in his theory of imagination we must in any case proceed to his religious ideas, and leave the epistemology of Locke and Berkeley for the more rarefied atmosphere of Swedenborg.

VII

M. H. Abrams

Mechanical and Organic Psychologies of Literary Invention

In the word *Reason* may be seen one of that numerous set of names of *fictitious entities*, in the fabrication of which the labours of the Rhetorician and the Poet have been conjoined. In *Reason* they have joined in giving us a sort of *goddess:* a goddess, in whom another goddess, *Passion*, finds a constant antagonist. . . It is not by any such mythology, that any clear and correct instruction can be conveyed.

JEREMY BENTHAM

What thou are we know not;
What is most like thee?

SHELLEY, *To a Skylark*

What we now call the psychology of art had its origin when theorists in general began to think of the mind of the artist as interposed between the world of sense and the work of art, and to attribute the conspicuous differences between art and reality, not to the reflection of an external ideal, but to forces and operations within the mind itself. This development was, in large part, the contribution of the critics (and especially the English critics) of the seventeenth and eighteenth centuries, who expanded the passing allusions to the mental faculties in ancient and Renaissance theorists into an extensive psychology of both the production and appreciation of art. In this aspect, English criticism, of course, participated in the tendency of English

Except for the notes, which have been omitted here, this essay is Chapter VII, "The Psychology of Literary Invention: Mechanical and Organic Theories," in *The Mirror and the Lamp: Romantic Theory and the Critical Tradition* by M. H. Abrams (New York City, N. Y.), pp. 156-83. Copyright 1953 by Oxford University Press. Reprinted by permission of the author and the publisher. The title has been adapted by the editor.

empirical philosophy, which characteristically tried to establish the nature and limits of knowledge by an analysis of the elements and processes of the mind. Early in the seventeenth century, Francis Bacon included poetry in his great register of human knowledge as a part of learning which is to be explained by reference to the action of imagination. In the middle of the century, Thomas Hobbes, answering Davenant's Preface to *Gondibert*, introduced, on the basis of his earlier philosophical speculation, a brief and popularized account of the place of sense-experience, memory, fancy, and judgment in the production of poetry. The speed with which suggestions such as these were caught up and expanded was extraordinary. One hundred years later few philosophers omitted the discussion of literature and the other arts in their general investigations of the mind, while almost all systematic critics (in conformity with Hume's suggestion, in the introduction to his *Treatise*, that the science of human nature is propaedeutic to the science of criticism, as well as of logic, morals, and politics) incorporated into their aesthetic theory a general treatment of the laws and operations of the mind. By 1774, Alexander Gerard had published his *Essay on Genius*, which remained for a century the most comprehensive and detailed study devoted specifically to the psychology of the inventive process.

It should be remarked that there was less absolute novelty in this contribution to criticism than appears at first. Much of the procedure was, very simply, to translate the existing commonplaces of traditional rhetoric and poetic into the novel philosophical vocabulary of mental elements, faculties, and events. A glance at Alexander Gerard's footnotes, for example, will show that he relies on all the standard critics from Aristotle to Bishop Hurd, and that although he professes to found his theory entirely on experiment and induction, he usually establishes or bolsters his generalizations by citing the authority of experts, among whom Cicero and Quintilian bulk even larger than Locke and Hume. Furthermore, the psychological idiom is very often used normatively rather than descriptively, and serves the critic largely as a device for setting up standards of literary performance and evaluation. In such normative discussions, mental terms, such as fancy and judgment, are mainly surrogates for more or less precisely defined sets of opposing qualities in the objective work of art. As one instance, when Rymer wrote concerning "Oriental" poets: "*Fancy* with them is predominant, is wild, vast, and unbridled, o'er which their *judgment* has little command or authority: hence their conceptions are monstrous, and have nothing of exactness, nothing of resemblance or proportion"—he named the faculties not in order to describe the workings of the mind, but in order, summarily, to derogate what in art is wild and unconfined, and to laud the contrary qualities of exactness and decorum. Some seventy-five years later, Joseph Wharton, writing about the "imagination" exhibited in Shakespeare's *Tempest,* correlates this psychological term with approximately the same aesthetic qualities of wildness and irregularity: his preferences, however, have changed. Shakespeare, he says, "has there given the reins to his boundless imagination, and has carried the romantic, the wonderful, and the wild, to the most pleasing extravagance." The antithesis and changing balance between imagination, or fancy, and judgment was one of the chief frames of discussion within which eighteenth-century critics of art fought out their version of the enduring battle between convention and revolt.

Our sole concern in this chapter, however, will be with descriptive psychology—what some theorists liked to call "the science of the mind"—and specifically, with the attempt to describe what goes on in the mind in the process of composing a poem. If we penetrate through differences of terminology and detail, we are struck immediately with the extent to which eighteenth-century writers agreed in their basic conception of the psychology of invention. Against this uniform tradition of previous psychology in England, Coleridge was the center of revolt. Scholars have recently emphasized that Coleridge himself was indebted to English precedent for some of his leading ideas, but it is misleading to stress the continuity of Coleridge's mature psychology of art with that which was current in eighteenth-century England. In all essential aspects, Coleridge's theory of mind, like that of contemporary German philosophers, was, as he insisted, revolutionary; it was, in fact, part of a change in the habitual way of thinking, in all areas of intellectual enterprise, which is as sharp and dramatic as any the history of ideas can show.

I have spoken before of the role of analogy in shaping the structure of a critical theory. Nowhere is this role more conspicuous than in discussions of the psychology of art. The only direct evidence in regard to the nature of the mental processes are those shadowy and fugitive items available to introspection, and these are "modes of inmost being," as Coleridge said, to which we "know that the attributes of time and space are inapplicable and alien, but which yet can not be conveyed save in symbols of time and space." Expressed in the terms of our day: mental events must be talked about metaphorically, in an object-language which was developed to deal literally with the physical world. As a result, our conception of these events is peculiarly amenable to the formative influence of the physical metaphors in which we discuss them, and of the underlying physical analogies from which these metaphors are derived. The basic nature of the shift from psychological criticism in the tradition of Hobbes and Hume to that of Coleridge can, I think, be clarified if we treat it as the result of an analogical substitution—the replacement, that is to say, of a mechanical process by a living plant as the implicit paradigm governing the description of the process and the product of literary invention. I shall begin by sketching the main outlines of the theory that was dominant prior to Coleridge, against which his own writings after the year 1800 were a continuous protest.

THE MECHANICAL THEORY OF LITERARY INVENTION

It was of great moment to literary criticism that modern psychology was largely developed in the seventeenth century, during the smashing triumphs of the natural philosophers in the field of mechanics. For it is clear that the course of English empirical philosophy was guided by the attempt, more or less deliberate, to import into the psychical realm the explanatory scheme of physical science, and so to extend the victories of mechanics from matter to mind. In the next century David Hume subtitled his *Treatise* "An attempt to introduce the experimental method of reasoning into moral subjects," and set himself to emulate Newton by eschewing hypotheses and ascending "from careful and exact experiments" to the simplest and most universal causes, in order to found a science of human nature, "which will not be inferior in certainty, and will be much superior in utility to any other of human comprehension." David Hartley explained that he had taken the doctrine of vibrations from Newton, and the doctrine of association from Locke and his followers, and professed to model his own research on "the method of analysis and synthesis recommended and followed by Sir Isaac Newton." Philosophers whose concern was with the operations of the literary mind also laid claim to the methods and certainty of natural science. Lord Kames believed that he had established his "elements of criticism" by examining "the sensitive branch of human nature" and ascending "gradually to principles, from facts and experiments"; and Alexander Gerard declared that his aim was to extend "the science of human nature" into the *terra incognita* of genius, and (despite the admitted difficulties of conducting experiments on the mind) "to collect such a number of facts concerning any of the mental powers, as will be sufficient for deducing conclusions concerning them, by a just and regular induction." To some optimists of the later part of the century, it seemed that their rules for composing and judging a poem had a sanction in a science of mind which was no less secure and determinative than the science of nature. James Beattie wrote in 1776:

> It would be no less absurd, for a poet to violate the *essential* rules of his art, and justify himself by an appeal from the tribunal of Aristotle, than for a mechanic to construct an engine on principles inconsistent with the laws of motion, and excuse himself by disclaiming the authority of Sir Isaac Newton.

Here, in summary, are the aspects of the eighteenth-century theory of literary invention, common to most writers in the empirical tradition, which reflect the nature of their mechanical archetype:

(1) *The elementary particles of mind.* The empirical psychology is unreservedly elementaristic in its method: it takes as its starting point, its basic datum, the element or part. All the manifold contents and goings-on of the mind are assumed to be analyzable into a very limited number of simple components, and the procedure of the theorist is to explain complex psychological states or products as various combinations of these atoms of mind. The sole elements, or "ideas," entering into the products of invention are assumed to be wholes or parts, literally, of *images*—exact, although fainter replicas of the original perceptions of sense.

The assumption that ideas are images is implied by Hobbes's characterization of the contents of mental discourse as "decaying sense." In Hume's locked internal world, the only differentia between sense impressions and ideas is the greater "force and vivacity" of the former. "The one," he says, "seems to be in a manner the reflection of the other..." Hume's implicit metaphor of an idea as a mirror-image of sensation, so pervasive in eighteenth-century discussions of the mind, becomes explicit in Gerard's description of the ideas in memory: "Like a mirrour, it reflects faithful images of the objects formerly perceived by us. ... It is in its nature a mere copier...."

To the philosophical school of Locke, the ultimate, unanalyzable particles of mental content were, of course, the replicas of the simple qualities of sense—blue, hot, hard, sweet, odor-of-roses—plus the replicas of the feelings of pleasure and pain. But when they talked of the making of poetry, both philosophers and literary theorists tended to take as the unit of the process that bundle of simple qualities constituting either the whole, or a splintered fragment, of a particular object of sense. Furthermore, in most discussions of poetic invention, these mental units were assumed to be primarily, if not exclusively, visual images, replicas of the objects of sight. Coleridge remarked acutely that the "mechanical philosophy" insists on a world of mutually impenetrable objects because it suffers from a "despotism of the eye"; and in literary theories this despotism was strengthened by the long rhetorical tradition that a speaker is most emotionally effective when he visualizes and evokes the scene he describes. As Addison said flatly, in *Spectator* 416, "We cannot indeed have a single Image in the Fancy that did not make its first Entrance through the Sight..." Later, Lord Kames held that because the ideas of all the other senses are "too obscure for that operation," the imagination, in "fabricating images of things that have no existence," is limited to dividing and recombining the "ideas of sight."

(2) *The motions and combinations of the parts.* Images move in sequence across the mind's eye. If these recur in the same spatial and temporal order as in the original sense-experience, we have "memory." But if the integral images of the objects of sense recur in a different order, or else if segmented parts of such images are combined into a whole never present to sense, we have "fancy," or "imagination"—terms almost always used synonymously to apply to all non-mnemonic processions of ideas, including those that go into the making of a poem.

To typify the action of imagination, theorists often adduced the ancient example of mythological grotesques which obviously lack a precedent in sense. In 1677 Dryden quoted Lucretius (who had early attempted to extend material atomism to the activities of the soul) in order to establish the possibility of imagining hippocentaurs, chimeras, and other "things quite out of nature" by "the conjunction of two natures, which have a real separate being." Similar instances of mental collocations had been cited by Hobbes, and were picked up by Hume, and they became a standard component in critical discussions of poetic invention. Gerard, for example, points out that even when the poet's imagination "creates" new wholes "such as are properly its own," the "parts and members of its ideas have been conveyed separately by the senses. . . ."

> When Homer formed the idea of *Chimera*, he only joined into one animal, parts which belonged to different animals; the head of a lion, the body of a goat, and the tail of a serpent.

The concept that the inventive process, in its boldest flights, consists in the severance of sensible wholes into parts and the aggregation of parts into new wholes, united even antagonistic schools of eighteenth-century philosophy. The Scottish philosopher, Dugald Stewart, followed the initiative of Thomas Reid in objecting to the tendency, from Locke through Hume, to disintegrate all of mental content into mere sequences of sensations and ideas, and in stressing instead the concept of mental faculties and "powers." He also anticipated (and perhaps influenced) Coleridge in distinguishing between the imagination and the fancy—the fancy, according to Stewart, constituting a lower faculty that proffers sensible materials upon which the imagination operates by its complex powers of "apprehension," "abstraction," and "taste." Yet Stewart's analysis of the poetic imagination follows the eighteenth-century pattern: its creative power consists only in the fact that it is able "to make a selection of qualities and of circumstances, from a variety of different objects, and by combining and disposing these to form a new creation of its own."

We must not project into Stewart's word, "creation," or into "original" and "plastic," which also became attached to the "imagination" in the second half of the century, a significance opposed to psychological atomism. All of these terms, as we shall see, carried important consequences for criticism, and "plastic" is especially interesting because it was adopted from cosmogonists who, in express opposition to a purely atomistic and mechanical philosophy, had employed the word to signify a vital principle, inherent in nature, which organizes chaos into cosmos by a self-evolving formative energy. As a term in the psychology of literature, therefore, "plastic" from the first carried the latent implications of Coleridge's creative "esemplastic" imagination. But in eighteenth-century usage, when the details get filled in, we recognize the standard imaginative process, consisting of the division and recombination of discretes to form a whole which may be novel in its order, but never in its parts. The word "create," as John Ogilvie warned, must not be interpreted "as relating to discoveries purely *original*, of which the senses receive no patterns." The ideas of sense and of reflection—

> these are indeed by what we term a plastic imagination associated, compounded, and diversified at pleasure. . . But in the whole of this process, the originality obviously results from the manner in which objects are selected and put together, so as to form upon the whole an unusual combination.

(3) *The laws of associative attraction*. As the principle governing the sequence and conjunction of ideas, and rendering the imagination "in some measure, uniform with itself in all times and places," Hume—building upon suggestions in Aristotle and in his English predecessors—posited the concept of the association of ideas. "The qualities, from which this association arises, and by which the mind is after this manner convey'd from one idea to another, are three, *viz.* Resemblance, Contiguity in time or place, and Cause and Effect." Ten years later, in 1749, David Hartley published a version of associative theory, developed independently of Hume, in which he set out to demonstrate rigorously that all the complex contents and processes of mind are derived from the elements of simple sensation, combined by the single link of contiguity in original experience. And very quickly the general concept of association, although with diverse predications of the number and kinds of associative connections, became incorporated into standard theories of the literary imagination.

There is a conspicuous parallelism between this basic pattern of mental activity and the elementary concepts of matter,

motion, and force composing Newton's science of mechanics—
although shorn, naturally, of the quantitative aspects of Newton's formulation. (1) The unit ideas of mind correspond to
Newton's particles of matter. Ideas, Hume pointed out, "may be
compar'd to the extension and solidity of matter," for, unlike
impressions, they "are endow'd with a kind of impenetrability,
by which they exclude each other, and are capable of forming
a compound by their conjunction, not by their mixture." (2)
The motion of ideas in sequence or "trains" is the mental equivalent of the motion of matter in physical space. (3) The "uniting
principle" or "gentle force" (as Hume characterized association) adds the concept of a force affecting that motion; while
the uniform operations of this force in "the laws of association"
are analogous to Newton's uniform laws of motion and gravitation.

So, at least, it seemed to some of the more systematic theorists
concerning the science of the mind. Hume himself drew the
parallel between the principles of association (even though he
regarded these as a statistical tendency rather than an "inseparable connection") and the law of gravitation.

> These are therefore the principles of union or cohesion among
> our simple ideas. . . Here is a kind of ATTRACTION, which in the
> mental world will be found to have as extraordinary effects as
> in the natural, and to shew itself in as many and as various forms.

In Hartley's system of psycho-physiological parallelism, the
association of ideas frankly becomes the introspective correlate
to the operation of the mechanical laws of motion in the
nervous system. And for a thoroughgoing materialistic monist
such as Holbach, of course, mind disappears entirely, and its
processes are reduced to the "action and re-action of the minute
and insensible molecules or particles of matter" in that particular
area of the universal machine which constitutes a human brain.

(4) *The problem of judgment and artistic design.* It is the
need for giving a satisfactory account of the order and design
in the completed work of art which perplexes, if it does not
confound, the attempt at a pure mechanism of mind. The problem was aggravated for the eighteenth-century phychologist of
invention because, as I have said, his procedure was mainly to
translate the existing theory of poetry into mental terms, and
this theory incorporated two elements entirely alien to elemen-

tarism and the mechanical categories of mind. One of these elements was the central Aristotelian concept of "form," and of an artistic "unity" in which the transposition, removal, or addition of any part will dislocate the whole. The other was the rhetorical and Horatian concept of art as, basically, a purposeful procedure, in which the end is foreseen from the beginning, part is fitted to part, and the whole is adapted to the anticipated effect upon the reader. But as Alexander Gerard, for one, pointed out, according to the principles of associationism any one idea "bears some relation to an infinite number of other ideas," so that the ideas collected merely according to this relation will "form a confused chaos," and "can no more be combined into one regular work, than a number of wheels taken from different watches, can be united into one machine." Otherwise stated: if the process of imagination is conceived as images moved by purely mechanical, or efficient causes of attraction— each present image pulling in the next automatically, according to the accident of its inherent similarity or of its contiguity in past experience—how are we to explain that the result is a cosmos instead of a chaos? And how are we to account for the difference between the incoherent associations of delirium and the orderly, productive associations of a Shakespeare?

The equivalent problem of explaining design in the physical universe had been the stumbling block of a mechanical philosophy ever since the atoms of Democritus. "How," Cicero had asked, can the Epicureans "assert the world to have been made from minute particles . . . coming together by chance or accident? But if a concourse of atoms can make a world, why not a porch, a temple, a house, a city, which are works of less labor and difficulty?" In the seventeenth century, the strong revival of atomism in the physical sciences made for a counteremphasis —hardly less pronounced among the atomists than among their opponents—on the need for a supplementary principle to account for the manifest order of the physical universe. Despite his reluctance to frame hypotheses, Newton himself, following the example of Boyle and other scientific predecessors, solved the problem of the genesis of law, order, and beauty in the world-machine by drawing, as it were, a *deus ex machina*. "This most beautiful system of the sun, planets, and comets," he said, "could only proceed from the counsel and dominion of an intelligent and powerful Being"—that is, from the execution of a design by a purposeful God. And of course, this theological argument from design in physical nature became one of the most familiar of philosophical concepts in both eighteenth-century prose and poetry.

In this respect, as in others, mechanical psychology repeated the pattern of mechanical cosmology. In his felicitous verses on the poems of Sir Robert Howard (1660), Dryden—who had studied Hobbes, and whose own imagination was enthralled by the Lucretian account of chaos falling into order by the chance concourse of atoms—considered, only to reject, the claim of mental atomism to have dispensed with the mental equivalent of Providence in explaining the creation of a poem:

> No atoms, casually together hurl'd,
> Could e'er produce so beautiful a world.
> Nor dare I such a doctrine here admit,
> As would destroy the providence of wit.

David Hume subjected the theological argument from design to a wonderfully acute critique in his *Dialogues concerning Natural Religion.* Yet in his *Enquiry,* after expounding the role of the association of ideas, he found it necessary to postulate the existence of a controlling design in the mind of the productive artist.

> In all compositions of genius, therefore 'tis requisite that the writer have some plan or object . . . some aim or intention in his first setting out, if not in the composition of the whole work. A production without a design would resemble more the raving of a madman, than the sober efforts of genius and learning.
> [Events or actions in narratives] must be related to each other in the imagination, and form a kind of *Unity,* which may bring them under one plan or view, and which may be the object or end of the writer in his first undertaking.

Alexander Gerard attempted to integrate his concept of a "main design" with the mechanical operation of imagination, by postulating that the presence of the supervisory design doubles the strength of certain associative links, and so enables relevant ideas to overrule their irrelevant rivals. Most theorists of mind, however, followed the model of physico-theological speculation in a very simple and direct way: they merely brought the intelligent Artisan of the world-machine indoors and converted him into a mental agent or faculty (called interchangeably "judgment," "reason," or "understanding") which supervises and reviews the mechanical process of association.

Even Gerard felt constrained to supplement, in this way, his concept of the "main design" as an automatic control over imaginative association.

> Every work of genius is a whole, made up of the regular combination of different parts, so organized as to become altogether subservient to a common end. . . But however perfectly the associating principles perform this part of their office, a person will scarce reckon himself certain of the propriety of that disposition, till it has been authorized by judgment. Fancy forms the plan in a sort of mechanical or instinctive manner: judgment, on reviewing it, perceives its rectitude or its errors, as it were scientifically; its decisions are founded on reflection, and produce a conviction of their justness.

The passage is perfectly representative; and except for a few stubborn mechanists like Hartley and Holbach, the eighteenth-century psychologist developed his scheme of the mind by combining two analogies. One was the analogy of a mechanism, in which the images of sense follow one another according to the laws of mental gravitation. The other was the analogy of an intelligent artisan, or architect, who makes his selection from the materials so proffered, and then puts them together according to his pre-existent blueprint or plan.

This concept of a teleological designer, superimposed on a mechanical scheme of mind, was achieved at considerable cost to the hoped-for "science of the mind." In Newton's world-system a final cause had been adduced only to explain the genesis of the universe, with God's omnipresent thereafter—except for his rare intervention in the way of a miracle, or to correct the irregularities of certain celestial bodies—serving mainly to guarantee the continuity of the mechanical laws of cause and effect. In the system of mind, however, final causes were permitted to interfere with the uniform operation of the laws of association in each several instance of purposive thinking. Furthermore, the very concept of a prior design (conceived to be a kind of master-image in the mind) posed a tacit challenge to the primary empirical assumption that there is no mental content which has not entered through the senses. Obviously, this design could not be an innate Idea. Neither could it be derived from direct perception, either of the works of nature or the works of earlier poets, for this is to set up a regress in which at some point original invention has to be introduced; and original invention, after all, is the very phenomenon we have set out to explain.

The endeavors of associationists to cope with these difficulties in the concept of aesthetic design is a most interesting aspect of their writings. Gerard, for example, following his normal routine of converting the topics of rhetoric into mental terms, comes, in due course, to the subject of "disposition," which (citing Cicero and Quintilian) he describes as the ordered arrangement of invented materials into "the economy of the whole." Here he discovers that the distinction between prior design and later fulfillment, and the underlying parallel between the internal process of genius and the deliberate and successive operations of an artisan, do not square with the facts of observation.

> The operations of genius in forming its designs, are of a more perfect kind than the operations of art or industry in executing them. . . . An architect contrives a whole palace in an instant; but when he comes to build it, he must first provide materials, and then rear the different parts of the edifice only in succession. But to collect the materials and to order and apply them, are not to genius distinct and successive works.

In the first stage of invention, "the notion of the whole is generally but imperfect and confused," and only emerges as the process goes on. Hence "this faculty bears a greater resemblance to *nature* in its operations, than to the less perfect energies of *art*." And to illustrate the special properties of the workings of "nature," Gerard hits upon an analogue pregnant with implications for literary psychology—the analogue of vegetable growth.

> When a vegetable draws in moisture from the earth, nature, by the same action by which it draws it in, and at the same time, converts it to the nourishment of the plant: it at once circulates through its vessels, and is assimilated to its several parts. In like manner, genius arranges its ideas by the same operation, and almost at the same time, that it collects them.

That is, when substituted for mechanism and artisanship as the paradigm for the inventive process, a plant yields the concept of an inherent potential design, unfolding spontaneously from within, and assimilating to its own nature the materials needed for its nourishment and growth. As we shall see, German theorists, under the spur of similar problems, were already beginning to explore the possibilities of the plant as the archetype of imagination, but this suggestion fell on stony ground in the England of 1774. Gerard himself, pursuing the analysis of literary design, at once reverts to the standard combination of mechanical association and supervisory architect. "Thus imagination," he says, "is no unskilful architect," for "it in a great measure, by its own force, by means of its associating power, after repeated attempts and transpositions, designs a regular and well-proportioned edifice."

COLERIDGE'S MECHANICAL FANCY AND ORGANIC IMAGINATION

Not until four decades after Gerard's *Essay on Genius* do we find in England a full development of the organism as aesthetic model. In order to sharpen the contrast between the categories of mechanical and organic psychology, I shall postpone, until the next chapter, discussion of the general history of organic theory, and go directly to its deliberate and elaborate application in Coleridge's description of the process and products of literary invention.

At the heart of Coleridge's theory is his laconic differentiation between fancy and imagination, in the thirteenth chapter of the *Biographia Literaria* (1817). As opposed to imagination, fancy

> has no other counters to play with, but fixities and definites. The Fancy is indeed no other than a mode of Memory emancipated from the order of time and space; while it is blended with, and modified by that empirical faculty of the will, which we express by the word CHOICE. But equally with the ordinary memory the Fancy must receive all its materials ready made from the law of association.

In his lengthy prolegomenon to this passage, in which he reviews and criticizes the history of mental mechanism through its culmination in Hartley, Coleridge expressly tells us that he intends his faculties of memory and fancy to incorporate everything that is valid in the associative theory of the eighteenth century, "and, in conclusion, to appropriate the remaining offices of the mind to the reason, and the imagination." And in fact, Coleridge's description of fancy skillfully singles out the basic categories of the associative theory of invention: the elementary particles, or "fixities and definites," derived from sense, distinguished from the units of memory only because they move in a new temporal and spatial sequence determined by the law of association, and subject to choice by a selective faculty —the "judgment" of eighteenth-century critics. Formerly, this had been the total account of poetic invention. But after everything which can be, has been so explained, Coleridge finds a residue which he attributes to the "secondary imagination." This faculty

> dissolves, diffuses, dissipates, in order to recreate; or where this process is rendered impossible, yet still at all events it struggles to idealize and to unify. It is essentially *vital*, even as all objects (*as* objects) are essentially fixed and dead.

The historical importance of Coleridge's imagination has not been overrated. It was the first important channel for the flow of organicism into the hitherto clear, if perhaps not very deep, stream of English aesthetics. (Organicism may be defined as the philosophy whose major categories are derived metaphorically from the attributes of living and growing things.) Consider first the antithetic metaphors by which Coleridge, in various passages, discriminates his two productive faculties. The memory is "mechanical" and the fancy "passive"; fancy is a "mirror-ment . . . repeating simply, or by transposition," and "the aggregative and associative power," acting only "by a sort of juxtaposition." The imagination, on the contrary, "recreates" its elements by a process to which Coleridge sometimes applies terms borrowed from those physical and chemical unions most remote, in their intimacy, from the conjunction of impenetrable discretes in what he called the "brick and mortar" thinking of the mechanical philosophy. Thus, imagination is a "synthetic," a "permeative," and a "blending, fusing power." At other times, Coleridge describes the imagination as an "assimilative power," and the "coadunating faculty"; these adjectives are imported from contemporary biology, where "assimilate" connoted the process by which an organism converts food into its own substance, and "coadunate" signified "to grow together into one." Often, Coleridge's discussions of imagination are explicitly in terms of a living, growing thing. The imagination is, for example, "essentially *vital*," it "generates and produces a form of its own," and its rules are "the very powers of growth and production." And in such passages, Coleridge's metaphors for imagination coincide with his metaphors for the mind in all its highest workings. The action of the faculty of reason Coleridge compares in detail to the development, assimilation, and respiration of a plant—thus equating knowing with growing and (to borrow a coinage from I. A. Richards) "knowledge" with "growledge."

Indeed, it is astonishing how much of Coleridge's critical writing is couched in terms that are metaphorical for art and literal for a plant; if Plato's dialectic is a wilderness of mirrors, Coleridge's is a very jungle of vegetation. Only let the vehicles of his metaphors come alive, and you see all the objects of criticism writhe surrealistically into plants or parts of plants, growing in tropical profusion. Authors, characters, poetic genres, poetic passages, words, meter, logic become seeds, trees, flowers, blossoms, fruit, bark, and sap. The fact is, Coleridge's insistence on the distinction between the living imagination and the mechanical fancy was but a part of his all-out war against the "Mechanico-corpuscular Philosophy" on every front. Against this philosophy he proposed the same objection which is found in the writings of a distinguished modern heir of organic theory, A. N. Whitehead. The scheme was developed, said Coleridge, under the need "to submit the various phenomena of moving bodies to geometrical construction" by abstracting all its qualities except figure and motion. And "as a *fiction of science*," he added, "it would be difficult to overvalue this invention," but Descartes propounded it "as *truth of fact:* and instead of a World *created* and filled with productive forces by the Almighty *Fiat*, left a lifeless Machine whirled about by the dust of its own Grinding . . ." What we need in philosophy, he wrote to Wordsworth in 1815, is

> the substitution of life and intelligence (considered in its different powers from the plant up to that state in which the difference in degree becomes a new kind [man, self-consciousness], but yet not by essential opposition) for the philosophy of mechanism, which, in everything that is most worthy of the human intellect, strikes *Death*, and cheats itself by mistaking clear images for distinct conceptions. . .

Coleridge, with considerable justification, has been called the master of the fragment, and has been charged with a penchant for appropriating passages from German philosophers. Yet in criticism, what he took from other writers he developed into a speculative instrument which, for its power of insight and, above all, of application in the detailed analysis of literary works, had no peer among the German organic theorists. And in an important sense, the elements of his fully developed criticism, whether original or derivative, are consistent—with a consistency that is not primarily logical, or even psychological, but analogical; it consists in fidelity to the archetype, or founding image, to which he has committed himself. This is the contradistinction between atomistic and organic, mechanical and vital —ultimately, between the root analogies of machine and growing plant. As Coleridge explored the conceptual possibilities of the latter, it transformed radically many deeply rooted opinions in regard to the production, classification, anatomy and evaluation of works of art. The nature of these changes can be brought to light if we ask what the properties are of a plant, as differentiated from those of a mechanical system.

Our listing of these properties is greatly simplified, because Coleridge has already described them for us, in the many, though generally neglected, documents in which he discusses the nature of living things. These begin with a long letter written at the age of twenty-four, two years before his trip to Germany and his study of physiology and natural science under Blumenbach; and they culminate with his *Theory of Life*, which incorporates various concepts from the German *Natur-Philosophen* and from the discoveries and speculations of English "dynamic" physiologists such as Hunter, Saumarez, and Abernethy. To place passages from Coleridge's biology and his criticism side by side is to reveal at once how many basic concepts have migrated from the one province into the other.

What, then, are the characteristic properties of a plant, or of any living organism?

(1) The plant originates in a seed. To Coleridge, this indicates that the elementaristic principle is to be stood on its head; that the whole is primary and the parts secondary and derived.

In the world we see every where evidences of a Unity, which the component parts are so far from explaining, that they necessarily pre-suppose it as the cause and condition of their existing *as* those parts; or even of their existing at all. . . . That the root, stem, leaves, petals, &c. [of this crocus] cohere to one plant, is owing to an antecedent Power, or Principle in the Seed, which existed before a single particle of the matters that constitute the *size* and visibility of the crocus, had been attracted from the surrounding soil, air, and moisture.

"The difference between an inorganic and organic body," he said elsewhere, "lies in this: In the first . . . the whole is nothing more than a collection of the individual parts or phenomena," while in the second, "the whole is everything, and the parts are nothing." And Coleridge extends the same principle to non-biological phenomena: "Depend on it, whatever is grand, whatever is truly organic and living, the whole is prior to the parts."

(2) The plant *grows*. "Productivity or Growth," Coleridge said, is "the first power" of all living things, and it exhibits itself as "evolution and extension in the Plant." No less is this a power of the greatest poets. In Shakespeare, for example, we find "*Growth* as in a plant." "All is growth, evolution, *genesis*—each line, each word almost, begets the following . . ." Partial and passing comparisons of a completed discourse or poem to an animal body are to be found as early as Plato and Aristotle, but a highly developed organismic theory, such as Coleridge's, differs from such precedents in the extent to which all aspects of the analogy are exploited, and above all in the extraordinary stress laid on this attribute of growth. Coleridge's interest is persistently genetic—in the process as well as in the product; in becoming no less than in being. That is why Coleridge rarely discusses a finished poem without looking toward the mental process which evolved it; this is what makes all his criticism so characteristically psychological.

(3) Growing, the plant assimilates to its own substance the alien and diverse elements of earth, air, light, and water. "Lo!" cries Coleridge eloquently, on this congenial subject:

> Lo!—with the rising sun it commences its outward life and enters into open communion with all the elements, at once assimilating them to itself and to each other. . . Lo!—at the touch of light how it returns an air akin to light, and yet with the same pulse effectuates its own secret growth, still contracting to fix what expanding it had refined.

Extended from plant to mind, this property effects another revolution in associationist theory. In the elementarist scheme, all products of invention had consisted of recombinations of the unit images of sense. In Coleridge's organic theory, images of sense become merely materials on which the mind feeds—materials which quite lose their identity in being assimilated to a new whole. "From the first, or initiative Idea, as from a seed, successive Ideas germinate."

> Events and images, the lively and spirit-stirring machinery of the external world, are like light, and air, and moisture, to the seed of the Mind, which would else rot and perish, In all processes of mental evolution the objects of the senses must stimulate the Mind; and the Mind must in turn assimilate and digest the food which it thus receives from without.

At the same time the "ideas," which in the earlier theory had been fainter replicas of sensation, are metamorphosed into seeds that grow in the soil of sensation. By his "abuse of the word 'idea,' " Locke seems to say "that the sun, the rain, the manure, and so on had made the wheat, had made the barley. . . If for this you substitute the assertion that a grain of wheat might remain for ever and be perfectly useless and to all purposes nonapparent, had it not been that the congenial sunshine and proper soil called it forth—everything in Locke would be perfectly rational." To Coleridge, the ideas of reason, and those in the imagination of the artist, are "living and life-producing ideas, which . . . are essentially one with the germinal causes in nature. . ."

   (4) The plant evolves spontaneously from an internal source of energy—"effectuates," as Coleridge put it, "its own secret growth"—and organizes itself into its proper form. An artefact needs to be made, but a plant makes itself. According to one of Coleridge's favorite modes of stating this difference, in life "the unity . . . is produced *ab intra*," but in mechanism, "*ab extra*." "Indeed, evolution as contra-distinguished from apposition, or super-induction *ab aliunde*, is implied in the conception of life. . ." In the realm of mind, this is precisely the difference between a "free and rival originality" and that "lifeless mechanism" which by servile imitation imposes an alien form on inorganic materials. As he says, echoing A. W. Schlegel:

   The form is mechanic when on any given material we impress

a pre-determined form . . . as when to a mass of wet clay we give whatever shape we wish it to retain when hardened. The organic form, on the other hand, is innate; it shapes as it develops itself from within, and the fullness of its development is one and the same with the perfection of its outward form.

In this property of growing organisms, Coleridge finds the solution to the problem which, we remember, had worried the mechanists, both of matter and of mind; that is, how to explain the genesis of order and design by the operation of purely mechanical laws. To say, Coleridge declares, that "the material particles possess this combining power by inherent reciprocal attractions, repulsions, and elective affinities; and are themselves the joint artists of their own combinations" is "merely to shift the mystery." Since, by Coleridge's analysis, an organism is inherently teleological—since its form is endogenous and automotive—his own solution of the mystery has no need for the mental equivalent of an architect either to draw up the preliminary design or to superintend its construction. For

> herein consists the essential difference, the contra-distinction, of an organ from a machine; that not only the characteristic shape is evolved from the invisible central power, but the material mass itself is acquired by assimilation. The germinal power of the plant transmutes the fixed air and the elementary base of water into grass or leaves. . .

Parenthetically, it may be pointed out that Coleridge resolved one problem only to run up against another. For if the growth of a plant seems inherently purposeful, it is a purpose without an alternative, fated in the seed, and evolving into its final form without the supervention of consciousness. "The inward principle of Growth and individual Form in every seed and plant is a *subject*," said Coleridge. "But the man would be a dreamer, who otherwise than poetically should speak of roses and lilies as *self-conscious* subjects." To substitute the concept of growth for the operation of mechanism in the psychology of invention, seems merely to exchange one kind of determinism for another; while to replace the mental artisan-planner by the concept of organic self-generation makes it difficult, analogically, to justify the participation of consciousness in the creative process. We shall see that, in some German critics, recourse to vegetable life as a model for the coming-into-being of a work of art had, in fact, engendered the fateful concept that artistic creation is primarily an unwilled and unconscious process of mind. Coleridge, however, though admitting an unconscious component in invention, was determined to demonstrate that a poet like Shakespeare "never wrote anything without design." "What the plant is by an act not its own and unconsciously," Coleridge exhorts us, "that must thou *make* thyself to become." In Coleridge's aesthetics, no less than in his ethics and theology, the justification of free-will is a crux—in part, it would appear, because this runs counter to an inherent tendency of his elected analogue.

(5) The achieved structure of a plant is an organic unity. In contradistinction to the combination of discrete elements in a machine, the parts of a plant, from the simplest unit, in its tight integration, interchange, and interdependence with its neighbors, through the larger and more complex structures, are related to each other, and to the plant as a whole, in a complex and peculiarly intimate way. For example, since the existing parts of a plant themselves propagate new parts, the parts may be said to be their own causes, in a process of which the terminus seems to be the existence of the whole. Also, while the whole owes its being to the coexistence of the parts, the existence of that whole is a necessary condition to the survival of the parts; if, for example, a leaf is removed from the parent-plant, the leaf dies.

Attempts to define such peculiarties of living systems, or the nature of "organic unity," are at the heart of all organismic philosophies. Sometimes Coleridge describes organic relation on the model of Kant's famous formula in the *Teleological Judgment;* in Coleridge's wording, the parts of a living whole are "so far interdependent that each is reciprocally means and end," while the "dependence of the parts on the whole" is combined with the "dependence of the whole on its parts." Or, following Schelling, he formulates it in terms of the polar logic of thesis-antithesis-synthesis. "It would be difficult to recall any true Thesis and Antithesis of which a living organ is not the Synthesis or rather the Indifference."

> The mechanic system . . . knows only of distance and nearness . . . in short, the relations of unproductive particles to each other; so that in every instance the result is the exact sum of the component qualities, as in arithmetical addition. . . In Life . . . the two component counter-powers actually interpenetrate

each other, and generate a higher third including both the former, "ita tamen ut sit alia et major."

Alternatively, Coleridge declares that in an organism the whole spreads undivided through all the parts. "The physical life is in each limb and organ of the body, all in every part; but is manifested as life, by being one in all and thus making all one. . ." These formulae, like the others, are duly transferred from natural organisms to the organic products of invention.

> The spirit of poetry, like all other living powers . . . must embody in order to reveal itself; but a living body is of necessity an organized one,—and what is organization, but the connection of parts to a whole, so that each part is at once end and means!

That function of synthesizing opposites into a higher third, in which the component parts are *alter et idem,* Coleridge attributes, in the aesthetic province, to the imagination—"that synthetic and magical power," as he describes it in the *Biographia Literaria,* which "reveals itself in the balance or reconciliation of opposite or discordant qualities." And the affinity of this synthesis with the organic function of assimilating nutriment declares itself, when Coleridge goes on at once to cite Sir John Davies' description of the soul, which "may with slight alteration be applied, and even more appropriately, to the poetic IMAGINATION":

> Doubtless this could not be, but that she turns
> Bodies to spirit by sublimation strange,
> As fire converts to fire the thing it burns,
> As we our food into our nature change.

To Coleridge, therefore, the imaginative unity is not a mechanical juxtaposition of "unproductive particles," nor a neoclassic decorum of parts in which (as Dryden translated Boileau), "Each object must be fixed in the due place"—

> Till, by a curious art disposed, we find
> One perfect whole of all the pieces joined.

Imaginative unity is an *organic* unity: a self-evolved system, constituted by a living interdependence of parts, whose identity cannot survive their removal from the whole.

It is a curious attribute of an organismic philosophy that on the basis of its particular logic, in which truth is achieved only through the synthesis of antitheses, it is unable to deny its metaphysical opposite, but can defeat it only by assimilating it into "a higher third," as Coleridge said, "including both the former." Accordingly, despite Coleridge's intoxication with the alchemical change wrought in the universe by his discovery of the organic analogy, he did not hesitate to save, and to incorporate into his own theory, the mechanical philosophy he so violently opposed. Mechanism is false, not because it does not tell the truth, but because it does not tell the whole truth. "Great good," he wrote in his notebook, "of such revolution as alters, not by exclusion, but by an enlargement that includes the former, though it places it in a new point of view." Coleridge's fully developed critical theory, therefore, is deliberately syncretic, and utilizes not one, but two controlling analogues, one of a machine, the other of a plant; and these divide the processes and products of art into two distinct kinds, and by the same token, into two orders of excellence.

Again and again, Coleridge uses his bifocal lens to discriminate and appraise two modes of poetry. One of these can be adequately accounted for in mechanical terms. It has its source in the particulars of sense and the images of memory, and its production involves only the lower faculties of fancy, "understanding," and empirical "choice." It is therefore the work of "talent," and stands in a rank below the highest; its examples are such writings as those of Beaumont and Fletcher, Ben Jonson, and Pope. The other and greater class of poetry is organic. It has its source in living "ideas," and its production involves the higher faculties of imagination, "reason," and the "will." Hence it is the work of "genius," and its major instances are to be found in the writings of Dante, Shakespeare, Milton, and Wordsworth. For while talent lies "in the understanding"—understanding being "the faculty of thinking and forming judgments on the notices furnished by sense"—genius consists in "the action of reason and imagination." As part of what it learns from sense-experience, talent has "the faculty of appropriating and applying the knowledge of others," but not "the creative, and self-sufficing power of absolute *Genius*." The "essential difference" is that between "the shaping skill of mechanical talent, and the creative, productive life-power of inspired genius," resulting in a product modified *"ab intra"* in each component part."

"The plays of B[eaumont] and F[letcher]," for example, "are mere aggregations without unity; in the Shakespearean drama there is a vitality which grows and evolves itself from within," so that "Shakespeare is the height, breadth, and depth of genius: Beaumont and Fletcher the excellent mechanism, in juxtaposition and succession, of talent." Similarly, Ben Jonson's work "is the produce of an amassing power in the author, and not of a growth from within." And to conclude, here is a passage epitomizing the analogical method of Coleridge's applied criticism. The lesser Elizabethans, he tells us, merely took objects available to sense and assembled them into new combinations of discrete parts.

> What had a grammatical and logical consistency for the ear, what could be put together and represented to the eye, these poets took from the ear and eye, unchecked by any intuition of an inward possibility, just as a man might fit together a quarter of an orange, a quarter of an apple, and the like of a lemon and of a pomegranate, and make it look like one round diverse colored fruit.

To this collocative activity Coleridge opposes the organic process: "But nature, who works from within by evolution and assimilation, according to a law, cannot do it." Immediately, these concepts of growth, assimilation, and biological law are translated from nature to the poetic mind.

> Nor could Shakespeare, for he too worked in the spirit of nature, by evolving the germ within by the imaginative power according to an idea—for as the power of seeing is to light, so is an idea in the mind to a law in nature.

The Associative Imagination in the Romantic Period

In spite of his valiant efforts, Coleridge failed to give any substantial check to the elementarist philosophy of mind in England. The attempt to account for all the contents and actions of the mind by a minimal number of sensory elements and a minimal number of associative laws continued to dominate the psychology of the age. Indeed, the system only achieved its most detailed and uncompromising statement in 1829, with the

Analysis of the Phenomena of the Human Mind of James Mill—
"the reviver and second founder," as his son said, of Hartley's
associationist psychology.

The elder Mill had little interest in poetry, and in formulating
the laws of association he felt no need to make special provision
for their poetic process. The associative connections of the poet
differ no whit from those of merchant, lawyer, or mathematician; poetic ideas "succeed one another, according to the same
laws. . . They differ from them by this only, that the ideas of
which they are composed, are ideas of different things." When,
in 1859, John Stuart Mill edited his father's book, although he
inserted corrections of many other passages, he let this observation pass without challenge. Some twenty-six years earlier, however, in that period when he had zealously applied himself to
solving the secret of poetry, he had written, in seeming contradiction to his father's doctrine:

> What constitutes the poet is not the imagery nor the thoughts,
> nor even the feelings, but the law according to which they are
> called up. He is a poet, not because he has ideas of any particular
> kind, but because the succession of his ideas is subordinate to
> the course of his emotions.

It turns out, however, that the younger Mill remained an associationist, more open-minded, though hardly less thoroughgoing, than his father. He merely adapted the earlier theory to
his own view that poetry is "the expression or uttering forth of
feeling" by delivering to the feelings the total control over the
associative process. That association may involve not only
sensory images, but also the feelings (themselves often regarded
as aggregates of elementary pleasures and pains), was a doctrine
coeval with the modern form of the theory itself. It had also
been noted by theorists in the associationist tradition that a
feeling or mood may help steer the course of association;
Gerard, for one, demonstrated that "a present passion" often
suggests "trains of ideas which derive their connexion, not from
their relation to one another, but chiefly from the congruity to
the . . . passion." Mill's innovation was merely to take what had
hitherto been a part and make it the total explanation of the
specifically poetic process of invention.

"Whom, then, shall we call poets?" Mill asks, and answers:
"Those who are so constituted, that emotions are the links of

association by which their ideas, both sensuous and spiritual, are connected together." He specifically substitutes a determining feeling for the determining design or plan posited by earlier associationists, in order to account for the formation of an aesthetic whole:

> At the centre of each group of thoughts or images will be found a feeling; and the thoughts or images are only there because the feeling was there. All the combinations which the mind puts together, all the pictures which it paints, the wholes which Imagination constructs out of the materials supplied by Fancy, will be indebted to some dominant *feeling*, not as in other natures to a dominant *thought*, for their unity and consistency of character—for what distinguishes them from incoherencies.

In this passage, Coleridge's organic imagination, although casually distinguished from the fancy, is reduced once more to a mechanical faculty combining particles of ideas, and the unity achieved by this process is not an organic unity, but a unity of emotional coherence. In the best poems of Shelley— the prime example, according to Mill, of the natural poet— "unity of feeling" is "the harmonizing principle which a central idea is to minds of another class . . . supplying the coherency and consistency which would else have been wanting."

Even when we turn to those contemporaries who were poets or critics by profession, we find little support or understanding of what Coleridge aimed to achieve by his theory of the imagination. We do find in characteristic romantic discussions of imagination a superlative evaluation of the function and status of this faculty; a frequent lapse of what had recently been an almost universal recourse to associative laws to explain its workings; a preoccupation with the office of the emotions in poetic invention; and a stress on the power of poetic imagination to modify the objects of sense. Not infrequently, we also hear echoes of Coleridge's antithesis between fancy and imagination, but the distinction is usually desultory and tends to collapse entirely, because unsupported by the firm understructure of Coleridge's philosophical principles.

Six years before the appearance of the *Biographia Literaria*, Charles Lamb used a concept of imagination to justify his preference of Hogarth's extraordinary engraving, "Gin Lane," over Poussin's celebrated "Plague of Athens":

> There is more of imagination in it—that power which draws all
> things to one—which makes things animate and inanimate, be-
> ings with their attributes, subjects and their accessories, take
> one colour, and serve to one effect. . . The very houses . . .
> seem drunk—seem absolutely reeling from the effect of that
> diabolical spirit of phrenzy which goes forth over the whole
> composition.

This passage was justly admired by Wordsworth; and it is safe
to assume that Coleridge would have agreed that this power of
coadunating every part, with no detail left irrelevant, and even
the houses made obeisant to the passion, is a gift of imagination—
the faculty, as he said, "that forms the many into one." But
Lamb, though a gifted and sensitive literary commentator, was
disinclined to speculation or theoretical construction, and has
little more to say on the matter.

Hazlitt, on the other hand, considered himself to be a philosopher as well as critic, and a number of his comments on the
poetic imagination also approximate those of Coleridge. "The
imagination is that faculty which represents objects, not as they
are in themselves, but as they are moulded by other thoughts
and feelings into an infinite variety of shapes and combinations
of power." Among the illustrations of this faculty Hazlitt includes Coleridge's favorite, the madness of Lear:

> Again, when [Lear] exclaims in the mad scene, "The little dogs
> and all, Tray, Blanche, and Sweetheart, see, they bark at me!"
> it is passion lending occasion to imagination to make every crea-
> ture in league against him. . .

In addition Hazlitt, like Coleridge, objected to the atomism and
analytic rationalism of eighteenth-century psychology. But his
own psychology, as we noticed in the preceding chapter, was
a dynamic one, focusing on the nisus, the intricate urgencies
underlying human behavior, and viewing the literary imagination both as the organ of sympathetic self-protection and as
a compensatory instrument which "gives an obvious relief to
the indistinct and importunate cravings of the will." For Coleridge's organic idealism, Hazlitt had no sympathy whatever. He
wrote a derisory review of Coleridge's *Statesman's Manual*, ending with a citation of the central passage in which Coleridge
analyzed a growing plant in order to read it "in a figurative
sense" for correspondences "of the spiritual world." This ex-

cerpt Hazlitt labeled "Mr. Coleridge's Description of a Green Field," and on it he commented: "This will do. It is well observed by Hobbes, that 'it is by means of words only that a man becometh excellently wise or excellently foolish.' "

We turn now to Wordsworth, whose poetry had first opened Coleridge's eyes to the need of positing the existence of a faculty of imagination, who had been in close communication with Coleridge at the very time when that theorist was maturing his antimechanistic philosophy, and who entirely agreed with his friend that the inveterate elementarism of eighteenth-century thought,

> Viewing all objects unremittingly
> In disconnection dead and spiritless;
> And still dividing, and dividing still,

wages "an impious warfare with the very life Of our own souls." It might confidently be expected that Wordsworth's extensive differentiation between fancy and imagination—developed to sanction the segregation, in the edition of 1815, of his "Poems of the Fancy" from his "Poems of the Imagination"—would show essential conformity to that of Coleridge.

On one point, Wordsworth, indeed, is unreservedly at one with Coleridge: in the opinion, as he gravely affirms, that he has himself demonstrated that he possesses imagination, in poems "which have the same ennobling tendency as the productions of men, in this kind, worthy to be holden in undying remembrance." Some of his descriptions of the faculty, too, are consonant with those of Coleridge. In an imaginative simile—or as he puts it, when the faculty is "employed upon images in a conjunction by which they modify each other"—"the two objects unite and coalesce in just comparison." In other instances, Wordsworth's imagination, like Coleridge's, "shapes and *creates*" by "consolidating numbers into unity . . ." Two of Wordsworth's examples of poetic imagination (Lear on the heath, and Milton's description of the coming of the Messiah to battle) were afterward cited by Coleridge as well. And upon first reading, it did seem to Coleridge, as he tells us in the fourth chapter of the *Biographia,* that Wordsworth's theory only differed from his own "chiefly perhaps, as our objects were different." Eight chapters farther along, however, Coleridge expressed a change of opinion: "After a more accurate perusal of Mr. Wordsworth's remarks on the imagination . . . I find that my conclusions are not so consentient with his as, I confess, I had taken for granted."

The reasons for Coleridge's disappointment with Wordsworth's discussion are not far to seek. The imagination, Wordsworth says, is creative; yet, he asks, "is it not the less true that Fancy, as she is an active, is also, under her own laws and in her own spirit, a creative faculty?" Worse still, Wordsworth indicates not only that fancy is creative, but that imagination is *associative:* both powers alike serve "to modify, to create, and to associate." At one point Wordsworth describes imagination as a mode of dissection and recombination in almost exactly the terms of Dugald Stewart, referred to earlier in this chapter. "These processes of imagination," he says, "are carried on either by conferring additional properties upon an object, or abstracting from it some of those which it actually possesses," thus enabling it to act on the mind "like a new existence." Finally, Wordsworth takes specific issue with Coleridge's differentiation, written for Southey's *Omniana* (1812), between the imagination as the "shaping and modifying power" and the fancy as "the aggregative and associative power." "My objection," Wordworth declares, is "only that the definition is too general."

> To aggregate and to associate, to evoke and to combine, belong as well to the Imagination as to the Fancy; but either the materials evoked and combined are different; or they are brought together under a different law, and for a different purpose.

To this Coleridge feels compelled to reply in the *Biographia* that "if, by the power of evoking and combining, Mr. Wordsworth means the same as, and no more than, I meant by the aggregative and associative, I continue to deny, that it belongs at all to the imagination. . ."

This dispute may seem much ado about a purely verbal difference. But from Coleridge's point of view, Wordsworth's vocabulary showed a regressive tendency to conflate the organic imagination with mechanical fancy, by describing it once again in terms of the subtraction, addition, and association of the elements of sensory images; and in doing this, Wordsworth had incautiously given the key to their position away to the enemy. According to A. N. Whitehead, "Wordsworth in his whole being expresses a conscious reaction against the mentality of the eighteenth century," and the nature-poetry of the romantic revival (of which *The Excursion* is Whitehead's prime example) "was a protest on behalf of the organic view of nature." The truth is, however, that in his critical writings, Wordsworth retained to a notable degree the terminology and modes of thinking of eighteenth-century associationism. But to Coleridge, the metaphoric failure to maintain the difference in kind between mechanism and organism, in the crucial instance of the faculties of fancy and imagination, threatened collapse to the dialectic structure of his total philosophy.

The further degeneration of Coleridge's distinction is plainly evident in Leigh Hunt's anthology, which he entitled *Imagination and Fancy*. In Hunt's introductory essay the difference between these faculties resolves into a difference between levity and gravity in the poet's attitude.

> [Poetry] embodies and illustrates its impressions by imagination, or images of the objects of which it treats . . . in order that it may enjoy and impart the feeling of their truth in its utmost conviction and affluence.
>
> It illustrates them by fancy, which is a lighter play of imagination, or the feeling of analogy coming short of seriousness, in order that it may laugh with what it loves, and show how it can decorate with fairy ornament.

A similar procedure has been followed by most commentators on Coleridge's theory of imagination, whether they deplore or admire Coleridge as a critic. As did the writers in Coleridge's lifetime, so many succeeding writers have either made the difference out to be a trivial one between serious and playful poetry, or else, on various grounds, have melted the two processes, that Coleridge so painstakingly separated, back into one. It is a final irony that I. A. Richards, who takes the crucial import of the distinction between fancy and imagination more seriously than any critic since Coleridge himself, and who attacks vigorously earlier efforts to conflate the distinction, goes on to do very much the same thing. Writing as a Benthamite or materialist "trying to interpret . . . the utterance of an extreme Idealist," he translates the difference between the products of the faculties into that of the number of "links" or "cross-connections" between their "units of meaning." These relations, quite comparable to the links of "similarity" between "ideas" in standard associationist analysis, serve once again to convert Coleridge's distinction in kind into a quantitative difference along a single scale. But Richards differs from other commentators in his awareness of what he is about. He undertakes deliberately to substitute for Coleridge's description one that he finds more congenial and, for his purposes, fruitful, however conscious that his "refreshed atomism—a counting of interrelations" might "sometimes have been repugnant, as suggesting mechanical treatment, to Coleridge himself."

The history of such philosophical disagreement makes it exceedingly dubious that this difference can ever be resolved by rational argument. Any logical and semantic analysis of the key terms in the dispute—"part," "unity, "relations," "links," "similarities," "coadunation," "growth,"—finally gets down to an appeal to the observed facts, and about these facts there is blank disagreement. When those of us whom Coleridge (with scant justice to the historical figure) called "Aristotelians" confront his example of an imaginative passage—

> Look! how a bright star shooteth from the sky
> So glides he in the night from Venus' eye—

we see a patent combination of parts; and we go on to explain its difference from Coleridge's illustration of fancy,

> Full gently now she takes him by the hand,
> A lily prison'd in a gaol of snow,
> Or ivory in an alabaster band;
> So white a friend engirts so white a foe,

as a matter of the multiplicity and intimacy of the relations between these parts. When Coleridge, speaking for the "Platonists" who for him constituted the remainder of the planet's population, looked at the first pair of lines, he saw a simple integral of perception, in which constituent parts are isolated, properly enough, for purposes of critical analysis, but at the price of altering their character and momentarily destroying the whole.

In our day those who wish to save the division between things-as-they-are and things as they appear to some other person, tend to account for Coleridge's stubbornness in this matter by referring to the nonrational elements of his personality; F. L. Lucas, for example, speculates that Coleridge's longing for unity "may be mere homesickness for the womb." Coleridge himself preferred to explain such differences in perception on rational grounds. "Facts, you know, are not truths; they are not conclusions; they are not even premisses, but in the nature and parts of premisses." The crucial difference lies in the choice of the initial premises (often, if I have not been mistaken, the analogical premises) of our reasoning, and the validity of the choice is measured by the adequacy of its coherently reasoned consequences in making the universe intelligible and manageable. If this criterion incorporates our need to make the universe emotionally as well as intellectually manageable, is not that the most important requirement of all?

VIII

GILBERT RYLE

Jane Austen and the Moralists

I

Jane Austen is often described as just a miniature-painter. Her blessed "little bit (two inches wide) of ivory" has too often set the tone of criticism. I mean to show that she was more than this. Whether we like it or not, she was also a moralist. In a thin sense of the word, of course, every novelist is a moralist who shows us the ways or *mores* of his characters and their society. But Jane Austen was a moralist in a thick sense, that she wrote what and as she wrote partly from a deep interest in some perfectly general, even theoretical questions about human nature and human conduct. To say this is not, however, to say that she was a moralizer. There is indeed some moralizing in *Sense and Sensibility* and she does descend to covert preaching in *Mansfield Park*. Here I do discern, with regret, the tones of voice of the anxious aunt, and even occasionally of the prig. But for the most part, I am glad to say, she explores and does not shepherd.

I am not going to try to make out that Jane Austen was a philosopher or even a philosopher *manquée*. But I am going to argue that she was interested from the south side in some quite general or theoretical problems about human nature and conduct in which philosophers proper were and are interested from the north side.

To begin with, we should consider the titles of three of her novels, namely, *Sense and Sensibility*, *Pride and Prejudice* and *Persuasion*. It is not for nothing that these titles are composed of abstract nouns. *Sense and Sensibility* really is about the relations between Sense and Sensibility or, as we might put it, between Head and Heart, Thought and Feeling, Judgment and

From *The Oxford Review* (February, 1966), 1: 5-18. Reprinted by permission of the author and the editor of *The Oxford Review*.

Emotion, or Sensibleness and Sensitiveness. *Pride and Prejudice* really is about pride and about the misjudgments that stem from baseless pride, excessive pride, deficient pride, pride in trivial objects, and so on. *Persuasion* really is or rather does set out to be about persuadability, unpersuadability, and over-persuadability.

To go into detail. In *Sense and Sensibility* it is not only Elinor, Marianne and Mrs. Dashwood who exemplify equilibrium or else inequilibrium between judiciousness and feeling. Nearly all the characters in the novel do so, in their different ways and their different degrees. John Dashwood has his filial and fraternal feelings, but they are shallow ones. They do not overcome his and his wife's calculating selfishness. Sir John Middleton is genuinely and briskly kind, but with a cordiality too general to be really thoughtful. What he does for one person he does with equal zest for another, without considering their differences of need, desert or predilection. He would be in his element in a Butlin's Holiday Camp. Mrs. Jennings, whose character changes during the novel, is a thoroughly vulgar woman who yet has, in matters of importance, a sterling heart and not too bad a head. Lucy Steele professes deep feelings, but they are sham ones, while her eye for the main chance is clear and unwavering. Like her future mother-in-law she has too little heart and too much sense of a heartless sort.

Marianne and Elinor are alike in that their feelings are deep and genuine. The difference is that Marianne lets her joy, anxiety or grief so overwhelm her that she behaves like a person crazed. Elinor keeps her head. She continues to behave as she knows she should behave. She is deeply grieved or worried, but she does not throw to the winds all considerations of duty, prudence, decorum or good taste. She is sensitive *and* sensible, in our sense of the latter adjective. I think that Elinor too often and Marianne sometimes collapse into two-dimensional samples of abstract types; Elinor's conversation occasionally degenerates into lecture or even homily. This very fact bears out my view that Jane Austen regularly had one eye, and here an eye and a half, on a theoretical issue. The issue here was this: must Head and Heart be antagonists? Must a person who is deeply grieved or deeply joyous be crazy with grief or joy? To which Jane Austen's answer, the correct answer, is "No, the best Heart and the best Head are combined in the best person." But Elinor sometimes collapses into a Head rather loosely buttoned on to a Heart, and then she ceases to be a person at all.

Jane Austen brings out the precise kinds of the sensibility exhibited by Elinor and Marianne by her wine-taster's technique of matching them not only against one another, but also against nearly all the other characters in their little world. The contrast between Lucy Steele and both Elinor and Marianne is the contrast between sham and real sensibility or emotion; the contrast between Willoughby and, say, Edward is the contrast between the genuine but shallow feelings of the one and the genuine and deep feelings of the other. Lady Middleton's feelings are few and are concentrated entirely on her own children. Her husband's feelings are spread abroad quite undiscriminately. He just wants everyone to be jolly.

I want briefly to enlarge on this special wine-taster's technique of comparative character-delineation. Jane Austen's great predecessor, Theophrastus, had described just one person at a time, the Garrulous Man by himself, say, or the Mean Man by himself. So the Garrulity or the Meanness are not picked out by any contrasts or affinities with contiguous qualities. Our view of the Garrulous Man is not clarified by his benig matched against the Conversationally Fertile Man on the one side, or against the Conversationally Arid Man on the other. The Meanness of the Mean Man is not brought into relief by being put into adjacency with the meritorious Austerity of a Socrates or the allowable Close Bargaining of a dealer. By contrast, Jane Austen's technique is the method of the vintner. She pinpoints the exact quality of character in which she is interested, and the exact degree of that quality, by matching it against the same quality in different degrees, against simulations of that quality, against deficiencies of it, and against qualities which though different, are brothers or cousins of that selected quality. The ecstatic emotionality of her Marianne is made to stand out against the sham, the shallow, the inarticulate and the controlled feelings of Lucy Steele, Willoughby, Edward and Elinor. To discriminate the individual taste of any one character is to discriminate by comparison the individual taste of every other character. That is to say, in a given novel Jane Austen's characters are not merely blankly different, as Cheltenham is blankly different from Helvellyn. They are different inside the same genus, as Cheltenham is different from Bath or Middlesbrough, or as Helvellyn is different from Skiddaw or Boar's Hill.

Thus in *Pride and Prejudice* almost every character exhibits too much or too little pride, pride of a bad or silly sort or pride of a good sort, sham pride or genuine pride and so forth. Elizabeth Bennet combines a dangerous cocksureness in her assessments of people with a proper sense of her own worth. Jane is quite uncocksure. She is too diffident. She does not resent being put upon or even realize that she is being put upon. There is no proper pride, and so no fight in her. Their mother is so stupid and vulgar that she has no sense of dignity at all, only silly vanities about her dishes and her daughters' conquests. Mr. Bennett has genuine pride. He does despise the despicable. But it is inert, unexecutive pride. He voices his just contempt in witty words, but he does nothing to prevent or repair what he condemns. It is the pride of a mere don, though a good don. Bingley has no special pride, and so, though a nice man, spinelessly lets himself be managed by others where he should not. His sisters are proud in the sense of being vain and snobbish.

Darcy is, to start with, haughty and snobbish, a true nephew of Lady Catherine de Burgh. His early love for Elizabeth is vitiated by condescension. He reforms into a man with pride of the right sort. He is proud to be able to help Elizabeth and her socially embarrassing family. He now knows what is due from him as well as what is due to him. Mr. Collins is the incarnation of vacuous complacency. He glories in what are mere reflections from the rank of his titled patroness and from his own status as a clergyman. He is a soap bubble with nothing at all inside him and only bulging refractions from other things on his rotund surface.

The same pattern obtains in *Persuasion*. Not only Anne Elliott but her father, sisters, friends and acquaintances are described in terms of their kinds and degrees of persuadability and unpersuadability. Anne has suffered from having dutifully taken the bad advice of the overcautious Lady Russell. Her father and sister Elizabeth can be persuaded to live within their means only by the solicitor's shrewd appeals to quite unworthy considerations. Her sister Mary is so full of self-pity that she can be prevailed on only by dexterous coaxings. Lydia Musgrove is too headstrong to listen to advice, so she cracks her skull. Her sister

Henrietta is so overpersuadable that she is a mere weathercock. Mr. Elliott, after his suspect youth, is apparently eminently rational. But it turns out that he is amenable to reason only so long as reason is on the side of self-interest.

This particular theme-notion of persuadability was, in my opinion, too boring to repay Jane Austen's selection of it, and I believe that she herself found that her story tended to break away from its rather flimsy ethical frame. Certainly, when Anne and Wentworth at last come together again, their talk does duly turn on the justification of Anne's original yielding to Lady Russell's persuasion and on the unfairness of Wentworth's resentment of her so yielding. But we, and I think Jane Austen herself, are happy to hear the last of this particular theme. We are greatly interested in Anne, but not because she had been dutifully docile as a girl. We think only fairly well of Lydia Musgrove, but her deafness to counsels of prudence is not what makes our esteem so tepid. Some of the solidest characters in the novel, namely the naval characters, are not described in terms of their persuadability or unpersuadability at all, and we are not sorry.

I hope I have made out something of a case for the view that the abstract nouns in the titles *Sense and Sensibility*, *Pride and Prejudice*, and *Persuasion* really do indicate the controlling themes of the novels; that Jane Austen wrote *Sense and Sensibility* partly, at least, from an interest in the quite general or theoretical question whether deep feeling is compatible with being reasonable; that she wrote *Pride and Prejudice* from an interest in the quite general question what sorts and degrees of pride do, and what sorts and degrees of pride do not go with right thinking and right acting; and that she wrote *Persuasion* from an interest—I think a waning interest and one which I do not share—in the general question when should people and when should they not let themselves be persuaded by what sorts of counsels.

I shall now become bolder. I shall now say what corresponding theme-notions constitute the frames of *Emma* and *Mansfield Park*, though no abstract nouns occur in their titles.

If cacophony had not forbidden, *Emma* could and I think would have been entitled *Influence and Interference*. Or it might have been called more generically *Solicitude*. Jane Austen's question here was: What makes it sometimes legitimate or even obligatory for one person deliberately to try to modify the course of another person's life, while sometimes such attempts are wrong? Where is the line between Meddling and Helping? Or, more generally, between proper and improper solicitude and unsolicitude about the destinies and welfares of others? Why was Emma wrong to try to arrange Harriet's life, when Mr. Knightley was right to try to improve Emma's mind and character? Jane Austen's answer is the right answer. Emma was treating Harriet as a puppet to be worked by hidden strings. Mr. Knightly advised and scolded Emma to her face. Emma knew what Mr. Knightly required of her and hoped for her. Harriet was not to know what Emma was scheming on her behalf. Mr. Knightley dealt with Emma as a potentially responsible and rational being. Emma dealt with Harriet as a doll. Proper solicitude is open and not secret. Furthermore, proper solicitude is actuated by genuine good will. Improper solicitude is actuated by love of power, jealousy, conceit, sentimentality and so on.

To corroborate this interpretation we should notice, what we now expect, that the novel's other characters also are systematically described in terms of their different kinds or degrees of concernment or unconcernment with the lives of others. Emma's father is a fusser, who wants to impose his own hypochondriacal regimen on others. But his intentions are kindly and his objectives are not concealed. He is a silly old darling, but he is not a schemer. He tries in vain to influence his friends' meals and his grandchildrens' holiday resorts. He is oversolicitous and solicitous about trivialities, but he does not meddle, save, nearly, once, and then John Knightley properly loses his temper with him. Mrs. Elton is silly and vulgar. Her fault is that of officiousness. She tries to force her services on other people. She is a nuisance, but there is nothing underhand about her; rather the reverse, she advertises too much the unwanted benefits that she tries to impose on her victims. John Knightley is somewhat refreshingly unconcerned with other people's affairs outside his own family circle. He is honest, forthright and perceptive, but, unlike his wife, her father and her sister Emma, he does not interest himself in things that are not his business. He is not brutal or callous, and only twice or three times is he even testy; but other people's affairs are not naturally interesting to him. Gossip bores him and social gatherings seem to him a weary waste of time. Mr. Elton differs from John Knightly in just this respect, that Mr. Elton affects solicitude without really feeling it, while John Knightley is frankly unsolicitous. By contrast, Miss Bates is an incessant, though entirely kindly natterer about other peoples' affairs. She cares very much about everybody's welfare, though her concern is, through no fault of her own, confined to talk. She is debarred from doing anything for anyone save her old mother, but all her little thoughts and all her little utterances are enthusiastically benevolent ones. She is the twittering voice of universal good will. Mr. Knightly is like her in good will, but unlike her in that his is executive and efficient good will. He says little; he just helps. He does what needs to be done for people, but he does not do it behind their backs, nor does he shout about it to the world. Finally, Frank Churchill is matched against Mr. Knightley in that while he too does things which make small or big differences to other people's lives, he often does surreptitious things. He does not hurry to come to meet his new stepmother; and when he does come it is because his crypto-fiancée has just returned to the village. He flirts with Emma, but does not let her know that he is only playing a game, and playing a game as a camouflage. He forces a piano on his fiancée without letting her know to whom she is indebted. He is not wicked, but he is not aboveboard, so many of his actions affecting others belong to the class of interference, and not of legitimate intervention. He is ready to make use of people without their knowledge or consent, in order to get himself out of difficulties. He is like Emma in being a bit of a schemer, but he is unlike her in that she tried to shape the whole life of Harriet; he tricked people only for momentary purposes. He did not want to make big or lasting differences to anybody's life, save his own and his fiancée's; but he was reckless of the danger of making such a difference without intending it. He meddled by covert gambling, she meddled by covert plotting. It is no accident that he was the adopted son of a domineering and wealthy old lady and her intimidated husband. In effect they had trained him not to be forthright. This theme-notion of *Emma*, that of Influence and Interference, is explicitly brought out in the conversation in which the heroine and hero first open their hearts to each other. These two abstract nouns both occur there, as they occur sporadically elsewhere in the novel.

Now for *Mansfield Park*, Jane Austen's profoundest, but also her most didactic novel. Its theme-notion is the connection, to use her own ugly phrase, between fraternal and conjugal ties. Here nearly all the characters are systematically described in terms of the affection which they feel, or do not feel, or which they only pretend to feel for their own flesh and blood. Their capacities or incapacities to make good husbands or wives are a direct function of their lovingness or unlovingness inside their own families. Fanny's devotedness to her brother William, her cousins, aunt and uncle gets its reward in happy marriage; while her coldheartedness at home results in marital disaster for Maria.

Jane Austen duly describes not only the major but also many of the minor characters in terms of their excellences and defects as brothers, aunts, daughters, cousins and parents. Sir Thomas Bertram is genuinely fond of his wife, children and niece. But he is too stiff and pompous to be intimate with them. He is affectionate at a distance. So his children do not love him and he does not understand them. Lady Bertram is drowsily fond of her family but is so bovine and inert that she seldom does anything or says anything to affect anybody. Her sister, Mrs. Norris, is an officious and mischief-making aunt and an unforgiving sister. Her eloquent professions of love for the Bertrams are a mere cover for self-importance. With such parents and such an aunt, Tom, Maria, and her sister grow up selfish and cold-hearted. Maria marries for the wrong reasons and destroys her marriage for worse ones.

The real hero of the story is Fanny's brother, William. He is gay, affectionate, vigorous, straight and brave, and he makes Fanny happy. It is their brother-sister love which is the paradigm against which to assess all the others. Fanny's love for her cousin Edmund had begun as a child's love for a deputy-William.

Henry and Mary Crawford have accomplishments, vitality, wit, artistic tastes, and charm. But they speak undutifully in public about the unsatisfactory uncle who had brought them up; they resent the unexpected return of Sir Thomas Bertram from Antigua to the bosom of his own family, simply because it puts a stop to their theatricals; and even between brother and sister the relations are cordial rather than intimate. Unlike William, Henry never writes a proper letter to his sister. Nor does he mind setting the Bertram sisters at loggerheads by flirting with both at once. He has little personal or vicarious family feeling. Critics have lamented that Henry Crawford does not marry Fanny. But this would have ruined the point. He has indeed everything that she or we could wish her husband to have—everything save two. He lacks high principles, and he lacks filial and fraternal lovingness. He is without those very qualities which make William the ideal brother. Henry could never be what Edmund was, a deputy-William. Though by no means without a heart, he was too shallow-hearted for him and Fanny ever to be the centers and circumferences of one another's lives.

Northanger Abbey is the one novel of the six which does not have an abstract ethical theme for its backbone. I think that when Jane Austen began to write this novel, it had been her sole intention to burlesque such novels as *The Mystery of Udolpho* by depicting a nice but gullible teenager looking at the actual world through, so to speak, the celluloid film of Gothic romances. But even here Jane Austen's ethical interest came quite soon to make its contribution. For we soon begin to find that Catherine, though a gullible ninny about how the actual world runs, is quite ungullible about what is right and wrong, decorous and indecorous. Her standards of conduct, unlike her criteria of actuality, are those of a candid, scrupulous and well-brought up girl, not those of the unschooled, novel-struck girl that she also is. Jane Austen began *Northanger Abbey* just poking fun at factual gullibility; but she soon became much more interested in moral ungullibility. Jane Austen the moralist quickly outgrew Jane Austen the burlesquer.

II

Jane Austen did, then, consider quite general or theoretical questions. These questions were all moral questions; though only in *Mansfield Park* and *Sense and Sensibility* did she cross over the boundary into moralizing. I am now going to be more specific and say what sorts of moral ideas were most congenial to her. I will try to bring out together both what I mean by this question and what its answer is.

In the eighteenth century, and in other centuries too, moralists tended to belong to one of two camps. There was what I shall call, with conscious crudity, the Calvinist camp, and there was what I shall call the Aristotelian camp. A moralist of the Calvinist type thinks, like a criminal lawyer, of human beings as either Saved or Damned, either Elect or Reject, either children of Virtue or children of Vice, either heading for Heaven or heading for Hell, either White or Black, either Innocent or Guilty, either Saints or Sinners. The Calvinists' moral psychology is correspondingly bi-polar. People are dragged upward by Soul or Spirit or Reason or Conscience; but they are dragged down by Body or Flesh or Passion or Pleasure or Desire or Inclination. A man is an unhappy combination of a white angelic part and a black satanic part. At the best, the angelic part has the satanic part cowed and starved and subjugated now, and can hope to be released altogether from it in the future. Man's life here is either a life of Sin or else it is a life of self-extrication from Sin. We find people being depicted in such terms in plenty of places. The seducer in *The Vicar of Wakefield* is Wickedness incarnate. So he has no other ordinary qualities. Fanny Burney's bad characters are pure stage-villains. Occasionally Johnson in the *Rambler* depicts persons who are all Black; and since they possess no Tuesday morning attributes, we cannot remember a thing about them afterward. They are black cardboard and nothing more. The less frequent angelic or saintly characters are equally unalive, flat and forgettable.

In contrast with this, the Aristotelian pattern of ethical ideas represents people as differing from one another in degree and not in kind, and differing from one another not in respect just of a single generic Sunday attribute, Goodness, say, or else Wickedness, but in respect of a whole spectrum of specific weekday attributes. *A* is a bit more irritable and ambitious than *B*, but less indolent and less sentimental. *C* is meaner and quicker-witted than *D*, and *D* is greedier and more athletic than *C*. And so on. A person is not black or white, but irridescent with all the colors of the rainbow; and he is not a flat plane, but a highly irregular solid. He is not blankly Good or Bad, blankly angelic or fiendish; he is better than most in one respect, about level with the average in another respect, and a bit, perhaps a big bit, deficient in a third respect. In fact he is like the people we really know, in a way in which we do not know and could not know any people who are just Bad or else just Good.

Jane Austen's moral ideas are, with certain exceptions, ideas of the Aristotelian and not of the Calvinist pattern. Much though she had learned from Johnson, this she had not learned from him. When Johnson is being ethically solemn, he draws people in black and white. So they never come to life, any more than the North Pole and the South Pole display any scenic features. Jane Austen's people are, nearly always, alive all over, all through and all round, displaying admirably or amusingly or deplorably proportioned mixtures of all the colors that there are, save pure White and pure Black. If a Calvinist critic were to ask us whether Mr. Collins was Hell-bound or Heaven-bent, we could not answer. The question does not apply. Mr. Collins belongs to neither pole; he belongs to a very particular parish in the English Midlands. He is a stupid, complacent and inflated ass, but a Sinner? No. A Saint? No. He is just a ridiculous figure, that is, a figure for which the Calvinist ethical psychology does not cater. The questions Was Emma Good? Was she Bad? are equally unanswerable and equally uninteresting. Obviously she should have been smacked more often when young; obviously, too, eternal Hell-fire is not required for her.

Let me now bring out my reservations. Jane Austen does, with obvious reluctance and literary embarrassment, use the criminal lawyer's Black-White process three or four times. Willoughby in *Sense and Sensibility* begins by being or at least seems to be, behind his attractive exterior, black-hearted. It turns out that he is only a bit grey at heart and not black. The latter shade is reserved for his fiancée, whom therefore we do not meet. In *Pride and Prejudice* Wickham and Lydia do become regulation Sinners, as do Mr. Elliot and Mrs. Clay in *Persuasion*. Fortunately London exists, that desperate but comfortingly remote metropolis; so Jane Austen smartly bundles off her shadowy representatives of vice to that convenient sink. It is in London that Henry Crawford and Maria enjoy or endure their guilty association. Thus Jane Austen is exempted by the width of the Home Counties from having to try to portray in her pastel-shades the ebony complexion of urban sin. Human saints and angels gave her no such literary anxieties. She just forgot that there were officially supposed to exist such arctic paragons, a piece of forgetfulness for which we are not inclined to reprove her.

As early as in *Northanger Abbey* Jane Austen explicitly relinquishes the Black-White, Sinner-Saint dichotomy. Catherine Morland, brought to her senses, reflects:

Charming as were all Mrs. Radcliffe's works . . . it was not in them, perhaps, that human nature, at least in the midland counties of England, was to be looked for. Of the Alps and Pyrenees, with their pine-forests and their vices, they might give a faithful delineation; and Italy, Switzerland and the South of France might be as fruitful in horrors as they were there represented. Catherine dared not doubt beyond her own country, and even of that, if hard pressed, would have yielded the northern and western extremities. But in the central part of England there was surely some security of existence even of a wife not beloved; in the laws of the land, and the manners of age. Murder was not tolerated; servants were not slaves, and neither poison nor sleeping potions were to be procured, like rhubarb, from every druggist. Among the Alps and Pyrenees perhaps, there were no mixed characters. There, such as were not spotless as an angel, might have the disposition of a fiend. But in England it was not so; among the English, she believed, in their hearts and habits there was a general though unequal mixture of good and bad. Upon this conviction she would not be surprised if even in Henry and Eleanor Tilney some slight imperfection might hereafter appear.

In *Persuasion* Jane Austen gives us what she would have been surprised to hear was a good rendering of Aristotle's doctrine of the Mean.

Anne wondered whether it ever occurred to him [Wentworth] to question the justness of his own previous opinion as to the universal felicity and advantage of firmness of character; and whether it might not strike him that like all other qualities of mind it should have its proportions and limits.

Not only was Jane Austen's ethic, if that is not too academic a word, Aristotelian in type, as opposed to Calvinistic. It was also secular as opposed to religious. I am sure that she was personally not merely the dutiful daughter of a clergyman, but was genuinely pious. Yet hardly a whisper of piety enters into even the most serious and most anguished meditations of her heroines. They never pray and they never give thanks on their knees. Three of her heroes go into the church, and Edmund has to defend his vocation against the cynicisms of the Crawfords. But not a hint is given that he regards his clerical duty as that of saving souls. Routine churchgoing on Sunday with the rest of the family gets a passing mention three or four times, and Fanny is once stated to be religious. But that is all. I am not suggesting that Jane Austen's girls are atheists, agnostics or

Deists. I am only saying that when Jane Austen writes about them, she draws the curtain between her Sunday thoughts, whatever they were, and her creative imagination. Her heroines face their moral difficulties and solve their moral problems without recourse to religious faith or theological doctrines. Nor does it ever occur to them to seek the counsels of a clergyman.

Lastly, her ethical vocabulary and idioms are quite strongly laced with aesthetic terms. We hear of "Moral· taste," "Moral and literary tastes," "Beauty of mind," "the beauty of truth and sincerity," "delicacy of principle," "the Sublime of Pleasures." Moreover there is a prevailing correlation between sense of duty, sense of propriety and aesthetic taste. Most of her people who lack any one of these three, lack the other two as well. Mrs. Jennings is the only one of Jane Austen's vulgarians who is allowed, nonetheless, to have a lively and just moral sense. Catherine Morland, whose sense of what is right and decorous is unfailing, is too much of an ignoramus yet to have acquired aesthetic sensibility, but the two Tilneys have all three tastes or senses. The Crawfords are her only people who combine musical, literary and dramatic sensitivity with moral laxity; Henry Crawford reads Shakespeare movingly, and yet is a bit of a cad. Elinor Dashwood, Anne Elliot and Fanny Price have good taste in all three dimensions. Emma Woodhouse is shaky in all three dimensions, and all for the same reason, that she is not effectively self-critical.

III

So Jane Austen's moral system was a secular, Aristotelian ethic-cum-aesthetic. But to say all this is to say that her moral *Weltanchauung* was akin to that of Lord Shaftesbury. Shaftesbury too had, a century before, assimilated moral sense to artistic sense, aesthetic taste to moral taste. A Grecian by study and predilection, he had followed Aristotle in preference to Plato, the Stoics or the Epicureans. A Deist rather than a Christian, he had based his religion, such as it was, on his ethics and aesthetics, rather than these on his religion. So I now put forward the historical hypothesis that Jane Austen's specific moral ideas derived, directly or indirectly, knowingly or unknowingly, from Shaftesbury. Certainly she never mentions him by name; but nor is any moralist mentioned by name, even in those contexts in which her girl-characters are described as studying the writings of moralists. Anne Elliot does advise the melancholy Captain Benwick to read, *inter alios*, "our best moralists"; Fanny Price tutors her young sister, Susan, in history and morals; that teen-aged bluestocking, Mary Bennet, makes long extracts from the writings of moralists, and regales her company with their most striking platitudes. But the word "moralist" would cover Goldsmith or Pope as well as Hutcheson or Hume, Johnson or Addison as well as Shaftesbury or Butler. We cannot argue just from the fact that Jane Austen speaks of moralists to the conclusion that she has any accredited moral philosophers in mind.

My reasons for thinking that Shaftesbury was the direct or indirect source of Jane Austen's moral furniture are these: (1) I have the impression, not based on research or wide reading, that throughout the eighteenth and early nineteenth centuries the natural, habitual and orthodox ethic was, with various modifications and mitigations, that Black-White, Saint-Sinner ethic that I have crudely dubbed "Calvinistic." Hutcheson, Butler and Hume, who were considerably influenced by Shaftesbury, all dissociate themselves from the Angel-Fiend psychology, as if this was prevalent. The essays, whether in the *Spectator*, the *Idler* or the *Rambler*, though I have only dipped into them, seem to me to use the Black-White process when very serious moral matters are discussed; but, perhaps partly for this reason, they tend not to treat very often such sermon-topics. The light touch necessary for an essay could not without awkwardness be applied to Salvation or Damnation. Fielding, who did know his Shaftesbury, was too jolly to bother much with satanic or angelic characters. There are many Hogarthian caricatures in his novels, but they are there to be laughed at. They are not Awful Warnings. That is, I have the impression that the secular and aesthetic Aristotelianism of Shaftesbury had not acquired a very wide vogue. It was not in the air breathed by the generality of novelists, poets and essayists. Perhaps there were latitudinarian sermons, other than Bishop Butler's, in which concessions were made to Shaftesbury and Hutcheson. I do not know. But I fancy that these ideas were current chiefly inside small, sophisticated circles in which "Deist" was not a term of abuse and in which one could refer without explanation or apology to Locke and Descartes, Hobbes and Aristotle, Epicurus and Spinoza. So, if I am right in my assimilation of Jane

Austen's moral ideas to those of Shaftesbury, then I think that she did not absorb these ideas merely from the literary, ecclesiastical and conversational atmosphere around her. I do not, on the other hand, insist that she got them by studying the writings of Shaftesbury himself, though if I was told that she got them either from Shaftesbury himself or from his donnish Scotch disciple, Hutcheson, I should without hesitation say "Then she got them from Shaftesbury." Of Hutcheson's epistemological professionalization of Shaftesbury there is not an echo in Jane Austen. She talks of "Moral Sense" without considering the academic question whether or not it is literally a Sixth Sense. Nor do I find any echoes in her from Butler or from Hume, who in their turn echo little or nothing of the aestheticism of Shaftesbury.

(2) Another thing that persuades me that Jane Austen was influenced fairly directly by Shaftesbury himself, besides the general secular and aesthetic Aristotelianism which she shares with him, is the vocabulary in which she talks about people. Her stock of general terms in which she describes their minds and characters, their faults and excellences is, *en bloc*, Shaftesbury's. Almost never does she use either the bipolar ethical vocabulary or the corresponding bipolar psychological vocabulary of the Black-White ethic. The flat, generic antithesis of Virtue and Vice, Reason and Passion, Thought and Desire, Soul and Body, Spirit and Flesh, Conscience and Inclination, Duty and Pleasure, hardly occur in her novels. Instead we get an ample, variegated, and many-dimensional vocabulary. Her descriptions of people mention their tempers, habits, dispositions, moods, inclinations, impulses, sentiments, feelings, affections, thoughts, reflections, opinions, principles, prejudices, imaginations and fancies. Her people have or lack moral sense, sense of duty, good sense, taste, good-breeding, self-command, spirits and good humor; they do or do not regulate their imaginations and discipline their tempers. Her people have or lack knowledge of their own hearts or their own dispositions; they are or are not properly acquainted with themselves; they do or do not practice self-examination and soliloquy. None of these general terms or idioms is, by itself, so far as I know, peculiar to Shaftesbury and herself. It is the amplitude of the stock of them, and the constant interplays of them which smack strongly of Shaftesbury. It had been Shaftesbury's business, so to speak, to Anglicize the copi-

ous and elastic discriminations of which Aristotle had been the discoverer. In Jane Austen Shaftesbury's Anglicization is consummated without his floridity.

Given the stilted bipolar vocabulary of, say, "Reason and Passion" or "Spirit and Flesh," then it is easy and tempting to reserve the top-drawer for the one and the bottom-drawer for the other. But given the copious, specific and plastic vocabulary of Aristotle or Shaftesbury, it then becomes a hopeless as well as a repellent task to split it up into, say, fifteen top-drawer terms and seventeen bottom-drawer terms, into a platoon of sheep-terms for angelic and a platoon of goat-terms for satanic powers, impulses and propensities. To the employer of a hundred crayons the dichotomy "Chalk or Charcoal" has no appeal. For example, John Knightley's occasional testiness was obviously not a Virtue. But nor was it a Vice. At worst it was a slight weakness, and in his particular domestic situation it was even a venial and rather likable condiment. Where the icing-sugar is too thick, a splash of lemon-juice is a welcome corrective. We would not wish to be surrounded by John Knightleys. But we would not wish to be without them altogether.

(3) There is one word which Shaftesbury and Jane Austen do frequently use in the same apparently idiosyncratic way, and that a way which is alien to us and I think, subject to correction, alien to most of the other eighteenth and early nineteenth century writers. This is the word "Mind," often used without the definite or indefinite article, to stand not just for intellect or intelligence, but for the whole complex unity of a conscious, thinking, feeling and acting person. I am not here referring to the philosophico-theological use of "Mind" for, roughly speaking, the Deist's or Pantheist's God. We do find this use occurring now and then in Shaftesbury, as in Pope.

Shaftesbury and Jane Austen both speak of the Beauty of Mind or the Beauty of a Mind, where they are talking about ordinary people; and when Shaftesbury speaks of the Graces and Perfections of Minds, of the Harmony of a Mind, or the Symmetry and Order of a Mind and of the Freedom of Mind he is talking in his jointly aesthetic and ethical manner just of laudable human beings. Jane Austen employs a lot of analogous phrases: "Inferior in talent and all the elegancies of mind," "delicacy of mind," "liberty of mind or limb" (all from *Emma*); "[he] has a thinking mind," ". . . in temper and mind," "Marianne's mind could not be controlled," "her want of delicacy, rectitude and integrity of mind" (all from *Sense and Sensibility*). In "one of those extraordinary bursts of mind" (*Persuasion*, Ch. VII) the word "mind" perhaps means "intelligence" or just "memory." Now I think that Shaftesbury used this term "Mind" as his preferred rendering of Aristotle's "ψυχὴ," for which the normal rendering by "Soul" would, I guess, have had for him too Christian or too parsonical a ring. He does once or twice use the disjunction "mind or soul." Jane Austen is even charier than Shaftesbury of employing the word "soul"; and she, I surmise, just takes over the Shaftesburian use of "Mind," very likely without feeling, what I think most philosophers would have felt, that this use was an irregular and strained one. If the Shaftesburian uses of the word "Mind" did not subsequently become current in literature, sermons or conversation, or even, as I am sure they did not, in the philosophical writings of Butler and Hume, then the fact that Jane Austen often makes the same and similar uses of it would be fairly strong evidence that she drew directly on Shaftesbury. But whether this is the case or not is a matter of philological history, in which field I am not even an amateur. I am primarily arguing for the general, if vague, conclusion that Jane Austen was, whether she knew it or not, a Shaftesburian. It is a dispensable sub-hypothesis that she had studied the rather tedious and high-flown writings of Shaftesbury himself. Shaftesbury had opened a window through which a relatively few people in the eighteenth century inhaled some air with Aristotelian oxygen in it. Jane Austen had sniffed this oxygen. It may be that she did not know who had opened the window. But I shall put an edge on the issue by surmising, incidentally, that she did know.

IX

JEROME B. SCHNEEWIND

Moral Problems and Moral Philosophy in the Victorian Period*

In the present essay an attempt is made to bring out some ways in which the understanding of a literary work may be assisted by an understanding of philosophical issues. The literary works here discussed are novels by a variety of nineteenth-century authors—Charlotte Yonge, Mrs. Gaskell, William Hale White, and George Eliot. The philosophical issues related to the novels are those involved in the controversy over ethics between the Utilitarians and the Intuitionists, a controversy which was at the center of English moral philosophy for more than a century following the writing of Jeremy Bentham's *Introduction to the Principles of Morals and Legislation.*[1] I do not mean to suggest

From *Victorian Studies,* Supplement to Volume 9 (September 1965): 29–46. Reprinted by permission of the author and the editors of *Victorian Studies.*

* The author wishes to express his gratitude to the University of Pittsburgh for its award of a Mellon Post-doctoral Fellowship, during the tenure of which (1963–64) much of the research on which this paper is based was done.

[1] The *Introduction* was printed but not published in 1781. It was not until the publication of Henry Sidgwick's *Methods of Ethics* (London, 1874; 1907) and F. H. Bradley's *Ethical Studies* (Oxford, 1876) that the basic terms of the controversy began to shift; and even these books, while marking important changes in methods of argument, are concerned to reconcile the Intuitionist and Utilitarian views. Bystanders and contenders see the controversy in the same way. Thus W. E. H. Lecky begins his *History of European Morals* (London, 1869; 1897) with a reference to "the great controversy, springing from the rival claims of intuition and utility to be regarded as the supreme regulator of moral distinctions"; and he goes on to give the epithets used to distinguish the schools: "One of them is generally described as the stoical, the intuitive, the independent or the sentimental; the other as the epicurean, the inductive, the utilitarian, or the selfish" (1: 1, 2–3). See also M. J. Guyau, *La Morale Anglaise Contemporaine* (Paris, 1879), pp. 190–191. Where two dates are given for a work, the second date is that of a later edition which I have used.

that interest in this philosophical issue was confined to the nineteenth century—far from it. But philosophers shift their emphases from time to time, and nineteenth-century English philosophers were concerned about the Utilitarian-Intuitionist debate in a way that differentiates them fairly clearly from both their predecessors and their successors.[2] William Whewell, H. L. Mansel, James Martineau, John Grote, J. S. Mill, and Henry Sidgwick, who, among others, carried on the debate, were all Victorian philosophers: this fact suggests that their work in moral philosophy may be used to explore the work of Victorian novelists concerned with moral problems. Thanks to J. S. Mill everyone is familiar with the Utilitarian position on the issues, but the Intuitionist standpoint is, quite surprisingly considering its importance for the thought of the period, almost completely neglected in histories of philosophy no less than in surveys of literature.[3] I begin, therefore, with a

[2] The break in interest can be dated fairly sharply at both ends. Bentham is the starting point for the nineteenth-century controversies, G. E. Moore for those of the twentieth. Bentham (like William Paley a few years later) lumps together as "principles adverse to that of Utility" almost all of the schools of thought of the eighteenth century. He dismisses the moral sense, the common sense, the understanding, right reason, the fitness of things, and laws of nature, under this heading *(Introduction,* ch. 2); while Paley, in his *Principles of Moral and Political Philosophy* (London, 1786), with equal scorn sweeps aside honor, custom, and scripture as rules of life, and the moral sense, innate maxims, natural conscience, instinctive love of virtue, and "perception of right and wrong intuition" as foundations of morality (1, chs. 4–5). The Benthamite simplification of the issues was taken as the relevant starting point for discussion during most of the nineteenth century, just as Moore's statement of issues in *Principia Ethica* (London, 1903) has been taken as the relevant starting point in recent discussion. But of course these were those in the years following the 1780s and in the years following 1903 who carried on the older modes of thought.

In this light it seems absurd to classify Bentham as "typically eighteenth century" because of his appeal to reason and his simplified view of human nature, just as it would be absurd to think of Moore as "typically nineteenth century" because of his appeal to intuition. So far as I know no one has said such a thing of Moore, but remarks of the type indicated are frequently made about Bentham.

[3] For Mill's views see especially the *Autobiography,* ch. 7. Harald Höffding and John Passmore have nothing to say about Intuitionist ethics. Oliver Elton and Samuel Chew do not discuss the Intuitionists at all, while Sherard Vines and Hugh Walker touch only on James Martineau. Neither Basil Willey nor Walter Houghton discusses the Intuitionist ethic, although each gives much space to the Utilitarians.

brief, and somewhat idealized, statement of the two views.

On the purely conceptual side of the debate, the differences between the two schools are as follows. (1) Methodologically the Utilitarians hold that to justify particular moral judgments is to show that there is *inductive evidence* for them, while for the Intuitionist no evidence is either necessary or possible for particular moral judgments: they must be known immediately, noninferentially, by direct awareness, or—at most—by simple deduction from a rule that is intuitively known.[4] Thus for the Intuitionist the paradigm cases of moral judgment are those in which we know straight off what we ought to do, while for the Utilitarian they are those in which we must figure out what to do. (2) Connected with this is the fact that for the Utilitarian the paradigm moral problems are those in which we do not know what we ought to do, and in which the solution comes as soon as we do know; while for the Intuitionist the central sort of problem is that in which the agent knows what he ought to do but finds it difficult to bring himself to do it. His problem is one of will or feeling.[5]

Even in specialized studies, where it would be relevant, the Intuitionist view is not mentioned: thus Humphry House in *The Dickens World* makes no reference to it, despite his frequent mention of Utilitarianism as something Dickens sometimes opposed.

[4] William Whewell in his *Elements of Morality, Including Polity* (Cambridge, 1845; 1864) thinks in terms of intuitively known rules or principles: see pp. 10–12. For a strong statement of the view that we intuit the moral quality of particular instances, see H. L. Mansel, *Letters, Lectures, and Reviews*, ed. Henry W. Chandler (London, 1873), pp. 126–29, 135 (an essay of 1854); 372–73 (an essay of 1866); and also James M'Cosh, *An Examination of Mr. J. S. Mill's Philosophy* (New York, 1866), p. 391: "Our intuitions are perceptions of individual objects or individual truths; and in order to reach an axiom or 'principle of morals,' there is need of a discursive process of generalization."

[5] John Grote, for example, in his *Examination of the Utilitarian Philosophy* (Cambridge, 1870) draws attention to this distinction, in his usual cautious way, when he remarks that "what is needed in respect of philanthropy, though to some extent *knowledge*, is still more *will* . . . such philosophies as by their principles are likely to strengthen the will are more valuable, and therefore perhaps likely to be more true, than such as go rather only to add to the knowledge" (p. 235). See also ch. 16, esp. p. 248: "utilitarianism is far from providing a complete remedy for the helplessness or igorance which [is] one of the chief obstacles to the promotion of the general happiness . . . . The other obstacle . . . indis-

(3) Perhaps the best-known point of dispute is the disagreement over the relative value or importance of motives and consequences, or of intentions and results. It is easy to get lost here. No Utilitarian ever denied that motives and intentions may have value, nor did the Intuitionists ever say that consequences are totally unimportant. They agree in separating the evaluation of an agent from the evaluation of an act, in distinguishing human acts and agents from other events and causes, and in holding that distinctively *moral* evaluation is only pertinent where human acts or agents are in question. The conceptual point of disagreement is brought out clearly by John Grote. Utilitarianism, he says, "considers actions to be of value in the universe, in the last resort, solely in respect of their usefulness. . . . Unless there is produced by them something which independently of them may be described as good or desirable, the universe, it is said, is no better for them."[6] But this is a gross oversimplification, for "there are two kinds of value . . . the value of usefulness or result, and the value of worthiness of feeling . . . which has gone towards the result," or, as he later puts it, "there are two separate and independent good qualities in regard of action, its generosity . . . and its usefulness." In the happiest cases these work together, but even if no good results are produced still "generous and self-forgetting action would be worth having in the universe" (pp. 72, 76–77). Since the Utilitarians think of the kind of value that results can have as the only kind of value there is, they are forced to evaluate motives or feelings solely in terms of their tendency to produce goodness of this kind. But for the Intuitionist this sort of value is "something in a manner pre-moral, something with the con-

---

position or want of kindly feeling, it will scarcely remedy at all: it is the other kinds of ethical philosophy, which utilitarianism despises, that really are occupied with the causes of this."

Utilitarians from Bentham through Sidgwick claim that one major superiority of their view over Intuitionism is that they provide a means for discovering in every case what one ought to do while the Intuitionist cannot give such a means. For strong criticism of this claim and of the general view of philosophy which it presupposes, see F. H. Bradley, *Ethical Studies* (London, 1876; Oxford, 1927), p. 193; and also Bradley's *Principles of Logic* (London, 1883; Oxford, 1922), 1: 269–71.

[6] John Grote, *Treatise on the Moral Ideals* (Cambridge, 1876), pp. 69–70.

sideration of which morality is not as yet properly begun."[7] The kind of value which only human willing or human motives can have is, for the Intuitionist, the distinctively moral, and therefore supremely authoritative, kind of value.

(4) The Utilitarians are all determinists, while their opponents take a strongly libertarian view. Martineau is stating a commonplace of the Intuitional position when he says that "either free-will is a fact, or moral judgment a delusion."[8] The Utilitarian's denial of this sort of freedom forces him to re-interpret key concepts of morality—duty, responsibility, personal merit—in Hobbesian terms, as referring ultimately to various ways of exerting social pressure to control individual actions. But to do this, the Intuitionist believes, is to pervert the terms from their central, and ordinary, sense.[9] The Util-

[7] Grote, p. 74. James Martineau, in his *The Seat of Authority in Religion* (London, 1890), says that what calculations of Utility supply "is not really *Moral* at all, distinguishing right from wrong; but simply *Rational*, distinguishing wise from foolish" (p. 81). The second and third chapters of Book I of this volume provide a useful short summary of Martineau's ethical views, the detailed exposition of which is given in *Types of Ethical Theory* (Oxford, 1885; 1891). Martineau's views were worked out, in substance, by 1845, and were first published in a review of William Whewell's *Elements* in the *Prospective Review* for 1845–46. He holds that what we intuit is always the relative value of two (or more) competing motives to action. Conscience tells us which of the motives present in us is higher, and thereby indicates the one from which we ought to act. Similar points are made by Mansel, pp. 365, 369–71, who argues that the consistent Utilitarian must deny the existence of morality altogether; and by Whewell, pp. 2, 12, 65–67.

[8] 2, 41. His defense of free will is to be found primarily in *A Study of Religion* (Oxford, 1887), 3, ch. ii. See also James M'Cosh, *The Intuitions of the Mind Inductively Investigated* (London, 1860; New York, 1869), pp. 266 ff.: "We have seen that conscience pronounces its decisions on acts of the will . . . . its judgments proceed on the supposition that . . . the will is free . . . . The possession of a free will is thus one of the elements which go to constitute man a moral and responsible agent." Mansel says that if there is no such thing as free will, then "no amount of special pleading will enable us to escape the inevitable conclusion that there is no such thing as morality. . . . there may be pleasure and pain . . . but other good or evil there can be none. . . . an Utilitarian morality —that is to say, the denial of any morality at all—is the necessary consequence of a determinist theory of the will—that is, of the denial of any will at all' (pp. 375–76).

[9] Martineau would have said of the view of J. S. Mill just what he said of those of Hutcheson, who, like Mill, was a determinist: "To his prepossession upon this question must be attributed the loose and unsatisfactory

itarian reply is that such an interpretation is the only way to preserve morality without committing oneself to a concept of freedom that entails denying the law of causation, and that is therefore either inapplicable or nonsensical. (5) Finally, the Utilitarian holds that moral knowledge as such carries with it no motivating force. One may know what one ought to do and still have no motive to do it. Hence sanctions—that is, reasons beyond the fact that something is a duty—must be attached to duties if men are to be led to act rightly. The Intuitionist typically denies this. On his view simply knowing what we ought to do gives us a motive for doing it, although, of course, that motive will not always be the one from which we act. No special sanctions or desires are needed to explain why a man does what he thinks he ought to do: the fact that he thinks he ought is a sufficient explanation.[10]

---

account which he gives of the central group of words in the Vocabulary of Morals; for example, 'Duty,' 'Ought,' 'Right,' 'Merit,' 'Approbation,' 'Reward,' and their opposites: a set of terms with which, it is plain, he feels himself ill at ease, and can hold no pleasant intercourse, till he has made converts of them, and baptised them into a non-natural sense. For him, perhaps, they may emerge regenerate; to the unconverted, they appear bereft of their wits" (2, 565). The position is a powerful one. Sidgwick admits not only that "the common retributive view of punishment, and the ordinary notions of 'merit,' 'demerit,' and 'responsibility' . . . involve the assumption of Free Will" (p. 71) but also that I cannot at the moment of decision think of my act as determined "without at the same time conceiving my whole conception of what I now call 'my' action fundamentally altered" (p. 66). Compare J. L. Austin, "Ifs and Cans" (1956), *Philosophical Papers* (Oxford, 1962): "Determinism, whatever it may be, may yet be the case, but at least it appears not consistent with what we ordinarily say and presumably think" (p. 179).

[10] For Martineau in knowing what we ought to do, insofar as this is purely *moral* knowledge, we have a motive to do it because what we know is the relatively greater worth of a motive already present and active. See Grote, *Examination of the Utilitarian Philosophy*, ch. viii; and *Treatise:* "I think that conscientiousness or deliberate reason is itself an original source of action" (p. 457 ff.). M'Cosh argues that Mill is wrong in representing Intuitionists as holding that the sanction of morality is a feeling. "It cannot be said to consist in 'feeling,' except we use the phrase in so wide and loose a sense as to include all mental operations, and the native principles of action from which they spring. . . . it points to and implies an objective reality, a real good and evil in the voluntary acts of intelligent beings," etc. (*Examination of Mr. J. S. Mill's Philosophy*, p. 392).
The fact that moral knowledge by itself is thought to have power to

This brief sketch of the major conceptual disagreements between typical Utilitarian and Intuitionist positions may show up the close unity of the different points on each side. The Utilitarian, not seeing anything ontologically special in human action, sees no special moral kind of value. He is thus forced to look to natural value for the differentia of action, and natural value can only be determined by calculation. Individual agents are no more moved internally to create the greatest possible amount of natural value than physical objects are moved internally to create the greatest possible amount of natural beauty, so that externally imposed adjustments are needed to bring about the desirable result. The Intuitionist sees human agency as being of a unique non-mechanical kind, and he sees it therefore also as bearer of a unique kind of value which is of higher authority than natural value. In this aspect man is by nature a moral agent and therefore necessarily moved by moral knowledge, and since moral value attaches to what man knows most directly—his own active powers—there is no need of calculation or inference to obtain such knowledge. There is rather need of the strength of will to overcome that aspect of man which is

---

move us to act (or, to put it another way, that it is thought to be a sufficient explanation of why a man did something to say that he believed he ought to) is responsible both for certain confusions on the part of the Intuitionists and (in part) for the Benthamite insistence on treating the rationalist and the sentimentalist—in contemporary terms, the cognitivist and the emotivist—forms of Intuitional doctrine as being equivalent. If it is held that reason or knowledge cannot alone move men to action, then either moral beliefs are not matters of reason or knowledge (since they move to action) or else a sanction is needed, in addition to the knowledge, to move one to do what reason tells one that one ought to do. Benthamites take the second alternative. It is possible to take the first view, and hold that what looks like moral *knowledge* is strictly speaking moral *feeling*. For there is no problem as to whether feeling can move men to action. The Benthamites see that their opponents do not happily take this alternative; and so they accuse them, often correctly, of being muddled, and of using sometimes a sentimentalist and sometimes a rationalist interpretation of morality. Hence it does not really matter to the Benthamite which view the Intuitionist takes, since from the Benthamite standpoint the Intuitionist really wants to have it both ways—and this does not strike the Benthamite as a possible position. For a recent restatement of the view that moral knowledge includes in its nature a motive to action, see W. D. Falk, " '*Ought*' *and Motivation*" in Wilfrid Sellars and John Hospers, *Readings in Ethical Theory* (New York, 1952), pp. 492–510.

moved only by desire for the non-moral natural values.[11]

The logical and conceptual portrayal of a controversy like that between Utilitarians and Intuitionists makes the philosophical debates seem far removed from the moral problems and moral attitudes of actual people in real situations. Yet each of the positions I have outlined articulates a definite moral attitude and can be viewed as a response to a certain kind of moral problem.

Our morality has two directions of concern. We must live in large groups and get along with people whom we do not know or with whom we have contact only in the course of business or in the accidental meetings of daily life. This is a pervasive feature of life, but so is the fact that a part of our lives involves extremely close contact with a very small number of people whom we know intimately. Morality may be involved in each sort of relationship, and consequently it is possible for the moral philosopher to take either sort as paradigmatic of human relations. In a variety of ways Utilitarianism presents a morality which is primarily impersonal, appropriate to the life of the large society or city and to the relations between strangers, while Intuitionism speaks more clearly for a personal morality, drawn from the life of the small group or the family, from the relations between old acquaintances or close friends.[12]

(1) Strangers are people whom one does not know, and among strangers one must either figure out what to do in each case or else act according to fairly definite rules which make little allowance for personal variations among individuals. To

[11] I have said nothing about the Utilitarian hedonism and the opposition to it on the part of Intuitionists, because this issue, insofar as it is not misunderstood, is the same as the issue over the existence or non-existence of a distinctively moral kind of value. The Utilitarian use of the terms "pleasure" and "pain" is extremely broad. They are meant to cover all the possible satisfactions and dissatisfactions or repulsions which enter into human experience, and not just those of which paradigm cases are the enjoyableness of having one's back scratched or the hurt of having a pin stuck into a finger. Whatever someone is *for* counts as a pleasure to him; whatever he is *against* counts as a pain. Anti-Utilitarians often misunderstand this, but the Utilitarians themselves are fairly clear about it.

[12] This theme is in some respects a well-known one, and references to it in Victorian literature itself could be multiplied endlessly: see, for example, the discussion and, references, in Walter E. Houghton, *The Victorian Frame of Mind* (New Haven, 1957), pp. 77–80.

know people well, to feel at home in a group, is on the other hand to know straight off what the others will do and what to do in response, and to be able, consequently, to act in ways closely fitted to distinct personalities. Calculations and rules come in only as personal relations resting on sympathetic understanding break down.

(2) Among strangers one may make mistakes because of miscalculation or because one does not know the rules, but the problems that arise in families or other intimate groups are not likely to be due simply to ignorance or intellectual error. They tend to be problems of adjusting the feelings and desires of the various members of the group, where these are all fairly well known to the members.

(3) John Stuart Mill's "estimate of what a philosophy like Bentham's can do" is suggestive. "It can teach," he says, "the means of organizing and regulating the merely *business* part of the social arrangements."[13] When I am engaged in a business transaction with someone, his motive for carrying out his part of the bargain is of no intrinsic concern to me: that he does what he agreed to do is the main point; and whether he does it from a sense of honor, a desire for profit, or a fear of punishment, does not matter. Still, in considering him for possible future transactions, I shall take his character into account: his reliability, his honesty, his firmness of purpose, are all relevant to an estimate of the way he will carry out his future commitments. Similarly, in one's relations with strangers one is concerned primarily with *what* they do, and only secondarily with *why* they do it. By contrast to this, in a closely knit family or among a group of good friends, one will not stand on one's rights or call in authorities to enforce promises. Resolutions of disagreements among divergent desires will be felt by everyone to be satisfactory only to the extent that they do not leave anyone feeling thwarted or hurt or angrily unwilling to accept the settlement. In contexts like these, then, it will matter relatively little what is actually done, but the motives and feelings of the persons involved will matter enormously.

(4) We cannot avoid predicting the actions of other people,

[13] J. S. Mill, "Bentham," *Dissertations and Discussions* (London, 1868), 1, 366. Mill goes on immediately to say that Bentham "committed the mistake of supposing that the business part of human affairs was the whole of them; all at least that the legislator and the moralist had to do with."

but the basis for prediction varies greatly from context to context. Where we do not know people well, we can, obviously, use as the basis for our predictions only facts that are likely to be true of all people and that do not involve highly individual characteristics. We cannot easily then see the acts of others as being much more than expected responses to standard sorts of situations, and we consequently tend to think even of our own acts in this way. But where we have intimate and detailed knowledge of other people, we can see their actions as natural expressions of their whole personalities, and our sense of the individuality of our own actions will consequently be heightened.[14] The contrast may be seen in a different light by noting that where impersonal social life is predominant, one tends to think of one's own actions as one thinks of those of others, in the third person, so that prediction is central and decision exceptional; while where there is a predominance of close and sympathetic contact with others, one tends to think of other people's actions as one thinks of one's own, so that decision is central and prediction secondary. The determinist, we might say, is impressed with the fact that we predict the actions of all but one person in the world; while the libertarian is struck with the importance of the fact that one's own actions result from one's decisions.[15]

[14] Both Bentham and Martineau speak of motives as "springs of action." In Bentham one has always the image of steel springs, triggered off by the releasing mechanism of some combination of circumstances. But in Martineau the association is with springs of water, so that one's actions flow from one as a stream. Cf. *The Seat of Authority in Religion*, p. 358.

[15] See for instance Sidgwick's *Methods of Ethics*, Bk. 1, ch. v, which gives a careful discussion of the reasons for accepting determinism, all involving the regularity and consequent predictability of events and actions, and then continues: "Against the formidable array of cumulative evidence offered for Determinism there is to be set the immediate affirmation of consciousness in the moment of deliberate action. Certainly when I have a distinct consciousness of choosing between alternatives of conduct, one of which I conceive as right or reasonable, I find it impossible not to think that I can now choose to do what I so conceive,—supposing that there is no obstacle to my doing it other than the condition of my desires and voluntary habits,—however strong may be my inclination to act unreasonably, and however uniformly I may have yielded to such inclinations in the past" (p. 65). It is mainly because of the strength of this point—i.e., the existence of decisions—that Sidgwick feels unable to settle the issue one way or the other. For a discussion of different kinds of bases

(5) In a large society or among strangers each man must look out mainly for himself. Insofar as there are socially sanctioned rules they will seem essentially external to the individual—reasonable enough, perhaps, as making the existence of the society possible, but to be obeyed only because of the social benefits and penalties involved. This is a consequence of the feeling that one's connections with a society of this sort are more or less accidental, that they do not contain what really pertains to oneself. It is what someone likes and wants that shows who he is: his duties are simply forced upon him by the world. Where, on the other hand, one lives in a small and stable group, one tends much more to think of oneself in terms of one's membership in the group. One is consequently more likely to think of moral demands as issuing from oneself, or from a part of oneself. The social and personal claims that one feels one ought to satisfy are at least as much made by oneself for others as they are by others for themselves. Difficulty in fulfilling such demands is not taken to suggest that they are unjust or too severe: it shows rather that the lower or worse part of oneself needs to be subdued by the higher and better part. Not one's merely natural wants and likes show one's character, but the duties one has and the way one carries them out. It is where the individual feels himself identified with a "station and its duties" that he will most clearly feel the call of duty as one which he is moved to obey simply because he hears it; and it is where this holds least that moral demands will be most apt to present themselves as external and as needing external sanctions.[16]

One more point needs to be added. In a small and stable society it is possible to make the kind of moral use of exemplary persons which has traditionally been made of the main figures in

---

for prediction and their consequences for our moral attitudes see F. H. Bradley, *Ethical Studies*, ch. i.

[16] Alexander Bain, *The Emotions and the Will* (London, 1859), ch. xv, gives the Utilitarian theory of conscience. In his view it is "an imitation within ourselves of the government without us . . . conscience . . . reproduces, in the maturity of the mind a facsimile of the system of government as practiced around us" (p. 313). "External authority" is thus "the genuine type and original of moral authority within" (p. 318). For the Intuitionist view see Martineau, *Types of Ethical Theory*, 2, 27 ff., and 401 ff., where the involvement of one's identity with one's social relations is stressed.

the Bible and of fictional characters like Bunyan's Christian. Models or patterns like these have an important social function. In educating children into morality and in carrying on the deliberations of mature morality, these models provide a unifying center both for the instruction of activity and for the encouragement of effort. When moral goodness is held to consist in resemblance to the model, moral rules dictating specific kinds of act will matter mainly because of the shape they can give to character: the primary task will be to become a person like the pattern person. His knowledge of what to do cannot be put into any set of explicit formulae, just as the know-how of the skilled craftsman or artist cannot be summed up verbally.[17] Consequently, to understand and to follow the model, sympathy and intuition are necessary—the one enabling us to grasp his hidden motives, the other showing us the rightness of his practice. Since the model person responds to the uniqueness of each individual with the uniquely right action, he is beyond rules; and an appeal to what he would think or do can therefore serve as support for the criticism or modification of a rule that has become rigid and lifeless. The pattern person represents the culmination of that emphasis on the personal which I have suggested is central to one aspect of our morality and to its articulation in the Intuitionist philosophy.[18] In a world where rapid change and easy social movement predominate, however, and where traditional moral teaching is no longer widely maintained,

[17] See J. A. Froude's comments in "Representative Men": "In life, as in art, and as in mechanics, the only profitable teaching is the teaching by example. Your mathematician, or your man of science, may discourse excellently on the steam-engine, yet he cannot make one. . . . The master workman in the engine room does not teach his apprentice the theory of expansion, or of atmospheric pressure; he guides his hand upon the turncock, he practices his eye upon the index, and *he leaves the science to follow when the practice has become mechanical.* So it is with everything which man learns to do; and yet for the art of arts, the trade of *life*, we content ourselves with teaching our children the catechism and the commandments" (*Short Studies on Great Subjects,* 1 [London, 1867; New York, n.d.], 471–72; first italics are mine).

[18] James Martineau pays particular attention to the pattern or model person and to the importance of the kind of influence such persons have. His sermon on "Christ the Divine Word," in *Hours of Thoughts on Sacred Things,* 2 (London, 1896), is especially relevant. Though he there emphasizes the person of Christ as pattern, he uses principles derived from his whole philosophy. See, for example, *The Seat of Authority in Religion,* pp. 53–55.

it is much less feasible to center morality on pattern persons. More stress falls necessarily on action in accordance with moral rules, and an impersonal principle which can be applied by some impersonal technique takes the place of the embodiment of the spirit of morality as the source of justifiable reform of the rules. The Utilitarian may make a passing bow in the direction of the personal influence of a great moral figure, but he is not basically very interested in him.

"To imagine a language," Ludwig Wittgenstein says, "is to imagine a form of life."[19] Moral attitudes and orientations of the sort I have outlined are inseparable from concepts, and these in turn from the words—"person," "act," "decision," "responsibility," "right," "wicked"—which we use to express them. To analyze the key concepts embodied in a language is therefore to work toward one kind of understanding of the form of life which is lived in terms of that language. What Bradley says of metaphysics—that it is "the finding of bad reasons for what we believe upon instinct"—may be true of all philosophy; but it is equally true, as he adds, that "to find these reasons is no less than instinct."[20] Our desire for understanding moves us naturally toward the sort of abstract perspicuity which philosophy can give, and is not fully satisfied until it has attained it. And, consequently, where material of the sort that a philosopher attempts to understand is present, we will find ourselves trying to grasp it in a philosophical manner. When we do so it is frequently, though not always, helpful to avail ourselves of categories and concepts which have already been developed in purely philosophical contexts. We need not attempt to reduce a literary work to a message or convert it into a proof in order to find philosophical classifications useful in describing and analyzing it. True enough, the use of such terms will relate the work to something outside the realm of literature; and this relation need not be considered of importance for the description of the work as literature, whatever its interest may be for the historian or the student of culture. But if the work portrays human life, it cannot but portray it as existing in some form or other; and, consequently, it must embody at least some of the

[19] Ludwig Wittgenstein, *Philosophical Investigations* (Oxford, 1953), p. 80, par. 19.

[20] F. H. Bradley, *Appearance and Reality* (Oxford, 1893), p. xii.

data from which moral philosophers start. A writer primarily concerned with politics, or with the surface manners of his time, or with thrilling or frightening or extraordinary happenings, may not tell us enough about his characters and their world for a determination of their moral outlook to be possible at any level beyond that of the commonplace. But many writers do give us enough to go beyond this point, either because of their selective focusing on relevant material or because of the total richness and complexity of the world they construct. To describe a work of this sort in philosophical terms is to point up something in the work, and something essential to its being the work it is. And if the work presents or reflects problems which have analogs among the conceptual difficulties of philosophy, it can only add a level to our understanding of what is in the work if we see the moral problems in the light of the conceptual ones. To say that in giving this kind of description of a literary work we must often go beyond the range of the writer's knowledge or conscious intention is to say only what holds of most literary criticism.[21]

In discussing the Intuitionist and the Utilitarian I have tried to show that each of them presents a picture of morality which simplifies the reality even when it claims only to clarify it, and which offers a justification of one morality in the name of the truth about morality as such. There may perhaps be some realm of abstraction in which we can have that complete moral neutrality which philosophers occasionally profess—after all, in some sense we all speak the same moral language—but the two schools of the nineteenth century were working on a different level. Their theories each articulate a definite and limited attitude toward life. And the fact that this is so makes their philosophical positions all the more relevant to literature. For it is not simply in presenting morally relevant aspects of human life that a writer gives us occasion for discussing his work in philosophical terms. There is to be considered in addition his general attitude toward life or what Wallace Stevens calls his "sense of the world"[22] as this is shown not only in his explicit statements but in his style and vocabulary, his selection of material, his handling of images and themes, as well. The writer does not stand aloof

[21] See Northrop Frye, *Anatomy of Criticism* (Princeton, 1957), p. 100.
[22] See Stevens's essay, "Effects of Analogy," in *The Necessary Angel* (London, 1960), esp. pp. 118 ff.

and neutral, presenting without addition or modification a report on some segment of the world. Like the philosopher, he presents the world as justifying a certain attitude or outlook; and this attitude, much more than the details of the contents of the work as such, will determine what philosophy, if any, is likely to provide a useful set of concepts for the discussion of the work.

Charlotte Yonge's *The Heir of Redclyffe* (1853) is a clear and simple example of the way in which a morality can be presented and endorsed in a novel with a minimum of explicit statement. The world she shows is that of the Intuitionist, a world of close-knit families living in a peaceful countryside. The problems with which her people cope are all personal; and they all arise from personal failings or weaknesses, and not from any complexity in the situations of the agents. The imitation of a pattern person is the source of such intellectual structure as the book possesses. Every major character is either a pattern or a follower; and the character and actions of each follower are shown to be deeply influenced by his pattern, for good or, as in the case of Laura and Philip, for evil. Central, of course, is the tormented Heir, Guy de Morville, whose life is one long battle between his higher and his lower self. He is a model for Charles and for Ben Robinson, both of whom improve strikingly as a result of his presence.[23] Amy is Charles's pupil as Laura was Philip's, and Philip has a follower—his "young man"—to match Charles.

[23] See ch. xxix, where Charles himself says to Guy, "You must not think I have not felt all you have done for me. You have made a new man of me." See also ch. xliv: " 'As if you wanted a hero model,' whispered Charlotte. . . . 'I've had one!,' returned Charles, also aside." For Ben, see ch. xxiii, where Guy's courage in the face of great danger is the inspiration. Guy attributes Ben's reform, noted by the clergyman, to the night's adventure. But the clergyman knows better: " 'Yes,' thought Mr. Ashford, 'such a night, under such a leader! The sight of so much courage based on that foundation is what may best touch and save that man.' " In ch. xxiv Charles contrasts Laura as Philip's pupil with Amy who is his. It is interesting that Miss Yonge, like George Eliot, slips in an occasional remark on the educational value of novels. See ch. xxxii, where Amy, discussing Laura's concealment of her love from Mamma, says: "You know he [Philip] never would let her read novels; and I do believe that was the reason she did not understand what it meant." This of course is in perfect keeping with the emphasis on models and patterns for moral teaching.

For these lesser figures the function of the pattern is as much to instruct the mind as to encourage the will, but for Guy himself there is no problem of knowledge. His difficulty is always depicted as being that of bringing himself to do what his better self tells him he ought. In the key scene in which he fights the temptation to yield to his fierce anger against Philip, he has no doubt that he ought to forgive him, but he finds it very hard. He repeats over and over the relevant supplicatory words from the Lord's Prayer: "Coldly and hardly were they spoken at first; again he pronounced them, again, again,—each time the tone was softer, each time they came more from the heart. At last, the remembrance of greater wrongs, and worse revilings, came upon him; his eyes filled with tears, the most subduing and healing of all thoughts—part of the great Example—became present to him; the foe was driven back" (ch. xvi). The concentration on problems like this, as well as the tone in which they are portrayed, make it plain where Miss Yonge's sympathies are: her own attitude, corresponding as it does to an Intuitionist morality, is perfectly suited to the only world she sees. It is in part this too easy harmony which makes her work so insipid.

Mrs. Gaskell shows us another Intuitionist conscience without qualms in *North and South* (1855), but she shows us at the same time a world full of problems for it. When Margaret hears that other people would think the lie she told to save her brother quite justifiable, she replies, "What other people may think of the rightness or wrongness is nothing in comparison to my own deep knowledge, my innate conviction that it is wrong" (ch. xlvi). But Margaret must come to terms with Darkshire and with Mr. Thornton, whose life and views incarnate the Utilitarianism of the industrial North. To his belief in the sufficiency of the cash nexus between man and man is opposed her insistence on a closer personal relationship, and it is in conjunction with the growth of his personal feelings for her that his morality undergoes a change.[24] Thornton, after investigating the reasons Higgins gave for wanting a job, "was convinced that all that Higgins had said was true. And then the conviction went in, as if by some spell, and touched the latent tenderness of his heart; the patience of the man, the simple generosity of the motive . . .

[24] For Mr. Thornton's opinions see ch. x and ch. xv. The relation between Thornton and Margaret may be compared, with roles reversed, to that between Felix Holt and Esther Lyon.

made him forget entirely the mere reasoning of justice, and overleap them by a diviner instinct" (ch. xxxix). Mrs. Gaskell sees a wider world than Miss Yonge; and her confidence in the older morality is more hardly won, and more interesting, as a result.

The novels of William Hale White show neither the untroubled vision of Miss Yonge nor the hopeful firmness of Mrs. Gaskell. He presents repeatedly a world in which the Intuitionist view is beginning to be irrelevant; and his hero, Mark Rutherford, might be described briefly as an Intuitionist whose moral vision is failing or gone. For the agent who has not yet developed moral insight there is nothing to do but to follow rules and maxims derived from the practice of those who have. The same will hold for the man who has had insight and lost it; but where the one may follow such rules with confidence, the other will always feel them to be inadequate and will never have the direct sense of the rightness of an act which once he had. "I have at my command," says Mark Rutherford, "any number of maxims, all of them good, but I am powerless to select the one which ought to be applied."[25] This is a constant theme in Hale White's novels.[26] It appears again, for example, in *Mark Rutherford's Deliverance* (1885), when Rutherford contemplates marrying the girl whom he originally rejected because of Miss Arbour's advice. "How true that counsel of Miss Arbour's was!," he muses, "and yet it had the defect of most counsel. It was but a principle; whether it suited this particular case was the one important point on which Miss Arbour was no authority" (ch. vii). Miss Arbour shows us the sort of confidence Rutherford lacks. "The voice of God hardly ever comes in thunder," she says, "we can lay down no law by which infallibly to recognise the messenger from God. But . . . when the moment comes it is perfectly easy for us to recognise him" (*Autobiography*, ch. v). The conflict between insight and rule appears again in *Clara*

---

[25] *The Autobiography of Mark Rutherford* (1881), ch. v. He continues: "A general principle, a fine saying, is nothing but a tool, and the wit of man is shown not in his possession of a well-furnished tool-chest but in the ability to pick out the proper instrument and use of it." Cf. Froude's use of the concept of the skilled craftsman, note 18 above.

[26] His essay on "principles" discusses the problem quite explicitly and ends with remarks on the importance of the incarnation of principles in a man. The essay is printed at the end of some editions of *The Deliverance*, e.g., that published by Jonathan Cape (London, 1929).

Hopgood (1896), where it is made explicit in the dialogue in which Madge refuses to "give up my instinct for the sake of a rule" while Clara replies that she cannot "profess to know, without the rule, what is right and what is not" (ch. v). And the balance of the tale does not force us to decide between the two.

Mr. Cardew, in *Catherine Furze* (1893) preaches a sermon in which he shows us one form of what Mark Rutherford wanted:

> . . . it is absolutely necessary that you should have one and one only supreme guide. To say nothing of eternal salvation, we must, in the conduct of life, shape our behavior by some one standard, or the result is chaos. We must have some one method or principle which is to settle beforehand how we are to do this or that, and the method or principle should be Christ. Leaving out of sight altogether His divinity, there is no temper, no manner so effectual, so happy as His for handling all human experience. Oh, what a privilege it is to meet with anybody who is controlled into unity, whose actions are all directed by one consistent force![27]

But Rutherford cannot accept the old form of life, and he will not accept the impersonal substitute that the Utilitarian rule offers.[28] In the end he finds some sort of resting place in helping a few people, in the personal relations finally attained with a wife, and in a temporary revision of traditional faith. It is the best he can do to reconstruct a world in which intuition can survive, and significantly enough it is the rejected part of his life, the coldly impersonal business office to which he goes daily

[27] *Catherine Furze*, ch. vi; and compare the comment in *The Revolution in Tanner's Lane* (1887), ch. ix, when Zachariah stifles a momentary doubt that arises from the callous treatment he gets when looking for a job. He is treated "as if he were not a person, an individual soul, but an atom of a mass to be swept out anywhere, into the gutter," and he wonders if God really looks after him. "But as yet his faith was unshaken and he repelled the doubt as a temptation of Satan. Blessed is the man who can assign promptly everything which is not in harmony with himself to a devil, and so get rid of it. The pitiful case is that of the distracted mortal who knows not what is the degree of authority which his thoughs and impulses possess; who is constantly bewildered by contrary messages, and has no evidence as to their authenticity."

[28] See the rejection of "philosophy" in *The Deliverance*, ch. vi. Rutherford insists on a deeper distinction between the higher and lower parts of our nature, and between right and wrong, than philosophy is capable of.

to do work he cannot think of as truly part of himself, that kills him.

If in the novels of Hale White and Mrs. Gaskell it is mainly changes in society that challenge the Intuitional morality, in George Eliot it is something different and something deeper. That her fundamental moral attitude is Intuitional is shown by many recurring features in her novels: the constant appeal to sympathy and insight, the great importance given to the influence of a morally superior person in awakening the moral life of another, the stressing of motives and feelings rather than actions, the insistence on the distinction between a true conscience and a mere awareness of what others will think, are chief among them.[29] Nor does she construct a social world in which such a morality faces new sorts of problems. But throughout her work there is a strong sense of the influence of factors beyond the control of the individual agent in determining his choices. Thus in one of the most carefully analyzed decisions of the many George Eliot shows us, Gwendolen's decision to marry Grandcourt, we almost directly see the determining forces at work; and they do not include some mysterious fiat of will working in entire independence of Gwendolen's character and her past inclinations, and able to check or change their tendencies. We do not need to rely on George Eliot's letters and essays to attribute to her some kind of deterministic belief:

[29] "They would think her conduct shameful; and shame was torture. That was poor little Hetty's conscience" (*Adam Bede*, ch. xxxi). It is Arthur's also: we are constantly reminded of his dependence on the favorable opinion of others. It is significant that both Hetty and Arthur, who upset the moral balance of the community, are without strong family roots. It may be noted also that Arthur is rather Utilitarian in his outlook. He believes that an evil can be balanced by a greater good, so that one's transgressions can all in principle be made up for (cf. ch. xxix). This is a view Adam explicitly disavows (ch. xviii); and at the very end Arthur himself sees his mistake, and admits of Adam that "there is a sort of wrong that can never be made up for." Like Adam he comes to disavow moral arithmetic and to realize that "feeling's a kind of knowledge" (cf. ch. lii).

Felix Holt's reflection as the mob sweeps him into Treby Park is a miniature rejection of Utilitarianism: "As he was pressed along with the multitude into Treby Park, his very movement seemed to him only an image of the day's fatalities, in which the multitudinous small wickednesses of small selfish ends, really undirected towards any larger result, had issued in widely-shared mischief that might yet be hideous" (ch. xxxiii). And as others have noted, if Holt is a radical, he is certainly not a Philosophic Radical.

it is a strong element in the sense of the world pervading her novels.[30] I have pointed out that Intuitionists strongly reject determinism on the grounds that it makes truly moral distinctions impossible, while the determinist replies that an interpretation of morality is quite possible on his view, and that he at least is not burdened with the difficult concept of a contra-causal freedom. The concept of freedom is of course quite crucial for a moral view, even for a determinist one, and it is in her attempt to work out a satisfactory portrayal of human freedom that George Eliot comes closest to dealing in her novels with the conceptual tension between an Intuitionist attitude toward morality and a determinist attitude toward the universe (unless it is a fatalistic view, alloting no place at all to human choice or decision or effort; and this, it hardly needs saying, is not at all George Eliot's version of determinism).

For the deterministic Utilitarian, freedom exists when a man is not prevented by anything outside his body or by any limits of bodily strength from doing what he wishes or would choose to do.[31] A man is free when he can do what he wants to do: is this George Eliot's view of freedom? If we are to judge by her characters who do as they please, the answer must be negative. *Daniel Deronda* (1876) is the novel in which freedom is closest to being George Eliot's theme; and in Gwendolen she gives us a brilliant portrayal of one whose whole aim in life is to do as she likes. Time after time George Eliot shows us that Gwendolen

[30] This is well brought out in the excellent discussion by George Levine, "Determinism and Responsibility in the Works of George Eliot," *PMLA* 77 (1962), 268–79. The only difficulty with the article is that it does not show any reason why we should take, as the philosopher who best articulates George Eliot's position, J. S. Mill rather than someone like F. H. Bradley who also includes the points of her view that Levine brings out. Bradley, I think, is closer in general attitude to George Eliot than Mill is; and there is consequently a closer correspondence in detail between his views and hers than between hers and Mill's.

[31] Bain thinks the controversy between free-will and determinism is largely a verbal one, and recommends dropping both terms. "I am a moral agent," he says, "when I act at the instigation of my own feelings, pleasurable or painful, and the contrary when I am overpowered by force. . . . We are not moral agents as regards the action of the heart, or the lungs, or the intestines. Every act that follows upon the prompting of a painful or pleasurable state, or the associations of one or other, is a voluntary act, and is all that is meant or can be meant by moral agency" (*The Emotions and the Will*, p. 564).

thinks she is free when she is living in this way. "My plan is to do what pleases me," she tells Rex, just after objecting to those who predict the actions of other people and saying boastfully, "I do what is unlikely" (ch. vii). She sees marriage with Grand-court as "the gate into a larger freedom" (ch. xiv), because it will enable her to do more fully what she chooses. Just before accepting him she thinks that she can refuse him; and "Why was she to deny herself the freedom of doing this which she would like to do?" Then immediately after accepting him she "gains a sense of freedom" (ch. xxvi) as he tells her, and she believes, that "You shall have whatever you like" (ch. xxvii). After marriage, however, she rapidly finds out her mistake: "in seven short weeks her husband had gained a mastery" which she could not resist (ch. xxxv). Her submission to him is contrasted strongly with Mirah's very different kind of submission. Deronda says of Mirah that she is "capable of submitting to anything in the form of duty," and Gwendolen feels strongly the sense that "her own submission was something different . . . was submission to a yoke drawn on her by an action she was ashamed of" (ch. xlv).

The alternative to this dreary collapse of "doing as you like" into a slavery brought on oneself is presented through Deronda. To understand it we must understand his problem, which is precisely the problem one might expect to confront a sympathetic and imaginative determinist who is not prepared to be a Util-itarian. "His early awakened sensibility and reflectiveness," George Eliot tells us, "had developed into a many-sided sym-pathy, which threatened to hinder any course of action" because he saw the human self in everyone and so could not really op-pose anyone. Virtuous himself, yet "he hated vices mildly," being unable to separate them from pitiful human lives. And, finally, "a too reflective and diffusive sympathy was in danger of paralyzing in him that indignation against wrong and that selectness of fellowship which are the conditions of moral force." It is this last point which is what the libertarian fears from the determinist. If Gwendolen shows us the purely selfish private will incapable of seeing any but its own ends, Daniel shows us a will so impartial and so impersonal that it is in danger of becoming, like the universe, incapable of seeking any ends or even of making any moral distinctions. What Deronda needed, we learn, was "an influence that would justify partiality, and make him what he longed to be, yet was unable to make himself—an organic part of social life" (ch. xxxii). Daniel's hope is that "the very best of human possibilities might befall him—the blending of a complete personal love in one current with a larger duty" (ch. l). And what solves his problem is, of course, his discovery that he is a Jew. Here Sir Leslie Stephen dryly remarks, "Deronda's mode of solving his problem is not generally applicable," a complaint echoed by Dr. Leavis.[32] But this misses the point. What we are to see in Deronda, and in his mother as well, is that to be free is to bind oneself voluntarily to duty, to a task or calling. Daniel's mother, like Gwendolen, neglected family duties; but unlike Gwendolen she surrendered herself to the stern demands of art and so became the singer and actress she felt she was born to be. Daniel gives himself to duties he finds are hereditary because he can treat them as duties that he in particular was born to fulfill. The principle is the same in each case: one finds one's duty when one finds one's identity, whatever it may be; and one is free insofar as one is able to love one's duty and live for its sake. For one is then doing what one most desires to do, while at the same time, since this desire is the desire of the higher or better self, one is not a slave to one's passions.[33]

It is an interesting coincidence that George Eliot's most sustained attempt to bring together in one coherent vision both her intuitional morality and her determinist sense of the world should have appeared in the same year as Bradley's attempt to overcome the nineteenth-century English controversy between the two schools in a synthesis of a Hegelian variety, and only

[32] Leslie Stephen, *George Eliot* (New York, 1902), p. 189. F. R. Leavis, *The Great Tradition* (New York, 1954), p. 107.

[33] One may think here of Spinoza's concept of the free man, and one does not entirely lose the connection with Spinoza when one thinks also of F. H. Bradley's Hegelian version of Freedom, tentatively suggested in *Ethical Studies*, ch. i. The whole essay is relevant; I quote a paragraph from the notes appended to it: " '*My* self,' we shall hear, 'is what is *mine;* and mine is what is *not* yours, or what does not belong to any one else. I am free when I assert my private will, the will peculiar to me.' Can this hold? Apart from any other objection, is it freedom? Suppose I am a glutton and a drunkard; in these vices I assert my private will; am I then free so far as a glutton and drunkard, or am I a slave—the slave of my appetites? The answer must be, 'The slave of his lusts is, *so* far, not a free man. The man is free who realizes his *true* self.' Then the whole question is, 'What is this true self, and can it be found apart from something like law?' Is there any 'perfect freedom' which does not mean 'service'?"

two years after Sidgwick's more painstaking attempt to reconcile the two schools. The concept of freedom which she tries to develop in the novel may in the end be as unsatisfactory philosophically as the hero is aesthetically. But the fact that she attempts to portray the sort of reality that would justify such a concept of freedom illustrates in a striking manner the way in which conceptual difficulties may operate in a literary medium, and gives us, as a result, an important example of one more way in which philosophical understanding may help in the understanding of a work of art.

X

ALAN DONAGAN

Victorian Philosophical Prose: J. S. Mill and F. H. Bradley

Philosophy is a more ancient form of prose literature than fiction. The classics of ancient Greek and Latin prose are works of history, of philosophy, of oratory. Even of prose written in English, Yvor Winters has contended that, when compared with writers of fiction, "the superiority in achievement to date lies with the historiographers."[1] Probably no literary critic would make such a claim on behalf of philosophy. Yet T. S. Eliot has described the prose style of F. H. Bradley as "for his purposes—and his purposes are more varied than is usually supposed—a perfect style."[2] Whatever its comparative rank among the varieties of prose literature, Victorian philosophical prose deserves more study than it has received.

No serious challenge has been offered to the conventional judgment that English prose was perfected in the classical age begun by Dryden, Temple, and Halifax, and continued by Swift, Addison, and Steele. Yet the chief philosopher contemporary with Dryden and Halifax was Locke, whose style Saintsbury justly deplored as "a disgusting style, bald, dull, plebian, giving indeed the author's meaning, but giving it ungraced with any due apparatus or ministry."[3] True, the way to the literary achievement of Dryden and his followers had been pioneered by the philosopher Hobbes; and in the fullness of the classical age,

From *The Art of Victorian Prose*, edited by George Levine and William Madden (New York City, N. Y.,) pp. 53–72. Copyright 1968 by Oxford University Press. Reprinted by permission of the author and the publisher.

[1] Yvor Winters, *The Functions of Criticism*, Denver, 1957, p. 50.

[2] T. S. Eliot, *Selected Essays*, 3d ed., London, 1951, p. 445.

[3] George Saintsbury, "English Prose Style," in *Miscellaneous Essays*, London, 1892, p. 13.

Berkeley wrote three philosophical masterpieces which as prose bear comparison with Addison's essays. Berkeley, indeed, was singled out by Saintsbury, who said of him that "he, again with Hume as a second, is as unlikely to be surpassed in philosophical style as Hume and Gibbon are unlikely to be surpassed in the style of history."[4] But Berkeley's prose, admirable as it is, breaks no new ground. From a literary point of view, he is less interesting than Swift; for nothing he had to say as a philosopher called for a prose different from that of his nonphilosophical contemporaries.

By the nineteenth century, philosophy could no longer be written in the prose of Berkeley. There were new things to say, and they could not be said in old ways. Why then did a critic as intelligent as Saintsbury, in 1876—the year in which Bradley published *Ethical Studies*—denounce the "antinomian" decadence of philosophical writing? "Philosophy," he scolded, ". . . has now turned stepmother, and turns out her nurselings to wander in 'thorniest queaches' of terminology and jargon, instead of the ordered gardens wherein Plato and Berkeley walked."[5] Nor did the decade that followed change his opinion: "take almost any living philosopher," he complained in 1885, "and compare him with Berkeley, with Hume, or even with Mill, and the difference is obvious at once."[6]

Saintsbury's strength as a critic is technical. Nobody has better analyzed how Dryden and his successors, paying heed to the genius of colloquial English, reformed the long sentence by expelling imitations of Latin syntax for which an uninflected language is unfit; how they learned to balance and proportion their sentences, and to dispense with rhetorical ornament.[7] His weakness is that his theory is only technical. His literary criticism is criticism of style, and he was capable of defining style as "the choice and arrangement of language with only a subordinate regard to the meaning to be conveyed."[8] Hence he considered "the art of rhythmical arrangement" to be "undoubtedly the principal thing in prose," with "simplicity of

4 Ibid., p. 15.

5 "Modern English Prose" [1876], in *Miscellaneous Essays*, p. 94.

6 "English Prose Style," *Miscellaneous Essays*, p. 24. That this essay first appeared in 1885 is recorded in the Preface, p. x.

7 *Miscellaneous Essays*, pp. 10–18, 27–29.

8 Ibid., p. 84.

language, and directness of expression in the shorter clause and phrase" as the two most important of its "subsidiary arts."[9]

Saintsbury's practice was better than his theory. Many of his critical perceptions were sound. The classical prose he admired was indeed good, and the sins he denounced in Victorian prose —the ugly rhythms of Herbert Spencer, the gaudy epithets of J. R. Green, and the tub-thumping of the journalists—were indeed sins. But it does not follow that the principles he extracted from his perceptions were true. A theory is established by seeking and failing to find unfavorable evidence, not by accumulating evidence that is favorable. Saintsbury's theory was destroyed by the deluge of *belles lettres* at the close of the century, which demonstrated that all his criteria for rhythm and diction could be satisfied by work that was inane, pretentious, and corrupt.

Literary criticism cannot have "only a subordinate regard" to the meaning conveyed. Saintsbury's dictum might even be reversed, and style defined as the choice and arrangement of words having regard *solely* to the meaning to be conveyed. His own examples may be turned against him. Thus, his specimens of bungled rhythm and badly articulated syntax turn out to convey thoughts unformed or ill-formed, and emotions only partly clear.[10] Style, in a word, is expression. Every act of literary composition has its aesthetic side, the writer's effort to grasp something clearly, which is inseparable from his effort to make clear his emotions about it.

The inseparability of the expression of thought from the expression of emotion, which is presupposed by all serious criticism, is seldom fully recognized or clearly understood. Failing to discern the crucial difference between formulating a thought and repeating, perhaps in other words, a thought already formulated, some critics have written as though, even to the man who first arrives at it, a thought can exist before its expression. On the contrary, the stages through which the expression of a thought passes, from clumsy imitation to exact statement, are stages through which the thought itself passes. Finding better words is the same thing as refining a thought. Still other critics have written as though, having arrived at a thought about a certain subject, there is a further process of having emotions

[9] Ibid., p. 38.
[10] Cf. *Miscellaneous Essays*, pp. 17–18, 36–37.

about it. They have failed to perceive that a man's emotions about a thing depend on his awareness of it, and of how it is related to other things, himself among them. The way to change his emotions about it is to bring him to think differently of it.

Hence the theory of art as the expression of emotion does not imply that critics can attend to the emotion expressed by a work of art to the neglect of its thought: emotion and thought can only be studied together. Rather, it defines the special nature of a critic's interest in the *thought* a work embodies. He is interested in that thought only as it has to do with the expression of emotion. Genuine art is exploratory. In it, the artist simultaneously becomes aware of something he was unclear about before, and aware of his emotions about it. Bad art is the counterfeit, often not wholly conscious, of genuine art. In it, the artist only pretends to explore; and what he offers is a faked report, designed to present himself as thinking and feeling in some approved way. Its betraying symptom is *cliché*.[11]

This aesthetic theory, or something like it, I take to be embodied in the best work of critics both in the Romantic tradition (like Coleridge and Matthew Arnold) and in the partial post-Romantic reaction from it (like T. S. Eliot and F. R. Leavis). If it should be true, then it is possible to separate what is true from what is false in a deeply interesting antithesis once proposed by T. S. Eliot.

> I should say [Eliot wrote] that in one's prose reflections one may be legitimately occupied with ideals, whereas in the writing of verse one can only deal with actuality. Why, I would ask, is most religious verse so bad; and why does so little religious verse reach the highest levels of poetry? Largely, I think, because of a pious insincerity.[12]

Eliot's diagnosis of what ails most religious verse was definitive, but he mistook the nature of pious insincerity. It does not consist in being occupied with ideals, but in pretending to ideals you do not really have, or in pretending that your ideals are realities although you do not believe they are. Pious insincerity of these kinds is as fatal in prose as in verse. It is as common

---

[11] My debt here to Benedetto Croce, *Aesthetic*, trans. Douglas Ainslie, 2d ed., London, 1922, and to R. G. Collingwood, *The Principles of Art*, Oxford, 1938, will be evident.

[12] *After Strange Gods*, New York, 1933, p. 27.

in religious prose as in religious verse, and it is far from un-
common in philosophy.

Consider the following passage, fortunately uncharacteristic,
from Bertrand Russell, one of the first philosophers of our time.

> Brief and powerless is Man's life; on him and all his race the
> slow, sure doom falls pitiless and dark. Blind to good and evil,
> reckless of destruction, omnipotent matter rolls on its relent-
> less way; for Man, condemned today to lose his dearest, to-
> morrow himself to pass through the gate of darkness, it remains
> only to cherish, ere yet the blow falls, the lofty thoughts that
> ennoble his little day; disdaining the coward terrors of the slave
> of Fate, to worship at the shrine his own hands have built;
> undismayed by the empire of chance, to preserve a mind free
> from the wanton tyranny that rules his outward life; proudly
> defiant of the irresistible forces that tolerate, for a moment,
> his knowledge and his condemnation, to sustain alone, a weary
> but unyielding Atlas, the world that his own ideals have fash-
> ioned despite the trampling march of unconscious power.[13]

This declamation is philosophically puzzling, because Russell appears in it to embrace an epiphenomenalism that is neither novel
nor plausible. How, in his postulated "empire of chance," of
"omnipotent matter," could the free minds, whose "ideals" and
"lofty thoughts" he celebrates, exist at all? From a literary point
of view, it is worse than puzzling. It is piously insincere: "an
indulgence," as F. R. Leavis described it, "in the dramatization
of one's nobly suffering self."[14] Nor is it characteristic of Russell. The following passage, which expresses his usual attitude,
is also better prose:

> In religion, and in every deeply serious view of the world and
> of human destiny, there is an element of submission, a realization
> of the limits of human power, which is somewhat lacking in the
> modern world, with its quick material successes and its insolent
> belief in the boundless possibilities of progress. "He that loveth
> his life shall lose it"; and there is danger lest, through a too con-
> fident love of life, life itself should lose much of what gives it

[13] The concluding paragraph of Bertrand Russell's "A Free Man's
Worship," in *Mysticism and Logic*, London, 1917, 46–57. Russell records
that it was "written in 1902," and that it "appeared originally . . . in the
New Quarterly, November 1907" (ibid., p. v).

[14] F. R. Leavis, "Tragedy and the 'Medium': A Note on Mr. Santayana's 'Tragic Philosophy,'" *Scrutiny* 12 (1943–44); reprinted in F. R.
Leavis, *The Common Pursuit*, London, 1952.

its highest worth . The submission which religion inculcates in action is essentially the same as that which science teaches in thought; and the ethical neutrality by which its victories have been achieved is the outcome of that submission.[15]

There is not a particle of defiance here; yet here Russell's thought is genuinely courageous.

Suppose an objector were to make the following retort. "Your criticism is as arbitrary as it is unmethodical. Of the two passages you quote from Russell you praise the latter as expressive, and decry the former as insincere, faked, and attitudinizing. But your saying these things does not make them so. How could you show me to be wrong if I were to declare that the former is deeply moving, hard-headed, and nobly written, and the latter timid, commonplace, and flat?

It would be an easy matter to change ground, and appeal to Saintsbury's technical criteria. The passage from "A Free Man's Worship" might be condemned, as Saintsbury condemned certain passages in Ruskin, for too closely approaching the rhythm of verse.[16] It contains no fewer than five complete heroic verses:

> "The slow sure doom falls pitiless and dark"
> "For Man, condemned today to lose his dearest"
> "The coward terrors of the slave of Fate"
> "Free from the wanton tyranny that rules
> His outward life; proudly defiant of . . ."

Yet this but illustrates an observation already made, that the technical faults analyzed by Saintsbury derive from a deeper nontechnical disorder. They are symptoms, not the disease.

If literary criticism is at bottom about success or failure in expression, then no serious critical dispute can be settled by formal demonstration from agreed premises. This fact is sometimes advanced to show that critical differences are matters of taste, concerning which reason can pronounce no verdict. But that does not follow. Not all rational disputes are about what can be formally demonstrated. Literary criticism does not presuppose that all competent judges share the same ultimate premises, but only that they have had the universal experience of try-

[15] *Mysticism and Logic*, p. 31. The quotation is from the essay "Mysticism and Logic," which, Russell records, "appeared in the *Hibbert Journal* for July 1914" (ibid., p. v).

[16] *Miscellaneous Essays*, p. 36.

ing to express what they feel, and have been aware sometimes that they succeeded and sometimes that they failed. Critical judgments are the fruit neither of demonstration nor logical intuition. They are fallible, but we are reasonably confident that many of them are trustworthy. They can be refined by analysis, and corrected or confirmed by comparing them with judgments of similar successes and failures.

Just as a man learns to understand what others say in the course of learning to speak, so he learns to judge others' successes or failures of expression in the course of learning to judge his own attempts at it. It is impossible to separate either process from the other. Both rest, at bottom, on the same foundation: the comparison of cases that are doubtful with others that are less doubtful. Although questions about the relevance and adequacy of such comparisons can sometimes be settled by analyzing the passages compared, analysis in itself cannot settle critical questions. It clarifies what is to be judged; but it would be pointless if the critic had not the power to judge what his analysis has clarified. T. S. Eliot was, I think, right when he declared that "comparison and analysis . . . are the chief tools of the critic"; and right too, when he added: "They are not used with conspicuous success by many contemporary writers. You must know what to compare and what to analyse."[17]

In reply to the imaginary objector to my harsh judgment of Russell's "A Free Man's Worship," I can say no more than this. That there are those whom its rhetoric may move need not be questioned; whether they are deeply moved by it depends in part on how serious its philosophy is (I do not think it is serious), and in greater part, on what, if anything, it expresses. That the passage is "nobly written," all too nobly written, was part of my reason for saying that it is not expression, but counterfeit. Further comparisons are unnecessary, because every reader can provide them for himself.

II

The work of John Stuart Mill (1806–1873) must occupy a central place in any study of Victorian philosophical prose.

[17] "The Function of Criticism" (1923) in *Selected Essays*, pp. 32–33. I have examined the philosophical questions to which this conception of criticism gives rise in my *The Later Philosophy of R. G. Collingwood*, Oxford, 1962, ch. 5.

From the publication of *A System of Logic* (1843) until that of his posthumous *Three Essays on Religion* (1874), his philosophical writings were generally received as the most important appearing in England. And although in the sixty years after his death it was the academic fashion to scorn him, even in writings of that period by philosophers hostile to him, it is common "to find in the Index the acknowledgement which the Preface withholds."[18] At no time did Mill lose his hold on the educated middle class; and he was studied by the academic philosophers he would most have desired as readers: by William James at Harvard (who dedicated *Pragmatism* to his memory); by Henry Sidgwick, Venn and W. E. Johnson at Cambridge; and, on the Continent, by Brentano and his school. As an academic classic in philosophy his position is now unassailable.

As we have seen, Saintsbury contrasted Mill's prose with that of the late Victorian philosophers he denounced, recognizing it as belonging to the classical tradition of Berkeley and Hume: and indeed it has many of the classical virtues. However, I suspect that the passages in Mill's philosophical writings that are remembered most vividly are polemical; and, for all their formal propriety, Mill's polemics betray an influence that is not at all classical. Here he is on Professor Adam Sedgwick's argument that ultilitarianism is impossible as an ethical theory, because, in most situations, an agent has no time to make utilitarian calculations as he acts.

> Mr. Sedgwick is a master of the stock phrases of those who know nothing of the principle of utility but the name. To act upon rules of conduct, of which utility is recognized as the basis, he calls "waiting for the calculations of utility"—a thing, according to him, in itself immoral, since "to hesitate is to rebel." On the same principle, navigating by rule instead of by instinct, might be called waiting for the calculations of astronomy. There seems no absolute necessity for putting off the calculations until the ship is in the middle of the South Sea. Because a sailor has not verified all the computations in the Nautical Almanac, does he therefore "hesitate" to use it?[19]

[18] Reginald Jackson, *An Examination of the Deductive Logic of John Stuart Mill*, Oxford, 1941, p. v.

[19] "Professor Sedgwick's Discourse on the Studies of the University of Cambridge," in *Dissertations and Discussions*, 2 vols., London, 1859, 1: 146–47.

ALAN DONAGAN

It is evident from this that Mill had studied Macaulay's polemical use of concrete examples, although he avoids Macaulay's "hard, metallic movement" of which Matthew Arnold complained.[20] Here is Macaulay, in controversy with Bentham,

> Mr. Bentham seems to imagine that we have said something implying an opinion favourable to despotism. . . . Despotism is bad; but it is scarcely anywhere as bad as Mr. Mill says that it is everywhere. This we are sure Mr. Bentham will allow. If a man were to say that five hundred thousand people die every year in London of dram-drinking, he would not assert a proposition more monstrously false than Mr. Mill's. Would it be just to charge us with defending intoxication because we might say that such a man was grossly in the wrong?[21]

Yet despite the similarity of these passages in structure and polemical method, the difference they exhibit between Macaulay's and Mill's style of thought is striking. It is not merely in the contrast between "he would not assert a proposition more monstrously false than . . ." and "there seems no absolute necessity for putting off the cauculations until . . ."; for Macaulay can be sarcastic, and Mill positive. It is that Mill, whose opinion of Sedgewick's *Discourse* was no higher than Macaulay's of Mill's father's *Essay on Government*, entered into Sedgwick's thought in order to expose it; and so presented the considerations that demolish it, that the reader has the sense of producing them himself. Macaulay overwhelms, but Mill converts.

In polemical writing the object primarily contemplated is what your adversary has said, and the emotions expressed are such as go with exposing it as error. Even when done as well as Macaulay and Mill did it, sheerly polemical writing can no more be the highest kind of political or philosophical writing than can sheer satire be the highest kind of poetry. Philosophers ought certainly to express the emotions with which they remove the rubbish that lies in the road to knowledge; but we look to philosophy for more than that.

[20] Matthew Arnold, *Friendship's Garland*, 2d ed., London, 1897, p. 71. and with Mill's father, James Mill.

[21] "Westminster Reviewer's Defense of Mill" (June 1829), from *The Works of Lord Macaulay*, Albany ed., London, 1898, 7: 349. For J. S. Mill's opinion of this controversy see J. S. Mill, *Autobiography*, World's Classics ed., London, 1924, pp. 133–36.

Mill's philosophical work was essentially critical. He constructed a system of logic, but not of metaphysics. In philosophical theology, his results have been fairly described by Fr. F. C. Copleston as "a rational scepticism, which is more than sheer agnosticism, but less than firm assent."[22] Even his theory of the external world as consisting of "permanent possibilities of sensation" was developed in the course of an "examination" of the philosophy of Sir William Hamilton. Yet Mill's best critical writing is beyond polemics. In his essays on Bentham and Coleridge, in his *Autobiography*, and in less sustained passages in almost all his later philosophical writings, his purpose in criticizing other philosophers was less to disprove them, than by determining their shortcomings to define an approach by which philosophy may hope to discover truth. In fulfilling that purpose, as he largely did, he opened new possibilities for English prose.

The following well-known passage from the essay on Bentham points directly to the nature of Mill's achievement.

> Bentham failed in deriving light from other minds. His writings contain few traces of the accurate knowledge of any schools of thinking but his own; and many proofs of his entire conviction that they could teach him nothing worth knowing. For some of the most illustrious of previous thinkers, his contempt was unmeasured. In almost the only passage of the "Deontology" which . . . may be known to be Bentham's, Socrates, and Plato are spoken of in terms distressing to his greatest admirers; and the incapacity to appreciate such men, is a fact perfectly in unison with the general habits of Bentham's mind. He has a phrase, expressive of the view he took of all moral speculations to which his method has not been applied, or (which he considered the same thing) not founded on a recognition of utility as the moral standard; this phrase was "vague generalities." Whatever presented itself to him in such a shape, he dismissed as unworthy of notice, or dwelt upon only to denounce as absurd. He did not heed, or rather the nature of his mind prevented it from occurring to him, that these generalities contained the whole unanalysed experience of the human race.[23]

Although external marks betraying the nineteenth century can be removed, like the use of the word "thinkers" for what Berke-

---

[22] F. C. Copleston, *A History of Philosophy*, London, 1966, 8: 90.
[23] *Dissertations and Discussions*, 1: 350–51.

ley would have called "philosophers," this passage cannot be rewritten in Berkeley's style. To Berkeley, as to all the classical English prose-writers, the fundamental philosophical question to be asked of any opinion is: what reasons are there for accepting or rejecting it? His style is lucid and pure because it has but one function: to convey to the reader's intellect an intelligible object. W. B. Yeats once observed of Berkeley, that "though he could not describe mystery—his age had no fitting language—his suave glittering sentences suggest it."[24] In that respect Berkeley outdid not only Addison, but Mill as well. What Mill was aware of was not a mystery, but an intelligibility in things that is not directly intelligible to every mind.

If you concede that much of the experience of the human race is unanalyzed, and that no human mind is well-fitted to analyze all of it, when a pronouncement by a thinker of alien approach or tradition seems absurd to you, you cannot escape asking whether it seems absurd because it is so, or because it treats of something not directly intelligible to you. It may, indeed, be mere confusion or insolent bluff. But if it is not? Mill suggested—he was not, of course, the first to do so—that by carefully considering such apparent absurdities, you may come indirectly to recognize and understand things in human experience that are not directly intelligible to you. A philosophical method that in part studies its objects by studying what others have made of them calls for a style more complex than the classical: one that is less direct, and, in its treatment of others' thoughts, more sensitive.

Mill's most extended study of a thinker in an alien tradition is his essay on Coleridge. Unfortunately, specimens of philosophical analysis from it that would not be too short to exhibit Mill's style are too long to quote. Its spirit, however, is shown in the following appraisal of the "Germano-Coleridgean" school.

> Every reaction in opinion, of course, brings into view that portion of the truth which was overlooked before. . . . This is the easy merit of all Tory and Royalist writers. But the peculiarity of the Germano-Coleridgean school is, that they saw beyond the immediate controversy, to the fundamental prin-

[24] W. B. Yeats's introduction to *Bishop Berkeley*, by T. M. Hone and M. M. Rossi. I owe both quotation and reference to Bonamy Dobrée, "Berkeley as a Man of Letters" in *Hermathena* 82 (1953): 59.

ciples involved in all such controversies. They were the first (except a solitary thinker here and there) who inquired with any comprehensiveness or depth, into the inductive laws of the existence and growth of human society. They were the first to bring prominently forward the three requisites which we have enumerated, as essential principles of all permanent forms of social existence; as principles, we say, and not as mere accidental advantages inherent in the particular policy or religion which the writer happened to patronize. . . . They thus produced, not a piece of party advocacy, but a philosophy of society, in the only form in which it is yet possible, that of a philosophy of history. . . .[25]

Unfortunately, Mill did not perceive how much of his Benthamite inheritance his enlarged philosophical vision required him to renounce; and the greatest of his nineteenth-century adversaries, F. H. Bradley (1846–1924), gained his most enduring victories over him by pointing out what he had overlooked.

III

Not a little misunderstanding of what were the Benthamite errors that Mill failed to jettison can be laid at the door of T. S. Eliot's brilliant essay on Bradley.

Bradley did not [Eliot wrote] attempt to destroy Mill's logic. Anyone who reads his own *Principles* will see that his force is directed not against Mill's logic as a whole but only against certain limitations, imperfections and abuses. He left the structure of Mill's logic standing, and never meant to do anything else. On the other hand, the *Ethical Studies* are not merely a demolition of the Utilitarian theory of conduct but an attack upon the whole Utilitarian mind. For Utilitarianism was, as every reader of Arnold knows, a great temple in Philistia. . . . And this is the social basis of Bradley's distinction . . . : he replaced a philosophy which was crude and raw and provincial by one which was, in comparison, catholic, civilized, and universal.[26]

That the founder of Utilitarianism was a Philistine, and that Utilitarianism has numbered many a Philistine among its adherents, may be granted; but it does not follow that "the whole Utilitarian mind" was Philistine. Mill and Henry Sidgwick were

[25] *Dissertations and Discussions*, 1: 425.
[26] "Francis Herbert Bradley," in *Selected Essays*, p. 448.

Utilitarians, as well as Bentham and Frederic Harrison. If Utilitarians provided themselves with a temple in Philistia, so also did Roman Catholics and members of the Church Established.

Neither Mill, nor Henry Sidgwick, his most distinguished successor, was able to make Utilitarianism either theoretically satisfactory, or inoffensive to the "vulgar moral consciousness," which they respected at least as much as Bradley did. That Bradley, writing fifteen years later, should have made telling objections to Mill's *Utilitarianism* (1861) should therefore surprise nobody. Bradley's criticism of Sidgwick,[27] which exposes the inadequacy of Sidgwick's "suppression" of egoism, throws a harsh light on Bradley's own discussion of selfishness and self-sacrifice. Few idealists today would confidently maintain that as an ethical theorist Bradley bettered Sidgwick. In his recent Gifford Lectures, the most distinguished of contemporary American idealists endorsed C. D. Broad's judgement that Sidgwick's *Methods of Ethics* is "on the whole the best treatise on moral theory that has ever been written," and, in an extended discussion of it, found no occasion even to mention Bradley's criticism.[28]

Bradley advanced as "in the main . . . satisfactory," and as decidedly improving on the views of Mill and Kant, the moral theory of "my station and its duties." He never wearied in proclaiming the consonance of that theory with the ordinary moral consciousness: sometimes, as in the following passage, in a style he acknowledged to be "heated."[29]

> If the popularizing of superficial views inclines [the non-theoretical person] to bitterness, he comforts himself when he sees that they live in the head, and but little, if at all, in the heart and life; that still at the push the doctrinaire and the quacksalver go to the wall, and that even that too is as it ought to be. He sees the true account of the state (which holds it to be neither mere force nor convention, but the moral organism, the real identity of might and right) unknown or "refuted," laughed at and despised, but he sees the state every day in its practice refute every other doctrine, and do with the moral approval of all what the explicit theory of scarcely one will

27 F. H. Bradley, *Ethical Studies*, 2d ed., Oxford, 1927, pp. 126–28; *Collected Essays*, Oxford, 1935, 1: 71–132.

28 Brand Blanshard, *Reason and Goodness*, London, 1961, p. 90.

29 *Ethical Studies*, p. 202.

justify. He sees instincts are better and stronger than so-called "principles." He sees in the hour of need what are called "rights" laughed at, "freedom," the liberty to do what one pleases, trampled on, the claims of the individual trodden under foot, and theories burst like cobwebs. And he sees, as of old, the heart of a nation rise high and beat in the breast of each one of her citizens, till her safety and honour are dearer to each than life, till to those who live her shame and sorrow, if such is allotted, outweigh their loss, and death seems a little thing to those who go for her to their common and nameless grave.[30]

These sentiments were common enough in the German Empire after the Franco-Prussian War of 1870; and later in the century were to become still commoner. Unquestionably, states in time of war do, with the approval of large majorities, what the explicit theory of scarcely one will justify; but nobody in England before Bradley thought to make a moral theory out of it.

By Saintsbury's formal standards, the passage is magnificent as literature, except perhaps for its last sentence, the iambic-anapaestic rhythm of which is dangerously close to verse. Here again, a formal fault may be traced to a corruption of expression. I believe I will not be alone in finding a difference between the staccato—

He sees in the hour of need what are called "rights" laughed at, "freedom," the liberty to do what one pleases, trampled on, the claims of the individual trodden under foot, and theories burst like cobwebs—

and the final incantation, moving from ". . . he sees, as of old, the heart of a nation rise high," to its affecting climax. That the former is genuinely felt it is impossible to doubt, however little one may applaud it; but the latter is unashamed, and probably unconscious, pulpit oratory. To try, and fail, to express what few artists have ever expressed is no disgrace. But Bradley allowed his failure to stand, and it infects the whole passage. He offered to express the thought of intellectual scruples being overcome by a higher devotion. In failing imaginatively to realize that devotion, he betrayed his hatred of the scruples themselves: hatred in search of a justification.

How could Eliot have failed to discover the significance of such passages? They are not rare in *Ethical Studies*, although,

[30] *Ethical Studies*, p. 184.

writing in 1927, Eliot may not have known of things in Bradley's occasional papers even more disturbing: his crude pseudo-
Darwinism in "Some Remarks on Punishment,"[31] or his defense of "violence, and even extermination" now and then—
for the "good of mankind," of course—in "Individualism and
National Self-Sacrifice."[32] Eliot's moral obtuseness in matters
political goes some way to explain it: as an admirer of Charles
Maurras he may even have found Bradley tame. But there is
another reason. Eliot correctly perceived in *Ethical Studies* the
influence of the urbane and ironical style of Matthew Arnold's
Culture and Anarchy and *Friendship's Garland*. The supreme
specimen, quoted at length by Eliot, is the criticism of *Literature
and Dogma* in the Concluding Remarks. Eliot's contrast between the "crude and raw and provincial" Utilitarians and the
"in comparison, catholic, civilized, and universal" Bradley, rests
on a delusion to which critics with a horror of provinciality are
subject: the delusion that to be nonprovincial is to be civilized.
Mill and Sidgwick were, in their writings, stiff, earnest, and
upright. They could be witty, although in a manner intellectual
rather than urbane. These characteristics, no doubt, are limitations; but they are compatible with being catholic and civilized.
To be willing to write as Bradley sometimes wrote is not.

IV

It is not impossible that Bradley himself became aware of the
flaws, both philosophical and literary, in *Ethical Studies*. Desir-
ing to rewrite it, he withheld his consent to its reprinting; and in
the preface to the posthumous second edition there is said to
be "reason to believe that, had he been able to carry out his
intention of re-writing the book, much would have been softened or omitted."[33] Bradley's acknowledged pre-eminence as a
philosophical stylist, however, does not rest on his ethical
writings. Nor, admirable though it is, does it lie in his mastery
of Arnoldian irony.

The ordinary reader of Bradley's major works, *The Principles
of Logic* (1882) and *Appearance and Reality* (1893) probably
carries away an impression recorded by his best recent critic,

[31] Reprinted in *Collected Essays*, Oxford, 1935, 1: 149–64.

[32] Reprinted in *Collected Essays*, 1: 165–76. The passage in which the
quoted phrases occur is on p. 175.

[33] *Ethical Studies*, 2d ed., Oxford, 1927, p. vi.

Professor Richard Wollheim, of a "heavy, luxuriant growth of rhetoric and dialectic that is usually allowed to swell and sprawl across the pages often enough obscuring the true lines of the discussion."[34] But Bradley's "rhetoric and dialectic" are vigorously alive, and in *Appearance and Reality* their luxuriance is pruned. The following brief specimen, on the error of Cartesian dualism, gives their flavor:

> The soul and its organism are each a phenomenal series. Each, to speak in general, is implicated in the changes of the other. Their supposed independence is therefore imaginary, and to overcome it by invoking a faculty such as Will—is the effort to heal a delusion by means of a fiction.[35]

This is a little baroque for today's *Bauhaus* taste; but it perfectly expresses Bradley's passionate absorption in his thought. Thinking ought to be a passion in philosophers; and for those in whom it is, Bradley's mature prose will always be worth studying.

It must not be forgotten that, in Berkeley, the eighteenth century produced an unsurpassed rhetorician and dilectician; or that, unlike Mill at his best, Bradley in his treatment of his adversaries reverted to the methods of the eighteenth century. Yet as a writer, Bradley is more than a Victorian Berkeley. To identify his peculiar genius, we must examine another aspect of his relation to Mill.

In his *System of Logic*, Mill contrived to analyze the methodology of nineteenth-century science in terms of traditional British empiricism. Nothing so comprehensive has been done since; and his methodological analyses are still of value. Perhaps that is what Eliot meant when he said that "Bradley left the structure of Mill's logic standing, and never meant to do anything else." Yet it is absurd to say that Bradley's attack on Mill's logic is directed only against "certain limitations, imperfections, and abuses." Adopting Eliot's metaphor, it would be more accurate to say that Bradley left the wings and extensive outbuildings of Mill's logic standing, but destroyed its central block: its theory of terms and propositions.

Traditional empiricism had great difficulty in acknowledging the existence of anything except what Hume called "percep-

[34] Richard Wollheim, *F. H. Bradley*, Penguin Books, Harmondsworth, 1959, p. 110.

[35] F. H. Bradley, *Appearance and Reality*, 2d ed. corr., Oxford, 1946, p. 296.

tions" and Mill "feelings" or "phenomena" or "states of consciousness." In his *System of Logic*, Mill recognized only two kinds of nameable thing besides states of consciousness: substances and attributes. Following the Cartesian tradition, he acknowledged two kinds of substances—minds, which experience states of consciousness; and bodies, the unsentient causes that excite certain of those states. "But," he added, "of the nature of either body or mind, further than the feelings which the former excites, which the latter experiences, we do not, according to the best existing doctrine, know anything."[36] As for attributes, he declared that "if we . . . cannot know, anything of bodies but the sensations which they excite in us or in others, those sensations must be all that we can, at bottom, mean by their attributes."[37] In sum, except for something we know not what that causes states of consciousness, and something we know not what that experiences them, we cannot even think of anything but states of consciousness. A corollary of this doctrine is that philosophical studies like logic and epistemology are fundamentally branches of traditional psychology.

In *The Principles of Logic* (1883), a year before Frege in his *Grundlagen der Arithmetik* attacked psychologism in mathematical theory, Bradley demolished this impossible but tenacious theory.

> In England [he declared] . . . we have lived too long in the psychological attitude. We take it for granted and as a matter of course that, like sensations and emotions, ideas are phenomena. And, considering these phenomena as psychical facts, we have tried (with what success I will not ask) to distinguish between ideas and sensations. But, intent on this, we have as good as forgotten the way in which logic uses ideas. We have not seen that in judgment no fact ever *is* just that which it *means*, or can mean what it is; and we have not learnt that, whenever we have truth or falsehood, it is the signification we use, and not the existence. We never assert the fact in our heads, but something else which that fact stands for.[38]

This is less an argument than a reminder; and it is conclusive. The essential thing in any mental act is what Brentano called its

[36] J. S. Mill, *A System of Logic*, 5th ed., London, 1862, 1: 69.

[37] Ibid.

[38] F. H. Bradley, *The Principles of Logic*, 2d ed. corr., Oxford, 1928, 1: 2.

"intentionality": its reference to an object, not necessarily a real one.[39] No feeling, taken in itself, has intentionality, or means anything. Its meaning, if it has one, is conferred on it. A philosophical theory of mind is therefore a theory, not of psychical facts like Mill's "states of consciousness," but of the meanings conferred on them.

In the empiricist tradition, the fundamental relation that is believed to hold between a word and what it refers to is like that of a label to what it labels. This is not an implausible view of the relation between a proper name, like "John Stuart Mill" or "London," and whatever it names. But, as the empiricists themselves recognized, most words are not proper names. The word "man" does not stand for some individual man, or for anything individual at all, but rather for certain attributes or properties (being a rational animal, perhaps) that all men by nature exemplify. In philosophical jargon, such attributes or properties are *universal:* they can be exemplified by many individuals, but are not themselves individuals.

The precise status of universals is still a matter of contention. One thing, however, it cannot be. Universals cannot be individuals. Yet Mill's doctrine that certain sensations "must be all that we can, at bottom, mean" when we refer to the attributes of bodies, implies that attributes, which are universals, are individuals; for sensations are individual occurrences. It is remarkable that Mill did not see this, because in his theory of denotation and connotation he clearly distinguished proper names from "connotative" or attributive terms.

His failure to see it was disastrous. It led him to hold that all attributes are "grounded" in individual states of consciousness, and that what any proposition ultimately means is that certain individual states of consciousness are "associated" with certain others. This result, as Bradley pointed out, is bankruptcy.

> The ideas which are recalled according to [the] laws [of association] are particular existences. Individual atoms are the units of association. And I should maintain, on the contrary, that in all reproduction what operates everywhere is a common identity. No particular ideas are ever associated or ever could be. What is associated is and must be always universal.[40]

[39] Franz Brentano, *Psychologie vom empirischen Standpunkt,* Leipzig, 1874, 1: Book 2, Ch. 1.

[40] *The Principles of Logic,* 1: 304.

When I say that all men are mortal, I do not mean that the "individual atoms," Socrates, Plato, and the rest are mortal, but that individual *men* are mortal. Individual atoms are here of interest only as having a "common identity" as men; and that common identity Mill's individual states of consciousness cannot provide.

Bradley did not always write with the classical purity of his criticism of associationism. The variety of his prose is unequalled in English philosophical literature. Henry Sidgwick considered the style of *Ethical Studies* to be in bad taste. Bradley, however, refused to tidy up his thoughts to meet Victorian standards of decorum.

> I maintain that all association is between universals, and that no other association exists . . . "And do you really," there may here come a protest, "do you really believe this holds good with emotions? If castor-oil has made me sick once, so that I can not see it or even think of it without uneasiness, is this too a connection between universals?" I reply without hesitation that I believe it is so; and that I must believe this or else accept a miracle, a miracle moreover which is not in harmony with the facts it is invoked to explain. You believe then, I feel inclined to reply, that the actual feelings, which accompanied your vomiting, have risen from the dead in a paler form to trouble you. I could not credit that even if it answered to the facts.[41]

His contemporaries, and most of ours, would have censored this example, and curbed the inclinations to which Bradley gave free rein. But Bradley did not stop at outright black humor:

> What is recalled has not only got different relations; itself is different. . . . If then there is a resurrection, assuredly what rises must be the ghost and not the individual. And if the ghost is not content with his spiritual body, it must come with some members which are not its own. In the hurry of the moment, we have reason to suspect, that the bodies of the dead may be used as common stock.[42]

Bradley's twofold perception that what is essential to mind is not the psychical states that compose it, as they are in themselves, but rather their meanings, and that the meanings it is most important to study are universal, was a turning point in

[41] Ibid., pp. 307–8.
[42] *The Principles of Logic*, 2: 306.

British philosophy. Those who would not, or could not, learn from him forfeited all claim to be considered seriously as philosophers. The opening sentences of an early paper by G. E. Moore, already a formidable adversary, bear ample witness to the importance of his influence:

> Now to Mr. Bradley's argument that "the idea in judgment is the universal meaning" I have nothing to add. It appears to me conclusive, as against those, of whom there have been too many, who have treated this idea as a mental state. But he seems to me to be infected by the same error as theirs. . . .[43]

Not even Moore would criticize Bradley except on Bradley's own terms.

Just as Mill could not carry out his indirect investigation into "the unanalysed experience of the human race" in the direct style of the eighteenth-century classics, so Bradley could not write about mind in the style of Mill. Yet it is extremely difficult to state precisely what Bradley's stylistic problem was. If the fundamental problem about mind is the nature of intentionality, philosophers must find a way of speaking about how signs, mental images, and the like can be made to be *about* things other than themselves. Ordinary language, with its devices of quotation and *oratio obliqua*, enables us to talk about what we say, and so, indirectly, about what we think; but it does not enable us to talk about the intentionality in virtue of which something said expresses a thought. The familiar logico-philosophical notion that concepts, propositions, and the like must be postulated as intermediate between words and sentences on the one hand, and things and facts on the other, merely deepens the mystery. The natures of concepts and propositions turn out to be elusive. Frege's discovery that in order to talk about a concept we seem to be obliged to treat it as an object, which it demonstrably cannot be, is only one of the problems raised.

These problems are not merely philosophical; or, if they are philosophical, then solving them will solve a stylistic problem as well. To the present, formalized semantics offers little hope that salvation may be found in some artificial formalism; for the same problem arises about such formalisms as about the natural languages. The passages I have quoted from Bradley's *Principles of Logic* illustrate one of the earliest and most serious attempts

[43] G. E. Moore, "The Nature of Judgment," *Mind*, n.s., 8 (1899): 177.

to treat of the philosophy of mind, as it is now understood, in natural English prose. Bradley did not succeed, as his successors Bertrand Russell, G. E. Moore, and C. I. Lewis have not succeeded; but he did make progress, and his work continues to reward careful study.

It may be objected that prose that is concerned with the theory of meaning must be too abstract, too remote from any human emotion to engage the attention of students of literature. Even though argument is unlikely to persuade those who have remained unpersuaded by the above quotations from Bradley, I nevertheless recommend to their attention an observation of R. G. Collingwood. "The progressive intellectualization of language, its progressive conversion by the work of grammar and logic into a scientific symbolism, . . . represents not a progressive drying-up of emotion, but its progressive articulation and specialization. We are not getting away from an emotional atmosphere into a dry, rational atmosphere. We are acquiring new emotions and new means of expressing them."[44]

[44] R. G. Collingwood, *The Principles of Art*, Oxford, 1938, p. 269.

XI

GEORGE PITCHER

Wittgenstein, Nonsense, and Lewis Carroll

The philosopher Ludwig Wittgenstein (1889–1951) was always concerned, one way or another, about nonsense; and much more so in his later writings than in the early ones. Nonsense is construed in the *Tractatus*[1] in a narrow technical way: a combination of words is nonsensical when it cannot possibly be understood, because no sense is or can (except trivially) be accorded it.[2] As an example of a nonsensical question, Wittgenstein gives that of "whether the good is more or less identical than the beautiful" (*T* 4.003).[3] He thinks that "most of the propositions and questions to be found in philosophical works are not false but nonsensical" (*T* 4.003), not even excepting, sadly, those found in the *Tractatus* itself (*T* 6.54). One of his main objectives is to devise and justify a method for distinguishing sense from nonsense, so that the latter may be consigned, as it should be, to silence (*T* 7). Nonsense is thus viewed as the major target for the philosopher's destructive weapons.

In the later *Philosophical Investigations*, Wittgenstein still

From *The Massachusetts Review* 6, No. 3, pp. 591–611. Copyright 1965 by The Massachusetts Review, Inc. Reprinted by permission of the author and the editor of The Massachusetts Review.

[1] Wittgenstein completed the *Tractatus Logico-Philosophicus* in 1918: it was published in the original German in 1921, and a year later in a German-English parallel text.

[2] Wittgenstein distinguishes nonsensical utterances from those which simply lack sense: "Tautologies and contradictions lack sense" (*T* 4.461), but they are not nonsensical. They are *sinnlos*, but not *unsinnig*.

[3] The following abbreviations will be used in giving references to Wittgenstein's works: *PI*, *Philosophical Investigations*; *BB*, *The Blue and Brown Books*; *T*, *Tractatus Logico-Philosophicus*; *RFM*, *Remarks on the Foundation of Mathematics*.

The following will be used for Carroll: *AW*, *Alice's Adventures In Wonderland*; *TLG*, *Through the Looking Glass*; *SB*, *Sylvie and Bruno*; *SBC*, *Sylvie and Bruno Concluded*.

finds that philosophers—including the author of the *Tractatus*—are professionally given to uttering nonsense. Not obvious nonsense, but hidden nonsense: and he conceives the job of *good* philosophy to be that of revealing it for what it is. "My aim," he wrote, "is: to teach you to pass from a piece of disguised nonsense to something that is patent nonsense" (*PI* Sec. 464. See also Sec. 119). Disguised nonsense has a surface air of plausibility and naturalness about it, so that it can take in even a sensible man. It has the semblance of sense. But when one examines it carefully and follows out its consequences, its inherent absurdity becomes manifest. Wittgenstein is still as concerned as ever to exorcize nonsense from philosophy; he wants to cure us of the puzzlement, the deep disquietude, it engenders in our soul. But now he also *uses* it[4] like a vaccine that cures us of *itself*. He may, for instance, describe some state of affairs that, according to a certain harmless-looking view or picture which he is criticizing, ought to be perfectly unexceptionable: but in fact the alleged state of affairs is radically odd, inherently absurd. The hidden nonsense is thus uncovered.

It is through the bond of nonsense that Wittgenstein is closely linked with Lewis Carroll. What I shall seek in general to demonstrate is the remarkable extent and depth of the affinity between these two great writers with respect to nonsense. Since I do not want to embroil myself in controversies about matters that would be excessively difficult to establish with anything approaching certainty, I shall not draw the further conclusion that Carroll exerted a profound influence on the later Wittgenstein. That he did, is one of my firm convictions;[5] but I shall

---

[4] To be sure, even in the *Tractatus*, *some* nonsense—namely, Wittgenstein's own—was deemed to be profoundly useful:

My propositions serve as elucidations in the following way: anyone who understands me eventually recognizes them as nonsensical, when he has used them—as steps—to climb up beyond them. (He must, so to speak, throw away the ladder after he has climbed up it.) (*T* 6.54)

But whether this doctrine is a legitimate one or not—I think it is not—it still claims a radically different kind of use for nonsense from those uses found in the *Investigations*.

[5] Quite apart from the fact that anyone who lived in England, and particularly in Cambridge, during the time that Wittgenstein did, could not fail to have read Lewis Carroll—especially the *Alice* books—it is known with certainty that Wittgenstein did read and admire Carroll. Miss

content myself with pointing out what I believe to be the extraordinary and illuminating parallels between their treatments of nonsense.

What I aim to show in particular is, first, that some of the important general kinds of nonsense that the later Wittgenstein finds in the doctrines of philosophers are found also in the writings of Lewis Carroll. By "kinds of nonsense," I mean nonsense that has its source in certain fundamental confusions and errors. I shall try to show that the very same confusions with which Wittgenstein charges philosophers were deliberately employed by Carroll for comic effect. Second, I want to show that some quite specific philosophical doctrines that the later Wittgenstein attacks are ridiculed also by Carroll. (Certain of these specific doctrines will embody, naturally, some of the general *types* of nonsense just mentioned.) Third, I shall cite several examples used by Wittgenstein to illustrate his points that resemble, in varying degrees, examples that are found in the works of Carroll.

Does it seem paradoxical, or even perverse, to assert that philosophy and humor—especially *nonsense* humor—are intimately related? If so, I hasten to add that Wittgenstein himself was keenly aware of the connection:

> Let us ask ourselves: why do we feel a grammatical joke to be *deep?* (And that is what the depth of philosophy is.) (*PI*, Sec. 111.)

And Malcolm reports that

> . . . Wittgenstein once said that a serious and good philosophical work could be written that would consist entirely of *jokes* (without being facetious).[6]

G. E. M. Anscombe, Mr. R. Rhees, and Prof. G. H. von Wright, all friends of Wittgenstein, have kindly provided me with information about his acquaintance with the works of Carroll. All confirm that he read at least some of the works. Miss Anscombe and Mr. Rhees both report that Wittgenstein used to cite, as a good grammatical joke, the Mock Turtle's remark "We called him Tortoise because he taught us" (*AW*, ch. 9). Mr. Rhees recalls a conversation in 1938 in which Wittgenstein referred admiringly to a passage in *Sylvie and Bruno;* but he adds that in the last eight or ten years of his life, Wittgenstein no longer thought as highly of Carroll as he had earlier. Carroll is mentioned by name in *PI* Sec. 13 and p. 198; and it is a safe bet that the nonsense poems referred to in *PI* Sec. 282 are those of Carroll.

[6] N. Malcolm, *Ludwig Wittgenstein: A Memoir* (London: Oxford University Press, 1958), p. 29.

Wittgenstein undoubtedly had the works of Lewis Carroll in mind when he made those remarks.

Nor is it really very surprising to find some affinity between the nonsense of Carroll and that which bothered Wittgenstein: for both men were professional logicians and much of their nonsense, as we shall see, is grounded in just those matters connected with language that a logician must concern himself with —such matters, for example, as the meanings of terms and sentences, as the (logical) differences that exist amongst various sorts of terms, as the fact that sentences having the same (or at least *apparently* the same) grammatical form sometimes express propositions of radically different logical forms, and so on.

I shall present my case by starting with items of less importance and proceeding in the rough direction of those of more importance.

1. Wittgenstein makes the point that one must not be seduced into thinking that one understands a certain sentence simply because it is gramatically well-formed and consists entirely of familiar words: the sentence may, in fact, make no sense whatever, or be at least "fishy" in some important respect.

> "These deaf-mutes have learned only a gesture-language, but each of them talks to himself inwardly in a vocal language."— Now, don't you understand that?—. . . I do not know whether I am to say I understand it or don't understand it. I might answer "It's an English sentence; *apparently* quite in order—that is, until one wants to do something with it; it has a connexion with other sentences which makes it difficult for us to say that nobody really knows what it tells us; but everyone who has not become calloused by doing philosophy notices that there is something wrong here." (*PI*, Sec. 348.)

The same point is made in *The Blue and Brown Books:* there, instead of saying "It's an English sentence; *apparently* quite in order," he says "It sounds English, or German, etc., all right" (*BB*, p. 56). This point and even the forms of words in which it is expressed are reminiscent of Carroll. After the Hatter had said something (viz., "Which is just the case with *mine*") that he seemed to have thought answered Alice's criticism of his watch,

> Alice felt dreadfully puzzled. The Hatter's remark seemed to her to have no sort of meaning in it, and yet it was certainly

English. "I don't quite understand you," she said, as politely as she could. (*AW*, ch. 7.)

A similar scene occurs in *Sylvie and Bruno Concluded.* The Professor said:

"I hope you'll enjoy the dinner—such as it is; and that you won't mind the heat—such as it isn't."
The sentence *sounded* well, but somehow I couldn't quite understand it . . . . (*SBC*, ch. 22.)

2. Just as there are remarks that are nonsense, or nearly so, because one can "do nothing" with them, so there are acts which make little or no sense because nothing of the right sort follows from them; they do not have the consequences or connections that are needed to make them into the kinds of acts they purport to be. Two examples that Wittgenstein gives of such acts find parallels in Carroll:

(a) Why can't my right hand give my left hand money?—My right hand can put it into my left hand. My right hand can write a deed of gift and my left hand a receipt.—But the further practical consequences would not be those of a gift. . . . (*PI*, Sec. 268.)

When Alice, after having eaten a piece of magical cake, grew so tall that she could hardly see her feet, she contemplated the possibility of having to send presents to them.

And she went on planning to herself how she would manage it. "They must go by the carrier," she thought, "and how funny it'll seem, sending presents to one's own feet! And how odd the directions will look!

Alice's Right Foot, Esq.
Hearthrug,
near the Fender,
(with Alice's love).

Oh dear, what nonsense I'm talking!" (*AW*, ch. 2.)

(b) Imagine someone saying: "But I know how tall I am!" and laying his hand on top of his head to prove it. (*PI*, Sec. 279.)

Putting your hand on top of your head does not demonstrate that you know how tall you are, because it has no conceptual connections with anything beyond itself—for example, with acts of measuring with foot-rules, or of standing back to back with another person of known height. The same (vacuous) act could be performed by anyone, no matter how tall he was and whether or not he knew how tall he was. Similarly, if you should ever have occasion, like Alice, to wonder whether you are rapidly growing or shrinking, it will avail you nothing to put your hand on top of your head to find out: the same results will be achieved in either case—namely, none.

> She ate a little bit, and said anxiously to herself "Which way? Which way?", holding her hand on the top of her head to feel which way it was growing; and she was quite surprised to find that she remained the same size. (*AW*, ch. 1.)

Alice's procedure would not be fruitless, of course, if she had reason to think that *only* her head and/or neck were stretching or shrinking while the rest of her body was remaining the same size. But she had no such reason, nor, as far as I can tell, did she think she had. Her surprise, therefore, is entirely unwarranted.

3. I can detect no intimate connection between Carroll and the early Wittgenstein, and so virtually all my examples are drawn from the later Wittgenstein. Still, there is one point in the *Tractatus* with which Carroll would presumably agree. Wittgenstein maintains that tautologies, including the Law of Excluded Middle, say nothing.

> (For example, I know nothing about the weather when I know that it is either raining or not raining.) (*T* 4.461.)

Carroll relies on this truth for his laughs when he has the White Knight describe the song he intends to sing.

> "It's long," said the Knight, "but it's very, *very* beautiful. Everybody that hears me sing it—either it brings *tears* into their eyes, or else—"
> "Or else what?" said Alice, for the Knight made a sudden pause.
> "Or else it doesn't, you know." (*TLG* ch. 8.)

4. In both the *Tractatus* and the *Investigations*, Wittgenstein heaps scorn on the (alleged) proposition that "A thing is identical with itself."

> Roughly speaking, to say of *two* things that they are identical is nonsense, and to say of *one* thing that it is identical with itself is to say nothing at all. (*T* 5.5303.)

"A thing is identical with itself."—There is no finer example of a useless proposition, which yet is connected with a certain play of the imagination. It is as if in imagination we put a thing into its own shape and saw that it fitted. (*PI*, Sec. 216.)

Carroll, too, saw that there is something very peculiar about such propositions:

"I'm sorry you don't like lessons," I said. "You should copy Sylvie. *She's* always as busy as the day is long!"
"Well, so am *I!*" said Bruno.
"No, no!" Sylvie corrected him. "*You're* as busy as the day is *short!*"
"Well, what's the difference?" Bruno asked. "Mister Sir, isn't the day as short as it's long? I mean, isn't it the *same* length?" (*SB*, ch. 12.)

5. One of the points that Wittgenstein makes over and over again in his later writings is that certain words which seem to denote something momentary and fleeting—usually, a feeling or thought or sensation—actually signify something quite different—perhaps a disposition or ability, or at least a longer-range pattern of events. At one point, he uses the example of "grief": one is tempted to think that this word simply denotes an inner feeling which, although it usually endures for some time, may happen on occasion to last for only a few seconds or even for only one. To cast doubt on this whole idea, Wittgenstein asks

Why does it sound queer to say: "For a second he felt deep grief"? Only because it so seldom happens?
But don't you feel grief *now?* ("But aren't you playing chess *now?*") The answer may be affirmative, but that does not make the concept of grief any more like the concept of a sensation.—(*PI*, p. 174.)

Carroll, too, appreciates the absurdity of supposing that someone could feel deep grief for only a second. In Knot VIII of *A Tangled Tale*, we read:

"But oh, agony! Here is the outer gate, and we must part!" He sobbed as he shook hands with them, and the next moment was briskly walking away.
"He *might* have waited to see us off!" said the old man piteously.
"And he needn't have begun whistling the very *moment* he left us!" said the young one severely.

6. Two points that are constantly stressed in the later writings of Wittgenstein are the following: (a) that "an ostensive definition can be variously interpreted in *every case*" (*PI*, Sec. 28),[7] and (b) that from the fact that a person knows what a word W denotes in one linguistic construction, it does not follow that he knows what W denotes in a different construction. (This latter point is, of course, intimately related to point 1, above.) To illustrate point (b), Wittgenstein uses the example of "measuring": one may know very well what it is to measure distance or length, but from this it does not follow that he knows what it is to measure *time*. (See *BB*, p. 26, and N. Malcolm, *Ludwig Wittgenstein: A Memoir*, pp. 47 f.) In Carroll, there are passages in which these two points seem to play an essential part. During the trial of the Knave of Hearts,

> one of the guinea-pigs cheered, and was immediately suppressed by the officers of the court. (As that is rather a hard word, I will just explain to you how it was done. They had a large canvas bag, which tied up at the mouth with strings: into this they slipped the guinea-pig, head first, and then sat upon it.)
> "I'm glad I've seen that done," thought Alice. "I've so often read in the newspapers, at the end of trials, 'There was some attempt at applause, which was immediately suppressed by the officers of the court,' and I never understood what it meant till now." (*AW*, ch. 11.)

This was not, to be sure, a paradigm case of an ostensive definition, since no one pointed to the proceedings and said to Alice "That is what is known as 'suppressing a guinea-pig' "; but it was just like one, since Alice guessed, from her previous reading of the newspapers, that it was in fact a case of suppressing a guinea-pig. Although not explicitly stated, it seems clear enough that Alice thought the phrase "suppressing a guinea-pig" refers to the beast's being put head first into a large canvas bag and being then sat upon, rather than to its being restrained and its cheering quelled, by whatever means. She thus misinterpreted the "osten-

[7] Giving an *ostensive definition* of a general term (e.g., "two") consists in pointing to, or otherwise indicating, something to which the general term is applicable (e.g., two nuts) and saying "That is called 'two'," or something equivalent to it. Wittgenstein shows that the person to whom an ostensive definition is given *may* always interpret it wrongly: in our example, for instance, the person may think that "two" denotes that particular pair of nuts, or that *kind* of nut, or the color of the nuts, or their size, or any number of other things.

sive definition" (point (a)). It is not so clear what is to be made of the second paragraph. Did Alice think she understood what the phrase "suppressing the *people*" (i.e., those who attempt to applaud at the end of trials) means? If so, she was wrong—for such people are not generally put head first into large canvas bags and sat upon—and then the point of the passage would be to show just how drastic her misinterpretation of the ostensive definition was. Or, to read the passage more literally, did Alice rather think she understood what "suppressing an *attempt*" (e.g., at applause) means? If so, she was wrong again: for even if she knew what suppressing a *guinea-pig* was, it would not follow that she knew what suppressing *an attempt at applause* was (point (b)). Indeed, on her understanding of the phrase "suppressing a guinea-pig," the phrase "suppressing an attempt at applause" is nonsensical, for attempts cannot be put into bags and be sat upon.

The following passage from *Sylvie and Bruno Concluded* is, however, more clearly relevant to point (b):

> "You seem to enjoy that cake?" the Professor remarked.
> "Doos that mean 'munch'?" Bruno whispered to Sylvie.
> Sylvie nodded. "It means 'to munch' and 'to *like* to munch.' "
> Bruno smiled at the Professor. "I *doos* enjoy it," he said.
> The Other Professor caught the word. "And I hope you're enjoying *yourself*, little Man?" he enquired.
> Bruno's look of horror quite startled him. "No, *indeed* I aren't!" he said. (*SBC*, ch. 23.)

Sylvie's analysis of "to enjoy cake" seems to me to be masterful; at any rate, Bruno may be assumed to know what it is to enjoy *cake.* But he mistakenly thought this knowledge entailed a knowledge of what it is to enjoy *himself.* Hence the Other Professor's kindly enquiry, which Bruno wrongly construed as containing the imputation of auto-cannibalism, badly shocked him.

7. Wittgenstein shows that one cannot always with sense "make the easy transition from some to all" (*PI*, sec. 344): for example, although it certainly makes sense to say that people sometimes make false moves in some games, it does not make sense to suggest that everyone might make nothing but false moves in every game (*PI*, Sec. 345). Carroll also realizes the absurdity of such transitions from *some* to *all*. After Alice has recited the poem called "You are old, Father William" to the Caterpillar, the latter is highly critical:

"That is not said right," said the Caterpillar.

"Not *quite* right, I'm afraid," said Alice timidly: "some of the words have got altered."

"It is wrong from the beginning to end," said the Caterpillar; and there was silence for some minutes. (*AW*, ch. 5.)

During the silence, Alice was doubtless wondering just what was fishy about the Caterpillar's accusation. (Alice's "ear" for non-sense is infallible; but she is never able to locate the source of the trouble.) The answer is that the charge was much too harsh to be intelligible: for although it is quite possible to recite a poem and get some of the words wrong, it is not possible to recite a given poem and get *all* of the words wrong—for then one is not reciting *that poem* at all.[8] Similarly, when the Dodo announced that *everyone* had won the Caucus-race (*AW*, ch. 3), he was speaking nonsense. One of the contestants can win a race, or some of them can, but not all. All can be given prizes, or even *win* prizes, for running so well or just for taking part in the race at all or for some other reason; but they cannot all receive prizes for *winning the race*—for to *win* a race is to come out *ahead* of the others. (Carroll, of course, delighted in ridiculous extremes of all sorts. In chapter 11 of *Sylvie and Bruno Concluded*, for example, Mein Herr argued that since a map is better the larger its scale, the best map must be one drawn on a scale of a mile to the mile. His countrymen actually produced such a map, but they were unable to unfold it for fear of shutting out the sunlight; so they had to be content to use the country itself as its own map.)

8. Some of the later Wittgenstein's investigations were concerned with the relationship between, as we may put it, what a thing (quality, process, etc.) *is* and what it is *called*. One absurd extreme view is that a thing really *is* what a certain group of people (e.g. English speakers) call it, so that speakers of other languages are flatly wrong to call it by some other name ("How peculiar you Germans are to call it a 'Tisch' when it is so obviously a *table*"). But another extreme view is equally absurd—the view, namely, that *in all cases* what a thing really *is* is altogether different from, is wholly independent of, what it is

---

[8] Under these conditions, in fact, one is not reciting any poem whatever. Even if the (wrong) words that come out should happen, by chance, to constitute a poem, the speaker would not be *reciting* that poem.

called. Wittgenstein, as might be expected, maintains that the way the relation is to be characterized varies from case to case:

> First I am aware of it as *this;* and then I remember what it is called.—Consider: in what cases is it right to say this? (*PI*, Sec. 379. See also Secs. 380 and 381, and the illuminating discussion of colors and color-words at the beginning of Part II of *The Brown Book*, especially *BB*, pp. 133–35.)

There are two passages in Carroll in which the absurdity of the second extreme view, above, is demonstrated. In the first, the Cheshire-Cat explains to Alice why he is mad. After getting Alice to agree, reluctantly, that a dog is not mad, he goes on:

> "Well, then," the Cat went on, "you see a dog growls when it's angry, and wags its tail when it's pleased. Now *I* growl when I'm pleased, and wag my tail when I'm angry. Therefore I'm mad."
> "*I* call it purring, not growling," said Alice.
> "Call it what you like," said the Cat. (*AW*, ch. 6.)

The second is the famous passage in which the White Knight tells Alice what song he is about to sing to her:

> "The name of the song is called '*Haddocks' Eyes*'."
> "Oh, that's the name of the song, is it?" Alice said, trying to feel interested.
> "No, you don't understand," the Knight said, looking a little vexed. "That's what the name is *called.* The name really *is* '*The Aged Aged Man*'."
> "Then I ought to have said 'That's what the *song* is called'?" Alice corrected herself.
> "No, you oughtn't: that's quite another thing! The *song* is called '*Ways and Means*': but that's only what it's *called,* you know!"
> "Well, what *is* the song, then?" said Alice, who was by this time completely bewildered.
> "I was coming to that," the Knight said. "The song really *is* '*A-sitting On A Gate*': and the tune's my own invention." (*TLG*, ch. 8.)

If it is absurd to think that what a thing *is* is in every case *wholly* independent of what it is *called*, it is equally, and even more evidently absurd to suppose that the entire nature of a thing is *completely* dependent on what it is called. In Carroll, of course, we find just this absurdity beautifully exploited. Alice came to a forest where nothing had a name: she met a fawn which then walked trustingly by her side.

> So they walked on together through the wood, Alice with her arms clasped lovingly around the soft neck of the Fawn, till they came out into another open field, and here the Fawn gave a sudden bound into the air, and shook itself free from Alice's arm. "I'm a Fawn!" it cried out in a voice of delight. "And, dear me! you're a human child!" A sudden look of alarm came into its beautiful brown eyes, and in another moment it had darted away at full speed. (*TLG*, ch. 3.)

9. As is well known, the later Wittgenstein wages war against essentialism, the doctrine that there is a unique set of characteristics—constituting an essence—that is shared by all and only those individuals to which a certain general term (e.g., "table," "tree," "serpent") applies. Carroll pokes gentle fun at essentialism when he describes the Pigeon's interview with Alice, whose neck had just stretched to an alarming length:

> "Serpent!" screamed the Pigeon.
> . . . .
> "But I'm *not* a serpent, I tell you!" said Alice. . . . I—I'm a little girl". . . .
> "A likely story indeed!" said the Pigeon, in a tone of the deepest contempt. "I've seen a good many little girls in my time, but never *one* with such a neck as that! No, no! You're a serpent; and there's no use denying it. I suppose you'll be telling me next that you never tasted an egg!"
> "I *have* tasted eggs, certainly," said Alice, who was a very truthful child; "but little girls eat eggs quite as much as serpents do, you know."
> "I don't believe it," said the Pigeon; "but if they do, then they're a kind of serpent: that's all I can say." (*AW*, ch. 5.)

The Pigeon had very peculiar ideas about the essences of little girls and of serpents: indeed, her conceptions of these two essences represent two extremes. On the one hand, she thought that the essence of little-girlness contains a great many characteristics, including that of having a neck considerably shorter than poor Alice's stretched one. Since Alice lacked that essential characteristic, the Pigeon judged that she could not possibly be a little girl, despite the fact that she presumably had all the other required characteristics. On the other hand, the Pigeon seemed to hold that the essence "serpenthood" consists of only one characteristic—that of eating eggs: therefore, if little girls eat eggs, they must be a kind of serpent.

10. A variety of problems connected with *rules* occupy the later Wittgenstein's attention as much as anything else. Carroll, too, has something to say about these matters. In the well-known article, "What the Tortoise Said to Achilles," for example, Carroll attacks the problem of what it is to accept a rule of inference. He tries to show that if accepting a rule of inference is considered to be the same thing as accepting a premise of an argument, then absurdity, in the form of an infinite regress, results. As soon as the rule is added to the premises of an argument, it no longer applies to the argument, and new rules must forever be appealed to.[9] The issue raised here by Carroll is a near cousin to Wittgenstein's intimately connected worries about obeying or following a rule, applying a rule to a particular case, and interpreting a rule.

There are many other difficulties connected with rules. For example, suppose that one or more persons are engaged in something that may be called a rule-governed activity. How can an external observer determine what rules the participants are following? If it is a game, can he "read these rules off from the practice of the game—like a natural law governing the play?" (*PI*, Sec. 54.) But then "how does the observer distinguish in this case between players' mistakes and correct play?" (*PI*, Sec. 54.) Or, more troubling still: how can the outside observer—or the participants themselves, for that matter—determine the difference between the participants' acting (merely) *in accordance with* a rule and their (knowingly) *obeying* or *following* the rule. (See *BB*, p. 13. Kant, as everyone knows, stressed the importance of this distinction in the realm of morality.) That Carroll was also aware of these problems is clearly demonstrated in the following scene, in which the Red Knight and the White Knight fight to determine whose prisoner Alice shall be:

> "I wonder, now, what the Rules of Battle are," [Alice] said to herself, as she watched the fight, timidly peeping out from her hiding-place. "One rule seems to be, that if one Knight hits the other, he knocks him off his horse; and, if he misses, he tumbles

---

[9] I *think* this is what Carroll tried to show. I also think he does not succeed: see J. F. Thomson, "What Achilles should have said to the Tortoise," *Ratio*, 3, No. 1 (1960), 95–105.

off himself—and another Rule seems to be that they hold their clubs with their arms, as if they were Punch and Judy. . . ." Another Rule of Battle, that Alice had not noticed, seemed to be that they always fell on their heads; and the battle ended with their both falling off in this way, side by side. (*TLG*, ch. 8.)

11. One of the most deeply Wittgensteinian—or perhaps I should say "anti-Wittgensteinian"—characters in all of Lewis Carroll is Humpty Dumpty. Wittgenstein attacks the idea that what a person means when he says anything is essentially the result of his performance of a mental act of intending (or meaning) his words to mean just that. If this view were correct, it would seem to follow that a person could utter a word or group of words and mean *anything* by them, simply by performing the appropriate act of intention. Wittgenstein concedes that the possibility exists of a person's giving a special meaning of his own to a word or words which mean something quite different in the language; but to do that is not to perform a special mental act:

> But—can't I say "By 'abracadabra' I mean toothache"? Of course I can; but this is a definition; not the description of what goes on in me when I utter the word. (*PI*, Sec. 665.)

(See the principle of point 5, above, of which this is a special case.) But generally—and this is a necessary truth—what a person means by the words he utters is just what those words *do mean*. We do not have to wait for the speaker to tell us what, in virtue of the mental act of meaning he performed while he spoke, he meant by them: and indeed, if we did, we could *never* discover what he meant—for we would be in no better position to understand his explanation than we were to understand his original utterance! One could almost say that it is precisely Humpty Dumpty whom Wittgenstein is here opposing.

> "There's glory for you!"
> "I don't know what you mean by 'glory'," Alice said.
> Humpty Dumpty smiled contemptuously. "Of course you don't—till I tell you. I meant 'there's a nice knock-down argument for you!'"
> "But 'glory' doesn't mean 'a nice knock-down argument'," Alice objected.
> "When *I* use a word," Humpty Dumpty said, in a rather scornful tone, "it means just what I choose it to mean—neither more nor less."

> "The question is," said Alice, "whether you *can* make words mean so many different things."
>
> "The question is," said Humpty Dumpty, "which is to be master—that's all." (*TLG*, ch. 6.)

Some of Wittgenstein's examples sound extremely Humpty-Dumpty-ish in fact:

> Can I say "bububu" and mean "If it doesn't rain I shall go for a walk"?—It is only in a language that I can mean something by something. This shows clearly that the grammar of "to mean" is not like that of the expression "to imagine" and the like. (*PI*, p. 18.)

Underlying the Humpty Dumpty view of the use of language is the following picture: a person's ideas (which are non-linguistic) are formulated, more or less clearly, in his mind; in order to express them, he need only find some suitable words —and, if Humpty Dumpty is right, *any* old words will do. And so, as the Duchess saw, if you are sure that the idea itself is clearly formulated, the matter of translating it into words is no great problem:

> "Take care of the sense, and the sounds will take care of themselves." (*AW*, ch. 9.)

Wittgenstein describes the picture as follows:

> The phrase "to express an idea which is before our mind" suggests that what we are trying to express in words is already expressed, only in a different language; that this expression is before our mind's eye; and that what we do is to translate from the mental into the verbal language. (*BB*, p. 41.)

Wittgenstein regards the picture with suspicion, since it is dangerously apt to mislead the philosopher: Carroll, on the other hand, simply has fun with it.

We sometimes—and mothers of young children, quite often —speak of saying something and meaning it ("I told you to put on your overshoes and I *meant* it!"). This form of expression inevitably gives rise to the idea that the *saying* is one thing and the *meaning it* another—a mental act or private feeling or whatever, that accompanies the saying. Wittgenstein argues against this idea (see, for example, *BB*, p. 34f. and p. 145): in doing so, he is defending Alice—at least up to a point—against the March Hare and the Mad Hatter:

"... You should say what you mean," the March Hare went on.
"I do," Alice hastily replied; "at least—at least I mean what I
say—that's the same thing, you know."
"Not the same thing a bit!" said the Hatter. "Why, you might
just as well say that 'I see what I eat' is the same thing as 'I eat
what I see'!"
"You might just as well say," added the March Hare, "that 'I
like what I get' is the same thing as 'I get what I like'!" (*AW*,
ch. 7.)

12. Of the several techniques Wittgenstein uses to make his
philosophical points, two that are especially conspicuous are
that of describing worlds (or possible situations) in which
"certain very general facts of nature" are different from what
we are used to, and (perhaps a more special case of the first)
that of describing tribes of people whose institutions and practices are quite different from our own. What he says in the
following passage would apply to *both* of these methods:

> I am not saying: if such-and-such facts of nature were different
> people would have different concepts (in the sense of a hypoth-
> esis). But: if anyone believes that certain concepts are absolutely
> the correct ones, and that having different ones would mean not
> realizing something that we realize—then let him imagine cer-
> tain very general facts of nature to be different from what we
> are used to, and the formation of concepts different from the
> usual ones will become intelligible to him. (*PI*, p. 230.)

Thus, for example, Wittgenstein makes important points by
considering the possibility of pain patches (*PI*, Sec. 312); of one
mathematician's always being convinced that a figure in another's proof had altered unperceived—presumably where there
is no way of ascertaining whether it had or not (*PI*, p. 225); of
a chair's suddenly disappearing and reappearing (*PI*, Sec. 80);
of all peoples' "shape, size and characteristics of behavior peri-
odically undergo[ing] a complete change" (*BB*, p. 62); and so
on. And here are some examples of the second method: Wittgenstein images tribes of people who measure things with elastic
foot-rules made of very soft rubber (*RFM*, p. 4); or who have
slaves that they think are automatons, although they have human
bodies and even speak the same language that their masters do;[10]
or who have no common word for (what we call) light blue and

[10] See N. Malcolm, "Wittgenstein's *Philosophical Investigations*," *The
Philosophical Review*, 63, No. 4 (1954): 548f.

dark blue (*BB*, p. 134f.); or who show no outward signs of pain (*PI*, Sec. 257); and so on.

I do not think it overly speculative to suggest that Wittgenstein *might* have gotten the original idea of these devices from his reading of Carroll: for what are any of Carroll's worlds but worlds in which certain "very general facts of nature" are radically different and in which people (or at least *beings*) act in very strange ways? One or two of Carroll's actual fancies, indeed, closely resemble some of Wittgenstein's: the ontological behavior of the Cheshire-Cat (*AW*, chs. 6 and 8) is like that of Wittgenstein's disappearing and re-appearing chair; and in *Sylvie and Bruno*, Bruno measures garden beds with a dead mouse (*SB*, ch. 15), which, although not elastic, shares some salient characteristics with foot-rules made of very soft rubber. Countless other of Carroll's fancies are Wittgensteinian in spirit: for example, the White Queen screamed in pain *before* she pricked her finger (*TLG*, ch. 5); and the Other Professor described certain people who do not feel pain when burned by a red-hot poker until years later, and who *never* feel it if they are (merely) pinched—only their unfortunate grandchildren might feel it (*SB*, ch. 12).

13. I have saved until last the respect in which Wittgenstein and Carroll are most deeply "at one," in which they become true spiritual twins. If any theses can be said to lie at the heart of Wittgenstein's later philosophy, one of the plausible candidates would certainly be the doctrine that much of the nonsense and puzzlement to be found in philosophy is the direct result of one fundamental kind of mistake—namely, that of wrongly treating a word or phrase as having exactly the same kind of function as another word or phrase, solely on the basis of the fact that they exhibit superficial grammatical similarities.

> When words in our ordinary language have prima facie analogous grammars we are inclined to try to interpret them analogously; i.e. we try to make the analogy hold throughout. (*BB*, p. 7. See also *PI*, Sec. 90.)

We thus "misunderstand . . . the grammar of our expressions" (*BB*, p. 16), and fall victim to misleading analogies (*BB*, pp. 26 and 28). Numerous examples of this pernicious, but completely natural, tendency are presented by Wittgenstein. Quite as many are scattered throughout the works of Carroll: indeed, I venture to suggest that the single major source of Carroll's wit lies precisely in his prodigious ability to exploit this particular human frailty. I do not propose to burden the reader with long lists of examples drawn separately from Wittgenstein and Carroll: I content myself with giving a handful (five, in fact) that I have chosen from among those found in *both* authors.

(a) Wittgenstein would maintain that the absurdity of Humpty Dumpty, already discussed, stemmed from his being misled by grammatical similarities.

> ... What tempts us to think of the meaning of what we say as a process essentially of the kind which we have described is the analogy between the forms of expression:
> "to say something"
> "to mean something",
> which seem to refer to two parallel processes. (*BB*, p. 35.)

So Humpty Dumpty treated the phrase "to mean such-and-such" as if it meant something very like what the phrase "to say such-and-such" means, and hence as though it referred to a private process going on in his mind while he spoke, just as "to say such-and-such" seems to refer to the observable public process. (Humpty Dumpty was inordinately given to this vice: thus he treated the sentence "I can make words mean what I want them to mean" as though it were perfectly analogous to "I can make workers do what I want them to do.")

(b) The temptation to assimilate phrases with radically different uses to one another is especially great, of course, when one or more of the words involved are the same (or at least appear to be the same). Hence it is treacherously easy to confuse empirical and logical necessity, since words like "must" or "can't" or "won't" occur typically in expressions of both:

> ... It is somewhat analogous to saying: "3 x 18 inches won't go into 3 feet." This is a grammatical rule and states a logical impossibility. The proposition "three men can't sit side by side on a bench a yard long" states a physical impossibility; and this example shows clearly why the two impossibilities are confused. (Compare the proposition "He is 6 inches taller than I" with "6 foot is 6 inches longer than 5 foot 6." These propositions are of utterly different kinds, but look exactly alike.) (*BB*, p. 56.)

Both Alice and the White Queen are guilty of this very confusion:

> "I'm sure *my memory* only works one way," Alice remarked.
> "I can't remember things before they happen."
> "It's a poor sort of memory that only works backward," the
> Queen remarked. (*TLG*, ch. 5.)

Alice thought that the statement "I can't remember things before they happen" stated an empirical necessity; that is, she
thought it was like "I can't break twigs before they are dry."
She thus supposed that if she had a better memory, she might
have been able to manage remembering things *before* they happened. But clearly it is not an empirical, but rather a logical, or
conceptual, necessity that one can't remember things before
they happen. Since the White Queen thought that Alice's inability to remember things before they happen was due to the
poor quality of the girl's memory, she too confused empirical
with logical necessity. The White Queen fell into this confusion
because in her world (if it *is*, in fact, a conceivable world),
time ran backwards and in that kind of world it would presumably make sense to speak of remembering "things that happened the week after next" (*TLG*, ch. 5). But she forgot that
her own memory, too, worked in only one direction (albeit in
the opposite direction from that in which Alice's memory
worked[11]), and had she remembered it, she would have been
blissfully unaware that this, too, was a matter of logical
necessity.[12]

(c) Wittgenstein points out that many of our forms of expression seduce us into thinking of time as "a *queer thing*" (*BB*,
p. 6) of one sort or another—for example, as a ghostly kind of
stream or river:

> ... We say that "the present event passes by" (a log passes by),
> "the future event is to come" (a log is to come). We talk about
> the flow of events; but also about the flow of time—the river on
> which the logs travel.

[11] Let us leave unasked the question: How could the White Queen,
for whom time ran backwards, converse with Alice, for whom time ran
forwards?

[12] Ignoring some minor qualifications, we can say that in Alice's world
it is logically necessary that one can remember only things in the past,
while in the White Queen's world, it is logically necessary that one can
remember only things in the future. Here we may begin to see, if only
dimly, the (very important) connections between (i) the distinction between logical and empirical necessity (point 13) and (ii) certain very
general facts of nature being what they are (point 12).

Here is one of the most fertile sources of philosophic puzzlement: we talk of the future event of something coming into my room, and also of the future coming of this event. (*BB*, pp. 107f.)

We would not expect Carroll to pass up the opportunities presented by this sort of confusion—and he doesn't.

Alice sighed wearily. "I think you might do something better with the time," she said, "than wasting it in asking riddles that have no answers."

"If you knew Time as well as I do," said the Hatter, "you wouldn't talk about wasting *it*. It's *him*."

"I don't know what you mean," said Alice.

"Of course you don't!" the Hatter said, tossing his head contemptuously. "I dare say you never even spoke to Time!"

"Perhaps not," Alice cautiously replied; "but I know I have to beat time when I learn music."

"Ah! That accounts for it," said the Hatter. "He won't stand beating. . . ." (*AW*, ch. 7.)

"In *your* country," Mein Herr began with a startling abruptness, "what becomes of all the wasted Time?"

Lady Muriel looked grave, "Who can tell?" she half-whispered to herself. "All one knows is that it is gone—past recall!"

"Well, in *my*—I mean in a country *I* have visited," said the old man, "they store it up: and it comes in *very* useful, years afterwards! . . . By a short and simple process—which I cannot explain to you—they store up the useless hours: and, on some *other* occasion, when they happen to *need* extra time, they get them out again." (*SBC*, ch. 7.)

(d) Although it is not a very easy trap to fall into, someone might conceivably construe "nobody" as if it were a proper name, because of certain grammatical similarities, some of which are indicated in the following passages from Carroll:

"Just look along the road, and tell me if you can see either of them."

"I see nobody on the road," said Alice.

"I only wish *I* had such eyes," the king remarked in a fretful tone. "To be able to see Nobody! And at that distance too! Why, it's as much as I can do to see real people, by this light!" (*TLG*, ch. 7.)

"Who did you pass on the road?" the King went on, holding out his hand to the Messenger for some hay.

"Nobody," said the Messenger.

> "Quite right," said the King: "this young lady saw him too. So of course Nobody walks slower than you."
> "I do my best," the Messenger said in a sullen tone. "I'm sure nobody walks much faster than I do!"
> "He can't do that," said the King, "or else he'd have been here first." (*TLG*, ch. 7.)

Wittgenstein imagines a language in which it would be much easier to succumb to this temptation:

> Imagine a language in which, instead of "I found nobody in the room," one said "I found Mr. Nobody in the room." Imagine the philosophical problems which would arise out of such a convention. (*BB*, p. 69.)

(e) Finally, Wittgenstein warns us that just as "now" is not a "specification of time," despite the apparent similarities between such utterances as "The sun sets at six o'clock" and "The sun is setting now" (*BB*, p. 108), so

> The word "today" is not a date, but isn't anything like it either. (*BB*, p. 108.)

The White Queen needs to learn this lesson—or else she has learned it very well and is not above applying it for her own advantage. She offers to engage Alice as her maid at wages of "Two pence a week, and jam every other day":

> "It's very good jam," said the Queen.
> "Well, I don't want any *to-day*, at any rate."
> "You couldn't have it if you *did* want it," the Queen said. "The rule is, jam to-morrow and jam yesterday—but never jam *today*."
> "It *must* come sometimes to 'jam to-day'," Alice objected.
> "No, it can't," said the Queen. "It's jam every *other* day: to-day isn't any other day, you know."
> "I don't understand you," said Alice. "It's dreadfully confusing!" (*TLG*, ch. 5.)

Wittgenstein and Carroll, as we have seen, were both professionally concerned with nonsense—and with very much the same sort of nonsense. It is the kind of nonsense that results from the very natural confusions and errors that *children* might fall into, if only they were not so sensible. It is nonsense, in any case, that can delight and fascinate children. It is significant, I think, that both Wittgenstein and Carroll understood the way

children's minds work: this is obvious in the case of Carroll, and
as for Wittgenstein, one must remember that he spent six years
(1920–26) teaching in village elementary schools. (Note, too,
that this period came *between* his earlier and later phases—that
is to say, just *before* his conception of nonsense took a Carrollian
turn.)

Wittgenstein's and Carroll's nonsense both produce extreme
puzzlement: Alice is constantly bewildered and confused by the
nonsense she hears in the course of her adventures, just as philosophers, according to Wittgenstein, are puzzled and confused
by the nonsense that they themselves unknowingly utter. In
both cases, the nonsense takes on the form of something like
madness. Alice's world is a mad one, and she is a victim of it:
she is utterly powerless against the nonsense of the mad ones
she encounters—she *never* wins! The philosopher's mind, on
Wittgenstein's view, is just Alice's mad world internalized.

> The philosopher is the man who has to cure himself of many
> sicknesses of the understanding before he can arrive at the no-
> tions of the sound human understanding.
> If in the midst of life we are in death, so in sanity we are
> surrounded by madness. (*RFM*, Part IV, Sec. 53.)

Like Alice, the philosopher is a helpless victim of the madness
(the non-sense)—until, also like Alice, he awakens, or is awakened, into sanity.

To be sure, Wittgenstein and Carroll had radically different
attitudes towards nonsense: it tortured Wittgenstein and delighted Carroll. Carroll turned his back on reality and led us
happily into his (wonderful) world of myth and fantasy. Wittgenstein, being a philosopher, exerted all his efforts to drag us
back to reality from the (horrible) world of myth and fantasy.
But the two men cover much the same ground: we may even
look upon Wittgenstein as conceptualizing and applying to
philosophy many of the points that Carroll had simply *intuited*.
But the attitude, certainly, is fundamentally different. The same
logical terrain that is a playground for Carroll, is a battlefield
for Wittgenstein. That is why, although standing very close to
one another, they may appear to the superficial eye to be worlds
apart.

XII

ANNE C. BOLGAN

The Philosophy of F. H. Bradley and the Mind and Art of T. S. Eliot: An Introduction[1]

The release of Eliot's Ph.D. dissertation of 1916 under its new title *Knowledge and Experience in the Philosophy of F. H. Bradley* was an event long awaited and of notable importance. The remarkable thing is that a piece of work so vibrant with relevance to every aspect of Eliot's life, thought, and art can have been suppressed for so long. By reprinting, as appendixes to the same volume, the two philosophical articles that he contributed to the *Monist* during the same year, Eliot has in effect made it possible for his readers to examine these early philosophical writings together, and really for the first time. In doing so, he has put us in possession of those primary documents that alone make possible the exploration of the nature and full ex-

This hitherto unpublished essay constitutes the introductory chapter of a forthcoming study entitled "Visions and Revisions: The Philosophy of F. H. Bradley and the Mind and Art of T. S. Eliot."

[1]The following abbreviations are used to identify publications cited in the body of the text:

KE	T. S. Eliot, *Knowledge and Experience in the Philosophy of F. H. Bradley,* edited with Notes and A Selected Bibliography by Anne C. Bolgan (London: Faber and Faber, 1964).
ETR	F. H. Bradley, *Essays on Truth and Reality* (Oxford: The Clarendon Press, 1914).
OPP	T. S. Eliot, *On Poetry and Poets* (New York: Farrar, Straus and Cudahy, 1957).
PIV	B. Bosanquet, *The Principle of Individuality and Value* (London: Macmillan and Company, 1912).
SE	T. S. Eliot, *Selected Essays* (New York: Harcourt, Brace and Company, 1950).
TSW	T. S. Eliot, *The Sacred Wood* (London: Methuen and Company Limited, 1920).
UP	T. S. Eliot, *The Use of Poetry and the Use of Criticism* (London: Faber and Faber Limited, 1933).

tent of Bradley's influence in the shaping of his mind and art. It would seem wise to undertake such an exploration if only because of the repeated references Eliot has made to the extent and depth of Bradley's influence upon him, and Eliot has a way, not only of meaning what he says, but of meaning it in very precise ways. When, for example, he says that upon those few "who will surrender patient years to the understanding of his meaning," the study of Bradley's philosophy "performs that mysterious and complete operation which transmutes not one department of thought only, but the whole intellectual and emotional tone of their being . . ."[2] he means just that. And if "the whole intellectual and emotional tone" of Eliot's being has been transmuted by some particular thing, I take this to be an important bit of news with some fairly obvious implications.

With his usual modesty, Eliot has offered the Bradley thesis to his readers "only as a curiosity of biographical interest . . ." and he suggests that "As philosophizing, it may appear to most modern philosophers to be quaintly antiquated" (*KE* 10). There is little doubt, I think, that these philosophical writings of Eliot's can now have at best only an incidental value for the professional philosopher, and that the importance which they in fact do have will come to rest finally in their use to the literary theorist and historian. To these, an almost inexhaustible mine to quarry has been given, for it is patently clear to anyone who has studied the work of both these men that it is Bradley's mind that lies behind the structuring principles of Eliot's poetry, as well as behind every major theoretical concept appearing in his literary criticism. One cannot hope to exhaust such an embarrassment of riches within the limits of any single study but what one can do is to break some ground and let the glittering ore shine through, if there is any.

We have for so long thought of Eliot as the literary dictator of the twentieth century that it is almost impossible for us now to believe that he was ever anything else. The mantle of philosophy slides uneasily over his shoulders and, as we have always done, we prefer to think of him instead as "wreathed in seaweed red and brown." We find it equally difficult to disabuse ourselves of the usual assumptions that cluster around the image of the man of letters—that is, the usual literary background, the

[2] T. S. Eliot, "A Commentary," *Criterion* 3, 9 (October 1924): 2. Signed: Crites.

youthful but "talented" scribblings, manifest excellence in the pursuit of literary studies, and so on. In Eliot's case, however, the facts are all to the contrary, and we might well begin our study of his mind and art, therefore, with a summary account of some of these important but neglected facts of Eliot's biography.

After the usual grammar and high school experience, Eliot entered Harvard in 1906 and was immediately introduced to that philosophical idealism that was to exert such a significant pressure in the formation of his mind and later in the innovative directions that both his poetry and criticism would initiate. The particular type of Idealism in which Eliot became immersed at Harvard, however, is that type which is known historically as Anglo-American Objective Idealism or, perhaps more simply, as the New Idealism—a type which, in very specific and important ways, is opposed historically to the philosophy of Subjective Idealism in England and America on the one hand, and opposed equally to ontological German Idealism on the other. This particular branch of idealistic philosophy came into being during the last decades of the nineteenth century and achieved its point of maximum influence at the turn, and during the early decades of, the twentieth. The main line of argument underlying it received its classic formulation at the hands of F. H. Bradley and Bernard Bosanquet in England and of Josiah Royce, Eliot's mentor at Harvard, in America.

For the next four years at Harvard, Eliot undertook a rigorous philosophical training under a brilliant roster of teachers that included such famous names as R. F. A. Hoernle, Irving Babbitt, George Santayana, Bertrand Russell, and, clearly the most influential of all, Josiah Royce himself. Eliot began to win recognition and praise from his teachers almost from the beginning for what they generally felt was his extraordinary competence. There is no evidence, on the other hand, that anyone at Harvard at that time considered him as displaying any serious or marked capacities as a potential man of letters. The young man elected as class poet of Eliot's year at Harvard, for example, was Edward Eyer Hunt of Mechanicsburg, Ohio.

At the end of his B.A. and M.A. training, Eliot, in the autumn of 1910, went off to Paris to continue reading philosophy at the Sorbonne where he also attended the lectures of Bergson. When he returned to Harvard after a year to begin his doctoral studies,

once again in philosophy, "The Love Song of J. Alfred Prufrock" was already in his pocket. One cannot help wondering
how anything so radically new, both in structure and intention,
could possibly come into being with such dramatic sudden-
ness. In effect, Eliot had gone to Paris a philosopher and returned an accomplished poet. The phenomenal nature of this
transformation can be felt even more clearly if one examines
some of Eliot's *juvenilia*. For an example, let us return to the
year 1905 that finds the young Eliot about to graduate from
Smith Academy at the age of seventeen. He had been asked by
his teachers and classmates to write a graduation ode for this
auspicious occasion, and in case it should be assumed that even
in Eliot's *juvenilia* there would undoubtedly be evidence of his
latent and poetic talent, I beg leave to quote the first stanza of
the ode recited that day:

> Standing upon the shore of all we know
> We linger for a moment doubtfully,
> Then with a song upon our lips, sail we
> Across the harbor bar—no chart to show,
> No light to warn of rocks which lie below,
> But let us yet put forth courageously.[3]

Had any of Eliot's teachers reading this ode been interested to
speculate as to which of their students might one day become
a major poet, it is probable that the only conviction they would
have shared in common would be that the young Eliot would
certainly not be he. What is almost unbelievable, however, is
that this ode was written in 1905 and that only five years later
"The Love Song of J. Alfred Prufrock" was an accomplished
fact. Clearly, this is not a case of gradual and increasing maturity along a straight line, but rather of a complete departure in
a new direction. It behooves us to inquire what it was that
forced the turn and, in its wake, brought the poetic Eliot to a
birth not unlike that of the phoenix from its own ashes. The
image itself suggests what had to happen before that new birth
could occur, but the record of events is not so simple or direct.

During 1913–14, Eliot's final year of graduate study at Harvard, he also served as a teaching assistant in the Department of
Philosophy and was awarded at the end of it a Sheldon Travel-

[3] T. S. Eliot, *Poems Written in Early Youth* (London: Faber and
Faber, 1967), p. 19.

ing Fellowship that he used to continue his philosophical studies in Germany during the summer immediately preceding the outbreak of the great war in 1914. At the end of the summer, he left Germany hurriedly to take up residence in England, first at Merton College, Oxford, where, in his words, he studied with "Harold Joachim, the disciple of Bradley who was closest to the master" (*KE* 9), and then, after his year there, in London where he became a schoolmaster at the Highgate Junior School. It was during these two years in England that Eliot wrote his doctoral dissertation on "Experience and the Objects of Knowledge in the Philosophy of F. H. Bradley"—the work that Josiah Royce referred to as "the work of an expert." (*KE* 10). That thesis, together with the two philosophical articles that Eliot contributed to the *Monist* in 1916, comprise the youthful but formative philosophical writings later adumbrated in Eliot's mind and art.

If some readers, at least, will be surprised to learn that Eliot, throughout much of his mature life, was a philosopher, what is surprising to me instead is that I can find so little in his early life and philosophical background to suggest that he would ever become anything else—least of all a poet, and almost overnight at that. His mother, even more disbelieving, apparently could not accept Eliot as a poet even after his impressive first volume of poetry had been published. In a letter to Bertrand Russell, she says:

> I am sure your influence in every way will confirm my son in his choice of Philosophy as a life work. Professor Wood speaks of his thesis as being of exceptional value. I had hoped he would seek a University appointment next year. If he does not I shall feel regret. I have absolute faith in his Philosophy but not in the vers libres.[4]

It would appear, however, that we must put aside the wilful desires both of myopic motherhood and of Procrustean scholarship as well and accept instead, and as gracefully as we can, the 20–20 vision with which the wisdom of hindsight so generously endows us. The dramatic transformation of T. S. Eliot from philosopher to poet did in fact occur. Our concern now must be with what is significant for literary history and criticism in this new and incontrovertible fact.

[4] Bertrand Russell, *Autobiography*, Vol. 2, 1914–1944 (Toronto: McClelland and Stewart, Ltd., 1968), pp. 58–59.

If, in one sense at least, Eliot's transformation faces us with a mystery we cannot hope to penetrate, yet it is a mystery that we can accommodate more easily if we recognize, by way of the argument of Eliot's philosophical writings, that there is an interior logic to it that it is worthwhile to explore. That logic, if it cannot finally be made responsible for the change, yet does serve to illuminate it in a somewhat surprising and significant way and thus serves to forge the lines of relation by which the first half of Eliot's life may be seen as at least connected to the second. We may put this another way by suggesting that if Eliot's philosophical training and background cannot be credited with having made him a poet, yet it can be shown to have played a major role in determining the particular kind of poet and critic he was finally to become. To delineate the shadow cast on Eliot's poetry and criticism by the central motifs of the New Idealism, generally, and by the argument of his philosophical writings, in particular, is thus the task we are about.

At an interesting juncture in his *Speculations*, T. E. Hulme introduces the following suggestive image:

> The fountain turned on. It has a definite geometrical shape, but the shape did not exist before it was turned on. . .
> But the little pipes are there before, which give it that shape as soon as the water is turned on.[5]

The view I have suggested above implies that Eliot's life and mind and art represent a mass of proliferous flesh that, if it is to be seen as composing one body, must be seen as gathered around the spinal cord of Bradley's philosophy. In short, "the little pipes . . . which give it the shape" and the order it has are his. I am reminded here of a delightful simile William James used to excoriate those readers who behave

> like myopic ant[s] crawling over a building, tumbling into every microscopic crack or fissure, finding nothing but inconsistencies, and never suspecting that a centre exists.

No one who has read very much of the commentary on Eliot's poetry and criticism can fail to see the analogy. Alternatively, if we place ourselves at the center of Eliot's philosophic vision, not

---

[5] T. E. Hulme, *Speculations*, ed., Herbert Read (2d ed.; New York: Harcourt, Brace and Company, 1924), p. 240.

256

only will we understand the many different things it has made him say throughout his life but we will see as well how undeviatingly true he has been to his philosophic beginnings.

Thus, in my view, any commentary—either on Eliot's poetry or his criticism—that proceeds in ignorance of the depth and pervasiveness of Bradley's influence, or that prefers to discount it, seems to me doomed from the start either to irrelevance or to ineptitude. To say this much, however, is not to have introduced us into Eliot's rose garden, where "all shall be well and/ All manner of thing shall be well" (*Little Gidding* V) but rather to impale us on the second horn of the peculiar dilemma that lies very near the heart of the present study. If irrelevance or ineptitude lies in one direction, then to suggest that the only way really to understand Eliot's poetry and criticism is by way of Bradley's dazzling ambiguities is tantamount to saying that "to be restored, our sickness must grow worse" (*East Coker* IV). If Bradley is the way to understand Eliot, how does one come to understand Bradley? In short, when Eliot's philosophical writings were given to us, a disproportion was given along with them as well and one that may perhaps prove fatal—a disproportion, that is, between the particular kind of understanding we seek and the mind-blowing methods necessary to achieve it. It is not unlike the attempt to protect a rose garden by means of an intercontinental ballistic missile—there is just too much strength by half, and while one is involved in the attempt to save a rose petal or two, the garden itself might well go down as a whole. The gift of Eliot's heavy artillery, however, somewhat like "the gifts reserved for age," is not to be denied and if it tends now and then to make the feet shuffle a bit, the hand to raise lamely, and the voice to appear unnaturally thin as we proceed, that is only because it is natural, if ineffectual, to wish that there were some easier way. But there is no easier way or, at least, before we can hope to find one, we "must go by a way wherein there is no ecstasy" (*East Coker* III) first. We must, that is, go by way of the history of ideas, and this despite the notorious difficulties involved.

One of the most oppressive of these difficulties is that, in interdisciplinary studies such as this one, what one finally writes must be too elementary for philosophers on the one hand, and too peripheral for literary critics on the other. To accept such a debilitating disjunction as final, however, is perhaps to seek,

ANNE C. BOLGAN

and certainly to find, one's deservedly modest place among the
scholarly unemployed. Alternatively, what one can do is to
throw up some bridges between the various disciplines involved
and thus encourage, in philosophers and in literary critics alike,
the occasional stroll into one another's territorial specialties. In
that way, the Chinese Wall that presently divides these specialties may perhaps be prevented from becoming an Iron
Curtain instead. This procedure, if it does not guarantee that
one will ultimately "fare well" does at least have the merit of
allowing us, like Eliot's voyagers, to "fare forward." The
remainder of this prefatory statement represents the first of
several of these nervous attempts at bridge work and does so
by suggesting some of the effects that might be expected to
follow if we were to introduce into our evaluation of Eliot's
mind and art the perspective allowed by his philosophical
writings.

II

The first thing that the perspective referred to above might
be expected to do is to reverse the judgment of Eliot as literary
critic that presently dominates the contemporary commentary
on his criticism. Before proceeding further, therefore, it may
be well to consider briefly this particular judgment of Eliot as
critic. It was conveniently summarized for us many years ago
by Leonard Unger, and it does not seem to have changed significantly since then. In his preface to *T. S. Eliot: A Selected
Critique,* Unger says:

> A common judgment made—with varying emphasis—by such
> critics was that Eliot was at his best when dealing with spe-
> cific subjects, but that he did not provide a general theory of
> aesthetics; and that when he did approach, or imply, the more
> inclusive generalizations he fell into contradictions.[6]

This judgment, I feel certain, derives mainly from John Crowe
Ransom's earlier book, *The New Criticism,* wherein Ransom
views Eliot's criticism as a set of "remarks"—sufficiently astute
in themselves but never extending to the level of principle. He
says:

> There is in Eliot's writings an immediate critical sense which
> is expert and infallible, but it consists with a theoretical inno-

[6] New York: Rinehart and Company, 1948, p. xiii.

258

cence. Behind it is no great philosophical habit, nor philosophical will, to push through it to definition. He rarely cares to
theorize in set passages about poetry. He is not what we call . . .
a "thinker."[7]

Ransom's way of looking at Eliot, a way that has now become
almost universal, is to see him as "a practitioner of Arnold's
touchstone method," and Ransom is apprehensive of what
would happen to any one of Eliot's "remarks" if "stiff critical
theorists should pounce upon it, remove it, put it technically,
and evaluate it."[8]

If Ransom's judgment was defensible almost thirty years ago
when he first stated it, it was so mainly because Eliot's extensive
philosophical training and history were virtually unknown at
that time and because these early but formative philosophical
writings of his had not yet been made available to the general
public. What is far less understandable is the persistence of
Ransom's judgment today when so much evidence to the contrary has been put before us. Yet that judgment continues to
make itself felt, for example, even in Kristian Smidt's *Poetry
and Belief in the Work of T. S. Eliot,* one of that increasing
number of books on Eliot's criticism that has been written with
some awareness of, and considerable reference to, Eliot's philosophical writings. Here is Smidt's variation of the Ransom
motif:

> That there should be inconsistencies and self-contradictions
> in a critic who had no coherent aesthetic theory is no more
> than is to be expected. Eliot admits them and thus takes the
> edge off any complaints that we may make. He might have
> done well to work out an aesthetic for himself, if only to avoid
> inconsistencies in his generalizations.[9]

Like Ransom, however, Smidt assures us that Eliot is, nevertheless, "one of the best arbiters of taste of our generation."[10] One
last quotation from Smidt will serve to sum up his final estimate of Eliot's critical powers:

> Eliot's power of relating the concrete and particular to the
> abstract and general may not be impressive; his capacity for

[7] Norfolk: New Directions, 1941, p. 145.
[8] Ibid., p. 145.
[9] Oslo: I Kommisjon Hos Jacob Dybwad, 1949, p. 16.
[10] Ibid., p. 17.

close reasoning may be limited; his loyalties and prejudices may be fortuitous in origin and subject to change; but his sensibility may be counted on. . . .[11]

And there we have it: the "immediate critical sense which is expert and infallible" on the one hand, and the "theoretical innocence" on the other; the "sensibility [that] may be counted on" but one that operates in a vacuum: "His capacity for close reasoning may be limited . . ."; "He is not what we call . . . a 'thinker.'" This is the considered opinion of many of the contemporary commentators on Eliot's criticism, yet it would be difficult to conceive a more erroneous judgment or a more unworthy charge. The objection that Eliot is obscure and that he has not given us "consistent principles," "valid generalizations," "a coherent aesthetic theory," is not, it seems to me, really a criticism at all but a persistent and, by now, a somewhat wearisome complaint arising from the confusion of two quite separate disciplines—that of literary criticism and that of literary theory. The slightest attention to Eliot's avowedly practical, and intentionally literary, purposes in these short essays, newspaper articles, and book reviews should be sufficient to obviate it—purposes that precluded a statement of aesthetic principle or the development of such a theory.

We must face it squarely. Eliot has not given us within his literary criticism a deliberately conceived or systematically formulated literary theory but, rather, "only hints and guesses," and the attempt to squeeze out of his texts the final "truths," "the more inclusive generalizations," the "coherent aesthetic theory" that those intentionally literary essays cannot supply is, therefore, both gratuitous and misguided. In short, Eliot must be allowed the prerogative of having written "workshop criticism," as he himself has called it (*OPP* 107), instead of systematic literary theory if that is what he wanted to do. And if Eliot, in his literary criticism generally and in "Tradition and the Individual Talent" in particular, chose "to halt at the frontier of metaphysics . . ." (*SE* 11) and thus, in effect, to write literary rather than aesthetic criticism, his readers in my view are left with only two legitimate alternatives. One is to halt with him and to content themselves with the astute critical perceptions, the "remarks," the "half-truths, or gnomic truths"

[11] Ibid.

that Ransom has found were sufficient "to have stocked the mind of a generation with his wisdom."[12] In this case, it is fruitless, and less than fair, to expand the theoretic implications of a remark oriented to a practical end, to compare it with another, equally dislocated from its own intention and context, and then, to convict Eliot of "theoretic innocence" if the two statements do not appear to be consistent with one another. Yet most readers will be aware that this is the method—a method that we may designate as the method of comparative quotation to murderous ends—that has almost universally been applied to convict Eliot of the defects of "confusion," "inconsistency," and "theoretic innocence."

Alternatively, if we do not choose to halt with Eliot himself "at the frontier of metaphysics" but wish instead to probe and expand the actual currency that Eliot's theoretical concepts have in his own mind, it helps considerably if we know precisely which metaphysical system those concepts were related to, and which system consequently determines the specific meaning Eliot intends them to have in his criticism. What is so remarkable about the release of Eliot's philosophical writings is that here, with an amplitude and in a manner that is unique in our literary history, we have given to us by a poet, critic, and philosopher that specific metaphysical framework of ideas in relation to which his literary principles emerged and his poetic practice was formed. R. S. Crane has taken more careful notice than has anyone else of the way in which literary concepts are frequently related to, and often derived from, those hidden but nonetheless controlling philosophical postulates that as a consequence determine in large part their actual meaning.[13] Thus, if we would enter more profoundly into the meaning of such literary concepts as those of the ideal order of poetry, the impersonality of the poet, unified sensibility, the nature of the objective correlative, and so on—concepts that have initiated such stubborn controversies in our time—it would seem clear that we must examine them, not as so many of our contemporary commentators have done, in wondrous ignorance of the philosophical antecedents by which they are everywhere controlled but, rather, within the context provided for them by

[12] Ransom, *The New Criticism*, pp. 145–46.

[13] See Ronald S. Crane (ed.), *Critics and Criticism, Ancient and Modern* (Chicago: University of Chicago Press, 1952), Introduction, pp. 1–24.

that particular philosophy in which they find their genesis and within which alone, as a consequence, their actual meaning can be determined—that is, the philosophy of F. H. Bradley and no other.

Thus, if we would safeguard Eliot's valuable perceptions from continued obloquy and from an obfuscation that could threaten them permanently, we must reassert the perennial methods of historical scholarship and invite a re-examination of Eliot's literary criticism in the light of those few but specific Bradleian doctrines that his philosophical writings make clear he made his own. Contrary to what Professor Kenner has told us, it is not to be thought that it was merely a "tonal influence" that Bradley exerted upon the young Eliot and that "It is as a colouring, [and] not as a body of doctrine that . . . [Bradley] stays in the mind. . ." and "is most discernible in Eliot's poetic sensibility."[14] (Nor, incidentally, can I possibly concur with him in the view that"Bradley has an attractive mind, though he perhaps has nothing to tell us. . . ," nor in that other quintessential Kennerism that Bradley "is an experience, like the taste of nectarines or the style of Henry James.")[15]

I would say instead that Eliot's major critical concepts, in every case, are but the literary equivalents of historically and systematically developed philosophical doctrines and that there is no way of coming to terms conceptually with the former except through the latter. What the philosophical writings make perfectly clear is that when Eliot, in his literary criticism, is called upon to "think," he can only do so in Bradleian terms and within the framework provided by the doctrinal convictions he came to share with Bradley in the course of his long and sensitive reading of his philosophy. Thus, if we are genuinely interested in entering into a fuller and deeper understanding of Eliot's critical thought, it would seem quite clear that our attention must first be focused on that philosophy in the light of which Eliot's entire intellectual being has been formed. It is only this philosophy that can provide for the theorist that larger context of systematic relations that is able to render Eliot's literary insights more meaningful in themselves

[14] Hugh Kenner, *The Invisible Poet: T. S. Eliot* (London: Methuen and Company, Ltd., 1965), p. 39.

[15] Ibid., p. 54.

as well as more productive *vis-à-vis* literary theory, and this brings me to my second point.

III

In the preceding section, I have expressed some dissatisfaction with the persistent objection that in his criticism Eliot "did not provide a general theory of aesthetics. . . ." In my view, the tradition of English letters has yet to produce a finer literary critic than T. S. Eliot, and it seems something less than fitting to have that phenomenon attended so often with the regret that he was not an aesthetician instead. If a systematically complete and internally self-consistent literary theory is a commodity so easily come by as some of our commentators would suggest, I could find little justification for the importance I would finally accord to Eliot's philosophical writings, for the preeminent value I would attribute to them rests primarily in the conviction that the "theory of objects" Eliot develops there, when read together with his literary criticism, can take us somewhat farther in the construction of a new and a post-expressionistic literary theory than anything else yet has, though perhaps not so far as many of our critics seem to think necessary. The first thing needful in this regard, however, is to be able to see Eliot's criticism with eyes unclouded by the regrets of others and to begin with the alternate assumption that, because of his extensive training as a philosopher and as a systematic "thinker," and because of "the great philosophical habit" these studies are inclined to develop, there is considerable presumptive ground for believing that Eliot's literary criticism is not likely to be so wholly confused and incoherent, so theoretically inchoate, as his critics seem to have found it. In short, a re-examination of Eliot's literary criticism seems necessary and one that is made with a view to assessing, somewhat more realistically than has been done in the past, exactly what contribution such a body of criticism can legitimately be expected to make to the systematic construction of a "coherent aesthetic theory."

What one finds in Eliot's literary criticism is not, it seems to me, a fully and systematically developed "Impersonal theory of poetry," but rather the richest and most extensive material yet given to us by an English poet and critic in support of it, material that is indispensable to its construction. And when that material is taken in conjunction with the hidden, but nonetheless controlling, metaphysical premises that the release of Eliot's philosophical writings has now made perceptible to us, the two together can cooperate to make possible what has never been possible before—that is, the systematic construction of Eliot's own "general theory of aesthetics," the theory that he has been so widely and so ironically condemned for not having given us. To proceed in this way would be to exploit to its fullest advantage, by way of the philosophical writings, the extraordinary susceptibility that I believe Eliot's criticism has to systematic development. Our first and primary concern, however, must be with Eliot's poetry and with the part that the perspectives of literary and philosophical history might be expected to play in illuminating it.

IV

The emergence in the twentieth century of a new and characteristically modern literary epoch was due primarily, it seems to me, to the influence of Eliot's literary writings, with the brilliant observations, the robust convictions, and the spirited aspirations concerning both poetry and criticism that they contain. The distinctive outlines of that epoch will, I believe, exhibit themselves most clearly when we relate the incisiveness of Eliot's literary enterprises to the equally new and equally radical innovations of the New Idealism. In this way, an initial step might be taken toward a distinctive characterization of *The Modern Tradition*[16] and one that views its literature, not as an extension of romanticism from the nineteenth into the twentieth century but one, rather, that relates the modern temper and sensibility to the lineaments of post-Kantian English and American philosophy instead of to post-Kantian German philosophy.

In his review of Peter Quennell's *Baudelaire and the Symbolists*, Eliot refers to "the insurgence of something which can hardly be called Classicism, but which may decently be called Counter-Romanticism."[17] It seems clear to me that it is in the central motifs of the New Idealism generally, and in the argu-

[16] Cf. Richard Ellman and Charles N. Feidelson, Jr., (eds.), *The Modern Tradition* (New York: Oxford University Press, 1965), pp. v–ix.
[17] *Criterion* 9, 35 (January 1930): 357.

ment of his own philosophical writings in particular, that we may seek most profitably for Eliot's own contributions to the counter-romantic movement—a movement intended to restore to poets and critics alike a voice that had lost itself in romantic effusion on the one hand, and in a critical impressionism on the other. The effort, then, to illuminate Eliot's poetry and criticism by relating them to the frame provided by his philosophy is, in some sense at least, an effort to order the philosophical and literary events of the past half century into some sort of meaningful synthesis. But how is this to be done?

The comprehensiveness of Eliot's mind and art provides four distinguishable, but hardly distinct, centers of interest to the student of modern literature—those deriving from his poetry, his literary criticism, his poetic theory, and his philosophical writings. My own particular critical interest, on the other hand, is directed not to any one of these taken alone or in isolation from the others but rather to the complexities of exchange among them, and this exchange I regard, not as matter for assertion or for argument, but as the matter to be shown. Whatever novelty of method and manner the following pages reveal derives entirely from that conception. The first thing needful, therefore, will be a loom on which the complexities of exchange may be woven, but what is even more necessary is some bright golden thread that, if it serves in part to create the fabric of exchange on the one hand can, at the same time, serve to lead us through its otherwise dark and labyrinthine ways on the other. If it is clearly the New Idealism that must provide me with my loom, the golden thread is one I have sought for myself and isolated, perhaps quite arbitrarily, in the dialectical conception of *the significant self* and of its temporal becoming that I see as perhaps the most significant contribution made by the New Idealism to post-Kantian philosophy. It is this conception that, in 1916, Eliot adumbrates in that theory of the "two souls" (*KE* 206) or selves that he outlines in the second of his two *Monist* essays (*KE* 198–207) and that, a year later, he will oppose to "the metaphysical theory of the substantial unity of the soul" that he is "struggling to attack" (*SE* 9) in "Tradition and the Individual Talent," thus separating himself systematically from the romantic conception of "personality" and from the expressionistic theory of poetry that follows from it. It is, of course, this same "metaphysical theory of the substantial unity of the soul" that the whole of Kantian and post-Kantian philosophy had attacked before him.

Perhaps the most difficult conception of all to grasp within post-Kantian philosophy is not so much that of the Absolute (or Transcendental Self, as it is called by such personalistic Absolutists as Josiah Royce, though not by Bradley), nor yet that of the empirical self revealed to introspection but, rather, that deeper and essentially paradoxical conception of *the significant self* that is progressively born of their interaction with one another in time and that consequently never really is but is always becoming. To define the true nature of *that* self— "Caught in the form of limitation/Between un-being and being" (*Burnt Norton* V)—was the major philosophical task set for the later Idealism by the logical inconsistencies implicit in Kant's *disjunction* of the two selves—phenomenal and noumenal —from one another. The nerve of Eliot's accepted faith, lived philosophy, and achieved art, on the other hand, rests in the *continuity* of the phenomenal or personal self with the noumenal or impersonal self and in the conviction that the first of these gains actual substance in time only to the extent that it enters into the becoming of the other in time. The dialectic implicit in this continuity, and of expansion through continuity, is what Eliot expresses both in his literary theory and in his poetic practice as well and this explains why the Quester Hero is the "generic Eliot character,"[18] and the process of his formation as such is the generic Eliot theme.

It was that same dialectic of significant self-creation, rather than of mere self-expression, to which Keats, in a striking anticipation of this aspect of the New Idealism, applied the memorable phrase "Soul-making"[19]—a phrase that Bosanquet, if not Bradley himself, took over and used almost a hundred years later as a way of signifying what Keats had called "the use of the world. . ."[20] Thus, when Bosanquet at that much later date could say:

> The universe is not a place of pleasure, nor even a place compounded of probation and justice; it is from the highest point

[18] The phrase is Hugh Kenner's, but I disagree with his attribution of it to Prufrock. See *The Invisible Poet: T. S. Eliot*, cited in n. 14.

[19] M. B. Forman (ed.), *The Letters of John Keats* (4th ed.; London: Oxford University Press, 1960), 2: 334.

[20] Ibid., p. 335.

of view concerned with finite beings, a place of soul-making.
. . . (*PIV* 26)

his main concern was to reformulate in systematic terms the primary insight that Keats had so clearly intuited before him. What I propose to do first, then, is to apply to a reading of Eliot's four major poems—"The Love Song of J. Alfred Prufrock," *The Waste Land, Ash Wednesday,* and *Four Quartets* —the historical and philosophical perspectives implicit in the consideration of Eliot's poetic world as, in Keats's phrase, a "vale of Soul-making." It is that phrase that shall serve me as the golden thread with which to weave the elaborate embroideries of Eliot's mind and art into one tapestry—a tapestry within which Eliot's poetry, criticism, and philosophy will all be seen "To become renewed, transfigured, in another pattern" (*Little Gidding* III)—the pattern of the Absolute. Thereafter, in the concluding part of my study, we shall explore some of the implications of that pattern for Eliot's "Impersonal theory of poetry" and, as a consequence, for our reading of literary history as well.

V

The significance of a turning point in literary history such as that delineated in the poetry of T. S. Eliot is that one can descry in the distance the end to which the new road leads and on which the first step has now already been taken. That end for Eliot was, to a great extent, predetermined by his early and profound absorption in the New Idealism of F. H. Bradley, and my concern, therefore, in this part of my study, must be to detail the relevance of Eliot's philosophical beginnings specifically to his poetic end. That relevance is not all of a piece nor, in each new poetic venture, is it of equal importance, but in one way or another the influence of Bradley's thought runs everywhere through Eliot's mind and art and may be discovered there simply by scratching the surfaces a bit.

Eliot's poetry is fortunate in having received the careful attention of many sensitive and discriminating critics who have been as responsive to its peculiar virtues as they have been generally sound in their critical judgments concerning it. What I hope to add now to this substantive body of Eliot criticism is a slight creative distortion—a tilt of the historical mirror, as it were—that will reveal the Bradleian filament running through the whole of Eliot's poetry and connecting poem to poem in a shadowed underpattern that is worthy of some relief and that, in brief and generalized terms, I must now attempt to resume here.

It is in the *Four Quartets* that Eliot finally attained the unique stature of a philosophical poet, thereby at a stroke rivaling Milton and approximating the grandeur of Dante, for it is in the *Four Quartets* that he gives consummate poetic expression to the significant historical lineaments of post-Kantian English and American philosophical thought and thus achieves in fact the composition of that philosophical poem to which the romantic poets before him could only aspire.

It is in the mandala whose structure underlies that of the *Quartets* that those lineaments can be most quickly and most clearly discerned; if the four quadrants of the mandala are created by the intersection of its horizontal diameter by a vertical one within a closed circle, that structure merely images in a concrete, visible form each of the pivotal doctrines within post-Kantian Absolute Idealism on which the wheel of that philosophy finally turns. Within the circle of the Absolute, it is "The dove descending. . ." (*Little Gidding* IV) that by its vertical descent into, and intersection with, the linear order of times establishes the cross as at the center of all absoluteness. Thus the Way of the Cross will become the one and only way for the self stretched upon its intersecting beams to enter, by degrees, and "With the drawing of this Love and the voice of this Calling" (*Little Gidding* V) into the life of the Absolute and the wheel of its Becoming. It is a life and a way within which the self, "in response to/The unheard music hidden in the shrubbery" (*Burnt Norton* I) and to "The dove descending. . . ," is progressively unhinged, as it were, from the merely linear world of "Time before and time after. . ." (*Burnt Norton* III) and urged into a spiral of ascent—an unsymmetrical movement that, being spiral, is therefore no longer either totally linear or totally vertical in nature but one whose ever-widening coil is created by the interactive tension of the opposing forces involved.

If Eliot, in the *Four Quartets*, has not so much embodied Bradley's philosophy as replaced it with "its complete equivalent in vision. . ." (*TSW* 161), he has in the three major poems that preceded the *Four Quartets* given expression to the impact

268

made upon him by one or another of the various doctrines within that philosophy that at the particular time involved was uppermost in his mind. Anyone attempting, therefore, to define the relation of Eliot's other major poems—"The Love Song of J. Alfred Prufrock," *The Waste Land*, and *Ash Wednesday* —to the *Four Quartets* may be reminded of Wordsworth's Preface to his own projected but never completed philosophical poem, *The Recluse*, a poem that he described in terms of a Gothic church. "[H]is minor Pieces," Wordsworth added,

> when they shall be properly arranged, will be found by the attentive Reader to have such connection with the main Work as may give them claim to be likened to the little cells, oratories, and sepulchral recesses, ordinarily included in those edifices.

And so it is, we may say, with Eliot's poetry as well, for if Eliot would not likely have compared the *Four Quartets* to a Gothic cathedral, yet he would certainly have approved the conception of a significant poet's work as comprising an *œuvre* that, in the unity it effects, expresses his total poetic vision.[21] In Eliot's case, the curve of that vision follows precisely that of the history of the self and of its mind as its anatomy had been progressively delineated by Bradley, and by others as well, in the various doctrines of late nineteenth- and early twentieth-century philosophical thought. We must, therefore, say something of that history.

It is, I think, no exaggeration to say that, from the time of Kant to the present, the New Idealism has primarily been concerned not only to formulate a philosophically exact conception of that Transcendental Self that sustains, at the same time that it impels, the pilgrims of the Absolute in the course of their never-ending quest, but also to help us perceive and understand the nature of that "relation" between pilgrim and Absolute that is internal to the definition of either and through which both are, in time, qualified and given substance. We must say a word next about that "relation."

In the course of this study, it will become progressively clear that if the "process of depersonalization" (*SE* 7) is as central to the mind and art of T. S. Eliot as it is to the philosophy of

---

[21] See Eliot's explication of the *œuvre* concept in his essay on John Ford in *Selected Essays* (New York: Harcourt, Brace and Company, 1950).

F. H. Bradley, it is a process that, in the various forms of itself in which it appears in the work of both these men, obeys a single logic—the triadic and stepladder logic of the concrete universal that the later idealism opposed to the dualistic logic of Kant. If the development of that logic was preeminently the achievement of Hegel in German philosophy and of Bradley and Bosanquet in English philosophy, yet it was Eliot who internalized for the first time in our literary history, and both in his literary theory and in his poetry, the radical alterations in vehicle, perspective, theme, and structure that are made necessary by it.

The essential point to understand within the logic of the concrete universal is the way in which it differs from the logic behind a nominal or "abstract" universal, and this must include as well an understanding of how each is arrived at.

The abstract universal is the end result of that sort of generalization that seeks identity apart from differences, and its operative method, therefore, is one of omission. Such a universal, Bosanquet tells us, is "framed by attending to the common qualities of a number of individuals, and [by] disregarding their differences" (*PIV* 35). Ultimately, therefore, it turns out to be a bare generality that, at best, is of indefinite "meaning," and if such a process of generalization is carried to its logical goal as regards any noun or individual whole, whether it be singular or collective in nature—man, poem, poetry, house, let us say—the resulting universal tends increasingly to vanish into complete emptiness. The universal man, for example, cannot as actually existent in one's conception of him be either tall or short, white or black, fat or thin. The universal man is, in fact, no man at all but merely an empty and "meaningless" generality.

The idealists, on the other hand—really from Plato on down—prefer to use "concrete universals," by which they mean universals that accommodate all the differences within them, as the paradigm of a true and genuine (rather than merely abstract) universality and the one that must, therefore, guide all logical inference during the progressive "course" of knowledge. If, then, we began our intellectual life, let us say, in a society where all the men were white and tall, our "idea" of man would include whiteness and tallness; if we later met men who were short and black and yellow and a number of other things, we should have to adjust our definition to include these differences. These new facts must be included in the concept and thus the "meaning" of the word "man"—the meaning, that is, intended by the Word itself as distinct from what *you* may or may not mean by it—progressively expands by taking account of the differences that are *internal* to the reality being defined or progressively being concretized in time.

The complete conception of man, then, must follow upon this progressive concretization and upon a real experience of it and will include *both* that universal by which all men are recognized as men and all the differences by which one particular man is distinguished from another as well. In short, a truly *concrete* universal is that total and systematic whole that is intended by every noun—man, gladness, house, poetry. Bosanquet has described it as:

> . . . a system of members, such that every member, being *ex hypothesi* distinct, nevertheless contributes to the unity of the whole in virtue of the peculiarities which constitute its distinctness (*PIV* 37).

Thus the "concrete universal"—even as already partially existent in time—is in its nature, and will always remain, an identity-in-difference or a many-in-one and that, in what is surely the most succinct expression possible, is precisely what Bradley means by the ultimate nature of the Absolute.

It should be clear, even from so cursory an account of it, that within the logic of the concrete universal a "relation" between the extratemporal Absolute or Universal Whole and any one of its own constitutive parts (the concrete particulars) is not, strictly speaking, possible anymore than a whole orange (or a whole anything)—either before or after segmentation into quarters—can be said to be capable of "relation" with any one of those quarters. Before segmentation, the parts that would make such a relation possible do not yet exist and, after segmentation, the whole that is equally necessary to such a relation does not exist. The only thing that can actually be said to exist, therefore, is not the relation of the whole orange to one of its own parts but, rather, the relation of one part of the orange to another, with all the parts together sharing in, at the same time that they comprise, the substance of the orange of which they are the "real" parts and that "ideally," therefore, they can "unite to form" (*SE* 8). Thus, what is involved is not the "relation" of the whole to part but, rather, the co-relation of parts within a whole that alone is Absolute and that alone, therefore, can serve as the ideal ground of the correlations involved.

Thus, when the logic of the concrete universal is applied to the conception of the individual self or soul, for example, one comes necessarily to view those selves—not as having each of them a "substantial unity" (*SE* 9) of its own but, rather, as constituting *together* the expression of an actually and concretely real Selfhood—not that "the Individual Talent" or self *is* but, rather, in the formation of which "the Individual Talent" or self *shares*. Within this context, the Absolute (or Transcendental Self) is a universal community of selves—a unity of selfhood that includes within itself the particular and individual selves of the many, but to speak of a "relation" between the particular and the universal, or between what we shall shortly hear Eliot call "the limited *Ich*" and "the *ueberindividuelles Ich*" (*KE* 72), or finally between the empirical and phenomenal self and the Transcendental and noumenal Self is, for the reasons given, not strictly possible. It is, nonetheless, that "relation" of "real" and "ideal," temporal and eternal, personal and impersonal, together with the *nisus* of the former progressively to substantiate itself by entering into the wholeness and universality of the latter, which must be posited and that lies at the heart of Bradley's philosophy, and lies as well at the structural base of each of the four poems to be reviewed here.

It is because of the impossibility of this metaphysical relation, therefore—what Eliot will call later "the impossible union/Of spheres of existence . . ." (*Dry Salvages* V)—that the Absolute or Transcendental Self always enters the world of Eliot's poetry in much the same way that it enters Bradley's philosophy—that is, tentatively and as a matter for faith,[22] for, as Eliot has said,

[22] We may recall here with profit Bradley's statement that "Philosophy demands, and in the end it rests on, what may fairly be termed faith. It has, we may say, in a sense to presuppose its conclusion in order to prove it. It tacitly assumes something in general to be true in order to carry this general truth out in detail" (*ETR* 15).

Eliot repeats what is essentially the same sentiment when he says: "A philosophy can and must be worked out with the greatest rigour and discipline in the details, but can ultimately be founded on nothing but faith: and this is the reason, I suspect, why the novelties in philosophy are only in elaboration, and never in fundamentals" (*KE* 163). Thirty-six

it is "a timeless unity which is not as such present either any-*where* or to any*one*" (*KE* 31). In the early poetry, the Absolute always appears suggestively, therefore, rather than in an explicit manner. It comes as a voice heard or as a presence felt and, in Bradley's words, "merely felt within me" (*ETR* 179), whereas later, as in the *Four Quartets*, it is presented to us in the form of a conceptual paradox to be thematically explored. In "The Love Song," the Absolute invades Prufrock's consciousness in the form of

> Streets that follow like a tedious argument
> Of insidious intent
> To lead you to an overwhelming question. . .

and also as the "human voices" that "wake" him in the end to a realization of his final dissolution amidst the wastes of time. In *The Waste Land*, the entry of the Absolute into the poem is announced in the "aethereal rumours" that "Revive for a moment a broken Coriolanus" and that, through him, revive as well the flagging efforts of the Quester Hero or *significant self* to "set my lands in order. . . ." In *Ash Wednesday*, the Absolute appears in the Christian variant of it that Bradley himself eschewed[23] but that Josiah Royce, Eliot's master at Harvard, and other personalistic Absolutists approved—that is as

---

years later, in his "Introduction" to J. Pieper's *Leisure, the Basis of Culture* (New York: Pantheon, 1952), p. 15, Eliot will refer once again to "the necessary relation between philosophy and theology, and the implication in philosophy of some religious faith."

[23] Bradley's position in this matter is clear, crisp, and consistent with his philosophy as a whole. He says: "I have not, I know, to repeat to those who are acquainted with my book that for me the Absolute is not God" (*ETR* 428). Contrast with this view, shared in by both Bradley and Bosanquet, the alternative views of such other Absolutist Idealists as Josiah Royce, Thomas Hill Green, Andrew Seth Pringle-Pattison, and A. E. Taylor, some of whose work Eliot refers to approvingly in a footnote (*UP* 135). Taylor says, for example:

"I have never disguised it from myself that when I speak of the 'Absolute' I mean by the word precisely that simple, absolutely transcendent, source of all things which the great Christian scholastics call God. I would add that when, following the tradition of my own teachers, I speak of the 'creatures' as 'appearances' of the Absolute, I mean by this precisely what St. Thomas, for example, meant by the doctrine that they have being by 'participation'" (A. E. Taylor, *Elements of Metaphysics* [7th ed.; London: Methuen and Company, Ltd., 1924] p. xiii).

> the Word unheard,
> The Word without a word, the Word within
> The world and for the world. . .

and against whose center "the unstilled world still whirled."
In the *Four Quartets*, finally, the Absolute appears variously
—sometimes, as earlier, in a suggestive way as, for example, in
the reference to that which is "heard, half-heard, in the still-
ness/Between two waves of the sea" (*Little Gidding* V), but
more often, and more significantly now, the Absolute appears
in the paradoxical form required both by Bradley's own formulation of its nature and by the Christian doctrine of Incarnation
as well. It appears, that is, as "The point of intersection of the
timeless/With time . . ." (*Dry Salvages* V) and its existence,
therefore, is metaphorically defined both as "the moment in and
out of time" (*Dry Salvages* V) and as "the still point of the
turning world . . ." (*Burnt Norton* II) except for which "There
would be no dance, and there is only the dance" (*Burnt Norton*
II).

To those who have never heard those whispers of immortality that are engendered within us by the presence there of
the Absolute, nor raised them if heard to the level of consciousness, Eliot must always remain a poet with little or nothing to
say, but Eliot's *personae* are not of these. They *have* heard them
and that is precisely their problem, for to have heard them is
ever after to be possessed by the requirement internal to the
experience of the Absolute—the need, that is, to endure that
"process of depersonalization" (*SE* 7) that its becoming makes
necessary for them. That process—a process of transmutation
in service of the whole and one "Costing not less than everything" (*Little Gidding* V)—is the process through which the
significant self, "Timeless, and undesiring" (*Burnt Norton* V),
itself finally comes to be.

Thus, at one end of Bradley's philosophy, and of Eliot's
poetry as well, is the Transcendental Self and, at the other, the
empirical self. The Quester Hero, or *significant self*, on the
other hand, is not identical in *substance* with either but is that
paradoxical organism that Eliot describes in his thesis as being
"a part of the world and yet . . . capable to a certain degree of
contemplating the world" (*KE* 156) of which it is itself a part.
It is this transcendental and self-generating organism, partially
in time but finally not of it, that is to be found at the center of

Eliot's mind and art and to which his poetry introduces us. It is also this same *significant self* that, throughout the whole of his literary career, Eliot went on everywhere to oppose, both suggestively and systematically, to the phenomenal "personality" he found at the base of romantic literary theory and practice.

In the task of formulating a philosophically exact conception of the Transcendental Self, and also of its first cousin—that "living copula" (*PIV* 371) or *significant self* by which its becoming is temporalized—unqualified success was hardly to be looked for. What was more often given to us instead by the philosophers was each time only "a different kind of failure" (*East Coker* V). It was, nonetheless, to that same task that Eliot devoted the entirety of his poetic art for, being both philosopher and poet, it was inevitable that the task of giving luminous and concrete expression to the subtle and difficult philosophical conceptions involved should devolve preeminently upon him:

> And so each venture
> Is a new beginning, a raid on the inarticulate
> With shabby equipment always deteriorating. . .
>
> (*East Coker* V)

When we apply to Eliot's poetic world the historical and philosophical perspectives implicit in the consideration of it as "a vale of Soul-making" what we shall find is that if, on the one hand, the poetry offers what is perhaps one of the easier, and assuredly the comeliest, of all possible vehicles for understanding at least something of the philosophy of Bradley and Eliot, an understanding of their philosophy on the other hand provides one of the more effective entrées into the layered depths of Eliot's poetry and into a clearer perception of just what is there to be perceived.

In "The Love Song of J. Alfred Prufrock," what is there to be perceived is the peculiarly Bradleian ambience created in Prufrock's person by the *continuity* of the two selves within it and by the spiral of ascent to which its dialectic urges him. The imperatives of Prufrock, however, being pre-Kantian and romantic in nature, are uncategorical ("No! I am not Prince Hamlet, nor was meant to be") and, as a consequence of the early nineteenth-century theory of the self and of its mind that underlies his Byronic postures, Prufrock forms within himself, not the character of the Quester Hero to which Eliot will eventually lead us but, rather, the character of the anti-hero in which he finds its precise literary foil. Thus, what Eliot gives us in "The Love Song" is a minor masterpiece of negation—a satiric commentary on an earlier and debased theory of the self-enclosed mind and of its debilitating effects on the man arrested within it and unable therefore "to force the moment to its crisis."

It is in *The Waste Land* that Eliot sought for the first time, but with only partial success, to delineate the character of the Quester Hero and to reveal that character to us in the process of its actual formation as such, but *The Waste Land* is Eliot's *Hamlet*, his most notable "artistic failure" (*SE* 123), and one in which the two selves—that of the poet-protagonist or Quester Hero and that of Tiresias—are seen as external to or disjoined from one another instead of as continuous with and integral to the formation of one another. The premises, in short, are once again dualistic and what Eliot gives us in *The Waste Land* is therefore "two souls" or selves (personal and impersonal, limited and all-inclusive) not as operative within one Whole of Experience that mediates the expansion of one through the progressive working of the other but, instead, two distinct protagonists whose points of view (as in romantic literary theory and practice) are essentially disjoined from one another and serve, therefore, to split the poem apart instead of as the dialectical vehicle through which its unity as a poem is achieved.

This technical defect is made up in *Ash Wednesday* wherein the substance of the two doctrines that Eliot tells us he accepts without reservations of any kind from "absolute idealism"—that is, "Degrees of Truth and Reality and the Internality of Relations" (*KE* 153)—is made manifest in the emergingly transcendent self of its *persona* as he "Jacob[s] to the stars"[24] in a spiral of ascent that, in this poem, is also and primarily a spiral of assent as well to the working of what Bradley calls "the indwelling will" of the divine within us (*ETR* 435).

Thus, what one finds in the poetry of T. S. Eliot is not so much the philosophy of F. H. Bradley as a precise literary variant of it and of its central motifs. Literal identity between the two is not to be looked for, for that is neither possible nor de-

[24] Dylan Thomas, "Altarwise by owl-light," *Collected Poems 1934–1952* (London; J. M. Dent and Sons, Ltd., 1952), p. 71.

sirable, even if it were. What a historical perspective allows instead to those who would apply it to the illumination of poetry is evidence of those mutative effects that result when the material of philosophy is transformed by its relocation in a different context and charged thereby with the new and visionary *telos* of poetry. Given this caveat we are now ready to examine Eliot's four major poems, beginning with "The Love Song of J. Alfred Prufrock"— the first note, as it were, in that transcendental melody that Prufrock himself will never sing but that it was Eliot's achievement to compose in his poetry as a whole.

XIII

DONALD DAVIE

Yeats, Berkeley, and Romanticism

"Romanticism," of course, is by this time quite unmanageable. By itself it gets us nowhere. When a reviewer of Yeats's *Collected Poems* (in *Adelphi*, November 1950) sees the volume as striking a blow for "the franker, simpler, more intelligible, and often, and even to the end, romantic ways of poetry," there is no way of rebutting him: since, among the unmanageably many meanings that have been given to "romantic" and "romanticism," there is doubtless one that does indeed relate it to frankness and simplicity. And I have no doubt that there are other meanings of "romantic" in terms of which one could quite properly regard all Yeats's poetry, first and last, as romantic. On the other hand I shall argue that there is another sense of "romantic," by which Yeats can be seen, in the 'twenties, to break quite deliberately with the romanticism of his youth. This again is not disputed; no one is likely to deny that in one sense "Among School Children" is a less romantic poem than "The Lake Isle of Innisfree." But I shall argue that this change in the poet goes deep; that the obvious and commonly recognized change in style testifies to a far-reaching and permanent change in a philosophic attitude. And this, I think, is less generally acknowledged.

There is obviously a conneciton here—or at least the possibility of a connection—with Yeats's interest, at the time he wrote "Among School Children," in the thought of Berkeley. For Berkeley too, until twenty or thirty years ago, was regarded as a proto-Romantic philosopher, one of the fathers of subjective idealism; and Yeats became interested in him at just about the time when Berkeleyans began to challenge this

From *Irish Writing*. Yeats special number. Edited by S. J. White, 31 (Summer 1955), 36–41. Reprinted by permission of the author and the editor.

reading of him, and to take seriously his own claim to be a philosopher of common sense. I shall argue, to buttress my claim for an anti-Romantic Yeats, that the poet's enthusiasm for the philosopher was not just a trailing of his Anglo-Irish coat (such as we find, for instance, in the Berkeleyan stanza of "Blood and the Moon"), but that it came out of a real grasp of Berkeley's significance as something other than what Coleridge, for instance, supposed.

The romanticism, then, that I am talking about, is the romanticism that Yeats explicitly discards in the last stanza of "Among School Children":

> "Labour is blossoming or dancing where
> The body is not bruised to pleasure soul,
> Nor beauty born out of its own despair,
> Nor blear-eyed wisdom out of midnight oil.
> O chestnut-tree, great-rooted blossomer,
> Are you the leaf, the blossom or the bole?
> O body swayed to music, O brightening glance,
> How can we know the dancer from the dance?"

In the second, third, and fourth lines the poet rejects three kinds of more or less deliberate self-division, willed mutilation or sickness, as ways toward beauty and wisdom. For instance "the body . . . bruised to pleasure soul" is surely a sort of shorthand not just for the flagellations and mortifications of religious asceticism, but also for that Romantic tradition of sexual passion which comes from the Courtly Love of the Middle Ages through the *Vita Nuova* and the Platonism of Sidney's "Astrophel and Stella." For to delay carnal consummation indefinitely, or to exclude it altogether, so as to screw up sexual desire into something "purer," more intellectual and spiritual, is a clear case of mortifying the flesh. And yet this was precisely the traditional spiritual discipline by which Yeats had schooled himself throughout his early life, in his wilfully exacerbated hopeless passion for Maud Gonne (who is, of course, much in evidence in earlier stanzas of this poem).

Again "beauty born out of its own despair" can refer, not only once again to Maud Gonne (if the poet's love for her had not been despairing, it would not have been beautiful, nor produced beauty in poems), but also to the "terrible beauty" that was born in 1916 out of the despair of a foredoomed enterprise.

It can also be taken to describe the whole of Yeats's earlier practice of quarreling with himself, in mask and antimask, calling up his own opposite, adopting a pose and then forcing himself to live up to it—in poetry, if not in life.

As for "blear-eyed wisdom out of midnight oil," the most revealing commentary on this was surely written by a great contemporary, Thomas Hardy, in his portrait of Clym Yeobright in *The Return of the Native:*

> The face was well shaped, even excellently. But the mind within was beginning to use it as a mere waste tablet whereon to trace its idosyncrasies as they developed themselves. The beauty here visible would in no long time be ruthlessly overrun by its parasite, thought, which might just as well have fed upon a plainer exterior where there was nothing it could harm. Had Heaven preserved Yeobright from a wearing habit of meditation, people would have said, "A handsome man." Had his brain unfolded under sharper contours they would have said, "A thoughtful man." But an inner strenuousness was preying upon an outer symmetry, and they rated his look as singular.
>
> Hence people who began by beholding him ended by perusing him. His countenance was overlaid with legible meanings . . . He already showed that thought is a disease of flesh, and indirectly bore evidence that ideal physical beauty is incompatible with emotional development and a full recognition of the coil of things. Mental luminousness must be fed with the oil of life, even though there is a physical need for it; and the pitiful sight of two demands on one supply was just showing itself here.
>
> When standing before certain men the philosopher regrets that thinkers are but perishable tissue, the artist that perishable tissue has to think.

Yeats in this place is plainly Hardy's artist who regrets "that perishable tissue has to think." And his thought is Hardy's thought—"thought is a disease of flesh." Behind them both, as often behind another contemporary, Thomas Mann, lies the conception of the artist or the thinker as an individual carrying the curse of a society, his gifts a sort of sacred sickness; and this is, as a fact of literary history, a conception thrown up by the Romantic movement in Europe.

Yeats in all three lines is probing that aspect of Romanticism misleadingly labeled "introspection." It is not Romantic to be capable of self-consciousness and hence of introspection; of making one part of the personality regard what some other part is thinking and feeling, even as it quite "sincerely" thinks and feels. Romanticism takes the further step from self-regarding to self-manipulating; and by harnessing the will to one half of the divided personality it induces the other half to think and feel as it wants to feel. Hence, ever since *Le Neveu de Rameau*, the Romantic fascination with the hypocrite, the actor, and the double; and its ever more frantic attempts to surprise itself into feeling what it is not prepared to feel. Hence too its search for primitive minds in which the vicious circles of self-consciousness have not yet appeared—the noble savage, the idiot, the naïf, the good and simple peasant. (But all this of course is just a dogmatic aside.)

Where does Berkeley stand in relation to this? Oddly enough he can be detected in at least one place considering the issue in just the homemade, unphilosophical terms I have adopted here. This comes in the fifth dialogue of the relatively late work, *Alciphron*, where Berkeley is attacking Shaftesbury. Berkeley's spokesman, Crito, is made to read from Shaftesbury's *A Soliloquy, or Advice to an Author*, mocking Shaftesbury's Ciceronian style by reading it as if it were loose and irregular dramatic verse. Euphranor, Crito's ally, carries on the joke by pretending that it is a play or a poem that is being read. And the freethinker Alciphron, Shaftesbury's apologist, falls into the trap:

> You are mistaken, it is no Play nor Poetry, replied Alciphron, but a famous modern Critic moralizing in Prose. You must know this great Man hath (to use his own Words) revealed a *Grand Arcanum* to the World, having instructed Mankind in what he calls *Mirrour-writing, Self-discoursing Practice, and Author Practice*, and shew'd "That by virtue of an intimate Recess, we may discover a certain Duplicity of Soul, and divide our *Self* into two parties, or (as he varies the Phrase) practically form the Dual Number." In consequence whereof he hath found out that a Man may argue with himself and not only with himself, but also with Notions, Sentiments, and Vices, which by a marvellous Prosopopoeia he converts into so many Ladies: and so converted, he confutes and confounds them in a Divine Strain. Can anything be finer, bolder, or more sublime?

Here Berkeley by implication condemns and derides the attitude behind Yeats's famous dictum that out of quarrels with others the poet makes rhetoric; out of quarreling with himself, poetry. As I should prefer to say, he stands with the later Yeats against the earlier. Berkeley derides proto-Romanticism in Shaftesbury, in the interests of Augustan common sense; the later Yeats, I think, also rejects Romanticism—and partly at least (in view of his enthusiasm at this period for Anglo-Irish Augustanism) in the interests of the same Berkeleyan ideal.

It would be disingenuous to take this passage of *Alciphron* (relaxed as it is, and wholly directed to scoring off an opponent) as a considered statement of the philosopher's central position. Yet it is thoroughly in line with the bearing of his thought as a whole. Notoriously, Descartes drove a wedge between that part of the personality which knows the world through the senses, and that other part which knows, as he maintains more reliably, by cogitation, deducing which of the reports made by the senses can be trusted. Locke drives the wedge a little deeper, deducing the existence of "matter," as to which, since it is colorless, scentless, soundless, tasteless, the senses give us no reports at all. The old-fashioned view of Berkeley was that he drove the wedge a little deeper still, and so took his place in the line of succession from Locke through Hume to Kant. But the modern reading is that Berkeley's criticism of Locke was more radical; that he refused as a psychological impossibility the Lockean and Cartesian view that the self which knows through perception and the self which knows through cogitation can be distinct and at variance in their findings. This revised view of his significance seems preferable on many counts—not only because it is, as Dr. Luce and others have shown, consonant with the argument of Berkeley's *Principles*; but also because it is consonant with the tone of his writing there, which is the tone of a man who believes himself to be irritably clearing away unnecessary refinements and false subtleties. Moreover this anti-Cartesian conservatism is what one would expect of a friend of Pope and Swift.

It is not easy to determine which view of Berkeley was held by Yeats. When he writes, in "Blood and the Moon," of "God-appointed Berkeley that proved all things a dream," he seems to lean towards the older view. Yet Dr. Luce himself (*Berkeley's Immaterialism*, Preface p. viii) contends that Yeats had "met the true Berkeley," when he wrote:

> Descartes, Locke, and Newton, took away the world . . . .
> Berkeley restored the world. Berkeley has brought back to us
> the world that only exists because it shines and sounds.

For our purposes, I believe, Yeats's position is made sufficiently clear by the characteristically wayward but often profound introduction he wrote, in 1931, to Hone's and Rossi's *Bishop Berkeley. His Life, Writings, and Philosophy*. Yeats here declares, "The romantic movement seems related . . . to Locke's mechanical philosophy, as simultaneous correspondential dreams are related, not merely where there is some traceable influence but through their whole substance." This may be to say no more than I have argued, that the split in the Romantic personality, between the part that feels and the part that manipulates itself feeling, is at bottom the split made by Descartes and widened by Locke. Yeats goes on, in a well-known passage, "The romantic movement with its turbulent heroism, its self-assertion, is over, superseded by a new naturalism that leaves man helpless before the contents of his own mind. One thinks of Joyce's *Anna Livia Plurabelle*, Pound's *Cantos*, works of an heroic sincerity, the man, his active faculties in suspense, one finger beating time to a bell sounding and echoing in the depths of his own mind. . . ." That Yeats was certainly wrong about Pound, and may have been no less wrong about Joyce, is here beside the point. We find him distinguishing his own attitude from theirs, in that he refuses to split himself into two halves, the one part listening to and recording what happens in the other. He claims Berkeleyan authority for this refusal and this claim is vindicated by the view of Berkeley which has gathered ground steadily since Yeats wrote. It is Berkeley he appeals to, along with Swift, Goldsmith, and Burke, when he protests further, "And why should I, whose ancestors never accepted the anarchic subjectivity of the nineteenth century, accept its recoil; why should men's heads ache that never drank?" We may, if we like, retort that not his ancestors but Yeats himself had joined in the Romantic bottle party; but his attitude now seems to be that his doing so was an aberration, that the Romantic phase was part of the logic of historical events for an English mind, but not for an Irish mind such as his own. At any rate, it seems clear that Yeats in 1931 was so far from considering himself a Romantic, that

he thought of his escaping Romanticism (and its consequences)
as part of his very Irishry.

And yet it is the poem that must have the last word. I have
said that the last stanza of "Among School Children" rejects
the characteristically Romantic ways toward wisdom and
beauty. But how should we understand this "rejection"? What
are the alternative ways that are accepted? It is easy to reply:
the Berkeleyan, the Anglo-Irish Augustan ways. And no doubt
when Yeats asks (rhetorically):

> "O chestnut-tree, great-rooted blossomer,
> Are you the leaf, the blossom or the bole?"

—he is evoking a way of life in which the self is not divided
against itself, in which art and life attain, in his own phrase
(again from the introduction to Hone and Rossi), "swiftness,
volume, unity." But if we put the stanza back in its place at the
end of the poem we have to see that the tree is growing, "La-
bour is blossoming or dancing," not under any circumstances
that man can bring about, but only in some realm of the ideal.
For "Among School Children" is largely a poem about what
it is like to grow old. And Yeats in the poem sees that the
knowledgeable will, probing to perjure the candid sense ("The
body . . . bruised to pleasure soul"), is not the product of any
human perversion, but an inescapable condition of life on any
terms. For what is old age but the decrepitude of sense defaced
by informed will?—if not by man's will, then by will of that
power which set him his course to run, which, in the course of
perfecting a few souls, mutilates all bodies. Thus Yeats, like
Hardy in the passage I have quoted, saw that the setting up of
soul or mind against body was a law of life, whether we like
it or not. There remains, I suppose, only the question whether
we should adopt this law for ourselves, furthering and hastening
the progress, aggravating the sickness to which we are born;
or whether we should (however vainly, in the last resort)
resist it. Yeats's early thought goes all by contraries: Robartes
and Aherne; man and mask; primary and antithetical tinctures.
This shows him taking for granted the self-division caused by
the introverted will, abetting it and embracing it as a technique
for dealing with experience. I have argued that the later Berkeleyan Yeats resented this law and protested against it, as Hardy
declares that the artist should.

XIV

MICHAEL L. ROSS

The Mythology of Friendship: D. H. Lawrence, Bertrand Russell, and "The Blind Man"

D. H. Lawrence completed the short story "The Blind Man" in November 1918. The war years had been for Lawrence years of bitter personal conflict, and it is appropriate that the story's composition should coincide so closely with the cessation of hostilities. "The Blind Man" reflects, powerfully if obliquely, the agony of the holocaust through which Lawrence, along with the rest of the world, had just passed. It also represents an attempt by Lawrence to arrive at a separate armistice for a battle that, since early in the war, had been raging within his own mind.

The writing of the story involved, for Lawrence, a gloomy reappraisal of a theme that had haunted him since the beginning of his career: the quest for an inviolable friendship, or *Blutbruderschaft*, between two men.

> I believe tremendously in friendship between man and man, a pledging of men to each other inviolably. But I have not ever met or formed such friendship. Also I believe the same way in friendship between men and women, and between women and women, sworn, pledged, eternal, as eternal as the marriage bond, and as deep. But I have not met or formed such friendship. . . .
>
> It seems to me, if one is to do fiction now, one must cross the threshold of the human people. I've not done "The Fox" yet—but I've done "The Blind Man"—the end queer and ironical. I realise *how* many people are just rotten at the quick. . . .
>
> I begin to despair altogether about human relationships—feel one may just as well turn into a sort of lone wolf, and have done with it.[1]

This essay is published for the first time in this anthology.
[1] *The Collected Letters of D. H. Lawrence,* ed. Harry T. Moore

Even a brief outline of "The Blind Man" suggests the bearing these remarks have on the central themes of the story. Maurice Pervin, a young Englishman, has lost his sight from a wound received during action in the Great War. Since his return to his farm in the English countryside, he has been living in a newly intensified intimacy with his Scottish wife Isabel, an intimacy that depends mysteriously on his loss of sight. Isabel is expecting a baby. Yet something is lacking in the marriage; the rural isolation allows no scope to Isabel's strong intellectual tendencies, and Pervin himself suffers from spells of violent despondency. When the story opens, Isabel is eagerly awaiting the arrival of her childhood friend, Bertie Reid, an eminent Scottish barrister. Bertie, with his urbane and dispassionate nature, represents Pervin's diametric opposite, and Isabel hopes that a companionship between the two may help to dispel her husband's painful sense of incompleteness. Bertie's entrance, however, at first provokes Pervin to an obstinate hostility; his alien presence seems to disrupt the intimacy between husband and wife, and his easy familiarity with Isabel makes Pervin feel snubbed and excluded. As the evening passes, the tension between the two men increases. After dinner, Pervin retires to work in the stables, his favorite haunt, leaving the other two together. Isabel, at length, asks Bertie to go fetch him back. When Bertie enters the stables, Pervin, in a sudden, desperate impulse of friendship, insists on passing his hand over the other man's head and arm. In return, he implores Bertie to place his hands upon his disfigured eyes. Bertie, though horrified, finds himself "under the power of the blind man," and is unable to refuse the demand,. When the two come back into the house, Pervin announces triumphantly to Isabel that they have "become friends." But the "queer and ironical" truth is that the encounter has been too much for the inhibited Bertie; he has, in some ultimate way, been crushed by the moment of contact.

As even this résumé should indicate, "The Blind Man" can be interpreted as a self-contained treatment of standard Lawrencean themes, without reference to any information not found in the narrative itself. This is, in fact, how it has custom-

---

(London: Heinemann, 1962), 1: 565–66. Letter to Katherine Mansfield [November 1918]. (Hereafter cited as *Collected Letters.*)

arily been regarded by Lawrence's critics. Nevertheless, when the text is read in the light of Lawrence's wartime experiences and correspondence, certain external points of reference irresistibly suggest themselves. The situation depicted in "The Blind Man" recalls, in particular, one of the most bizarre episodes in Lawrence's personal history: his friendship of 1915–16 with the philosopher Bertrand Russell. This connection, once demonstrated, becomes essential to a fully informed reading of Lawrence's story.

II

The actual relationship between Russell and Lawrence, like the fictional one between Maurice Pervin and Bertie Reid, had ended in a mutually frustrating impasse. It had, however, started off promisingly enough. Lawrence and Russell had been introduced by their common friend, Lady Ottoline Morrell, early in 1915, at a time when each man was ripe for a new form of close intellectual comradeship. Russell, troubled by accusations that he suffered from an "undue slavery to reason," hoped that Lawrence might provide him with "a vivifying dose of unreason."[2] Lawrence, conversely, lacked the sort of clarity and support an intellect like Russell's could presumably offer. The coming of war had put him under an enormous emotional strain. From all that was taking place in his own country, or for that matter in the rest of Europe, he felt an intense revulsion. The pointless slaughter ravaging the Continent, the rabid chauvinism gripping England, seemed to him the natural outcome of entrenched, perverted modes of thinking and feeling; yet so bloody a confirmation of his own prophetic rightness could only arouse him to sickened disbelief. Not long before his first letter to Russell, he had written: "The War finished me: it was the spear through the side of all sorrows and hopes."[3] He began repeatedly to describe himself in grandiose terms as having been crucified, betrayed, or (like Maurice Pervin) mutilated by the force of historical events. Wholeness, he now

[2] Bertrand Russell, *The Autobiography of Bertrand Russell* (Toronto and Montreal: McClelland and Stewart, 1968), 2: 23. (Hereafter cited as *Autobiography*.)

[3] *Collected Letters*, 1: 309. Letter to Lady Cynthia Asquith [?31 January 1915].

felt, more urgently than ever before, could be achieved only through a total upheaval, both within the state and, more immediately, within the life of each individual.

Russell, though by no means the likeliest ally in such a cause, for obvious reasons appeared to Lawrence a most desirable one. As both quickly realized, they were in agreement on a number of important issues. At the same time, Russell, profoundly though he detested arbitrary and undemocratic privilege, was himself the product of an established social and intellectual elite that to a man of Lawrence's background and temperament was ultimately quite alien. Lawrence hoped that, by overcoming such personal barriers, he might sway Russell to endorse his own idiosyncratic and somewhat hazy program. Russell's mission would be to translate Lawrence's beliefs into popularly understandable terms, and to see to their nationwide dissemination. Thus, through Russell's intervention, Lawrence would come to exercise a satisfying influence over his misguided fellow-countrymen. At the very least, the collaboration might invest his intuitions with a garb of philosophical respectability.

Despite all their differences of temperament, background, and outlook, the friendship prospered for a time. As Russell crisply puts it, "At first all went merry as a marriage bell."[4] In retrospect, it is perhaps less surprising than it might seem that such a peculiar union could have taken place. Both Lawrence and Russell were men of supremely great, if disparate, talents, and each was capable of recognizing and respecting the distinction of the other. Both men were courageously outspoken; both were in some sense visionaries; both were in radical rebellion against the Victorian orthodoxies that still dominated their society. Their solidarity was fostered by their common opposition to the war and to its attendant epidemic of chauvinism. Privately, each man quickly confessed to an uncommonly warm regard for the other. If the friendship was doomed to fail, the failure must be attributed to disruptive forces powerful enough to overcome the numerous and substantial cohesive ones.

These disruptive forces first emerged early in 1915, when Lawrence accompanied Russell, at the other's invitation, on a

4 *Autobiography*, 2: 20.

"honeymoon" to Cambridge. Lawrence's withering judgments upon the place and its inhabitants were contrary to what Russell had hoped and expected. John Maynard Keynes offers a plausible analysis of the causes of Lawrence's animosity: "Bertie gave him what must have been, I think, his first glimpse of Cambridge. It overwhelmed, attracted and repulsed him. . . . It was obviously a civilisation, and not less obviously uncomfortable and unattainable for him—very repulsive and very attractive."[5] Keynes goes on generously to acknowledge the partial truth of Lawrence's strident accusations of "deadness." Even by this time, Lawrence may have harbored some suspicion that a similar deadness was concealed by Russell's own attractive personality.

But, deeply as he had been shaken by the fiasco of his presentation to respectable intellectual society, he did not allow it seriously to interrupt the growth of his intimacy with Russell. At the end of May, he was still declaring strenuously to the other man: "We are one in allegiance, really, you & I. We have one faith, we must unite in one fight."[6] Ironically, it was just their attempt to "unite in one fight" that produced the crucial strain on the friendship. The two men became leagued in a cooperative venture to manufacture effective antiwar propaganda. For Lawrence, this meant working on what he unblushingly termed his "philosophy."[7] Eventually this was transformed into "The Crown," an essay that has little overt relevance to the war itself, but substantial bearing on what Lawrence considered its ultimate spiritual causes. Russell, meanwhile, was preparing a series of lectures which, though discursive, had to do more directly with current social issues. After consulting with Lawrence about his plans for the series, Russell sent him a detailed outline. Lawrence's scrutiny of this revealed to him that, although he could agree wholeheartedly

[5] *D. H. Lawrence: A Composite Biography*, ed. Edward Nehls (Madison: University of Wisconsin Press, 1957), 1: 287. (Hereafter cited as *Composite Biography*.)

[6] *D. H. Lawrence's Letters to Bertrand Russell*, ed. Harry T. Moore (New York: Gotham Book Mart, 1948), pp. 46–47 [29 May 1915]. (Hereafter cited as *Letters to Russell*.)

[7] See, for example, Lawrence's letter of ?20 June 1915, to Lady Ottoline Morrell (*Collected Letters*, 1: 349–50): "I send you what is done of my philosophy. Tell me what you think, exactly."

with many of Russell's specific proposals, the lectures would pay scant attention to the spiritual issues he thought most vital. Even worse, on at least one fundamental point—Russell's sympathetic treatment of democratic institutions—they threatened to contradict his most passionate convictions. He lost no time in making his dissatisfaction known to Russell. In addition, to Russell's astonishment, he returned his copy of the outline, crisscrossed with numerous and often violently critical marginal notations.[8]

In his own record of the friendship, Russell points, as the principal source of trouble, to Lawrence's unreasonable, despotic personality, and to the authoritarian social theories that he sees as merely the projection of Lawrence's egomania. Lawrence himself, needless to say, saw matters quite differently. For him, the pragmatic, issue-by-issue approach to social reform, so dear to the philosopher, was simply an evasion of what the times called for. Instead, the only cure for the evils besetting modern society was a profound and universal spiritual catharsis; any program that fell short of this would merely prolong the disease. Lawrence might subscribe to many of the specific measures on Russell's agenda; he could, however, muster little enthusiasm for a program that was no more than piecemeal. His baffled feeling that, by devising such a program, Russell had somehow betrayed their "faith," helps explain the savagely provoking tone of many of his subsequent letters. Even his most outrageous mistreatment of the other man sprang from his sincere—whether or not misguided—belief in the rightness of his own vision, and his panicky fear that Russell was shrugging away his most passionate attempts at persuasion. It is the product of his wild missionary zeal, of his exasperated impulse to have done with Russell once and for all, and of his chronic inability to leave his adversary alone.

All these conflicting tendencies are evident in Lawrence's astonishing tirade of 14 September 1915, in which he buries Russell under a landslide of vituperation. "Your basic desire is the maximum desire of war, you are really the super-war-spirit. What you want is to jab and strike, like the soldier with the bayonet, only you are sublimated into words. . . . The enemy

[8] For a transcription of Russell's outline with Lawrence's notations, including (facing p. 88) a photographic plate of one page of the typescript, see Appendix A of *Letters to Russell.*

of all mankind, you are, full of the lust of enmity."⁹ The brutal
insult to Russell's integrity is clearly Lawrence's means of re-
venging himself, by probing an insecurity he must shrewdly
have glimpsed behind the other man's composure. And yet,
savage and intemperate as it is, the letter can not be set down
as the product of pure, uncomplicated spite. Even in abusing
Russell, Lawrence betrays a desperate need to recapture his
lost sense of solidarity with him. He had arrived at the conviction that only a convulsive change in Russell's own nature
could render a genuine comradeship possible, a conviction he
voices in his letter of 16 August to Cynthia Asquith:

> I am so sick of people: they preserve an evil, bad, separating
> spirit under the warm cloak of good words. That is intolerable
> in them. . . . Bertie Russell talks about democratic control and
> the educating of the artisan, and all this, all this goodness, is just
> a warm and cosy cloak for a bad spirit. They all want the same
> thing: a continuing in this state of disintegration wherein each
> separate little ego is an independent little principality by itself.
> What does Russell really want? He wants to keep his own
> established ego, his finite and ready-defined self intact, free
> from contact and connection. He wants to be ultimately a free
> agent.¹⁰

Very possibly, by unearthing before Russell's startled eyes a
whole array of undreamed-of antisocial desires, Lawrence
hoped to shatter his "ready-defined," aseptic self-image, and so
open the way to a more genuine communion. If so, the attempt
was miscalculated. Initially, it succeeded (no doubt to Lawrence's grim satisfaction) in driving Russell to the verge of
suicide;¹¹ but it prompted him, on second thought, to consign
Lawrence and his gospel to the realm of philosophical insanity.

Although Russell's reaction is perfectly understandable, it
was inevitably based on a very partial insight into the workings
of Lawrence's mind. Ironically, some of the most offensive
phrases in his tirade to Russell recur subsequently in Lawrence's descriptions of himself. Almost exactly a year later, one
finds him announcing: "I am no longer an Englishman, I am
the enemy of mankind. . . . I hate humanity so much, I can only

⁹ *Letters to Russell*, pp. 59–60.
¹⁰ *Collected Letters*, 1: 360.
¹¹ See *Autobiography*, 2: 22–23.

think with friendliness of the dead."[12] The echo says much about the complexity of Lawrence's feelings toward Russell. It tends to confirm an admission that, in a rare moment of objectivity, he had made to the other man: "After all, my quarrelling with you was largely a quarrelling with something in *myself*, something I was struggling away from in myself."[13] By explaining away Russell's pacifism, Lawrence was in effect making him an unwilling party to his own increasingly bitter pangs of misanthropy. His designation of Russell as "the enemy of mankind" looks, in this light, like a last-ditch effort to assimilate the other man's identity to his own, to recast him as an alter ego capable of sharing his own suffocating hatred. Privately, he was harboring emotions quite different in nature from the fierce denunciation of 14 September. In a letter written on the same day, he confesses to Lady Ottoline Morrell: "To-day I wrote very violently to Russell. I am glad, because it had to be said some time. But also I am very sorry, and feel like going into a corner to cry, as I used to do when I was a child. But there seems so much to cry for, one doesn't know where to begin. And then, damn it all, why should one?"[14] The months that followed brought an answer, of sorts, to this last question. It is true that the immediate consequences of the letter to Russell were less dire than Lawrence apparently feared. But, even though the friendship wavered on for some months longer, the quarrel had clearly foreshadowed its eventual collapse. That collapse, when it did come, was signaled by no sudden dramatic event; nor did it restore calm after the stormy passage of the alliance. Rather, the anxieties the friendship had provoked continued to work, throughout the remainder of the war, as an irritant to Lawrence's imagination.

III

Lawrence's short story, "The Blind Man," represents one product of this unresolved irritation. One clue to the story's roots in Lawrence's personal experience is blatantly obvious.

[12] *Collected Letters*, 1: 470. Letter to Cynthia Asquith [1 September 1916].

[13] *Letters to Russell*, p. 61 [17 November 1915].

[14] *The Letters of D. H. Lawrence*, ed. Aldous Huxley (London: Heinemann, 1932), p. 254 [14 September 1915]. (Hereafter cited as *Letters.*)

Bertie Reid, "Bertie" Russell—the resemblance cannot be dismissed as coincidental; too many other clues point to Russell as the original of the fictional character. Yet the portrait is anything but a simple photographic likeness. The Scottish barrister of the story differs from Russell both in his calling and in his national origin, and many of his personal mannerisms seem to be invented, not drawn from memory. Lawrence had elsewhere taken off Russell in a fashion that is strikingly different. The elderly baronet, Sir Johsua Malleson, who appears in the novel *Women in Love*, is readily recognizable as a deliberate and waspish caricature of Russell. Some of Sir Joshua's mannerisms—his rapid-fire, witty conversation, and his readiness to guffaw at his own jokes—correspond to established particulars of Russell's behavior.[15] The fashionable setting in which he appears, Hermione Roddice's estate of Breadalby, clearly recalls Lady Ottoline Morrell's estate of Garsington, which Russell had on occasion visited. But, although the harshness of the caricature doubtless reflects Lawrence's smoldering animosity, Sir Joshua's presence serves mainly to fill in a suitable background for Rupert Birkin's crisis with Hermione. The baronet's clever, mechanical chatter and saurian appearance are simply a part of the suffocating Breadalby atmosphere, from which Birkin at length runs for his life. The portrait is a flat, satirical sketch, subordinated to Lawrence's larger artistic purposes in the novel. For all the malice with which it is drawn, little about the sketch would suggest that Lawrence's involvement with Russell had been more serious than Birkin's casual acquaintance with Sir Joshua.

"The Blind Man" represents something entirely different: a veiled record of the emotional stresses that had convulsed the friendship itself. The "Bertie" of the story corresponds, not to the Russell any detached observer might have seen, but to a Russell transformed by Lawrence's resentment and frustration. Upon closer inspection, even some of Bertie Reid's apparently neutral features suit such a subjectively filtered portrayal. His Scottishness, for example, is linked with an intellectual sharpness that appeals to one side of Isabel Pervin's divided personality. Bertie's profession has similar implications; for Lawrence, Russell's passion for progressive legislation was the hallmark

[15] See Alan Wood, *Bertrand Russell: The Passionate Sceptic* (London: Allen and Unwin, 1957), p. 28, p. 241.

of a barrenly legalistic spirit. And, even though Bertie's "insane reserve" may seem a far cry from Russell's urbane sociability, it does correspond to the invincible personal caution that had been one of Lawrence's chief grievances against his disappointing ally.

By the end of 1915, Lawrence was coming to see Russell categorically as the embodiment of all those forces he most detested in the modern world. As Russell puts it: "I came to feel him a positive force for evil and . . . he came to have the same feeling about me."[16] The conviction that Russell's nature and his own were somehow mystically opposed may have contributed to the increasing polarization of Lawrence's thought, a tendency traceable in many of his letters of this time. To Russell, to Lady Ottoline, and to others, he advances a view of human experience as divided into two antithetical realms: the conscious life of "light" and "vision," and the unconscious life of "darkness" and "blindness." The use of such symbolism was by no means new to Lawrence; it appears, in one form or another, throughout his work, virtually from the beginning of his literary career. At the time of his acquaintance with Russell, however, Lawrence was coming to give to symbolism of light and darkness a new and more specific kind of relevance. In one of the first of his letters to Russell, Lawrence had resorted to symbolism of this type, in a groping attempt to communicate his feeling of personal isolation:

> All the time I am struggling in the dark—very deep in the dark— and cut off from everybody & everything. Sometimes I seem to stumble into the light, for a day, or even two days—then in I plunge again, God knows where & into what utter darkness of chaos. I don't mind very much. But sometimes I am afraid of the terrible things that are real, in the darkness, and of the entire unreality of these things I see. It becomes like a madness at last, to know one is all the time walking in a pale assembly of an unreal world—this house, this furniture, the sky & the earth—whilst oneself is all a while a piece of darkness pulsating in shocks, & the shocks & the darkness are real. The whole universe of darkness & dark passions . . . the subterranean black universe of the things which have not yet had being—has conquered for me now, & I can't escape. So I think with fear of having to talk to anybody, because I can't talk.[17]

16 *Autobiography*, 2: 21.
17 *Letters to Russell*, pp. 41–42 [?15 March 1915].

Lawrence, as Russell's guest, had just made his first visit to Cambridge, where he had felt profoundly shaken by his lack of rapport with the intellectual luminaries to whom he had been introduced. If, afterward, he speaks of his terrifying sense of enclosure within a subterranean "universe of darkness," the connection can hardly be accidental. In his next letter to Russell he reverts, more prosaically, to the same symbolic associations: "It is true Cambridge made me very black and down."[18]

The feeling of entrapment to which Lawrence confesses in these early letters to Russell, and the almost pathetic urgency with which he appeals to the other man for comradeship or release, strongly recall the predicament of Maurice Pervin, the blinded hero of Lawrence's story. To Pervin, blindness has a literal meaning closely resembling the figurative meaning given it by Lawrence: it cuts him off from the ordinary, "visible" world, and causes him to long for communion with a man who enjoys free access to visual reality. Lawrence's desperate invitation to Russell to enter "his world" could easily stand as an epigraph to the blind man's history:

> I feel quite sad, as if I talked a little vulgar language of my own which nobody understood. But if people all turn into stone or pillars of salt, one must still talk to them. You must put off your further knowledge and experience, & talk to me my way, & be with me, or I feel a babbling idiot & an intruder. My world is real, it is a true world, & it is a world I have in my measure understood. But no doubt you also have a true world, which I can't understand. It makes me sad to conclude that. But you must live in my world, while I am there. Because it *is* also a real world. And it is a world you can inhabit with me, if I can't inhabit yours with you.[19]

Metaphorically, the situation presented in the short story matches the one described in the letter: Bertie is free to "join" Pervin simply by shutting his eyes, even if the blind man is incapable of opening his.

Yet the symbolism of blindness in the story is not associated solely with terror, isolation, and longing. It has still more important, positive implications, which can best be explained with reference to letters Lawrence wrote later, in the autumn of

18 Ibid., p. 43 [?19 March 1915].
19 Ibid., pp. 37–38 [26 February 1915].

MICHAEL L. ROSS

1915. Here, he dwells lyrically on the importance of the fabulous dark underworld of the psyche, in which reality is ultimately to be sought. Where earlier he had associated darkness with a fearful sense of personal entrapment, now—spurred, perhaps, by Russell's skepticism—he rhapsodically extoles the liberating properties of the "invisible world." "One must put away all ordinary common sense, I think, and work only from the invisible world," he declares to Lady Cynthia Asquith on 2 October. "The visible world is not true. The invisible world is true and real. One must live and work from that."[20] In a subsequent letter he amplifies his meaning: ". . . The conscious life —which you adhere to—is no more than a masquerade of death: there is a living unconscious life. If only we would shut our eyes; if only we were all struck blind, and things vanished from our sight, we should marvel that we had fought and lived for shallow, visionary, peripheral nothingnesses. We should find reality in the darkness."[21] To Lady Ottoline Morrell, on 7 December, he rings elaborate changes on the same theme, making still more explicit the connection between the sense of sight and intellection. The letter, with its ostinato style, sounds like an attempt at hypnosis:

> Do not struggle, with your will, to dominate your conscious life—do not do it. Only drift, and let go—let go, entirely, and become dark, quite dark—like winter which mows away all the leaves and flowers, and lets only the dark underground roots remain. Let all the leaves and flowers and arborescent form of your life be cut off and cast away, all cut off and cast away, all the old life, so that only the deep roots remain in the darkness underground, and you have no place in the light, no place at all. . . .
> Do not keep your will in your conscious self. Forget, utterly forget, and let go. Let your will lapse back into your unconscious self, so you move in a sleep, and in darkness, without sight or understanding. Only then you will act straight from the dark source of life, outwards, which is creative life.[22]

As Lawrence must by now have realized, Russell, who placed a high priority on will and discipline, could hardly have been expected to receive such theories with enthusiasm. In his letters,

[20] *Letters*, pp. 259–60 [2 October 1915].
[21] Ibid., p. 279 [28 November 1915].
[22] Ibid., p. 286 [7 December 1915].

296

Lawrence generally displays an extremely keen awareness of his correspondent's personality; the passage quoted above, for example, is nicely calculated to appeal to Lady Ottoline's feminine susceptibility to powerful emotional suggestion. When, on the following day, he wrote to Russell, he made a laborious attempt to present the same ideas under a semblance of philosophic discourse:

> Now I am convinced of what I believed when I was about twenty—that there is another seat of consciousness than the brain & the nerve system: there is a blood-consciousness which exists in us independently of the ordinary mental consciousness, which depends on the eye as its source or connector. There is the blood-consciousness, with the sexual connection holding the same relation as the eye, in seeing, holds to the mental consciousness. One lives, knows, and has one's being in the blood, without any reference to nerves and brain. This is one half of life, belonging to the darkness. And the tragedy of this our life, and of your life, is that the mental and nerve consciousness exerts a tyranny over the blood-consciousness and that your will has gone completely over to the mental consciousness, and is engaged in the destruction of your blood-being or blood-consciousness, the final liberating of the one, which is only death in result. Plato was the same. Now it is necessary for us to realise that there is this other great half of our life active in the darkness, the blood-relationship: that when I *see*, there is a connection between my mental-consciousness and an outside body, forming a percept; but at the same time, there is a transmission through the darkness which is never absent from the light, into my blood-consciousness: but in seeing, the blood-percept is perhaps not strong. On the other hand, when I take a woman, then the blood-percept is supreme, my blood-knowing is overwhelming. There is a transmission, I don't know of what, between her blood & mine, in the act of connection. So that afterwards, even if she goes away, the blood-consciousness persists between us, when the mental consciousness is suspended; and I am formed then by my blood-consciousness, not by my mind or nerves at all.[23]

One can hardly imagine what response Russell might have made to this bizarre setting-to-rights of Plato's kingdom of the soul. The letter embodies, in any event, Lawrence's most systematic exposition of the symbolic antinomies he had been devel-

[23] *Letters to Russell*, pp. 63–64 [8 December 1915].

oping. In the way it links together darkness, blood-knowledge, and sexuality, it strongly foreshadows the path he would follow in "The Blind Man." So, in an even blunter fashion, do some of his subsequent messages to Russell: "Do stop working & writing altogether and become a creature instead of a mechanical instrument. Do clear out of the whole social ship. Do for your very pride's sake become a mere nothing, a mole, a creature that feels its way & doesn't think."[24] This seems little else than one more calculated act of provocation; even if he had been disposed to heed such advice, Russell was as incapable of "becoming a mole" as Lawrence of becoming a professional logician.

Yet, whether or not he really expected Russell to obey it, Lawrence undoubtedly saw such a command as a matter of life-and-death urgency. By making such contrasts between feeling and thinking, blood-knowledge and vision, moles and mechanical instruments, he was giving universal meaning to the mystic antagonism he now felt to exist between himself and Russell. What happens in "The Blind Man" provides a clear parallel: in the story, too, a similar clash of personalities assumes a momentous importance. Pervin, the protagonist, is—though for no reason of his own choosing—all too literally "a mole, a creature that feels its way and doesn't think." Bertie Reid, his antagonist, is firmly associated with the opposed qualities of sight and intellectual abstraction. This interplay of opposing elements determines the design of the entire narrative. The symbolic contrast between vision and blindness tends, in some degree, to underscore the pain and frustration that Pervin's wound causes him. In the company of the other, sighted characters, Pervin seems pathetically helpless and clumsy. He is condemned to act out in reality the emotional ordeal Lawrence had been compelled to endure inwardly, the ordeal of "struggling in the dark . . . cut off from everybody and everything."

And yet, paradoxically, the story reveals Pervin's wound as at bottom a source of power. Lawrence's insistence on what is positive in Pervin's blinded groping echoes, with startling exactness, his own directives to Russell:

> Pervin moved about almost unconsciously in his familiar surroundings, dark though everything was. He seemed to know

[24] Ibid., p. 70 [? 19 February 1916].

the presence of objects before he touched them. It was a pleasure to him to rock thus through a world of things, carried on the flood in a sort of blood-prescience. He did not think much or trouble much. So long as he kept this sheer immediacy of blood-contact with the substantial world he was happy, he wanted no intervention of visual consciousness. In this state there was a certain rich positivity, bordering sometimes on rapture. Life seemed to move in him like a tide lapping, lapping, and advancing, enveloping all things darkly. It was a pleasure to stretch forth the hand and meet the unseen object, clasp it, and possess it in pure contact. He did not try to remember, to visualise. He did not want to. The new way of consciousness substituted itself in him.[25]

Such a passage, which at first sounds naïvely descriptive, really amounts to a programmatic recasting of Lawrence's letter to Russell about "blood-consciousness." The similarities are almost uncomfortably numerous; to a hostile critic they might even provide grounds for treating the story as merely a platform for Lawrence's doctrinaire theories. What is most surprising, however, is Lawrence's real measure of success in translating a piece of pseudoscientific rigmarole into a believable portrayal of character. Because Pervin's behavior calls to mind the way blinded persons do actually go about adjusting to their loss of sight, the symbolic overtones of the passage do not seem too obviously "planted." By presenting blindness with an air of unassuming, literal authenticity, Lawrence forces the reader to identify himself closely with Pervin, and thereby to acknowledge the supreme necessity of pure and immediate contact.

IV

Throughout "The Blind Man," Lawrence objectifies his abstract and highly personal theory of blood-consciousness by embodying it in a convincingly imagined fictional situation. He reinforces the main symbolic polarities—blindness and vision, darkness and light—with other related contrasts.[26] Isabel's

[25] D. H. Lawrence, "The Blind Man," in *The Complete Short Stories of D. H. Lawrence* (London: Heinemann, 1955), 2: 355. (Hereafter cited as "The Blind Man.")

[26] For useful discussions of Lawrence's development of symbolic patterns in the story see Mark Spilka, "Ritual Form in 'The Blind Man,'" in *D. H. Lawrence: A Collection of Critical Essays*, ed. Spilka (Englewood Cliffs: Prentice-Hall, 1963), p. 112–16; and Nancy Abolin, "Lawrence's

MICHAEL L. ROSS

parlor, with its order and gentility, is poised against Maurice's stable, full of the palpable darkness of animal warmth. Isabel feels half an intruder within Pervin's sacred precincts; Bertie Reid is a far more flagrant intruder, and his entry into the stable constitutes a rash act of trespassing. Bertie's own temperament includes all those qualities that are forever shut out of Pervin's world; he lives as tightly enclosed within his realm of sight as Pervin within his realm of blindness. His limitations are emphasized by his physical appearance: "He was a little dark man, with a very big forehead, thin, wispy hair, and sad, large eyes."[27] Lawrence keeps alive the association of sight with understanding by calling repeated attention to Bertie's most prominent features: "[Isabel] looked at his dark grey eyes, with their uncanny, almost child-like intuition, and she loved him. He understood amazingly—but she had no fear of his understanding."[28] By pitting Bertie as a foil against his blind protagonist, Lawrence delivers a damning judgment upon the barrister's world of "understanding"—a world that appears to be hospitable and humane, but is essentially devoid of feeling or purpose. Pervin's blind vitality so dominates the scene that Bertie comes unexpectedly to seem, by contrast, the truly "handicapped" person. The feebleness of Bertie's "sight" is established dramatically in the concluding pages, where the barrister is stunned by his direct contact with Pervin's blindness and by his simultaneous exposure to Pervin's passionate friendship.

By forcing such contact on Bertie, the blind man has at last succeeded in penetrating the other's "insane reserve." In doing so, however, Pervin has in effect destroyed him—"He was like a mollusc whose shell is broken."[29] Bertie's shell stands as the symbolic equivalent of Pervin's blindness; it epitomizes the barrister's brittle and self-protective egoism, just as Pervin's sightlessness epitomizes his sensuous, instinctual groping toward a knowledge of the surrounding world. This metaphor, too,

'The Blind Man': The Reality of Touch," in *A D. H. Lawrence Miscellany*, ed. Harry T. Moore (Carbondale: Southern Illinois University Press, 1959), p. 215–20.

[27] "The Blind Man," p. 357.

[28] Ibid., pp. 359–60.

[29] Ibid., p. 365.

can be traced back to the time of Lawrence's friendship with Russell; its occurrences serve, in fact, as a partial index to the course of Lawrence's feelings about the other man. In "The Crown," Lawrence equates the shell with rigid and ready-made definitions of the self, which cramp the spirit, preventing it from growing into its natural form and shielding it from a full and vivifying exposure to emotional reality. Such a shell encloses those orthodox liberals who yearn for peace in order to preserve obsolete democratic institutions:

> We may give ourselves utterly to destruction. Then our conscious forms are destroyed along with us, and something new must arise. But we may not have corruption within ourselves as sensationalism, our skin and outer form intact. To destroy life for the preserving of a static, rigid form, a shell, a glassy envelope, this is the lugubrious activity of the men who fight to save democracy and to end all fighting.

By allowing man's destructive impulses to exhaust themselves, even bloodshed may shatter the old forms and lead to a rebirth. Liberal humanitarianism, by contrast, acts simply to perpetuate destructiveness; its "shell" remains intact and sterile, rather than allowing a passage to living impulses:

> We shall need to live again, and live hard, for once our great civilized form is broken, and we are at last born into the open sky, we shall have a whole new universe to grow up into, and to find relations with. . . . But let us watch that we do not preserve an enveloping falsity around our destructive activity, some nullity of virtue and self-righteousness, some conceit of the "general good" and the salvation of the world by bringing it all within our own conceived whole form. This is the utter lie and obscenity. The ego, like Humpty Dumpty, sitting for ever on the wall.[30]

According to Lawrence, "The Crown was written in 1915, when the war was already twelve months old, and had gone pretty deep."[31] The entire essay is, almost certainly, an elaboration of the "philosophy" he had been trying out on Russell and Lady Ottoline during the summer of 1915. Its composition thus coincides precisely with the quarrel over Russell's pro-

---

[30] D. H. Lawrence, "The Crown," in *Reflections on the Death of a Porcupine* (Bloomington: Indiana University Press, 1963), pp. 78–79.

[31] Ibid., prefatory note.

posed lecture series; and, in the passage quoted above, echoes of that dispute are plentiful. Russell was, after all, Lawrence's one intimate acquaintance among "the men who fight to save democracy and to end all fighting," and his general verdict upon such men closely corresponds to many of his explicit pronouncements about the philosopher. Just at this time, he was coming to view Russell as a man who shielded his "destructive activity" within a shell of "enveloping falsity." In his angry letter of 16 August to Lady Cynthia Asquith, he complains that Russell cherishes (much like "Humpty Dumpty") his "own established ego, his finite and ready-defined self," sitting primly on a wall in order to escape the peril of breakage and the responsibility of growth. His bitterness extends to Lady Ottoline as well; she and Russell have joined forces against him in a conspiracy of misunderstanding:

> I've got a real bitterness in my soul, just now, as if Russell and Lady Ottoline were traitors—they are traitors. They betray the real truth. They come to me, and they make me talk, and they enjoy it, it gives them a profoundly gratifying sensation. And that is all. As if what I say were meant only to give them gratification, because of the flavour of personality, as if I were a cake or a wine or a pudding. . . .
> All that is dynamic in the world, they convert to a sensation, to the gratification of what is static. They are static, static, static, they come, they say to me, "You are wonderful, you are dynamic," then they filch my life for a sensation unto themselves, all my effort, which is my life, they betray. . . . The result is for them a gratifying sensation, a tickling, and for me a real bleeding.[32]

Like the liberal humanitarians whom Lawrence attacks in "The Crown," Russell and Lady Ottoline "have corruption within themselves as sensationalism"; they, too—on the level of personal relations—"destroy life for the preserving of a static, rigid form, a shell." The angry sense of betrayal that was to wreck the friendship with Russell lies just below the apparently impersonal surface of Lawrence's essay.

In his very first letter to Russell, Lawrence had introduced the same image, but without implying any judgment on his correspondent's own personality:

[32] *Collected Letters*, 1: 362 [16 August 1915].

There comes a point when the shell, the form of life, is a prison to the life. Then the life must either concentrate on breaking the shell, or it must turn round, turn in upon itself. . . . Now either we have to break the shell, the form, the whole frame, or we have got to turn to this inward activity of setting the house in order & drawing up a list before we die.[33]

Before long he began to apply the shell metaphor to specific persons of his acquaintance. In April, he writes to Lady Otto-line Morrell about Francis Birrell and the younger Bloomsbury set, with whom Russell had some connections: "They are cased each in a hard little shell of his own, and out of this they talk words. There is never for one second any outgoing of feeling, and no reverence, not a crumb or grain of reverence."[34] By late summer, he had mournfully concluded that his ally Russell, far from being a man he could count on for help in breaking the shell of the established form of life, was snugly ensconced within a shell of his own; that even he was too thoroughly "sublimated into words" to be able to "get into a boat and preach from out of the waters of eternity."[35] Partly in reaction, perhaps, against the philosopher's uncooperativeness, he began to couple his pet metaphor with an ever more uncompromising antirationalism. "I am bored with coherent thought. Its very coherence is a dead shell."[36]

Writing "The Blind Man" provided Lawrence with an op-portunity to complete vicariously the job he had once under-taken in fact—to smash Russell's protective "shell," to demolish for good and all the other man's provoking armor of com-posure. The resounding bang that climaxes the fiction compen-sates for the disappointing whimper with which the actual friendship had expired; here, at least, dynamic feeling can triumph conclusively over static intellectual abstraction. In its indebtedness to Lawrence's private compulsions, "The Blind Man" incorporates many elements of fantasy, the familiar sort of wish-fulfillment revery in which a stinging and indelible wrong can be beautifully righted. In the fiction Pervin—though

[33] *Letters to Russell*, pp. 34–35. [12 February 1915].

[34] *Collected Letters*, 1: 332 [19 April 1915].

[35] *Letters*, p. 240 [9 July 1915].

[36] *Collected Letters*, 1: 373. Letter to H. O. Meredith [2 November 1915].

in a very special and qualified sense—seems to figure as a dream-surrogate for Lawrence himself; and here, again, the evidence of Lawrence's letters confirms the connection.

In a note of consolation to Lady Cynthia Asquith, written during the turbulent autumn of 1915, Lawrence declares:

> I am English, and my Englishness is my very vision. But now I must go away, if my soul is sightless for ever. Let it then be blind, rather than commit the vast wickedness of acquiescence.
>
> Don't think I am not sorry about your brother—it makes me tremble. Don't think I want to hurt you—or anybody—I would do anything rather. But now I feel like a blind man who would put his eyes out rather than stand witness to a colossal and deliberate horror.[37]

If Lawrence had by now begun to imagine himself in the role of "blind man," there are several reasons why that role might have strongly suggested itself to him. One reason is his tendency, during the war, to describe his personal feelings in terms of mutilation and crippling bodily injury. Such hyperbole captures both his response to the war as a direct personal blow and his desolate sense of separation from his countrymen, who were enthusiastically taking part in an orgy of patriotic frenzy. Much like the blind man of his story, Lawrence felt a desperate need for "some further connection with the outer world."[38] To picture himself as a casualty of war must have been both easy and tempting. Much as the mob might scorn those who would not risk their lives in the trenches, Lawrence obviously felt he was risking something still more important—his integrity of soul, even his sanity. To do poetic justice to his real though inconspicuous suffering, he required a dream self-image that could compete, in its drama and its pathos, with the literal heroism of the war's recognized martyrs.

But what made the stance of "blind man" especially attractive to him was surely its appropriateness to his emerging theories of consciousness, as set forth in his letters to Russell and Lady Ottoline. In "The Blind Man," both phases of Lawrence's thinking—his frightened sense of entrapment within his world of darkness, and his eager conviction of that world's rich promise—are powerfully blended. The figure of Maurice Pervin

---

[37] *Collected Letters*, 1: 371 [21 October 1915].
[38] "The Blind Man," p. 348.

joins together Lawrence's haunting sense of frustration and incompleteness with his embattled trust in the supreme authenticity of his newly discovered, dark psychic underground. Pervin is thus uniquely suited to bear Lawrence's standard against the forces of light and intellection.

According to John Middleton Murry, "Lawrence was always prone to construct a dream-figure of himself who bore singularly little relation to the actual man."[39] If Pervin does represent such a dream-figure, his resemblance to the dreamer is certainly far from obvious:

> Bertie was a barrister and a man of letters, a Scotsman of the intellectual type. . . . Maurice Pervin was different. He came of a good old country family—the Grange was not a very great distance from Oxford. He was passionate, sensitive, perhaps over-sensitive, wincing—a big fellow with heavy limbs and a forehead that flushed painfully. For his mind was slow, as if drugged by the strong provincial blood that beat in his veins. He was very sensitive to his own mental slowness, his feelings being quick and acute. So that he was just the opposite to Bertie, whose mind was much quicker than his emotions, which were not so very fine.[40]

Apart from Pervin's passionateness and quickness of feeling, little in this description would call to mind Lawrence himself. Yet it is quite understandable that Lawrence could have been tempted to associate himself with just such a figure; to make of it, half-consciously perhaps, a vehicle for some of his most cherished fantasies. There could be, above all, no more apt antagonist for the cerebral, sophisticated Bertie Reid. Bertie's Scottishness—he is an outlander, alien to the locale of the story —can be played off, to his disadvantage, against Pervin's firm local "roots."[41] Pervin's "strong provincial blood" connects him squarely with the English countryside and, by extension, with the folk-wisdom of its inhabitants, while his dwelling-place lies

---

[39] *Composite Biography*, 1: 324.

[40] "The Blind Man," p. 349.

[41] In this respect, the contrast between Maurice Pervin and Bertie Reid closely resembles the opposition, in Thomas Hardy's novel *The Mayor of Casterbridge*, between the blindly impulsive Saxon, Michael Henchard, and the shrewdly rationalistic Scot, Donald Farfrae. In view of Lawrence's long-standing interest in Hardy's novels, the resemblance may not be entirely accidental.

handily within shouting distance of the theater of English culture. Embarrassed as he had been by his own provincialism, and by his sense of exclusion from Russell's and Lady Ottoline's inner circle, Lawrence was naturally inclined to recast Russell as the outsider, and himself as the exemplar of English local traditions ("My Englishness is my very vision"). Though he might declare grandly that he was "no longer an Englishman," he could never, in his heart, be reconciled to feeling himself anything else.

The dreamlike transformations of fact extend still further. There are few overt resemblances between Isabel Pervin and Lady Ottoline Morrell; it was, in fact, Catherine Carswell who claimed to recognize herself as Isabel's "original."[42] Nevertheless, Isabel's role in bringing together her husband and her childhood friend corresponds suggestively to Lady Ottoline's role in introducing Lawrence to Russell.

> Isabel felt that they *ought* to get on together. But they did not. She felt that if only each could have the clue to the other there would be such a rare understanding between them. It did not come off, however. Bertie adopted a slightly ironical attitude, very offensive to Maurice, who returned the Scotch irony with English resentment, a resentment which deepened sometimes into stupid hatred.[43]

By changing a few names and adjectives, one could make this serve as a roughly true-to-life resumé of what had happened among the flesh-and-blood trio of acquaintances. The situation recalls Lawrence's insecurity in the company of Russell and Lady Ottoline—members of a social and intellectual elite hitherto foreign to his experience—while it reflects his need to affirm the validity of his own more plebeian heritage.

At Cambridge, in the company of G. E. Moore, Keynes, and the others, Lawrence doubtless had seen himself as all too precisely the "babbling idiot and intruder" he had begged Russell to save him from feeling. In the company of Russell and Lady Ottoline, who were bound together by their common

---

[42] See *Composite Biography*, 1: 475 and note. Although Mrs. Carswell apparently did not suspect it, her husband Don—a Scottish barrister—may also have suggested a few of the external particulars of Isabel's friend Bertie Reid. Otherwise, however, there are no detectable resemblances between the man and the fictional character.

[43] "The Blind Man," p. 349.

causes, their common circle of acquaintances, and their common social backgrounds, and who were also (as Lawrence was probably unaware) in the midst of a love affair, he must have felt an even more stinging sense of idiocy and intrusion. At moments, "The Blind Man" obliquely recaptures his embarrassment:

> They moved away. Pervin heard no more. But a childish sense of desolation had come over him, as he heard their brisk voices. He seemed shut out—like a child that is left out. He was aimless and excluded, he did not know what to do with himself. . . . He fumbled nervously as he dressed himself, in a state almost of childishness. He disliked the Scotch accent in Bertie's speech, and the slight response it found on Isabel's tongue. He disliked the slight purr of complacency in the Scottish speech. . . . He was fretful and beside himself like a child, he had almost a childish nostalgia to be included in the life circle. And at the same time he was a man, dark and powerful and infuriated by his own weakness. By some fatal flaw, he could not be by himself, he had to depend on the support of another. And this very dependence enraged him. He hated Bertie Reid, and at the same time he knew the hatred was nonsense, he knew it was the outcome of his own weakness.[44]

Such a passage, when viewed in isolation from its fictional context, reveals an unexpected array of confessional overtones. Pervin's desolation—literally explained, of course, by his blindness—strikingly parallels Lawrence's own private sentiments. Even the blindness itself is poignantly expressive of his frustration at being painfully "handicapped" in his dealings with his two distinguished friends. Similarly, Pervin's annoyance at "Scottish" speech suggests Lawrence's easily imaginable sensitivity, as a Midlander, to the difference in accent between himself and the others, and his understandable annoyance at the "purr of complacency" in their upper-caste British speech. Still more revealing, however, is the "fatal flaw" that compels Pervin—like Lawrence—to seek a companionship that at the same time he shrinks from as potentially humiliating. The blind man's panicky childishness recalls the nervous reaction induced in Lawrence by the quarrel with Russell: "I am very sorry, and feel like going into a corner to cry, as I used to do when I was a child." The whole complex assortment of Pervin's feelings—

[44] Ibid., pp. 356–57.

his sense of helpless dependence and unusable power, his vindictive rage and his own disgust with it—can be read, distinctly enough, in and between the lines of Lawrence's correspondence during his friendship with Russell.

V

At the conclusion of his story, the blinded Maurice Pervin gains a total, dreamlike supremacy over the sighted Bertie Reid:

> Now Bertie quivered with revulsion. Yet he was under the power of the blind man, as if hypnotised. . . .
> Bertie could not answer. He gazed mute and terror-struck, overcome by his own weakness. He knew he could not answer. He had an unreasonable fear, lest the other man should suddenly destroy him. Whereas Maurice was actually filled with hot, poignant love, the passion of friendship. Perhaps it was this very passion of friendship which Bertie shrank from most.[45]

Plainly enough, it was just such a thoroughgoing supremacy that Lawrence had aspired, and failed, to gain over the wary Russell. Pervin's "triumph" is, as the text indicates, an undesired and therefore basically a hollow one. The communion he thinks he has achieved by physical contact with the other man has little to do with the sheer terror and revulsion Bertie actually feels. As Nancy Abolin rightly says, "It is part of the irony of Lawrence's vision that the very same nature which would make Bertie a complementary fulfillment for Maurice's character also makes him totally incapable of accepting Maurice's urgent and poignant offer of friendship."[46] In fact, the irony is a part, not only of Lawrence's vision, but of the painful personal memories that the vision to some extent duplicates. And yet, for all its irony, the story's conclusion represents a clear dream-reversal of Lawrence's own experience; a willed dénouement whose ringing finality serves to compensate for the frustrating, inconclusive outcome of the actual friendship between Lawrence and Russell. Into this fantastically altered version, nothing of the intellectual give-and-take that had gone on between the two men is permitted to enter. By excluding all secondary issues, Lawrence has diverted the struggle between his dream-antagonists into the channel where

[45] Ibid., p. 364.
[46] Abolin, "The Reality of Touch," pp. 217–18.

his own greatest power was concentrated—the capacity for feeling, for "blood-brotherhood" itself. In the consoling world of fantasy, Pervin can overwhelm Bertie by pitting—as Lawrence had never managed to do with Russell—his primary strength against the other man's primary vulnerability.

Linked with this contest, predictably, is a match of sexual potency, which also works in Bertie's disfavor. His inadequacy is dramatized by the oblique rivalry between the two men for Isabel's allegiance. Initially, Bertie might appear to have the advantage. He is, of course, not disabled; in addition, he shares childhood memories with Isabel, and can offer her an outlet for the intellectual tendencies her intimacy with Maurice has stifled. Yet this sort of companionship is proven to be sterile. Bertie's entrapment within the shell of his ego renders him as immune from sexual involvement as from the passionate comradeship for which Pervin longs: "He had his friends among the fair sex—not lovers, friends. So long as he could avoid any danger of courtship or marriage, he adored a few good women with constant and unfailing homage, and he was chivalrously fond of quite a number. But if they seemed to encroach on him, he withdrew and detested them. . . . He was ashamed of himself, because he could not marry, could not approach women physically."[47] Pervin's blindness, by contrast, is strongly identified with uninhibited sexual fulfillment.[48] Unlike Bertie's sad-eyed, disembodied power of vision, it brings to Isabel a profound and enlivening satisfaction, the fruit of which is her unborn child—a living rebuke to the sterility of Bertie's shell-enclosed egoism.

The picture Lawrence presents of Bertie Reid, inhibited by his special nature from sexual contact, is almost comically at variance with the established truth about Russell himself, whose

[47] "The Blind Man," p. 359.

[48] A similar connection between blindness and healthy sexuality is made in Lawrence's poem "These Clever Women," which begins with the injunction: "Close your eyes, my love, let me make you blind!" and concludes with the question:

> Am I doomed in a long coition of words to mate you?
> Unsatisfied! Is there no hope
> Between your thighs, far, far from your peering sight?

The entire poem is closely relevant to Lawrence's intentions in "The Blind Man." See *The Complete Poems of D. H. Lawrence*, ed. Vivian de Sola Pinto and F. Warren Roberts (London: Heinemann, 1964), 1: 118–19.

sexual career was for more adventurous than Lawrence's own. Here, once again, Lawrence has simply projected the image of Russell best calculated to flatter his own injured ego. In many respects, "The Blind Man" strikingly confirms the opinion of William H. Gass: "Lawrence wrote novels, stories, essays, of challenge and revenge, composed elaborate and desperate daydreams, disposing of his problems and his friends, recreating himself, rewriting his forlorn history."[49] Almost every word of this might have been aimed specifically at "The Blind Man." And yet, even conceding the truth of Gass's statement, one can read the story as something more than an "elaborate and desperate daydream" in which a bafflingly complex and painful episode from Lawrence's "forlorn history" has been battered, at all costs, into the appropriately gratifying fictional shape. The reshaping not only affords Lawrence the consolations of fantasy; it also enables him to spotlight certain essential truths that lay, half-buried, beneath the intricacies of the life history. Although Lawrence never succeeded in cracking Russell's "shell" with his onslaughts, he did come dangerously close to destroying the other man's belief in the value of his own existence. And for Lawrence, as for his fictional protagonist, this sort of "victory" could provide at best a hollow consolation for his failure to find the union he was desperately seeking. His predicament, essentially, was equivalent to the blind man's: to break down the barriers separating him from the other man, he would have had to demolish the other's ego; yet such violence automatically ruled out, instead of guaranteeing, any further contact. The ending of the story suggests, more poignantly than could any ordinary biographical record, the grief caused Lawrence by the stalemate between his own "blindness" and Russell's hopelessly incompatible "sight." "The Blind Man" embodies both Lawrence's compulsion to bypass the reality of his failure, and his sober recognition that the failure had been irrevocable. Despite its heavy freight of self-vindication, the fiction reflects, even while it distorts, the historical truth.

To test the relevance to fact of Lawrence's strange fable, one need look no further than Russell's own *Autobiography*. In some of his cited letters, and at times in those portions of the

[49] William H. Gass, "From Some Ashes No Bird Rises," *The New York Review of Books* (1 August 1968), p. 4.

narrative that were composed by 1931,[50] Russell confesses to a painful sense of isolation within his own personality, a self-enclosure that coincides strikingly with Lawrence's presentation of Bertie Reid. He writes, for example, to Ottoline Morrell on 11 June 1915: "How passionately I long that one could break through the prison walls in one's own nature. I feel now-a-days so much as if some great force for good were imprisoned within me by scepticism and cynicism and lack of faith. But those who have no such restraint always seem ignorant and a little foolish. It all makes one feel very lonely." His next words pinpoint the reference: "I can't make head or tail of Lawrence's philosophy. I dread talking to him about it. It is not sympathetic to me."[51] Clearly Russell, too, suffered, perhaps as acutely as Lawrence, from the breakdown of their alliance; yet he seems to have been equally helpless to overcome those differences of temperament and belief that raised a barrier between them.

How rigidly Russell was bound by his self-enclosure is amusingly suggested by Lady Ottoline Morrell's description of him, dancing at one of her "Thursday evenings": "When there was a general *mêlée*, Bertie Russell would be dragged in by one of the Aranyis. It was very comic to see him—a stiff little figure, jumping up and down like a child, with an expression of surprised delight on his face at finding himself doing such an ordinary human thing as dancing. It seemed to liberate him from himself, and made him very happy for a short time at least."[52] Despite the substantial truth in Russell's charges about Lawrence's mania for personal tyranny, what exasperated Lawrence

[50] See, for example, Russell's statement in his *Autobiography*, 2: 38: "Underlying all occupations and all pleasures I have felt since early youth the pain of solitude. I have escaped it most nearly in moments of love, yet even there, on reflection, I have found that the escape depended partly upon illusion." In a footnote dated 1967, Russell qualifies this admission as being "no longer true," but there is no reason to think it untrue for the Russell Lawrence knew in 1915. (On p. 159 of Volume II, Russell reveals that a short autobiographical memoir, dictated to his secretary in May and June 1931, "has formed the basis of the present book down to 1921." The "epilogue" to that memoir, which then follows on pp. 159–60, contains sentiments very similar to those quoted above.)

[51] *Autobiography*, 2: 53.

[52] *Ottoline: The Early Memoirs of Lady Ottoline Morrell*, ed. Robert Gathorne-Hardy (London: Faber and Faber, 1963), p. 277.

was at bottom the failure of his campaign to "liberate" Russell from himself in a permanent and serious fashion. What Lady Ottoline says of Lawrence himself has a bearing on that failure: "Many people are interested in others in a superficial way, but [Lawrence's] interest would penetrate and lay hands on his object, breaking down barriers. No wonder that there were those that resented it, and resented what they thought was his interference in their private lives, that he would tell them that he knew better than they did what was good for them. He was not the child of an old cultivated family who inherits a natural restraint and respect for his neighbour's hidden and secluded lives. . . ."[53] Such observations recall—all the more vividly because inadvertently—the impasse depicted in Lawrence's short story. What Russell, like his fictional counterpart, could not bear was having another man "penetrate and lay hands on" his own "hidden and secluded life," violating the sanctity of his well-bred reserve through a lack of innate restraint. For Russell, such liberties put any lasting intimacy out of the question.[54]

---

[53] Ibid., pp. 273–74.

[54] Russell's much more satisfying friendship with another great novelist, Joseph Conrad, helps to clarify by contrast his inability to enter into a *Blutbruderschaft* with Lawrence. See *Autobiography*, 1: 207 ff. Conrad, whom Russell met in 1913, also through Lady Ottoline, turned out to be "an aristocratic Polish gentleman to his fingertips"—whereas Lawrence's fingertips were distinctly those of a Nottingham miner's son. Again, Conrad's "romantic love . . . from a certain distance" for England was quite unlike Lawrence's fiercely immediate mixture of love and hatred for his native country, a blend of emotions Russell may have found more disquieting. More important still was Conrad's settled distrust of unconscious impulse, an attitude that is leagues removed from Lawrence's: "He thought of civilized and morally tolerably human life as a dangerous walk on a thin crust of barely cooled lava which at any moment might break and let the unwary sink into fiery depths." Such a vision was obviously far more congenial to Russell than Lawrence's contemptuous rejection of discipline, and his identification of the "fiery depths" as the vital source of human reality. Finally, Conrad's commitment to discipline was mirrored in the tactful restraint of his personal manner, just as Lawrence's antirationalist bias was paralleled by his unceremonious directness. Such a restraint was far likelier to put Russell at his ease, enabling him at once to enter into an intimacy that Lawrence's impetuous familiarity always ruled out: "We [Russell and Conrad] seemed to sink through layer after layer of what was superficial, till gradually both reached the central fire. . . . The emotion was as intense as passionate love, and at the same time all-embracing." The resemblance between this recognition and the sort of blood-brotherhood Lawrence longed for is strangely ironic.

Revealing as all these connections are, however, "The Blind Man" can hardly have been intended by Lawrence simply as a fanciful commentary on the relationship between himself and Russell. The story's intrinsic interest depends on literary qualities that transcend such personal references. It is ultimately Lawrence's transforming artistic vision that promotes the story from the level of a private document to the level of impersonal myth. Russell, in his *Autobiography*, dismisses Lawrence flatly as a compulsive and ineffectual daydreamer: "Most of the time he lived in a solitary world of his own imaginings, peopled by phantoms as fierce as he wished them to be."[55] What Russell neglects, significantly, to mention is that precisely the same could be said of almost any major literary artist. The artist, unlike any routine dreamer, has the power to communicate the truth of his "solitary world," to make "his own imaginings" a vital part of the reader's reality. "The Blind Man," even while it compensates for Lawrence's private feelings of resentment and insufficiency, embodies those feelings in a fictional design that has an impersonal logic of its own. Both Lawrence's failure with Russell and the psychological theorizing it helped to stimulate stand behind the story; but it is Lawrence's artistic conscience that governs his fiction's shape.

Perhaps the most striking evidence of Lawrence's artistic control is his avoidance of that quality that most often colors wish-fulfillment fantasy, the tendency to melodrama. Lawrence's treatment of his protagonist is, in general, quite judiciously and effectively distanced. Secretly, in his creator's mind, Pervin may have figured as an avenging Samson; but, as with Milton's Samson, his weakness and frustration are presented as fully as his latent power. The double-sidedness of Pervin's handicap is suggested most brilliantly by Lawrence's adept handling of point-of-view, a technical matter that is, for obvious reasons, of signal importance in this story. What happens to Pervin is transmitted, neither exclusively through the blind man's own senses, nor from a standpoint exterior to him. In-

---

For general discussions of Lawrence's relations with Russell see James L. Jarrett, "D. H. Lawrence and Bertrand Russell," in *A D. H. Lawrence Miscellany*, pp. 168–87; and Edward Alexander, "Thomas Carlyle and D. H. Lawrence: A Parallel," in *University of Toronto Quarterly* 37, Number 3 (April 1968): 248–67, especially 260ff.

[55] *Autobiography*, 2: 23.

stead, Lawrence deftly alternates frequent glimpses into Pervin's darkened consciousness with occasional shifts into Bertie Reid's brightly lighted psyche and into Isabel's painfully divided one. Through his skillful managing of juxtaposition, he stops the reader from responding in any simple or conventional way to Pervin's predicament.

Isabel's role is crucial in maintaining the needed balance between distance and identification. At moments, she cannot help pitying her husband as a piece of human wreckage: "She watched him enter, head erect, his feet tentative. He looked so strong-blooded and healthy, and, at the same time, cancelled. . . . Perhaps it was his scars suggested it."[56] But at other times, rather than "looking" in this fashion, she is drawn helplessly to empathize with Pervin's darkened, sensuous life:

> The loud jarring of the inner door-latch made her start; the door was opened. She could hear and feel her husband entering and invisibly passing among the horses near to her, in darkness as they were, actively intermingled. The rather low sound of his voice as he spoke to the horses came velvety to her nerves. How near he was, and how invisible! The darkness seemed to be in a strange swirl of violent life, just upon her.[57]

By responding so intensely to her husband's world of darkness, Isabel clinches for the reader its relevance to the life of the sighted as well. Her feeling of nearness depends on those "lower" senses—hearing and touch and smell—they can still share, and her perceptions become blended (Maurice's "velvety" voice is one example of this) to transmit a powerful effect of synesthesia. Pervin—who is introduced in his most congenial surroundings, the rank, unlighted stables—is himself emphatically invisible. The darkness that blankets both man and wife images the contact that binds them together, with a bond far stronger than ordinary pity or affection.

By such means, Lawrence elicits a balanced response to what is singular in Pervin's condition. This makes it all the easier for him to induce the reader to accept "blindness"—with all the symbolic associations that cluster around the idea—as standing for a compelling and reachable "new way of consciousness." Far from sensing that the conflict between "blindness" and

---

[56] "The Blind Man," p. 357.
[57] Ibid., p. 353.

"sight" has its source in some inveterate personal grudge of the author's, the reader accepts it as a timeless and universal parable about two fundamentally opposed ways of experiencing the world. Notions which, in Lawrence's letters, seem incoherent or essentially private, are here given an irresistible fictional cogency. Psychologically, "The Blind Man" may have closed a chapter in Lawrence's personal history. Artistically, it elaborates Lawrence's brooding resentment into something utterly different, replacing the narrow rancor of personal antagonism with the kind of openness and anonymity that belong to genuine myth. And yet, had the antagonism itself not continued to trouble Lawrence's consciousness—had he not been impelled to do a peculiar sort of "poetic justice" to his quarrel with Russell—the myth might never have been born, or might never have attained to the compulsive vigor it in fact possesses. What the present discussion has tried to establish—the rootedness of "The Blind Man" in Lawrence's private experience—is far from being the only reason for the story's excellence, yet it is also anything but irrelevant to Lawrence's artistic accomplishment.

XV

S. P. ROSENBAUM

The Philosophical Realism of Virginia Woolf

"Why don't you contribute to the Queen's Doll's house,
Virginia?"
"Is there a W. C. in it, Vita?"
"You're a bit hoity-toity, Virginia."
"Well, I was educated in the old Cambridge school. Ever
hear of Moore?"
"George Moore the novelist?"
"My dear Vita, we start at different ends."
    (Conversation with Vita Sackville-West reported by
Virginia Woolf in a letter to Clive Bell, January 1924)[1]

During the past thirty or forty years a number of studies have
found the fiction of Virginia Woolf to be philosophically significant, though she has seldom been called outright a philosophical novelist. Perhaps the tendency to identify the philosophical novel with the novel of ideas is the reason why critics
appear to be reluctant to think about her in those terms. That
there were other ways of using philosophy in fiction besides
the novel of ideas is clearly implied by Virginia Woolf in her
essay on George Meredith. She complained that his teaching
was obtrusive in his fiction,

> and when philosophy is not consumed in a novel, when we can
> underline this phrase with a pencil, and cut out that exhorta-
> tion with a pair of scissors and paste the whole into a system,
> it is safe to say that there is something wrong with the philoso-
> phy or with the novel or with both (1:230).[2]

This essay is part of a work in progress tentatively entitled The
Bloomsbury Group: A Study in Literature and Philosophy.

[1] From an unpublished letter quoted with the permission of Professor
Quentin Bell and Mrs. Angelica Garnett. I am especially indebted to
Professor Bell for his great kindness and help.

[2] Volume and page numbers following references to Virginia Woolf's
essays refer to *Collected Essays* (London, 1966), 4 vols.

These remarks were not written by someone hostile or even indifferent to philosophy and its importance for fiction. They suggest, on the contrary, that Virginia Woolf had her own ideas about the nature of philosophy as well as the novel. This essay is an attempt to examine some of those ideas and the ways in which they are "consumed" in her fiction.

I

If many critics have agreed that Virginia Woolf's novels have philosophical meanings of one kind or another, they have disagreed as to what the philosophy actually is. Bergsonism, empiricism, idealism, and existentialism have all been brought to bear on her work but with unconvincing results.[3] The publication of John Maynard Keynes's *Two Memoirs* in 1949 introduced a different and more important philosophical dimension to the interpretation of Virginia Woolf. Keynes does not mention her specifically in his second memoir entitled "My Early Beliefs," but his brilliant, partial generalizations cover the impact of G. E. Moore's ethics and personality on himself, his friends, and their circle, which of course included Virginia Woolf. Keynes discusses how he and his friends accepted Moore's "religion" as set forth in *Principia Ethica*. It consisted of "timeless, passionate states of contemplation and communion," the greatest of which were, according to Moore, "certain states of consciousness, which may be roughly described as the pleasures of human intercourse and the enjoyment of beautiful objects." Moore himself, says Keynes, was "a puritan and a precisian," but his followers ignored his morals, his concern with the relation of ethics to conduct. Keynes marveled that Moore was so oblivious to the life of action, that the basic intuitions of his ethics were so limited, and that his influence on them was so much of a piece with Edwardian individualism.[4]

Keynes's account, which has been cited by friend and foe

---

[3] Maxime Chastaing's misleadingly entitled *La philosophie de Virginia Woolf* (Paris, 1951) is the most extended attempt to relate philosophy to Virginia Woolf's work, but the results are paradoxical. Ignoring the evidence of Virginia Woolf's nonfiction, Chastaing extracts from contextless quotations taken from Virginia Woolf's novels a philosophy of redemption and grace that condemns empiricism by espousing it and showing the unendurable results.

[4] John Maynard Keynes, "My Early Beliefs," *Two Memoirs, Essays and Sketches in Biography* (New York, 1956), pp. 239–56.

alike in discussions of the importance of *Principia Ethica* for the Bloomsbury Group,[5] was authoritatively challenged and modified in 1960 by Leonard Woolf's first volume of autobiography, *Sowing*. Woolf found Keynes "quite wrong" in saying that Moore's disciples separated his morals and religion or that Moore ignored action for contemplation.[6] The details of the disagreement, together with memoirs and interpretations by Clive Bell, Desmond MacCarthy, Bertrand Russell, and others, need not be gone into here. The point is that in assessing Moore's influence on his Cambridge circle, it is not sufficient to rely on Keynes's memoir. Leonard Woolf's account is also indispensable.

Virginia Woolf once wrote to a critic that she had no training in philosophy; such knowledge of it as she possessed came "simply from listening to people talking. . . ."[7] In addition to her father, those people included a brother, a brother-in-law, a husband, and at least one close friend, all of whom had seriously concerned themselves with philosophy at Cambridge, and all of whom, with the exception of Leslie Stephen, had come under the influence of G. E. Moore and to a lesser extent Bertrand Russell and J. McT. E. McTaggart. Leonard Woolf has well described how he and a number of friends—including Roger Fry—were "permanently inoculated with Moore and Moorism," and through them, others who were not at Cambridge or did not belong to the Apostles—Vanessa and Virginia Stephen, Clive Bell, Duncan Grant—were also

> deeply affected by the astringent influence of Moore and the purification of that divinely cathartic question . . . 'What do you mean by that?' Artistically the purification can, I think, be traced in the clarity, light, absence of humbug in Virginia's literary style and perhaps in Vanessa's painting.
>
> . . . The colour of our minds and thought had been given to us by the climate of Cambridge and Moore's philosophy. . . . But we had no common theory, system, or principles which we wanted to convert the world to. . . ."[8]

[5] The fullest treatments to date of the importance of *Principia Ethica* for Virginia Woolf's work are to be found in Irma Rantavaara's *Virginia Woolf and Bloomsbury* (Helsinki, 1953) and J. K. Johnstone's *The Bloomsbury Group* (London, 1954).

[6] Leonard Woolf, *Sowing* (London, 1960), pp. 146–49.

[7] Quoted in Floris Delattre, *Feux d'automne* (Paris, 1950), p. 239.

[8] Leonard Woolf, *Beginning Again* (London, 1964), pp. 24–25.

To this revealing assertion of G. E. Moore's importance for Virginia Woolf can now be added the information that she read Moore himself carefully. In August 1908, when she was twenty-seven years old and at work on *The Voyage Out,* Virginia Stephen wrote to Saxon Sydney Turner that she was making headway with Moore and what must have been *Principia Ethica,* "though I have to crawl over the same page a number of times, till I almost see my own tracks." To her brother-in-law Clive Bell she wrote in the same month,

> I split my head over Moore every night, feeling ideas travelling to the remotest parts of my brain, and setting up a feeble disturbance hardly to be called thought. It is almost a physical feeling, as though some little coil of brain unvisited by any blood so far, and pale as wax, had got a little life into it at last; but had not strength to keep it. I have a very clear notion which parts of my brain think.

Finally, on 29 August she wrote to her sister,

> I finished Moore last night; he has a fine flame of arrogance at the end—and no wonder. I am not so dumb founded as I was; but the more I understand, the more I admire. He is so humane in spite of his desire to know the truth. . . .⁹

Leonard Woolf's statements along with these letters show the extent to which Virginia Woolf was educated, as she said to Vita Sackville-West, in "the old Cambridge school" where one George Moore was not to be confused with another. And it would seem reasonable that an examination of the philosophical bases of her fiction should begin for once at the same end that she did. Philosophically, G. E. Moore influenced Virginia Woolf more than anyone else, but in addition to this direct influence on her and her circle Moore's philosophy is also *representative* of the intellectual milieu in which Virginia Woolf was born and bred. Many of the ideals and ideas in or underneath Virginia Woolf's novels were shared by Moore with such diverse persons as Leslie Stephen, McTaggart, Roger Fry, Lowes Dickinson, and Bertrand Russell. Candor, clarity, analysis, art, love, logic, and commonsense are among the more important features of a family resemblance among these men, though they did not value all of these things equally.

⁹ These excerpts from Virginia Woolf's unpublished letters are quoted with permission of Professor Bell and Mrs. Garnett.

In his "Reply to My Critics" written at the end of his career, Moore divided his responses into three categories that reflect the nature of his achievement. They were sense-perception, ethics, and philosophic method.[10] It is not possible to examine in the space that I have here the way these divisions correspond to Moore's significance for Virginia Woolf, and I have had to select what seems to me to be the most important of them, namely sense-perception. Moore's ethics, though of crucial significance in Virginia Woolf's art and life, depend fundamentally on his epistemology. Similarly, in her fiction ethical assumptions rest on epistemological ones.

II

The term "blue" is easy enough to distinguish, but the other element which I have called "consciousness"—that which sensation of blue has in common with sensation of green—is extremely difficult to fix. That many people fail to distinguish it at all is sufficiently shown by the fact that there are materialists. And, in general, that which makes the sensation of blue a mental fact seems to escape us: it seems, if I may use a metaphor, to be transparent—we look through it and see nothing but the blue; we may be convinced that there *is something* but *what* it is no philosopher, I think, has yet clearly recognised.[11]

This passage from G. E. Moore's famous "The Refutation of Idealism," which he published at the age of thirty in 1903—in the same year as *Principia Ethica*—illustrates the relevance of Moore's epistemology for Virginia Woolf's fiction. But first the general context of the quotation needs to be understood. When Moore came up to Cambridge he was apparently a Lucretian materialist.[12] Under the influence of McTaggart he became an idealist. But already in the early idealist essays that he published before the turn of the century Moore was distinguishing between mind and ideas, "and this was the beginning, I think, of certain tendencies in me which have led some people to call me a 'Realist'. . . ."[13] In "The Refutation of Idealism," Moore

[10] *The Philosophy of G. E. Moore*, ed. P. A. Schilpp (New York, 1952), p. 535.

[11] G. E. Moore, "The Refutation of Idealism," *Philosophical Studies* (London, 1922), p. 20.

[12] Bertrand Russell, *Autobiography* (London, 1967), 1: 73.

[13] G. E. Moore, "Autobiography," *The Philosophy of G. E. Moore*, p. 22.

as a modern philosophical realist criticized not the idealists' contention that reality was spiritual (he said he devoutly hoped it was) but their central assumption that everything was mental because to be is to be perceived. Moore argued that the assumption is contradictory: it affirms that "being" is identical with "being perceived," and at the same time it distinguishes between them in making the statement. If a color and the perception of a color were identical, then the statement that a color was being perceived would be the same as a statement saying that a color is a color. Moore concluded that we must distinguish between consciousness and the objects of consciousness that exist independently of it, and thus he maintained the position of modern —as opposed to medieval—philosophical realism. He is not a materialist here because he asserts the nonmaterial reality of consciousness; he is not an idealist because he asserts the separate reality of material objects. Throughout his earlier philosophy Moore's most basic point is the distinction between the act and the object of consciousness. Or as Russell summarized it, "What I think at first chiefly interested Moore was the independence of fact from knowledge and the rejection of the whole Kantian apparatus of *a priori* intuitions and categories, moulding experience but not the outer world."[14]

In later years Moore came to think little of "The Refutation of Idealism," but he did not alter his assumption of the basic dualism of consciousness and its objects. Much of his work in epistemology was spent in struggling with the nature of those objects. He had almost nothing to say, however, about the act itself, the nature of consciousness, apart from the passage just quoted and a later description of it in the same essay as "diaphanous."[15] Nevertheless, Moore is, along with William James and Bergson, a philosopher of consciousness. The very ideals of his ethics are states of consciousness. But it is the epistemological dualism, with its distinction of fact from knowing, that becomes a basic philosophical presupposition of Virginia Woolf's criticism and fiction.

The significance of Moore's realism for Virginia Woolf's critical theory can be seen in her well-known essay, "Modern Fiction," which she first published in 1919. In attacking literary

[14] Bertrand Russell, *My Philosophical Development* (New York, 1959), p. 12.

[15] "The Refutation of Idealism," p. 25.

materialists, as she called Bennett, Wells, and Galsworthy, Virginia Woolf uses the same distinction that Moore did in refuting philosophical materialists. By attending only to material reality both overlook that other reality that Moore called "transparent" and "diaphanous" and that Virginia Woolf described as "a luminous halo, a semi-transparent envelope." The literary materialists have also ignored the life of consciousness; they have attended to the fabric of things instead of recording "the atoms as they fall upon the mind in the order in which they fall . . . the pattern, however disconnected and incoherent in appearance, which each sight or incident scores upon the consciousness" (2: 106–7). These familiar words have misled several critics into describing Virginia Woolf as an empiricist. One says he does not wish to get involved in philosophical distinctions yet finds it "worth insisting that Mrs. Woolf was of all writers the least justified in using the word 'materialist' as a term of abuse" because her own view of consciousness "is in fact an expression of pure, crude, mechanical Lockean materialism."[16] It is worth getting involved in philosophical distinctions when they are muddled, however, and when the writer's work is partly misconceived as a result. Materialism and empiricism are being confused here. Furthermore, neither was maintained by Virginia Woolf or G. E. Moore. Moore might be thought of as belonging to a broadly conceived empirical tradition in his approach to knowledge and in his concern with sense data; but in his insistence that consciousness included more than just sensory experience and in his refusal to accept skeptical conclusions that conflicted with common sense, Moore was not an empiricist.[17] In "The Refutation of Idealism" Moore rejected alike both the psychologism of empiricism and the subjectivity of idealism. In these ideas the representativeness of Moore's thought can be seen. In a very general way he is in the same philosophical tradition as Leslie Stephen; his criticism of materialism he could have adopted from McTaggart. But in his epistemological realism the influence on Virginia Woolf seems to have been direct. Through his ideas it should be clear that her emphasis on consciousness and her critique of literary material-

16 Arnold Kettle, *An Introduction to the English Novel* (New York, 1960), 2: 106n.

17 John O. Nelson, "Moore, George Edward," *The Encyclopedia of Philosophy*, ed. Paul Edwards (New York, 1967), 5: 378–79.

ists are no more an indication that Virginia Woolf is an idealist than her concern with sense impressions make her an empiricist or materialist. For her and for Moore the most accurate and useful philosophical classification here is realism.

The significance of G. E. Moore's epistemology for Virginia Woolf's fiction can be seen most clearly to begin with in the experimental stories and sketches published in *Monday or Tuesday*. How Moore's realism helped her to write about the life of consciousness that the Edwardian materialistic novelists had neglected appears in them and in the novels that followed. Even the slightest pieces in the collection, the two impressionistic sketches called "Blue and Green," appear to be exercises in the rendering of consciousness. In the passage quoted above Moore described consciousness as "that which sensation of blue has in common with sensation of green"; by juxtaposing the descriptions of a series of blue and then green impressions, Virginia Woolf implies consciousness (which Moore said was so difficult to fix) through what the two sets of impressions have in common. Most of the stories in *Monday or Tuesday* are studies of the way consciousness combines with what it perceives to produce those states of mind that Virginia Woolf felt fiction should be about. The combining sometimes brings in the question of what is truth. Moore's realism involved a correspondence rather than an idealistic coherence theory of truth, and while Virginia Woolf was not directly concerned with anything so abstruse, we shall see later in her novels that truth is to be found in both the correspondence of the deliverances of consciousness with external reality and the coherence of mystical moments. Virginia Woolf's first published story, "The Mark on the Wall," shows very well how Moore's philosophical realism together with the correspondence theory of truth underlies her early fiction. It is not a difficult story and yet it and "An Unwritten Novel" have frequently been misunderstood. "The Mark on the Wall' consists of a narrator sitting in a chair wondering what a certain mark on the wall is, and engaging in various reveries that start from the possibility that the mark is one thing or another. Only at the end of the story does the narrator learn from another character that the mark is a snail. The reveries, or trains of thought as they are called in the story, are represented by a technique that Virginia Woolf said in her diary allowed "one thing [to] open out of another"

(23)[18] and that her commentators have described as the stream of consciousness technique. It is undoubtedly too late in the day to protest against a label that is indiscriminately affixed to such different writers as Joyce, Faulkner, and Virginia Woolf, but it may still be worth noting what Virginia Woolf herself meant by the phrase. In her essay "Middlebrow" she refers parenthetically to "lapsing into that stream which people call, so oddly, consciousness, and gathering wool from the sheep. . ." (2: 202). This kind of stream is not represented in her fiction. What is called her stream of consciousness technique resembles, say, Joyce's, only in its depiction of internal, subjective awareness and in the representation of thoughts and feelings as opening out of one another. In these sequences she never abandons punctuation or syntax and rarely tries to represent the subconscious. They are usually presented in the third person— "one," not "I," is her favorite pronoun—and the most accurate description of them was the one Virginia Woolf used in her diary when she referred to her technique in *To the Lighthouse* as "oratio obliqua" (100). Her technique in *The Waves* she described as "soliloquies" (159). The sequences she represents in these novels and in her short stories owe more to Locke and Sterne than they do to Freud, though Virginia Woolf does not engage in the empiricists' atomization of experience that William James was criticizing in his famous phrase. It is more useful on the whole to think of Virginia Woolf's representations of consciousness in terms of states rather than streams. In these states, consciousness is not chopped up but represented as organic wholes in G. E. Moore's sense of the term meaning a whole that has no regular relation to the sum of its parts.[19] William James also used the images of a halo and a penumbra to illustrate his conception of consciousness, both of which give a better general notion of consciousness as Moore and Virginia Woolf conceived of it than a stream.

In "The Mark on the Wall" the technique and content of the trains of thought started by the mark have led to misinterpretations of their function. The story presents not merely these ideas but also the ludicrous discrepancy between them and their cause, between the ranging speculations and the mark that the

[18] Page numbers following references to Virginia Woolf's diary refer to *A Writer's Diary*, ed. Leonard Woolf (London, 1953).

[19] G. E. Moore, *Principia Ethica* (Cambridge, 1965), p. 27.

narrator cannot be bothered to identify. A recent critic is as wide of the mark as the narrator when he reads this and other stories as an "assertion of subjectivity or idealism"[20] in which the snail is unimportant and the ideas all important. There is no denying the significance in Virginia Woolf's subsequent work of such ideas as the masculine conception of reality, the mysteriousness of life, or the impersonal world that exists apart from us, but these ideas and the methods by which they are presented must be seen in the context of the story. The point of view in the story, the personality of the narrator who speculates on the impossibility of knowing anything because she cannot be troubled to stand up and see just what exactly is the mark on the wall, is an element in the story that should not be overlooked. Sanity and sense involve the interrelations of thought *and* external reality, of consciousness *and* the objects of consciousness. In "An Unwritten Novel" there is the same silly discrepancy between the trains of thought and their cause, between imagined and actual reality. And there is the same plunging from ridiculing to being ridiculous in the narrator's sequence of ideas. There is also the same deflating revelation at the end of the true nature of external reality.

A number of the stories in *Monday or Tuesday* could be described as epistemological tales. Moore's dualistic theory of perception underlies their representation of the acts and objects of consciousness. In stories like "The Mark on the Wall" and "An Unwritten Novel," as well as in essays like "Modern Fiction," Virginia Woolf is exploring the world through these assumptions and criticizing views of reality that ignore or minimize either half of the dualism.

III

In Virginia Woolf's first two novels, *The Voyage Out* and *Night and Day*, G. E. Moore's ethics appear in various interesting guises,[21] but his epistemology is only latent. Not until

[20] Jean Guiguet, *Virginia Woolf and Her Works* (London, 1965), p. 385.

[21] *Principia Ethica* is even quoted, though not named, in *The Voyage Out*, p. 82. (All references to Virginia Woolf's fiction as well as to *A Room of One's Own* refer to the uniform edition of her works published by the Hogarth Press, 1929–53. In the cases of *Jacob's Room, Mrs. Dalloway*, and *The Waves*, the second uniform editions are used, the first now being out of print.)

the experiments of *Monday or Tuesday* that led to *Jacob's Room*, the third and most epistemological of her novels, does Moore's realism become crucial for Virginia Woolf's art. A key to *Jacob's Room* can be found again in the essay "Modern Fiction" where Virginia Woolf maintained that if a writer were free to

> base his work upon his own feeling and not upon convention, there would be no plot, no comedy, no tragedy, no love interest or catastrophe in the accepted style . . . (2: 106).

There is little or no plot, comedy, tragedy, or love interest in *Jacob's Room*. The catastrophe of Jacob's death is not even given. *Jacob's Room* is an anti-novel. Echoes of *Tristram Shandy* can be heard in the visits of Captain Barfoot to the widowed Mrs. Flanders. Jacob's name—Jacob means supplanter—alludes not only to the famous place where so many of his generation were buried but also to that celebrated heroine of another eighteenth-century novel that Virginia Woolf described in 1919 as "indisputably great": *Moll Flanders* (1: 63). "The Fortunes and Misfortunes of the Famous Moll Flanders" are replaced by a modern quest for Jacob himself. The direction of the quest follows Jacob's education into the ways of mind and matter. The title names a room, not an occupant. At the beginning Archer is calling " 'Ja—cob! Ja—cob!' " (6). At the end Bonamy cries " 'Jacob! Jacob!' " (176). Other characters call him throughout the novel. Everyone who loves Jacob seems to lose him at one time or another; the shifting dislocations of time and especially place help to convey this absence or remoteness. On one level *Jacob's Room* is an author in search of her character. The quest is also elegiac because Jacob resembles Virginia Woolf's brother Thoby who died at twenty-six. Epistemologically, the novel is a quest for the nature of consciousness. Is not the task of the novelist, Virginia Woolf asked in "Modern Fiction," "to convey this varying, this unknown and uncircumscribed spirit" (2: 106) that is consciousness? But what *is* consciousness and how can the novelist convey it? These questions to which *Jacob's Room* is addressed are distinct because Virginia Woolf does not present a narrator introspecting his own consciousness. She wanted to avoid what, in a diary entry made before the beginning of her third novel, she called "the damned egotistical self" that spoiled the work of

James Joyce and Dorothy Richardson for her. She wanted a technique instead that would "enclose the human heart" but without also enclosing the scaffolding and bricks of the materialistic novelists; all was to be "crepuscular, but the heart, the passion, humour, everything as bright as fire in the mist" (23). When she went on in this entry to note that the theme of her new novel "is a blank to me," Virginia Woolf was closer than she realized to what *Jacob's Room* is all about.

Twice in *Jacob's Room*, once as he is going up to Cambridge and then after his return from Greece, the narrator observes in the identical words, "It is no use trying to sum people up. One must follow hints, not exactly what is said, nor yet entirely what is done" (29, 153). People cannot be summed up in *Jacob's Room* because people are not sums but Moorean organic unities that may be better or worse, greater or less, than the sums of their parts. "Of all futile occupations," the narrator observes, "this of cataloguing features is the worst. One word is sufficient. But if one cannot find it?" (69). Thus do problems in epistemology become problems in poetics for Virginia Woolf. Nor is there any essence of character, any "unseizable force" that novelists never catch; this crude vitalism of cabinet and club men who say character-drawing is a frivolous art "enclosing vacancy" allows them to contemplate with equanimity the destruction of lives such as Jacob's (154–55). Though he may not be knowable, Jacob is killable. Another reason why people cannot be summed up is the translucent character of consciousness. One of the ways that Virginia Woolf describes consciousness throughout her work is in metaphors of translucence. It is a halo, a semi-transparent envelope, a mist, through which light is dispersed. In *Jacob's Room* consciousness is referred to once as a darkening glass: "We start out transparent, and then the cloud thickens. All history backs our pane of glass. To escape is vain" (47). The sorrow of human experience is what darkens us. The translucence of consciousness keeps us from comprehending our own as well as other peoples'; we can never be sure their consciousnesses respond in the same way as ours do. Uncertainties and inconsistencies in the point of view of the novel somewhat obscure this in *Jacob's Room*. At one point the narrator says "Whether we know what was in his mind is another question" (93), yet there are places in the novel —at King's College Chapel, at the Parthenon—where we are unambiguously presented with the contents of Jacob's mind. These occasional inside views do not seriously detract from the difficulties that the narrator presents of understanding another person's mind.

In 1905 Moore published a long and difficult paper entitled "The Nature and Reality of Objects of Perception," which caused considerable excitement among such friends as Keynes and Strachey.[22] Starting with the assumption that "there is a sense in which no man can observe the perceptions, feelings or thoughts of any other man," Moore tried to answer the question "*What* reason do my observations give me for believing that any other person has any particular perceptions or beliefs?" His answer involved the postulation of "sense-contents" (later called sense-data) that Moore argued were independent of our private perceptions of them.[23] Moore's question, if not exactly his answer, underlies the quest for Jacob's consciousness. We can describe what Jacob looks like and how he acts, yet "there remains over something which can never be conveyed to a second person save by Jacob himself. . . . Even the exact words get the wrong accent on them. . . . What remains is mostly a matter of guess work. Yet over him we hang vibrating" (71–72). Why we have to hang vibrating is explained a page or so before in a passage that eloquently summarizes the epistemological and the elegaic aspects of the quest:

> In any case life is but a procession of shadows, and God knows why it is that we embrace them so eagerly, and see them depart with such anguish, being shadows. And why, if this and much more than this is true, why are we yet surprised in the window corner by a sudden vision that the young man in the chair is of all things in the world the most real, the most solid, the best known to us—why indeed? For the moment after we know nothing about him.
>
> Such is the manner of our seeing. Such the conditions of our love (70–71).

What can the novelist do with these conditions of perception and love? The answer is in the novel's title. We must attend not

---

[22] R. F. Harrod, *The Life of John Maynard Keynes* (London, 1951), pp. 112–13.

[23] G. E. Moore, "The Nature and Reality of Objects of Perception," *Philosophical Studies*, pp. 53, 60, and 70ff.

merely to what Jacob says and does but also to what he perceives. We must go to Jacob's room.

Jacob's room represents what he perceives in two ways. First, it is his immediate environment. From his rooms in Cambridge, London, Patras, we follow hints about his thoughts and feelings by becoming conscious of what he has been conscious of. Second, Jacob's room is symbolic of his consciousness itself. Critics have noted Virginia Woolf's use of windows as epistemological symbols;[24] the rooms from which one looks out through these windows are often symbolic of a consciousness perceiving external reality. Twice the word "room" appears in titles of her works. In *A Room of One's Own* Virginia Woolf argued that to be a good writer one had to have an independent consciousness of one's own in order to attend to worthwhile ends and not be distracted by goods that were only means to these ends.[25] The two meanings of room as symbol of consciousness are not completely separable, of course. The symbolic room often includes objects of perception inside or outside itself; mere consciousness is as difficult to fix as Moore said it was. But both meanings are consistent with Moore's realism. Jacob's rooms are symbols of the acts and the objects, the form and the content, of consciousness. Jacob's rooms are also where epistemology and poetics come together again. On the first page of the notebook in which Virginia Woolf wrote *Jacob's Room* (she had the title from the start), she asked and then answered, "Yet what about form? Let us suppose that the Room will hold it together."[26]

The dualistic realism that is the principal philosophical presupposition underlying *Jacob's Room* can also be seen in the novel's concern with mind and body. Jacob's education makes him aware, through such different people as Cambridge dons and London prostitutes, of the indispensable value of mind, but the discussion of all this belongs to the examination of Moore's

[24] See for example Ralph Freedman, *The Lyrical Novel* (Princeton, 1963), pp. 229–30.

[25] Virginia Woolf's criticism of Joyce's method in *Ulysses* is also put in terms of "our sense of being in a bright yet narrow room, confined and shut in, rather than enlarged and set free" outside and beyond the consciousness he represents (2: 107–8).

[26] Quoted in John D. Gordan, *New in the Berg Collection*, 1959-1961 (New York, 1964), p. 31.

ethical influence on Virginia Woolf. Epistemologically, the dualism of mind and body in the novel is unmistakable in *Jacob's Room*'s pervasive concern with death. Jacob's consciousness is so difficult to apprehend not only because of its unity, translucence, and privacy, but also because of its transience. The room as symbolic of consciousness and the objects of consciousness is so appropriate here because the room can be emptied, as the title suggests, leaving only the objects. The question asked of Jacob's father—described on his tombstone as a merchant of the city because, though he had only been one for three months, he had to be called something—is a question that haunts the narrator and the novel: "Had he then been nothing?" The question applies to Jacob as well, as does the reply: "An unanswerable question, since even if it weren't the habit of the undertaker to close the eyes, the light so soon goes out of them" (14). *Jacob's Room* is finally a novel about the perception of mortality. It tries to present how we perceive what it is that dies, and in doing this the novel again assumes the rudiments of a realistic theory of perception. Consciousness dies; things like rooms and shoes endure. Death as an ultimate problem in epistemology was not, however, a concern of Moore's. His few published remarks on immortality show that he did not believe in it and found attempts such as McTaggart's to theorize about it incomprehensible.[27] There are no whispers of immortality in *Jacob's Room* either.[28] The quest for the mysterious and transient consciousness of another is bewildering if not futile, and these are the conditions of our love and our perceiving. The only epistemological certainty concerning death seems to be the way that the thoughts and facts of death can alter our perceptions of external reality. At the beginning of the novel Mrs. Flanders's tears make the bay she sees quiver, and the original last line of the novel describing her in *Jacob's*

[27] See G. E. Moore, "Mr. McTaggart's 'Studies in Hegelian Cosmology,'" *Proceedings of the Aristotelian Society* 2 (1901–2): 177–214, and "A Defense of Commonsense," *Philosophical Papers* (New York, 1962), pp. 32–59.

[28] There are echoes of both the techniques and images of T. S. Eliot's poetry in *Jacob's Room* and other novels of Virginia Woolf, especially those with settings in London. "Whispers of Immortality" was among the poems published by the Woolfs in 1919; it provides an interesting contrast to *Jacob's Room* in its use of philosophy.

Room was, "The room waved behind her tears."[29] In Virginia Woolf's third novel a tear is an epistemological thing.

IV

The rooms of *Mrs. Dalloway* like those of Jacob are symbolic. Clarissa's attic bedroom represents her virginal perceptions and reactions to certain things. When Septimus Smith's consciousness is about to be invaded by a soul-forcing doctor, he throws himself out of his room to death. And there is the old lady living across from Clarissa. Two-thirds of the way through *Mrs. Dalloway*, the heroine stands at her drawing-room window watching the lady and brooding over her daughter's somewhat fanatical tutor and an old lover just back from India:

> Why creeds and prayers and mackintoshes? when, thought Clarissa, that's the miracle, that's the mystery; that old lady, she meant, whom she could see going from chest of drawers to dressing-table. She could still see her. And the supreme mystery which Kilman might say she had solved, or Peter might say he had solved, but Clarissa didn't believe either of them had the ghost of an idea of solving, was simply this: here was one room; there another. Did religion solve that, or love? (140–41).

E. M. Forster has quoted this passage to illustrate how wrong it is to describe Virginia Woolf's work in terms of "mysticism, unity beneath multiplicity, twin souls. . . ," and he concludes, "As far as her work has a message, it seems to be contained in the above paragraph. Here is one room, there another."[30] Forster's comments, made when *Mrs. Dalloway* was Virginia Woolf's latest novel, are as relevant to his own work as to his friend's. Both staunchly represent in their fiction the marvelous, irreducible otherness of people, the plurality of souls, the obduracy of matter. Both are philosophical realists, and there is something of the mystic in each as well. Ignoring either aspect results in misinterpretation, though in fact it is the realistic assumptions that are most often overlooked.

How Virginia Woolf contrives to base a novel on both mys-

[29] Quoted in Charles G. Hoffmann, " 'From Lunch to Dinner': Virginia Woolf's Apprenticeship," *Texas Studies in Literature and Language* 10 (Winter 1969): 626.

[30] E. M. Forster, "The Early Novels of Virginia Woolf," *Abinger Harvest* (London, 1953), p. 130.

ticism and philosophical realism can be seen in the climax of *Mrs. Dalloway* when there recurs the scene that Forster called the embodiment of Virginia Woolf's message. Just before the scene Mrs. Dalloway hears of Septimus Smith's suicide. She goes into a little room away from the party and thinks,

> A thing there was that mattered; a thing, wreathed about with chatter, defaced, obscured in her own life, let drop every day in corruption, lies, chatter. This he had preserved. Death was defiance. Death was an attempt to communicate, people feeling the impossibility of reaching the centre which, mystically, evaded them; closeness drew apart; rapture faded; one was alone. There was an embrace in death (202).

This nearly mystical response to the suicide is anticipated earlier in the novel when Clarissa is thinking about her own inadequacies; they are presented as sexual but the experience described is not to be confined to that. "She could see what she lacked. It was not beauty; it was not mind. It was something central which permeated; something warm which broke up surfaces and rippled the cold contact of man and woman, or of women together." Sometimes she could yield to the charm of a woman: "Then, for that moment, she had seen an illumination; a match burning in a crocus; an inner meaning almost expressed. But the close withdrew; the hard softened. It was over —the moment" (36). Something that mattered; a mystical center of some kind, momentary in duration and ecstatic in character—this becomes familiar in Virginia Woolf's work from *Mrs. Dalloway* onward. (The mystical moments of *Night and Day* are somewhat different.) In *Mrs. Dalloway*, however, the experience is tied to the separate lives of other people in their rooms. This clearly appears in the climactic scene of the novel when Mrs. Dalloway draws the curtains apart and sees again the old lady in her room across the street; Mrs. Dalloway's thoughts here recapitulate the novel's themes:

> It was fascinating, with people still laughing and shouting in the drawing-room, to watch that old woman, quite quietly, going to bed alone. She pulled the blind now. The clock began striking. The young man had killed himself; but she did not pity him; with the clock striking the hour, one, two, three, she did not pity him, with all this going on. There! the old lady had put out her light! the whole house was dark now with this

going on, she repeated, and the words came to her, Fear no more the heat of the sun. She must go back to them. But what an extraordinary night! She felt somehow very like him—the young man who had killed himself. She felt glad that he had done it; thrown it away while they went on living. The clock was striking. The leaden circles dissolved in the air. But she must go back. She must assemble. She must find Sally and Peter. And she came in from the little room (204–5).

Just what other rooms and their occupants have to do with the mystical experience of closeness in Virginia Woolf's art can be seen in Moore's and Russell's early philosophical realism; other people and the mystical center are both independent of our consciousness of them. Mystically, Virginia Woolf could be described as extroverted rather than introverted[31] and her realistic epistemology is consistent with this.

In addition to the mysticism of *Mrs. Dalloway* there are two other major differences in the treatment of consciousness between it and *Jacob's Room*. First, instead of a quest for the consciousness of the central character there is postulated representation of different people's consciousnesses. This is not simply a change in point of view. Both novels contain limited and omniscient narration, but in *Mrs. Dalloway* there is a change in emphasis from the outside observer-narrator to the private consciousnesses of Clarissa Dalloway, Septimus Smith, Peter Walsh, and others. (The observer also remains, as can be seen in the scathing description of the Bradshaws.) The second major difference between the two novels comes out of the first. Between the distinct, directly represented minds in *Mrs. Dalloway* there are crucial connections and disconnections. Through these relations Virginia Woolf is able to maintain her realistic outlook while confining her narration principally to individual subjective awarenesses. What the characters are conscious *of*, what they perceive in common, binds them and the novel together. Virginia Woolf touched on both these differences when she asked herself in her notes for the novel, "whether the inside of the mind in both Mrs. D. and S. S. can be made luminous— that is to say the stuff of the book—lights on it coming from

---

[31] See the discussion of the distinction between introvertive and extrovertive mysticism in Ronald W. Hepburn, "Mysticism, Nature and Assessment of," *Encyclopedia of Philosophy*, 5: 429.

external sources."³² The degree to which she succeeded in *Mrs. Dalloway* measures the degree to which she met Arnold Bennett's criticism that it was all very well to attack Edwardian materialism but her own approach had not managed to create character.³³ The quest for Jacob's consciousness left little time for any other characters in the novel, and one result is that our understanding of Jacob's own perceptions of others is limited by the little we know about those people. Virginia Woolf's well-known reply to Bennett, which she wrote while at work on *Mrs. Dalloway*, accepts his premise that novels are written to create character but complains that it is *his* characters who are not real enough.

> In one day thousands of ideas have coursed through your brains; thousands of emotions have met, collided, and disappeared in astonishing disorder. Nevertheless, you allow the writers to palm off upon you a version of all this, an image of Mrs. Brown, which has no likeness to that surprising apparition whatsoever (1: 336).

That surprising apparition, Mrs. Dalloway, is Virginia Woolf's Mrs. Brown. *Jacob's Room* ends with empty shoes in a tenantless room; the last line of *Mrs. Dalloway* is "For there she was."

Yet in representing the consciousnesses of several characters rather than concentrating on the pursuit of one, Virginia Woolf does not forsake the privacy of consciousness that so interested her in *Jacob's Room*. *Mrs. Dalloway* is organized around private souls. Even the culminating party is a collection of individuals essentially alone. Each central consciousness is isolated with his own frigidity, madness, or sentimentality that others can perceive but not alter. Septimus and Clarissa are linked in their isolating inability to love, though they feel more intensely than the other characters. They are consoled somewhat in their awareness of the isolation of others and in the value of their own integrity that must be protected from the soul-forcers, be they lovers or psychiatrists. But these essentially ethical matters cannot be discussed here apart from noting that the change from one consciousness to several makes per-

---

³² Quoted in Charles G. Hoffmann, "From Short Story to Novel: The Manuscript Revisions of Virginia Woolf's *Mrs. Dalloway*," *Modern Fiction Studies* 14 (Summer 1968): 174.

³³ *A Writer's Diary*, p. 57.

sonal relations and thus ethics much more important for Virginia Woolf's fourth novel than for her third.

Individual consciousnesses in *Mrs. Dalloway* relate to one another directly through their perceptions of one another and indirectly through their perceptions of their common environment. The direct relations develop from scattered encounters at the beginning of the novel to the party at the end. The general effect is similar to that in *The Years* where everything is described as coming over again yet differently. Consciousnesses are indirectly related to one another in *Mrs. Dalloway* by a web of their perceptions. The warp and the woof of·this web are their various perceptions of space and of time. The image of a web is actually used in the novel to describe Lady Bruton's consciousness, a thread of which attaches to her luncheon guests after they leave; it stretches and finally snaps when she sleeps (124). A few pages later the web reappears with Richard Dalloway: "And as a single spider's thread after wavering here and there attaches itself to the point of a leaf, so Richard's mind, recovering from its lethargy, set now on his wife. . ." (126). The spatial perceptions that link consciousnesses are often of an external event that provides a transition in the novel from one mind to another. The prime minister's car, the airplane, the pattern of clouds are some of the examples that London provides. The pervasiveness of London in *Mrs. Dalloway* comes from Virginia Woolf's concern with her characters' awareness of their environment; a city is a very convenient setting in which to represent shared objects of perception and different responses to them. A skywriting advertisement for toffee is a thing of exquisite beauty for the insane Septimus. But perception is not merely a relative matter in the novel, and even Septimus knows at times his madness from his sanity: "He began, very cautiously, to open his eyes, to see whether a gramophone was really there. But real things—real things were too exciting. He must be cautious" (156).

One of the ways that Clarissa Dalloway thinks of herself is as a mist spread out between her friends (11–12). Peter Walsh recalls her idea that

> to know her, or any one, one must seek out the people who completed them; even the places. . . . It ended in a transcendental theory which, with her horror of death, allowed her to believe, or say that she believed (for all her scepticism), that

since our apparitions, the part of us which appears, are so momentary compared with the other, the unseen part of us, which spreads wide, the unseen might survive, be recovered somehow attached to this person or that, or even haunting certain places, after death. Perhaps—perhaps (168).[34]

Clarissa's is a theory of perception as well as immortality. Its translucent metaphor of consciousness and its epistemological dualism are familiar features of Virginia Woolf's representations of perception. Less familiar is the notion of consciousness being defined or completed by what it is conscious of—a notion that in *Mrs. Dalloway* suggests how individual consciousnesses are related to one another through their perceptions of a common environment. The temporal perceptions of the characters illustrate this very clearly. One of Virginia Woolf's working titles for the novel was "The Hours." Views of time appear in the "timeless" yet transitory moments of joy and despair that the central characters experience in the hours struck off on the bells of London's clocks, in the passage of a single day during which the forward action of the novel is set, and in the patterns of the lives of Clarissa, Septimus, and Peter. These different uses of time are interrelated variously; the moment, for example, is connected with death through the recurring quotation from *Othello*, "if it were now to die 'twere now to be most happy." But there is no one unifying theme or theory of time in *Mrs. Dalloway*. Time as moment, hour, day, or life is a condition of existence.

The uses of time in *Mrs. Dalloway* are worth belaboring a little because they have often been taken as philosophically very important—the philosophy being Bergson's. Time in Virginia Woolf's fiction ought not to be reduced to a dichotomy of scientific time and *durée réelle*. Mind time in *Mrs. Dalloway* is synchronized with clock time; the bells of the clocks fit naturally into the rhythm of the heroine's life, even coinciding with her final insights. Only the clocks of Harley Street are appropriately "shredding and slicing, dividing and subdividing"

[34] Clarissa Dalloway's idea of acts of consciousness detached from the perceiver is not unlike G. E. Moore's description of a belief (in the common sense view of the world) "that there *may* have been a time when acts of consciousness were attached to *no* material bodies anywhere in the Universe, and *may* again be such a time . . ." *Some Main Problems of Philosophy* (London, 1953) (p. 11).

(113). The exaltation of the moment is a static not a dynamic experience; the consciousness of time is sequential, spatialized. All of which Bergson said it should not be. Time in *Mrs. Dalloway* does not so much flow as spread; rather than a river it is a sea in which the characters live like fish and experience in their different places the rippling circles of the hours. One of the most extraordinary things about *Mrs. Dalloway* is the water imagery in which Virginia Woolf describes the London existences of her characters. Even the function of time past in *Mrs. Dalloway* is part of the novel's philosophical realism that presents time as something that is experienced by consciousnesses, something that is outside themselves and that they share in the perception of. A number of critics have taken, as indications of a theory of memory similar to Bergson's, the tunnels of time that Virginia Woolf said in her diary she was digging out behind her characters when she needed their pasts (61). That they are not can be seen in the acute criticism of Bergson's theory that Bertrand Russell made in 1912:

> The whole of Bergson's theory of duration and time rests throughout on the elementary confusion between the present occurrence of a recollection and the past occurrence which is recollected. . . . What Bergson gives is an account of the difference between perception and recollection—both *present* facts—and what he believes himself to have given is an account of the difference between the present and the past.[35]

The consciousnesses of Clarissa and Peter move from perception to recollection and back again, but all the action of the novel is in the present. Through both perception and recollection Clarissa observes not only the pattern of her own life but also Peter's and even Sally Seaton's. The tunnels of time like the clocks of London are part of the novel's web of perceptions.

V

A discussion of the epistemology of *Mrs. Dalloway* is an incomplete way of approaching that novel because so many of its philosophical concerns are also ethical. This is true as well of

---

[35] Bertrand Russell, *History of Western Philosophy* (London, 1961), p. 764. Russell's critique of Bergson originally appeared in *The Monist* in 1912.

Virginia Woolf's most overtly philosophical novel, *To the Lighthouse*. Yet here too philosophical realism shapes the novel. In Virginia Woolf's fifth novel we have for the first and last time a major character who *is* a philosopher. Despite this fact the philosophy in the novel has been overlooked because *To the Lighthouse* is also Virginia Woolf's most autobiographical novel. Mr. Ramsay has been recognized as a philosopher only insofar as Leslie Stephen was one. With the evidence of Virginia Woolf's diary and Stephen's own "sentimental autobiography"[36] it is as certain as these things ever are that Mr. Ramsay is a close portrait of the author's father, just as Mrs. Ramsay is modeled on her mother. One of the uses of biography in the study of fiction is the emphasis it can give to dissimilarities; with Mr. Ramsay the ways in which he differs from Leslie Stephen are at least as interesting as the ways in which he resembles him. Leslie Stephen appeared once before in Virginia Woolf's fiction as the classical scholarly Ridley Ambrose in *The Voyage Out*. Both could pass as good likenesses of Leslie Stephen—except for the significant difference of their occupations. Leslie Stephen's achievements were those of a historian of thought, a biographer, a literary critic, and a moral philosopher, in approximately that order of importance. Mr. Ramsay is none of these. He resembles Leslie Stephen in his sentimentality, his sense of failure, his implicitly agnostic stoicism, and in what his daughter once in an essay called his "intemperate candour" (2: 48). But as close as as he comes to the pursuits of the author of *English Thought in the Eighteenth Century* is when he has promised "to talk 'some nonsense' to the young men of Cardiff about Locke, Hume, Berkeley, and the causes of the French Revolution" (73). Philosophically, Leslie Stephen's major work was an amalgam of Darwin and Mill entitled *The Science of Ethics*. Moore's demolition of Spencer's ethics in *Principia Ethica* destroyed it too. Nothing of *The Science of Ethics* survives in *To the Lighthouse* except maybe the faint echo of utilitarianism in Mr. Ramsay's thoughts on Shakespeare and the average man (70). Furthermore, Leslie Stephen does not appear to have been very interested in Mr. Ramsay's philosophical preoccupations.

[36] See *A Writer's Diary*, pp. 76–77; Noel Annan's *Leslie Stephen* (Cambridge, Mass., 1952), 98ff; and Quentin Bell's "The Mausoleum Book," *A Review of English Literature* 6 (January, 1965), 9–18.

He was not an epistemologist and no one could call him "the greatest metaphysician of the time" (62).

Once Lily Briscoe asked Andrew Ramsay what his father's books were about.

> "Subject and object and the nature of reality", Andrew had said. And when she said Heavens, she had no notion what that meant. "Think of a kitchen table then", he told her, "when you're not there" (40).

Brief, vague, and fanciful as it is, this is an account not of Leslie Stephen's empiricism but of G. E. Moore's realism, where kitchen tables exist apart from our perceptions of them. "The Refutation of Idealism" is on this very subject. It even has an example of a table existing in space. And certain features of Ramsay's career resembles Moore's. Mr. Ramsay is described by Mr. Bankes as " 'one of those men who do their best work before they are forty' "; his definite contribution had been a little book when he was twenty-five, and "what came after was more or less amplification, repetition" (41). Moore was thirty when *Principia Ethica* appeared, and his subsequent career was an anticlimax for some of his friends. Ramsay also suggests Moore rather than Stephen in his method of thought. His attempts "to arrive at a perfectly clear understanding of the problem" (56) is like the method of no philosopher Virginia Woolf read or knew of so much as Moore. These similarities between Moore and Ramsay have perhaps been obscured by the recurrent misunderstanding of the symbolization of Mr. Ramsay's thinking in the letters of the alphabet of thought. When she describes Mr. Ramsay's futile struggle to get from Q to R, Virginia Woolf is not displaying what has been called "some cerebral etiolation" in the portrait of a philosopher who " 'thinks' with the most helpless particularity."[37] She is doing precisely the opposite. By representing Mr. Ramsay's thinking as proceeding in the very general form of conventional logical symbols, Virginia Woolf is wittily extending the standard letters used to symbolize the conditional type of argument, If P then Q. Mr. Ramsay on the frontiers of thought is struggling to get from Q to R. As E. M. Forster remarked about a scene in

[37] M. C. Bradbrook, "Notes on the Style of Mrs. Woolf," *Scrutiny* 1 (May 1932): 37.

Jacob's Room, Virginia Woolf is describing not what the character is thinking of but something rarer: the process of thought itself.[38]

In certain respects, of course, Ramsay resembles G. E. Moore because Moore and Stephen belong to that general philosophical orientation inadequately described as Cambridge Rationalism. A discussion of Mr. Ramsay's ethical convictions could show the extent to which Moore and Stephen agree and disagree, but this is unimportant here because the significance of Mr. Ramsay's philosophy is his realism rather than his ethics. Moore's ethics did not accompany his epistemology into Mr. Ramsay's thought; *Principia Ethica* is fundamental to the novel as a whole rather than to the part that is Mr. Ramsay's moral thought. Just what the philosophical importance of Mr. Ramsay is can be seen in the dichotomies running throughout *To the Lighthouse*. Mr. and Mrs. Ramsay can be viewed as embodying not only the masculine and feminine principles but also reason and intuition, analysis and synthesis, farsightedness and nearsightedness, thought and action, truth and beauty, perhaps even realism and idealism in some sense or other. These poles are not simply positive and negative values. Mr. Ramsay's logic is a counter-weight to his wife's instinct; she must yield to his truth and he pay homage to her beauty. Beneath the dichotomies is love, the fundamental value of the novel that they share and in which their differences are resolved at the end of the first part of *To the Lighthouse*. The Ramsays are individuals as well as a couple, and each has the capacity to lose his personality in something outside himself. The lighthouse symbolizes and is a symbol for both. Its strokes of light bring Mrs. Ramsay from a "wedge-shaped core of darkness" (99) into ecstasy; its physical isolation and purpose imply Mr. Ramsay, who is described as being "out thus on a spit of land which the sea is slowly eating away. . . . marking the channel out there in the floods alone" (71–72).

Autobiographically, the truism that *To the Lighthouse* offers is that Virginia Woolf was the daughter of Julia *and* Leslie Stephen. If *Mrs. Dalloway* can be regarded as Virginia Woolf's *Ulysses*, *To the Lighthouse* is her *À la recherche du temps perdu*. She wanted a new name for the kind of book she was writing after *Mrs. Dalloway* and thought of calling it an elegy,

[38] *Abinger Harvest*, p. 132.

according to her diary (80). Love and death are its main concerns, though in ways quite different from the elegaic *Jacob's Room*. Philosophically, the novel displays the indispensableness —as well as the incompleteness—of philosophical realism, and this is brought out by the third major character in the novel, Lily Briscoe. For all its dualisms, *To the Lighthouse* is also a novel of triads. It is emphatically divided into three parts, being the only novel of Virginia Woolf's with a table of contents and named rather than simply numbered sections. Even the lighthouse has three flashes. Set against the antitheses that the different consciousnesses of Mr. and Mrs. Ramsay include is the ultimate extinction of consciousness presented in the second part of the novel. In the third part Lily Briscoe struggles to harmonize the Ramsays' dichotomies through her own love and art. She finally balances Mr. Ramsay's philosophy with what Mrs. Ramsay has taught her. Form is finally combined with color in her vision, and thus she is able to resolve at the end the last dichotomy of the novel, that of time and space.

In calling the first section of the novel "The Window" Virginia Woolf indicates once more her concerns with the innerness and outerness of perception. Behind the window sits Mrs. Ramsay on whose consciousness much of this section is focused. Outside, in front of the window, Mr. Ramsay paces among the objects of perception. The inner-outer dualism is also represented, as in *Mrs. Dalloway*, by relating perceivers through their perceptions. The beam of the lighthouse functions in a similar way to the bell of Big Ben. Erich Auerbach has been one of the few critics to recognize that Virginia Woolf's "multipersonal" rather thant "unipersonal" method places her work in the broad tradition of literary realism by virtue of the way it investigates objective reality.[39] Here is one point at which

[39] Erich Auerbach, *Mimesis: The Representation of Reality in Western Literature* (Princeton, 1953), p. 536. Two recent studies of *To the Lighthouse* both use Auerbach's insight and emphasize the perspectives or viewpoints in the novel, but neither discusses the necessary objective reality on which these focus. Avrom Fleishman's "Woolf and McTaggart," *ELH*, argues that McTaggart influenced Virginia Woolf through his ideas about selfhood, love, time, and psychic communication. McTaggart's ethical ideas may have influenced Virginia Woolf to some extent through their importance for the Apostles (including Moore), but McTaggart's idealism, which entailed a denial of the reality of time, space, and matter, is remote from her fictional world. Fleishman's principal

literary and philosophical realism touch. The most memorable use of this "multipersonal" method so far in her fiction is to be found in the dinner party of *To the Lighthouse*. By moving from one person's private state of consciousness to another while still maintaining the public conversations, Virginia Woolf is able to juxtapose the different awarenesses without sacrificing the realities of the party. The Boeuf en Daube is as real as the subjective anxieties of its eaters. "Subject and object and the nature of reality" is the philosophical basis of the party; the nature of reality appears not only in the individual awarenesses and what they are aware of but also more generally in the dualism that is symbolized throughout the novel in images of light and water. The lighthouse surrounded by the sea is an unmistakable example, but not only the lighthouse. When the candles are lit at the party, the characters become aware of the contrast of "order and dry land" inside, and "outside, a reflection in which things wavered and vanished, waterily." They were all "conscious of making a party together in a hollow, on an island; had their common cause against that fluidity out there" (151–52). Later in the party Mrs. Ramsay feels "there is a coherence in things, a stability; something, she meant, is immune from change, and shines out . . . in the face of the flowing, the fleeting, the spectral. . ." (163). The light of consciousness can transcend the fluidity of matter, for a while anyway.

In the second section of *To the Lighthouse* the dualisms are extended beyond modes of perception, beyond mind and matter, to the poles of the human and the nonhuman. For all its obscure lyricism, "Time Passes" is still the most sustained impersonal meditation on man and nature, on consciousness and its nonconscious environment, anywhere in Virginia Woolf's fiction. Amid the passing of time, the deaths of the old and the

---

illustration is *To the Lighthouse*, but his interpretation does not take into account Mr. Ramsay's role in the novel. Mitchell A. Leaska's *Virginia Woolf's Lighthouse: A Study in Critical Method* (London, 1970) is one of the few studies of the novel to give Mr. Ramsay his due and reduce Mrs. Ramsay to human proportions. Leaska's method of analyzing points of view in the novel (and analyzing samples from them stylistically) does not consider the realistic philosophical implications of the multipersonal novel and thus does not recognize, for example, how Lily Briscoe's final synthesis depends upon them.

young, we are presented with the ineluctable separateness of
nature from man's consciousness of it. The difference between
the human and the nonhuman pervades the whole section, even
though "the pool of time" that the house of the Ramsays is
temporarily rescued from by Mrs. McNab eventually includes
people together with things.

> Did Nature supplement what man advanced? Did she com-
> plete what he began? With equal complacence she saw his
> misery, condoned his meanness, and acquiesced in his torture.
> That dream, then, of sharing, completing, finding in solitude
> on the beach an answer, was but a reflection in a mirror? . . .
> (207–8).

But if nature is independent of man, he is not independent of
her, for nature's moods affect him and at times "it was impossible to resist the strange intimation . . . that good triumphs,
happiness prevails, order rules; or to resist the extraordinary
stimulus to range hither and thither in search of some absolute
good. . ." (205). In other words, the nature of reality is such
that objects are not dependent upon subjects but subjects are
affected, at least, by their objects. This abstract conclusion is
born out in the different perceptions of the Ramsays in "The
Window." Mr. Ramsay insists on the contingent nature of
reality: the facts of weather cannot be changed by human
wishes. Mrs. Ramsay's mystical experience is, however, an inner
state brought about by an outer reality.

The best commentary on "Time Passes" is the last section of
the novel, "The Lighthouse." Through the double action of
Mr. Ramsay's ritual journey to the lighthouse and Lily's painted
vision, the oppositions between kinds of consciousness and between consciousness and temporal nature are brought together.
Mr. Ramsay completes the action of the novel's title and receives his children's love, as he received his wife's at the end of
part one. Lily is finally able to paint her post-impressionist, non-
representational balancing of colored shapes. The trains of
thought and feeling that accompany the creating of this picture involve philosophy in important ways. The stages of what
could be called Lily's philosophical painting are worth looking
at closely.

As Mr. Ramsay and the two children go down to the boat
Lily recalls her symbol for him and his philosophy:

> The kitchen table was something visionary, austere; something bare, hard, not ornamental. There was no colour to it; it was all edges and angles; it was uncompromisingly plain.

Mr. Ramsay, Lily feels, had concentrated on this table until he "partook of this unornamented beauty which so deeply impressed her" (240–41). Next, Lily faces her canvas and confronts "this formidable ancient enemy of hers—this other thing, this truth, this reality, which suddenly laid hands on her, emerged stark at the back of appearances and commanded her attention." Then doing what the Ramsays in their different ways have done, she exchanges "the fluidity of life for the concentration of painting" (245). Finally, when Lily asks the question of herself, "What is the meaning of life?" the first stage in the thinking that accompanies her philosophical painting is reached. The answer has frequently been cited as one of the central passages in Virginia Woolf's fiction:

> The great revelation had never come. The great revelation perhaps never did come. Instead there were little daily miracles, illuminations, matches struck unexpectedly in the dark; here was one. . . . Mrs. Ramsay saying "Life stand still here"; Mrs. Ramsay making of the moment something permanent (as in another sphere Lily herself tried to make of the moment something permanent)—this was of the nature of a revelation. In the midst of chaos there was shape; this eternal passing and flowing . . .was struck into stability. Life stand still here, Mrs. Ramsay said. "Mrs. Ramsay! Mrs. Ramsay!" she repeated. She owed this revelation to her (249–50).

In addition to the connections between art and ethics that it suggests, this revelation is very significant in *To the Lighthouse* not so much because of its novelty—something quite like it had been said in *Night and Day* and *Mrs. Dalloway*—as because of its incompleteness. Moments of illumination are no longer enough. As Lily struggles with her painting, "tunnelling her way into her picture, into the past" (267), thinking of love and of death, Lily repeats her question about the meaning of life:

> What was it then? What did it mean? Could things thrust their hands up and grip one; could the blade cut; the fist grasp? Was there no safety? No learning by heart of the ways of the world? No guide, no shelter, but all was miracle, and leaping from the pinnacle of a tower into the air?

If, she goes on silently addressing the old poet Carmichael (according to Ramsay he could have been a great philosopher), the two of them could demand an explanation of why life was so inexplicable, then the space of her canvas would fill and Mrs. Ramsay would return (277). But without an explanation Mrs. Ramsay's teaching is not enough; a life of matches struck in the dark is a life mainly spent in the dark. "The waters of annihilation" (278) that Lily feels she has stepped off into with these questions are like those Mr. Ramsay and his children sail over to reach that tower symbolizing miraculous insight in the midst of water—but from which one leaps when the miracle ends.

No explanations come, and Lily struggles with her painting, thinking of Mr. Ramsay sailing farther away to the lighthouse. "For whatever reason she could not achieve that razor edge of balance between two opposite forces; Mr. Ramsay and the picture; which was necessary" (296). Something is missing from the design, just as something is missing from Mrs. Ramsay's moments of illumination. Continuing to recall the events of ten years ago (the marriage of the Ramsays was "no monotony of bliss—she with her impulses and quicknesses; he with his shudders and glooms" [305]), Lily's concentration on her painting suddenly returns as something flutters at the window, Mrs Ramsay's window. Lily now attains the final stage of her thought and her painting:

> One wanted, she thought, dipping her brush deliberately, to be on a level with ordinary experience, to feel simply that's a chair, that's a table, and yet at the same time, It's a miracle, it's an ecstasy. The problem might be solved after all.

But then something moves at the window; a wave of white goes over the pane.

> "Mrs. Ramsay! Mrs. Ramsay!" she cried, feeling the old horror come back—to want and want and not to have. Could she inflict that still? And then, quietly, as if she refrained, that too became part of ordinary experience, was on a level with the chair, with the table. Mrs. Ramsay—it was part of her perfect goodness to Lily—sat there quite simply, in the chair. . . .

Lily's response is to walk to the edge of the lawn and look out over the bay: "Where was that boat now? Mr. Ramsay? She wanted him" (309–10). Lily realizes he must have reached the lighthouse. She can now draw the line at the center of her balanced picture. The painting and the novel are finished.

What completes Lily's vision and brings about the reappearance of Mrs. Ramsay is Mr. Ramsay's philosophy. It is only when Lily is able to combine Mr. Ramsay's epistemology of ordinary experience and Mrs. Ramsay's illuminations that her problem is solved, the Ramsays balanced, the picture finished. The kitchen table when you are not there provides the common sense ground, the safety, for miracles of illumination. Mr. Ramsay's realism, when recalled by Lily, results in the most unreal return of Mrs. Ramsay—but a return, it should be remembered, that is also dependent upon the supreme values of *Principia Ethica*, art and love.

VI

Of the extended piece of fiction that she wrote between *To the Lighthouse* and *The Waves*, Virginia Woolf said in her diary that, among other things, *Orlando* taught her "how to keep the realities at bay" (136). The plural is not to be confused with the singular here; the realities were to be kept at bay so that reality would have more scope. "Philosophic words, if one has not been educated at a university, are apt to play one false," Virginia Woolf half-mockingly noted in *A Room of One's Own*. She knew very well that a great deal of G. E. Moore's work had shown how such words played philosophers false. *A Room of One's Own* was written right after *Orlando* and provides a kind of commentary on it in the way that *Three Guineas* comments on *The Years*. After her remark about philosophic words, Virginia Woolf went on,

> What is meant by "reality"? It would seem to be something very erratic, very undependable—now to be found in a dusty road, now in a scrap of newspaper in the street, now a daffodil in the sun. It lights up a group in a room and stamps some casual saying. It overwhelms one walking home beneath the stars and makes the silent world more real than the world of speech—and then there it is again in an omnibus in the uproar of Piccadilly. Sometimes, too, it seems to dwell in shapes too far away for us to discern what their nature is. But whatever it touches, it fixes and makes permanent. That is what remains over when the skin of the day has been cast into the hedge; that is what is left of past time and of our loves and hates (165–66).

To live "in the presence of reality" she concludes one must be independent, one must have a room and all that it symbolizes of one's own. Reality here approaches the Ideal in *Principia Ethica* through the exaltation of shared and recollected moments of insight and illumination. In *Orlando* some of Moore's ethical ideas are explored and occasionally satirized; his epistemology is playfully distorted through the manner with which Virginia Woolf fends off the realities by separating consciousness from sexual and temporal realities. Orlando's metamorphosis and immortality allow her an impossible variety of states of consciousness. Virginia Woolf's notion of the androgynous mind, as developed in *A Room of One's Own*, appears to be based on a theory of mind that postulates changing states of mind rather than a single form of mental being. In *Orlando* these states are manifested in one's different selves; identity depends on a master conscious self which paradoxically assumes control only when one becomes unselfconscious. The distinction here between consciousness and self-consciousness, between awareness and self, becomes very important in *The Waves*. In *Orlando*, however, it serves as mainly a comic examination of the possibilities of the androgynous mind when attached to a body that has an androgynous past.

Yet time is more important than sex in *Orlando*. The absence of death in *Orlando* removes the mainspring of Virginia Woolf's preoccupation with time in her fiction, and her interest in the remembrance of things past and in the difference between change and our awareness of it becomes correspondingly emphasized. With three hundred years to draw on, Orlando has a rich store of recollection with which to back her perceptions. The distinction in *Orlando* between mind and clock time is, again, the distinction between consciousness of change and change itself. When Virginia Woolf writes of how an hour once lodged in "the queer element of the human spirit" may be stretched to days or shrunk to a second, she is assuming a dualism of the act and objects of perception in order even to describe what she calls "this extraordinary discrepancy between time on the clock and time in the mind" (91).

Time in *The Waves* appears both within and without "the queer element of the human spirit" that consciousness is for Virginia Woolf. As the dust jacket of the first English edition of the novel puts it,

In Mrs. Woolf's new novel each character speaks in soliloquy
against the background of the sea. Several lives thus appear as in
a pageant detached from the framework of daily life, but they
change and grow old as time goes on. In the end one of the
characters sums up the effect of their lives as a whole.

Enough is known from Leonard Woolf's autobiographies about
the operations of the Hogarth Press to make it more than likely
that the person who wrote this account of *The Waves* was
either the author or her husband. It is a just summary, and in
using dramatic terms such as "pageant" and "soliloquy" it points
up the drama of consciousness that the novel presents. *The
Waves* is the culmination of Virginia Woolf's progress that
began more than ten years before when she called upon novelists to exclude the extraneous and convey the semi-transparent
envelope of consciousness.[40] This novel is her own fulfillment
of a prophecy about the future of the novel that she wrote after
To the Lighthouse. In "The Narrow Bridge of Art" she wrote
that the novel to come,

> will give, as poetry does, the outline rather than the detail. It
> will make little use of the marvellous fact-recording power.
> . . . It will have little kinship with the sociological novel or the
> novel of environment. With these limitations it will express the
> feeling and ideas of the characters closely and vividly, but from
> a different angle. It will resemble poetry in this that it will give
> not only or mainly people's relations to each other and their

[40] In an illuminating criticism of *The Waves* based on a study of the
two earlier complete versions of the novel that differ basically from the
published third version, J. W. Graham argues in "Point of View in *The
Waves*: Some Services of the Style," *University of Toronto Quarterly*
39 (April 1970): 193–211, that beginning with *Orlando* and essays written
around the same time Virginia Woolf became increasingly dissatisfied
with the use of psychology and personality in her fiction and sought to
represent more the impersonality that appears in *The Waves*. In support
of this interpretation of her development, Graham discusses how *The
Waves* grew out of the framework of a mind thinking the novel—an ur-
narrator whose vestiges can be found in the lyrical interludes and in the
uniform style of the different soliloquies. But underneath the change
from personality to impersonality lies a continuing preoccupation with
consciousness that develops steadily from Virginia Woolf's early work
and that is another reason why Virginia Woolf is more accurately to be
described as an epistemological novelist rather than a psychological one.
The concern with perception underlies the growth of *The Waves* as
well, for there Virginia Woolf moves from an ur-consciousness to the
six that finally are dramatized in the novel.

activities together, as the novel has hitherto done, but it will give the relation of the mind to general ideas and its soliloquy in solitude (2: 224–25).

All of this is done in *The Waves* through the form of six soliloquizing consciousnesses that are preoccupied, at various periods in their lives, with their individual awareness of both outer and inner reality. The six are concerned not only with the impingement of others and the sea on their consciousnesses but also with their individual identities, their separate developing selves that are distinguishable from their consciousnesses. The philosophical realism of *The Waves* is, in short, both external and internal.

The external is the familiar dualism of consciousness and external reality, and nowhere in her fiction is this made more explicit than in the soliloquies and their lyrical, stage-direction settings of the sea—settings that Virginia Woolf described in her diary as "insensitive nature" (153). The same dualism underlies what the author once saw as the essential conflict of the novel: Bernard's final speech was, again according to her diary, to show "the theme effort, effort, dominates: not the waves: and personality: and defiance . . ." (162). Human consciousness is confronted with its impending extinction by the natural. The brevity of life is symbolized by the one day of consciousness that the rising and setting sun of the intervals represents as the duration of the six lives. Death has returned from its holiday in *Orlando*. Halfway through dinner at Hampton Court, the six— their egotism blunted by food and wine—share an experience of momentary extinction in which, as Louis says, " 'Our separate drops are dissolved; we are extinct, lost in the abysses of time, in the darkness.' " But when Bernard cries " 'Fight!' " and Neville says " 'Oppose ourselves to this illimitable chaos,' " time returns with their consciousness of it, and the six move to a very different kind of moment in which they become one conscious life, a six-sided flower, as they did when they last dined with Percival. This moment is opposed to the non-consciousness of the natural order. " 'Let it blaze against the yew trees,' " says Bernard. " 'One life. There. It is over. Gone out' " (159–62). The same dualism with the same urgency of conscious effort and the same inevitable result occurs at the end of the novel. Bernard flings himself, unvanquished, unyielding, against death —but the last line of the novel is *"The Waves broke on the shore"* (211).

Almost paradoxically there is something of a dualism in the extrovertive mysticism of *The Waves*. Bernard's mystical experience of a "Fin in a waste of waters" (134–35) and Rhoda's losses of identity both parallel strikingly the remarks on her mystical experiences that Virginia Woolf made in her diary on 30 September 1926 (101–2). In all these experiences something— it is called "reality" in her diary—lies outside rather than within one's consciousness. This "reality" attracts consciousness, as it were, until at the height of the experience the awareness of everything else except it is lost. Even here, however, there seems to be a distinction between the awareness and what one is aware of. This seems to be true, at any rate, of Bernard's experience when he sees something essential, something that is described as making Tahiti possible, out in the midst of "a waste of waters."

The internal philosophical realism of *The Waves* is a less familiar feature of Virginia Woolf's fiction than the external, but in this novel it is at least as important. G. E. Moore's argument for the logical independence of what is perceived from the action of perceiving can be applied to distinguish self from consciousness of self. Moore criticized the idealists in "The Refutation of Idealism" for denying the possibility of self-consciousness:

> I think it may be seen that if the object of an Idealist's sensation were, as he supposes, *not* the object but merely the content of that sensation, if, that is to say, it really were an inseparable aspect of his experience, each Idealist could never be aware either of himself or of any other real thing. . . . The fact is, on his own theory, that himself and that other person are in reality mere *contents* of an awareness, which is aware *of* nothing whatever.[41]

In *The Waves* internal perceptions are no more mere contents of awareness than external perceptions. To be self-conscious is to be aware of something independent of consciousness. The meditations of the soliloquizing consciousnesses on their identities illustrates how basic this distinction is to *The Waves*. It can be seen in the uniform way in which the different consciousnesses speak, because consciousness lies too deep for the tears of personality and style. The effect of a monotone in the soliloquies helps to represent the existence of an awareness separate from

[41] "The Refutation of Idealism," p. 28.

the six highly individualized personalities of the novel. It is this awareness, common to the six characters, that is present when they are able at the two dinners to separate themselves from their egos and commune for a moment as one consciousness, one life. At these moments the novel is fully a drama of consciousness as well as consciousnesses.

At the center of the one life that the six petals momentarily at least arrange themselves around is the impressive but illusive figure of Percival. He closely resembles Jacob Flanders, and behind both is Thoby Stephen. (When she finished *The Waves* Virginia Woolf wondered in her diary [169] if she could put "Julian Thoby Stephen 1881–1906" on the first page of the novel.) Looking back to *Jacob's Room* we can see other significant similarities and differences. *Jacob's Room* is a quest for consciousness itself; *The Waves* is an exploration of *self*-consciousness. The earlier work tries to determine what Jacob was and what he was conscious of, the later novel tries to show what Percival meant to his friends and how he existed in their consciousnesses. If *Jacob's Room* is about the problem of other minds, *The Waves* is about the problem of our own. These different aims require different forms for each novel, but not different epistemologies. All of this can be illustrated in the preoccupations of the six characters with apprehending their developing identities.

Bernard, the most inclusive and various of the six, is continually thinking about his different selves. At college Bernard notes, " 'The complexity of things becomes more close. . . . What am I? I ask. This? No, I am that' " (54). After an orgy of self-consciousness accompanying his engagement, Bernard ceases to be himself for a while and is caught up in the lives of others—but only for a while. The description of his returning identity diagramatically separates consciousness and the objects of consciousness:

> "Yet behold, it returns. One cannot extinguish that persistent smell. It steals in through some crack in the structure—one's identity. I am not part of the street—no, I observe the street. One splits off, therefore" (82).

Unlike Louis' or Rhoda's, Bernard's identity also depends upon other people's identities. Louis is obsessively self-aware; with his success in business comes a new self that he affirms as he

signs his name again and again and thinks how he must concentrate his consciousness on what he is now and not be distracted by his imagination or the uncommercial world around
him. Only when past inferiorities have been completely shed
will he be free to write his poetry. In her solitude Rhoda is
even more insecure than Louis, but her identity is something
that she is always losing. As a young girl she is conscious that,

> "I have no face. Other people have faces; Susan and Jinny
> have faces; they are here. Their world is the real world. The
> things they lift are heavy" (30–31).

Her solitude torments her and yet she would have nothing else.
Her final comment on consciousness without a self is suicide.
Louis and Rhoda resemble each other—they are lovers for a
time—in their isolated awareness of their uncertain identities;
with both the independence of self from awareness is manifest.
Jinny and Neville also resemble each other in the ways they
fix their identities on love. Neville's homosexuality is more
tormented than Jinny's heterosexuality, however. Susan invests
her identity in nature and motherhood, yet as with all the others
she too perceives the difference between her awareness and this
self. On her farm she asks,

> "But who am I, who lean on this gate and watch my setter
> nose in a circle? I think sometimes (I am not twenty yet) I am
> not a woman, but the light that falls on this gate, on this
> ground" (70–71).

It is Percival, says Louis, " 'who makes us aware that these
attempts to say, "I am this, I am that," which we make, coming
together, like separated parts of one body and soul, are false' "
(98). Fear and vanity motivate the attempts, but still the communion of the six selfless, merged consciousnesses is inevitably
transitory. The loss and recovery of self is also the crucial experience in Bernard's long summing-up that appears almost as
an epilogue to the drama of consciousness. Bernard's purpose in
his final soliloquy is to explain the meaning of his life, but his
inclusiveness and the way in which the six lives have been experienced as one enable him, in the words of the dust jacket, to
summarize "the effect of their lives as a whole." As with the
rest of *The Waves*, the explanation is not so much in social,
religious, psychological, or even moral terms as it is in percep-

tual ones. Bernard's explanation consists of a review of the principal perceptions of his life. His identity as a child developed from the "arrows of sensation" that struck his unprotected consciousness. " 'A shell forms upon the soft soul, nacreous, shiny, upon which sensations tap their beaks in vain' " (181). Another epistemological symbol used by Bernard and illustrative of his philosophical realism is a tree: " 'The mind grows rings; the identity becomes robust; pain is absorbed in growth' " (182–83). Growth teaches the independence of nature from mind—if only in death. Percival's death shows to Bernard the realities of the world outside one's consciousness; experiencing the first morning that the dead Percival would not know leads Bernard " 'to see things without attachment, from the outside, and to realize their beauty in itself—how strange!' " (187). The sources of ethical and aesthetic value in the realism of *The Waves* appear here.

After the Hampton Court reunion and communion, Bernard suffers an appalling experience. He addressed his self and nothing happened. He is conscious, but of nothing. There is not even the fin in the waste of waters, as there was when he realized he had lost his youth and shed one of his "life-skins" (134). He realizes he is a man without a self. Earlier in his life Bernard had noticed the expression of old men in clubs—" 'they had given up calling for a self who does not come' "—and now that he is old, it happens to him. In this crisis Bernard is reduced to mere consciousness:

> "So the landscape returned to me; so I saw fields rolling in waves of colour beneath me, but now with this difference; I saw but was not seen. I walked unshadowed; I came unheralded. . . . Thin as a ghost, leaving no trace where I trod, perceiving merely, I walked alone in a new world. . ." (203).

This experience is the background to Bernard's final dinner with an acquaintance. During it Bernard becomes aware first of his mere physical self and then of the immense receptivity of his being. In the midst of this celebration of himself, Bernard sees what he is reflected in his companion's eyes. His physical self-awareness returns with a sickening blow reminiscent of his collision with the pillar box after his engagement. Insensitive matter, the enemy of consciousness, has to be confronted once more; the wave has tumbled over him again, scattering the contents of consciousness. The struggle must begin yet again, and as Bernard begins it, things gradually come together. Consciousness of self, of others, of external reality all fuse and he can conclude to his companion, " 'I regain the sense of the complexity and the reality and the struggle, for which I thank you' " (208). This is the meaning of his life.

The three things that Bernard regains his sense of at the end of *The Waves* summarize Virginia Woolf's philosophy in the novel. The complexity entailed in the perception of the individual's changing identity, the reality that in various ways is independent of one's awareness, and the struggle that the individual must make against the extinguishing chaos of external nonconscious nature—all are central philosophical matters in the novel. There are others as well, such as the supreme values of artistic beauty and love, that derive from consciousness and fit into the perspectives of philosophical realism.

One of Virginia Woolf's contemporaries who had also read some G. E. Moore and was probably aware of his influence on the Bloomsbury Group seems to have recognized some of these perspectives in *The Waves*. In the introduction to his play, appositely titled *Fighting the Waves*, William Butler Yeats observed the year after *The Waves* was published that,

> Certain typical books—*Ulysses*, Virginia Woolf's *The Waves*, Mr. Ezra Pound's *Draft of XXX Cantos*—suggest a philosophy like that of the *Samkara* school of ancient India, mental and physical objects alike material, a deluge of experience breaking over us and within us, melting limits whether of line or tint; man no hard bright mirror dawdling by the dry sticks of a hedge, but a swimmer, or rather the waves themselves.[42]

Shortly before the publication of *The Waves* Yeats had written that "The romantic movement seems related to the idealist philosophy; the naturalistic movement, Stendhal's mirror dawdling down a lane, to Locke's mechanical philosophy, . . ." and the work of Joyce, Pound, and Proust to "that form of the new realist philosophy which thinks that the secondary and primary qualities alike are independent of consciousness. . . ."[43] Yeats has a footnote at this point citing Moore's "The Refutation of Idealism" as a source of this philosophy. Without going into Yeats's

[42] *Explorations* (New York, 1962), p. 373.
[43] *Essays and Introductions* (New York, 1961), pp. 404–6.

extraordinary reading of Moore and Russell or being put off by Yeats's finding realism under the beds of Joyce, Pound, Proust, and Virginia Woolf (he may have been only responding to the fact that none of them was a romantic idealist or mechanical empiricist), we can recognize that Yeats was right about the philosophical presuppositions of *The Waves*.

VII

In her last two novels Virginia Woolf is less preoccupied with consciousness and perception than in her four preceding ones. *The Years* and *Between the Acts* are closer to *The Voyage Out* and *Night and Day* in the kinds of life they represent. In each the content of consciousness is more important than the act; literary realism is more evident in them than philosophical realism. *The Years* and *Between the Acts* share the same philosophical assumptions with the more epistemological works in Virginia Woolf's canon but they are not about perception in the same way that her middle novels are. The remarkable otherness of people's consciousnesses and the spatial, temporal relations their perceptions have in common, the need to combine miracles of intuition with realities of ordinary experience, the drama of transient consciousness that is both a struggle for identity and against enduring, nonconscious nature—these are the epistemological concerns of *Monday or Tuesday, Jacob's Room, Mrs. Dalloway, To the Lighthouse*, and *The Waves*. The stories and novels are not, of course, reducible merely to accounts of sense-perception. Yet if her assumptions about consciousness and its relations to external and internal reality are ignored, we may well misconceive the art and the values of Virginia Woolf's fiction.

If a symbol were needed for the significance of G. E. Moore's epistemological realism for Virginia Woolf's work, it could be found perhaps in the manuscript of one of her earliest diaries. The manuscript consists of holograph pages from a paper notebook that have been pasted over or tipped into a leather-bound copy of Isaac Watts's famous *Logick*. In a preface to this diary, Virginia Stephen, then aged seventeen, explains that she embedded the pages of her diary in a book that she found in a country bookshop in order to have a binding for it. She denied that the subject of the book had any influence on her choice. The size of its pages and her paper were the principal considerations.[44] Despite this disclaimer, one might remain a little skeptical. Certainly it was fortuitous that the daughter of a philosopher and literary critic would choose for merely material reasons the logic text of an author famous for his hymns and children's poems. But whatever her motives at seventeen, the diary she made symbolizes her later use of Moore's philosophy in her writing. As Watts's *Logick* became the material basis for the palimpsest that was her early diary, so Moore's *Principia Ethica* became the epistemological as well as the ethical basis for her mature art.

[44] A page from this diary containing Virginia Stephen's almost illegible explanation is reproduced in the *Bulletin of the New York Public Library* 73 (April, 1969), facing p. 247.

BIBLIOGRAPHY

The works listed below were selected to represent various periods and approaches to the study of English literature and British philosophy. The intention of the bibliography is illustrative rather than exhaustive. Works mentioned in the Introduction are included but not those given in the notes of the essays. No single work of general reference can be listed for English literature, though the volumes of the still incomplete *The Oxford History of English Literature* and both *The Cambridge Bibliography of English Literature* (1940; supplement 1957), five volumes, and *The New Cambridge Bibliography of English Literature* (1969–   ) are the most comprehensive series with which to begin. For British philosophy the recent *The Encyclopedia of Philosophy*, edited by Paul Edwards *et al.* (New York and London, 1967), eight volumes, is the indispensable tool. In addition to studies of individual philosophers by various experts, *The Encyclopedia of Philosophy* contains numerous general articles as well as detailed bibliographies and a very extensive index. It contains articles on the philosophical importance of Arnold, Blake, Butler, Carroll, Carlyle, Coleridge, George Eliot, T. S. Eliot, Emerson, Hazlitt, Johnson, Milton, More, Pope, Shelley, Swift, and Thoreau and various discussions relevant to the history of ideas such as John Passmore's "The Historiography of Philosophy" (6: 226–30).

Three general collections of essays by diverse hands deserve special mention here, even though two of them have provided essays for this anthology. These collections contain a number of very interesting studies by scholars of various persuasions in the history of ideas, and each coincidentally was dedicated to a most distinguished literary historian of ideas. *Reason and the Imagination: Studies in the History of Ideas, 1600–1800*, edited by J. A. Mazzeo (New York, 1962) honored Marjorie Hope Nicolson. *Essays in English Literature from the Renaissance to the Victorian Age*, edited by Millar MacLure and F. W. Watt (Toronto, 1964) was presented to A. S. P. Woodhouse. And *The English Mind: Studies in the English Moralists*, edited by Hugh Sykes Davies and George Watson (Cambridge, 1964) was a tribute to Basil Willey.

Abrams, M. H. "Belief and Disbelief," *University of Toronto Quarterly* 27 (January 1958): 117–36.
Alexander, Samuel. *Philosophical and Literary Pieces*. London, 1939.
Beardsley, Monroe C. *Aesthetics: Problems in the Philosophy of Criticism*. New York, 1958.

Braudy, Leo. *Narrative Form in History and Fiction: Hume, Fielding, and Gibbon.* Princeton, 1970.

Brennan, Joseph. *Three Philosophical Novelists: Gide, Joyce, Mann.* New York, 1964.

Brett, R. L. *The Third Earl of Shaftesbury: A Study in Eighteenth-Century Literary Theory.* London, 1951.

Cameron, J. M. *The Night Battle: Essays.* London, 1962.

Crane, R. S. "Notes on the Organization of Locke's *Essay*," *The Idea of the Humanities and Other Essays Critical and Historical* (Chicago, 1967): 1: 288–301.

———. "Philosophy, Literature, and the History of Ideas," *The Idea of the Humanities* 1: 173–87.

Crompton, Louis. *Shaw the Dramatist.* Lincoln, 1969.

Davie, Donald. *The Language of Science and the Language of Literature, 1700–1740.* London, 1963.

Dobrée, Bonamy. "The Philosophers," *English Literature in the Early Eighteenth Century* (Oxford, 1959), pp. 257–302, 605–6.

Eliot, T. S. *Selected Essays.* New York, 1950.

Ellmann, Richard and Charles Feidelson, Jr. *The Modern Tradition: Backgrounds of Modern Literature.* New York, 1965.

Greenwood, E. B. "Literature and Philosophy," *Essays in Criticism* 20 (January 1970): 5–17.

Hall, Roland. "D. H. Lawrence and A. N. Whitehead," *Notes and Queries* 207 (1962): 188.

Hampshire, Stuart. *Modern Writers and Other Essays.* London, 1969.

Holloway, John. *The Victorian Sage: Studies in Argument.* London, 1953.

James, D. G. *The Life of Reason: Hobbes, Locke, Bolingbroke.* London, 1949.

Jones, Richard Foster. "The Background of 'The Battle of the Books,'" *The Seventeenth Century*, ed. Jones *et al.* (Stanford, 1951), pp. 10–40.

Kaehele, Sharon and Howard German. "The Discovery of Reality In Iris Murdoch's *The Bell*," *PMLA* 82 (December 1967): 554–63.

Kermode, Frank. *Romantic Image.* London, 1957.

Krook, Dorothea. *Three Traditions of Moral Thought.* Cambridge, 1959.

Laird, John. *Philosophical Incursions into English Literature.* Cambridge, 1946.

Leavis, F. R. "'English'—Unrest and Continuity," *Times Literary Supplement* (29 May 1969), pp. 569–72.

———. "Literary Criticism and Philosophy," *The Common Pursuit.* London, 1953.

Leyburn, Ellen Douglass. "Bishop Berkeley, Metaphysician as

Moralist," *The Age of Johnson Essays Presented to Chauncey Brewster Tinker* (New Haven, 1949), 319–28.

Lovejoy, Arthur O. *Essays in the History of Ideas*. Baltimore, 1948.

———. *The Great Chain of Being: A Study of the History of an Idea*. Cambridge, Mass., 1936.

MacLean, Kenneth. *John Locke and English Literature of the Eighteenth Century*. New Haven, 1936.

Miller, J. Hillis. *Poets of Reality: Six Twentieth-Century Writers*. Cambridge, Mass., 1965.

Mintz, Samuel I. *The Hunting of the Leviathan*. Cambridge, 1962.

Moore, C. A. "Berkeley's Influence on Popular Literature—A Review of a Review," *The South Atlantic Quarterly* 14 (1915): 263–78.

Moore, Virginia. *The Unicorn: William Butler Yeats' Search for Reality*. New York, 1954.

Murdoch, Iris. "Against Dryness: A Polemical Sketch," *Encounter* 16 (January 1961): 16–20.

Nicolson, Marjorie H. "Milton and Hobbes," *Studies in Philology* 23 (October 1926): 405–33.

Quinton, Anthony. "Philosophy and Literature," *Times Literary Supplement* (27 July 1967), pp. 673–74.

———. "Thought," *Edwardian England, 1901–1914*. Edited by Simon Nowell-Smith (Oxford, 1964), 253–302.

Richards, I. A. *Coleridge on Imagination*, London, 1934.

———. *Principles of Literary Criticism*. London, 1926.

Santayana, George. *Three Philosophical Poets: Lucretius, Dante, Goethe*. Cambridge, Mass., 1910.

Scott, William O. "Shelley's Admiration for Bacon," *PMLA* 73 (June 1958): 228–36.

Sparshott, F. E. *The Concept of Criticism*. Oxford, 1967.

Stallknecht, Newton P. *Strange Seas of Thought: Studies in William Wordsworth's Philosophy of Man and Nature*. Durham, 1945.

Torchiana, Donald T. "God-Appointed Berkeley," *W. B. Yeats and Georgian Ireland* (Evanston, 1966), pp. 222–65.

Tuveson, Ernest. *The Imagination as a Means of Grace: Locke and the Aesthetics of Romanticism*. Berkeley, 1960.

———. "The Importance of Shaftesbury," *ELH* 20 (1953): 267–99.

Trilling, Lionel. "The Meaning of a Literary Idea," *The Liberal Imagination* (New York, 1953), pp. 268–87.

———. "The Two Environments: Reflections on the Study of English," *Beyond Culture: Essays on Literature and Learning* (New York, 1965), pp. 209–33.

Wasserman, Earl R. "The English Romantics: The Grounds of Knowledge," *Studies in Romanticism* 4 (Autumn 1964): 17–34.

Watt, Ian. *The Rise of the Novel.* London, 1957.

Wellek, René. *Immanuel Kant in England, 1793–1838.* Princeton, 1931.

Wellek, René and Austin Warren. "Literature and Ideas," *Theory of Literature* (New York, 1956), pp. 98–113, 279 82, 324 25.

Whitehead, Alfred North. *The Concept of Nature.* Cambridge, 1920.

———. *Science and the Modern World.* New York, 1925.

Wiley, Margaret L. *Creative Sceptics.* London, 1966.

Willey, Basil. *Nineteenth Century Studies.* London, 1949.

———. *The Eighteenth Century Background.* London, 1940.

———. *The English Moralists.* London, 1964.

———. *The Seventeenth Century Background.* London, 1934.

Wilson, Edmund. *Axel's Castle: A Study of the Imaginative Literature of 1870–1930.* New York, 1931.

Young, Helen Hawthorne. *The Writings of Walter Pater: A Reflection of British Philosophical Opinion from 1860 to 1890.* Privately printed, Lancaster, Pa., 1933.

INDEX

This index is confined to the names of writers, philosophers, and critics.

Index